Financial and Fiscal Policies

Financial and Fiscal Policies

Crises and New Realities

Second Edition

Y. V. REDDY
PARTHA RAY
PINAKI CHAKRABORTY

OXFORD
UNIVERSITY PRESS

Great Clarendon Street, Oxford, OX2 6DP,
United Kingdom

Oxford University Press is a department of the University of Oxford.
It furthers the University's objective of excellence in research, scholarship,
and education by publishing worldwide. Oxford is a registered trade mark of
Oxford University Press in the UK and in certain other countries

First Edition published in 2014
Second Edition published in 2024

Published in the United States of America by Oxford University Press
198 Madison Avenue, New York, NY 10016, United States of America

British Library Cataloguing in Publication Data

Data available

Library of Congress Control Number: 2024946834

ISBN 9780198934257

DOI: 10.1093/9780198934288.001.0001

Printed and bound in India by
Replika Press Pvt. Ltd.

Preface to the 2014 Edition

Mainstream economists and influential economic policymakers are struggling to fully appreciate, for the future, the far-reaching implications of the global financial crisis since 2007. What started as a financial crisis is still running its course, transforming itself into an economic, if not a sociopolitical crisis. The uneven recovery that followed the threatened collapse of financial markets and institutions in the global economy is proving to be fragile. The impact of the crisis, though global, is varied among countries. There is a plethora of research and analyses emanating out of the crisis in the financial sector but it encompasses several other areas of public policy. There are signs of fatigue about the pronouncements on the causes and cures of the global financial crisis. Hence, one more book on the subject warrants a few words from the authors justifying the venture.

The book started with a conversation between Y.V. Reddy (YVR) and Narayan Valluri (NV) in 2010 about the fiscal nature of the financial crisis. Both YVR and NV felt at that time that the focus of the debates was on avoiding collapse of financial markets and on stimulating economies to avoid depression in the short run while addressing issues of reforms of the financial sector and global imbalances. They felt that the fiscal implications of the financial crisis and its management were yet to be fully appreciated. A book on the subject was conceived at that time, keeping in view the background of YVR in money and finance, and of NV in fiscal management. However, as the crisis unfolded, the role of fisc became central. Further, the way the euro crisis was unravelling, the significance of the links between fiscal and financial sectors appeared to get reinforced. Partha Ray (PR) joined the team in late 2011, initially for working on debt restructuring but later for a variety of country experiences and for deciphering the patterns of the crisis in the global context and contagion globally. PR had exposure to global experiences while he was at the International Monetary Fund during most of the relevant period. So, finally the outcome became a product of three authors, though major contributions to the first, second, and third sections were from NV, PR, and YVR, respectively. We are convinced that while the role of fisc was not clear in understanding the reasons for the crisis, the centrality of public finance in global finance had become evident as the crisis and its management unfolded—across nations as well as inter-temporally. Depending on the country-specific circumstances and the quality of fiscal management, the fisc was arguably a cause but undeniably also a victim of the current crisis and contagion. While the financial roots of the crisis and the need for initiating fiscal–monetary stimulus in miti-gating the hangover from the crisis are well known, we thought the fiscal–financial–monetary link needs some further exploration. As far as contagion is concerned, the channels of propagation of the crisis and contagion across countries can be discerned at three levels: (a) contagion of the crisis from one country to another, (b) spread of the crisis from one sector to another within a country (due to sector linkages within a country), and (c) centrality of fisc in both (a) and (b).

Paul Krugman once famously said that there are three kinds of eco-nomics, namely, Greek letters (i.e., the academic); up-down (e.g., typical policy documents saying GDP turned out to be higher at 8 per cent and inflation turned out to be lower at 4 per cent); and airport (e.g., the books that one gets in an airport bookstore, predicting the world economy is coming to an end in 2020 or so). True to this spirit, the research on the global financial crisis and its fallout have followed varied traditions—popular account, academic research, and policy briefs. While we have consciously avoided Greek letters (even when we discuss Greece!), we are unsure whether the present book can be characterized as a convex combination of up-down and airport varieties of economics. Against the backdrop of an analytical account of the crisis (deciphering various stylized facts) and various policy measures across countries, we have attempted a conjecture about the fiscal–financial–monetary link and emerging issues. In the absence of any unifying theory of financial or eco-nomic crisis, we do not have a single story of the crisis countries. If the narration appears inconclusive, it reflects the complex reality that is not amenable to simplification. Finally, the book deals with some aspects of what may be described as live history. Events that are occurring and their associated policies are work-in-progress characterized to some extent by learning by doing. Consequently, there are elements of imprecision in the book and predominance of phrases 'perhaps', 'emerging', or 'going forward'. The descriptive illustrative analytical account reflects the current state of significant uncertainty in both the prospects for the global economy and thinking on economic policies. The book is addressed to a wide readership comprising market participants, academia, and policymakers, though each section may be of special interest to different segments of readership. In writing the book, we benefitted immensely from the available literature, from participation in seminars and conferences, and professional interactions with eminent scholars and respected policymakers. They are too numerous to be listed; and suffice it to say in Telugu 'Endaro Mahanubhavulu, Andariki Vandanamulu' (Our salutations to all of the several eminent experienced and wise persons). We record our appreciation for the services rendered by Sunil Nagpal in the various stages of work specifically related to the book. In particular, we are indebted to the editorial team at Oxford University Press (OUP) for ensuring our work was carried out in a very professional manner. We also express our gratitude to the two anonymous reviewers of the book to whom it was sent by OUP. We are indebted to Soumyen Sikdar for his comments on an earlier draft of Chapter 9.

Needless to say, we are responsible for any errors that remain in the book. Also, views expressed in the book are our personal views and do not necessarily reflect those of any institution that any of us is or has been associated with.

We dedicate this book to our respective spouses, Geetha, Rajani, and Shyamali, for their encouragement in all our endeavours.

In a lighter vein, in a book such as this with three authors, there could be ample scope for including three prefaces—but good sense prevailed upon us and we chose to write a single simplified preface to an oversimplified account of the particularly complex reality of the global crisis and its fiscal context.

Y.V. Reddy
Narayan Valluri
Partha Ray

Preface to the Revised (2024) Edition

The 2014 edition of the book, 'Financial and Fiscal Policies: Crises and New Realities' (Y.V. Reddy, Narayan Valluri, and Partha Ray) was published against the backdrop of the global financial crisis and euro area crisis.

But much water has flowed under the bridge since then; we have witnessed developments like the US-China trade war, Brexit, the pandemic, Russia-Ukraine war, return of inflation—to name a few. Thus, when Shri Dhiraj Pandey from Oxford University Press got in touch with us for a revised edition of the book, we readily agreed. As Shri Narayan Valluri decided to opt out from the revision on account of his preoccupations, with his permission, and at our request, Pinaki Chakraborty joined Y.V. Reddy and Partha Ray in revising the book.

The present edition (Y.V. Reddy, Partha Ray, and Pinaki Chakraborty) revises the 2014 book in two specific aspects. First, it updates the information context of the book covering the major developments during the period 2014–2022 and analyses their policy implications, namely, Brexit; the US-China trade war; the pandemic; the Russia-Ukraine war; and the current apprehension of stagflation. Second, while we felt while the broad messages of the 2014 book are by and large valid, nuances are added, in the revised draft, wherever necessary.

Thus, while the chapter scheme of the original and the revised edition remains more or less the same, we make two changes. First, in view of its revised topicality and developments, we combine the erstwhile Chapters 6 and 7 on the euro area crisis into one single Chapter 6, covering 'Euro Area Economies'. Second, we also introduce a 'China's bilateral lending to developing countries' as a separate section in Chapter 11.

We thank Shri Dhiraj Pandey and Ms. Amrita Brahmo for painstakingly pursuing us and for all his perseverance in getting the revised edition of the book finalized. We thank Kaushik Bhadra for helping us in updating a part of the dataset.

We hope the revised edition of the book will be received well by the readers as in case of the first edition.

Y.V. Reddy
Partha Ray
Pinaki Chakraborty

Contents

List of Illustrations   xiii
List of Abbreviations   xvii

1. Introduction   1

2. Background: The Global Financial Crisis   23

3. Impact of the Crisis on Fiscal Positions   43

4. Response to the Crisis and Fiscal Implications   61

5. The Crises and the Global Economy in the
   Twenty-First Century   83

6. Euro Area Economies: The Crisis and Thereafter   119

7. India: Crisis and the Economic Stimuli   187

8. Public Debt, National Income, and Growth   229

9. Crisis and Public Debt Management   241

10. Fiscal Implications and Central Banking   257

11. Sovereign Debt Restructuring   277

12. Taxation and Regulation of the Financial Sector   301

13. Sub-national Finance and Crisis   311

14. Emerging Challenges   321

References   329
Index   343

Illustrations

Box

11.1. The Nature of Chinese Loans to Low- and Middle-Income Countries   293

Charts

5.1. Real GDP Growth and Share in Global GDP (at PPP)   85

5.2. Global Inflation (%)   97

5.3. Fiscal Balance and Current Account Balance (Percentage of GDP)   100

5.4. Share of the US, the EU, and China in World GDP (Based on Purchasing Power Parity, Percentage)   104

6.1. USD to Euro Spot Exchange Rate   124

6.2. ECB's Monetary Policy Rates   169

6.3. ECB's Net Asset Purchases by Programme under APP   171

7.1. Impact on the Money Market   197

7.2. GFD of the Centre, of the States, and Combined (Percentage of GDP)   210

7.3. Real and Nominal GDP and Inflation Rate (Based on GDP Deflator)   219

Figure

6.1. Nature of Crises in Euro Area Countries that are Severely Affected   157

Tables

3.1. Overall Fiscal Balances (% of GDP)   49

3.2. Primary Balance of G20 Countries (% of GDP)   52

3.3. General Government Debt (% of GDP)   54

3.4.   Components of Consolidated Government and Central Bank Debt, 2011   57

3.4A. Components of Consolidated Central Government and Central
       Bank Debt, 2020   59

4.1.   Discretionary Fiscal Stimulus in G20 Countries During the Global
       Financial Crisis   69

4.2.   Fiscal Stimulus During COVID-19: Advanced Economies   70

4.3.   Fiscal Stimulus During COVID-19: Emerging Economies   71

4.4.   Fiscal Stimulus During COVID-19: Low-Income Developing
       Economies (Estimates as of 5 June 2021)   72

5.1.   Incidence of the COVID-19 Pandemic in the 25 Most-Affected Countries   92

5.2.   Subtitles of IMF's World Economic Outlook (WEO), 2008–2022   93

5.3.   Different Estimates of the Impact of Brexit on the GDP Growth of the
       UK Economy   108

5A.1. GDP Growth (%) across the G20 Economies   112

5A.2. Inflation (%) across the G20 Economies   113

5A.3. Fiscal Balance (% of GDP) across the G20 Economies   114

5A.4. Current Account Balance (% of GDP) across the G20 Economies   115

5A.5. Growth in Some Non-Euro Area Advanced Economies (%)   116

5A.6. Inflation in Some Non-Euro Area Advanced Economies (%)   117

6.1.   Euro Area Countries' Share in World GDP at PPP; Percentage   121

6.2.   Major Macroeconomic Variables of the Euro Area   123

6.3.   Select Indicators in Centre Euro Area Economies   126

6.4.   Greece: Select Macroeconomic Indicators   132

6.5.   Ireland: Select Macroeconomic Indicators   136

6.6.   Portugal: Select Macroeconomic Indicators   139

6.7.   Italy: Select Macroeconomic Indicators   142

6.8.   Spain: Select Macroeconomic Indicators   148

6.9.   Iceland: Select Macroeconomic Indicators   150

6.10. Indebtedness and Leverage in Selected Euro Area Economies, 2012   162

6.11. EU's New Fiscal Rules   178

7.1.   India: Select Macro Indicators   191

7.2.   Liquidity Injection/Availability during September 2008–9   200

7.3.   Pandemic-related Liquidity Measures (INR Billion)   204

7.4. Key Fiscal Indicators of States   214

7.5. Institutional Fiscal Reforms by State Governments in India   215

7.6. Major Deficit Indicators of the State Governments (Per cent to GDP)   218

9.1. Evolution of G20 Agenda   250

9.2A. Select Fiscal Indicators for the G20 Countries: IMF Forecasts   252

9.2B. Select Fiscal Indicators for the G20 Countries: IMF Forecasts   253

10.1. Examples of Central Bank Unconventional Balance Sheet Policies
during the Global Financial Crisis   268

12.1. Pledging for Financial Sector Support during the Global Financial
Crisis (as of end 2009; percentage of 2009 GDP)   303

Abbreviations

ADR	American Depository Receipts
AFS	available-for-sale
APT	ASEAN plus three
APP	Asset Purchase Programme
ASA	ASEAN Swap Arrangement
ASEAN	Association of Southeast Asian Nations
BIS	Banks for International Settlement
BOP	Balance of Payments
BSA	bilateral swap arrangement
CBPP	covered bond purchase program
CD	Certificate of Deposit
CDS	Credit Default Swaps
CIFS	Credit Institutions Financial Support Scheme
CIGI	Centre for International Governance Innovation
CMI	Chiang Mai Initiative
CMIM	Chiang Mai Initiative Multilateralization
CMIM-PL	Chiang Mai Initiative Multilateralization-Precautionary Line
CP	Commercial Paper
CRAR	capital-to-risk adjusted assets ratio
CRR	cash reserve ratio
CST	Central Sales Tax
EBA	European Banking Authority
EC	European Commission
ECB	European Central Bank
ECF	Extended Credit Facility
ECSC	European Coal and Steel Community
EDA	European Debt Agency
EDP	Excessive Deficit Procedure
EEA	European Economic Area
EEAG	European Economic Advisory Group
EEC	European Economic Community
EFF	Extended Fund Facility
EFSF	European Financial Stability Facility
EFSM	European Financial Stabilisation Mechanism
EIOPA	European Insurance and Occupational Pensions Authority
ELG	Eligible Liabilities Guarantee

EMDE	emerging market and developing economies
EMI	European Monetary Institute
EMU	European Monetary Union
ERM	Exchange Rate Mechanism
ESCB	European System of Central Banks
ESFS	European System of Financial Supervision
ESM	European Stability Mechanism
ESMA	European Securities and Markets Authority
ESRB	European Systemic Risk Board
FAAF	Financial Assets Acquisition Fund
FCL	Flexible Credit Line
FCNR(B)	Foreign Currency Non-resident (Bank)
FETA	European Free Trade Association
FII	foreign institutional investors
FIT	Flexible Inflation Targeting
FME	Financial Supervisory Authority, Iceland
FRBM	Fiscal Responsibility and Budget Management
FRED	Federal Reserve Economic Data
FRFA	Fixed Rate Full Allotment
FSAP	Financial Sector Assessment Program
FSB	Financial Stability Board
GCC	Gulf Cooperation Council
GDP	Gross Domestic Product
GFD	Gross Fiscal Deficit
GDR	Global Depository Receipts
GIIPS	Greece, Italy, Ireland, Portugal, and Spain
GNP	Gross National Product
HFT	held-for-trading
HICP	Harmonised Index of Consumer Prices
HTM	Held-to-Maturity
ICSID	International Centre for Settlement of Investment Disputes
IIF	Institute of International Finance
IIFCL	India Infrastructure Finance Company Limited
IIP	index of industrial production
IMF	International Monetary Fund
INET	Institute for New Economic Thinking
IPO	Initial Public Offering
LAF	Liquidity adjustment facility
LIBOR	London Interbank Offered Rate
LSE	London School of Economics
LTRO	long-term refinancing operations
MENA	Middle-East and North Africa
MSME	Micro, Small, and Medium Enterprises

MSS	Market Stabilisation Scheme
NBFC	Non-Banking Financial Companies
NPA	Non-performing assets
NPV	Net Present Value
NREGA	National Rural Employment Guarantee Act
NR(E)RA	Non-Resident (External) Rupee Account
OCA	optimum currency area
OECD	Organization for Economic Co-operation and Development
OMO	Open Market Operations
OTS	one-time settlement
PCL	Precautionary Credit Line
PLL	Precautionary and Liquidity Line
PPP	Purchasing Power Parity
PSB	public sector banks
QE	Quantitative Easing
RCF	Rapid Credit Facility
RE	Revised Estimate
RET	Ricardian equivalence theorems
SBA	Stand-By Arrangements
SBI	State Bank of India
SDM	Sovereign Debt Management
SDRM	Sovereign Debt Restructuring Mechanism
SGP	Stability and Growth Pact
SLR	statutory liquidity ratio
SME	Small and Medium Enterprises
SMP	Securities Market Programme
SOE	State-Owned Enterprises
SPV	Special Purpose Vehicle
SSM	Single Supervisory Mechanism
TARP	Troubled Asset Relief Program
TFC	Total Fixed Cost
TFP	Total Factor Productivity
UNCTAD	United Nations Conference on Trade and Development
USTR	US Trade Representative
VAT	value added tax
WTO	World Trade Organization

1

Introduction

Slicing the timeline is a useful way of starting a narrative. Writing the story of the global economy during the twenty-first century in 2024 allows us to discern a number of phases. While the twenty-first century began with some anxiety with regard to growth and stability due to Y2K-related problems, this anxiety was short-lived and was perhaps followed by unprecedented growth in output at the beginning of the century.[1] But this high growth phase during 2001–7 was followed by two major crises in quick succession—first the global financial crisis, followed by the euro area crisis. Both these crises witnessed the initiation of massive fiscal and monetary stimulus and demonstrated the linkage between the financial and fiscal sectors. While the period covering 2014–19 was one of return to the growth trajectory albeit of the new normal variety, there were various headwinds affecting growth—the US-China trade war, initial confusing signals of Brexit finally culminating in the UK's exit from the European Union—to name a few.

In 2020, the world witnessed the emergence of the COVID pandemic that culminated in a once-in-a-century type of human tragedy and a return to more aggressive fiscal and monetary stimuli. As the world economy was limping back to a semblance of normality in early 2022, the Russian invasion of Ukraine added additional complications to the nascent recovery. As observed by the IMF (2022), '(With) Russia's invasion of Ukraine, war is back in Europe. The world is facing renewed uncertainty, as war comes on top of the persistent and still-evolving COVID-19

<hr>

[1] Refers to the problems widely anticipated to have surfaced in the year 2000 (also known as the Millennium bug, the Y2K bug, or simply Y2K). It was a problem for both digital (computer-related) and non-digital documentation and data storage situations which resulted from the practice of abbreviating a four-digit year to two digits) (*Source*: Wikipedia; Thomas, Martyn. 2017. "What Really Happened in Y2K?", available at https://www.regulation.org.uk/library/2017-y2k_bug_evaluation.pdf)

Financial and Fiscal Policies. Second Edition. Y. V. Reddy, Partha Ray, and Pinaki Chakraborty, Oxford University Press. © Y. V. Reddy, Partha Ray, and Pinaki Chakraborty 2024. DOI: 10.1093/9780198934288.003.0001

pandemic.[2] The war in Gaza, which started in October 2023, also added to this uncertainty and has the potential to dent recovery.

The COVID pandemic and measures to deal with it have created a set of complex multidimensional macroeconomic challenges. As the pandemic struck, coordinated fiscal and monetary policy action provided critical support to households and firms affected by the lockdown. It resulted in large government deficits and an increase in the money supply. The Russia-Ukraine war has added to the complexity by putting pressure on prices and by disrupting the global supply chain. Against the backdrop of these crises, the present book is focused on financial and fiscal policies.

Take, for example, the period of 2001–7. The growth of the economies was globally impressive, which was experienced by both developed and developing economies. At the same time, volatility in output, employment, and prices was conspicuously subdued. There were very few voices of discomfort regarding growth in the early years of the century with what should have been considered a boom. On the contrary, monetary authorities took credit for what has been described as the Great Moderation. The increasing globalization, which witnessed considerable alleviation of poverty, was also admittedly helpful. The financial sector, especially global finance, was at the forefront in claiming a large share of benefits from the significant growth in output. The performance of emerging and developing economies was particularly impressive. Their achievements were attributed to sound macroeconomic policies, and possibly global finance, but less so to the development of financial markets and deregulations.

However, pressures in financial stability were observed in 2007, culminating in the global financial crisis in 2008. The euphoria about particular growth models relating to money, finance, and fiscal affairs that prevailed in the mid-1990s was punctured. The global crisis manifested itself in the financial sector in late 2008 and 2009, requiring monetary actions, and these were followed by fiscal and monetary stimulus. It is interesting that what started as a crisis in the financial sector transformed into sovereign debt crises in several countries and later resulted in uneven and uncertain recovery. Developing countries, in particular emerging

---

[2] https://www.imf.org/en/Publications/FM/Issues/2022/04/12/fiscal-monitor-april-2022

market economies, where the adoption of the new orthodoxy (relating to a leading role of the financial sector) of the mid-1990s, was still work-in-progress, were also affected though considerably less than advanced economies. No doubt there are exceptions in both categories.

As the global economy was about to come out of the aftermath of the global financial crisis, the euro area sovereign debt crisis surfaced. Interestingly, both these crises (i.e., the global financial crisis and the euro area crisis) witnessed unprecedented usage of monetary and fiscal stimuli. It is noteworthy that the links between monetary policies, financial sector policies, and fiscal policy, particularly in managing the crisis, have become evident during the crisis with implications for institutional arrangements for the future. The earlier preference for monetary and fiscal policies being conducted independently of each other is being questioned and coordination in such public policies is gaining attention.

While the period 2014–19 started witnessing some withdrawal of the monetary and fiscal stimuli, there were a number of headwinds affecting growth locally. Two phenomena are important in particular, namely, Brexit and the US-China trade war.

First, the intention for the UK to leave the European Union (EU) got an initial seal of approval in a referendum on 23 June 2016, in which 51.89 per cent voted in favour of leaving the EU and 48.11 per cent voted to remain a member. After British Prime Minister David Cameron resigned, the formal notification to the EU about the UK's decision to exit the EU was notified by the new Prime Minister Theresa May in March 2017. Subsequently, there was a series of deadlocks in the formal process of exit, and it was only on 31 January 2020 that the UK finally exited the EU. While the economic impact of Brexit is yet to be estimated firmly, it had immense implications for the UK's trade openness, foreign investment inflows, and immigration growth.

Another shock that had profound implications for the global economy was the initiation of the US-China trade war. Under the then-new US Presidency of Donald Trump, the US Trade Representative (USTR) was directed to investigate the allegation of adopting unfair trade practices by China. The March 2018 report of the USTR made a serious attack on a number of aspects of the Chinese trade policy. Following the report, US President Trump ordered various actions against China in July 2018; these included imposing tariffs on Chinese products, and restrictions on

Chinese investment in high-tech sectors of the US economy. What followed during the next two years were moves and countermoves on the parts of the US and China. Industries like solar panels, washing machines, steel and aluminium, automobiles, and semiconductors were affected in particular. There were also issues relating to technology and intellectual property rights. The trade war eventually led to tariffs on some US$550 billion of Chinese goods and US$185 billion of US goods. Contrary to the popular expectation of a possible end of the trade war after the change of the US presidency, US President-elect Biden affirmed in December 2020 that he would not make any immediate moves to lift tariffs. While the trade war narrative is still on, as of mid-2022, there seems to be a thawing of the trade tensions between the US and China.

Despite occurrences like Brexit or the US-China trade war, the growth scenario during 2014–19 was somewhat benign. But, the advent of the pandemic changed all that. Looking at the unprecedented impact of the pandemic (both in terms of human lives and economic ramifications), authorities all over the world changed the course of macroeconomic and financial sector policies and adopted a stance of 'whatever it takes' to mitigate the impact of the crises. In other words, the policy toolbox to tackle the global financial crisis and the euro area crisis was put to use in a liberal manner as a key ingredient of the pandemic mitigating strategy.

Admittedly, the current pandemic is a health crisis; but while its primary solution came from the science of epidemiology and virology, a consequence of the pandemic as well as its solution package tends to have critical monetary and fiscal elements. In terms of the economic implications of the pandemic, various channels can be identified. First, along with the loss of human lives and the prolonged and uncertain treatment of the infection/ailment, there was an associated health cost with its consequent burdens on personal finance, health insurance companies, and/ or the Exchequer. Second, in order to reduce the extent of the spread of the pandemic, most of the countries declared nationwide lockdowns of varying degrees and duration. Such lockdowns, in turn, had confined labour to the boundaries of home and/or places without much mobility. Consequently, unemployment shot up and labour income went down substantially in many geographies, pushing the poorest people in some countries to the verge of destitution. Unless significant online work was possible in a specific field, such lockdowns led to the stoppage of production in various sectors with supply going down and the global supply chain was affected. Third, since there was low demand out of low income, along with a deep recession, both repayment capacity as well as the loan demand of the households and firms were affected with associated adverse implications for the banking sector. Finally, with a huge expansion of the central banks' balance sheet and fiscal stimuli, the burden on the monetary authorities, as well as treasuries, went up by leaps and bounds.

Specifically, the solution package of the pandemic-induced economic crisis witnessed a return of the aggressive fiscal and monetary policy stimuli that were part of the global economic crisis and euro area crisis. Quantitative easing measures and central banks' asset purchase programmes were pursued actively in the face of low/negative interest rates. Governments all over the world became hugely indebted. In fact, in quantitative terms, the size of the economic stimuli package in the case of the current pandemic was a multiple of similar packages pursued during the global financial crisis. That is to say, despite being a mortality and morbidity crisis, the current pandemic exposed the fault lines of the linkage between financial and fiscal policies.

It is against this backdrop that the book describes the observed linkages between finance and fiscal issues in the context of the crises, with several illustrations and anecdotal evidence. It attempts to explore emerging issues in the policies relating to the management of public debt, central banking, taxation, and regulation of the financial sector. In view of their contemporary relevance, issues relating to sovereign debt restructuring and sub-national finance arising from the crisis are also discussed. In brief, the book argues that an important lesson for public policy is that sound fiscal management is at the heart of maintaining financial stability consistent with growth. Further, sound fiscal management demands adequate space for the conduct of public policy at the national level, while navigating the forces of globalization, in particular of finance. An equally complex challenge is to reconcile the considerable advantages of independence of monetary authorities and regulators with the compulsions of coordination of public policies, without ignoring the criticality of fiscal policies.

Given that this is part of live and contemporary history, there are no finalities but several obvious questions are thrown up. How did the global financial crisis happen? What was the link between the global financial crisis and the euro area crisis? Are there general lessons or does the devil lie in the details of country-specific circumstances? What is the relationship between modern-day private sector finance with the fisc?[3] How has the financial sector been 'slapped by the invisible hand' (Gorton 2010)? How is the world coping with the huge monetary and fiscal stimuli that have been injected during the pandemic? Is inflation here to stay? Is the possibility of a debt crisis looming large? Without any claim to being exhaustive, this book seeks to probe some of these questions.

The Theme

While the book discusses the details of country-specific circumstances, in terms of broad generalizations, three givens may be highlighted. First, the channels of propagation of the crisis and contagion across countries can be discerned at three levels, namely, (a) contagion of the crisis from one country to another; (b) spreading of the crisis from one sector to another within a country (due to sector-linkages within a country); and (c) centrality of fisc both with regard to (a) and (b). Second, there is an element of circularity of the fisc and the crisis in the sense that fisc can be both a cause and a victim of the crisis. Third, patterns of contagion could vary a great deal between advanced and developing countries, depending upon the structural characteristics of the economies concerned and the extent of openness and sophistication of the financial sector in particular. Interestingly, despite the clamour for globalization and its actualization, nation-states continue to remain responsible for the welfare of their citizens and the stability of their societies, so that while finance is global, financial regulation and fisc are essentially domestic. This general idea underlies the three givens enumerated before. To illustrate, the Greek crisis in the government bond market could affect German banks if their balance sheets have substantial exposure to Greek bonds. On the other hand, the crisis can spread from the banking sector in Ireland or in Spain to the government sector in these economies, depending upon the extent of nationalization of the banking sector or the span and quantum

---

[3] Fisc is the shortened form for fiscal (which includes situation, authorities, and management).

of rescue packages. Finally, 'when all else fails', the government could emerge as the 'ultimate risk manager' regardless of the dominance of the private sector in any economy (Moss 2002).

The book deals with its grand theme at three levels. First, it examines the emerging linkages between money, finance, and fisc.[4] Second, it looks at the cross-country experiences of the current crisis, particularly in the context of the euro area debt crisis. Third, in this light, the book raises a number of emerging policy challenges. What follows in the subsequent sections of this introduction is a brief outline of the remaining chapters of the book focusing on this theme.

Money, Finance, and Fisc: Nature of Linkages in the Crisis

Chapter 2 ('Background') seeks to provide a broad overview of the causes of the crises, their global fiscal impact, responses to the crises, and their fiscal implications, including the larger fiscal consequences on public debt. While loose monetary policies, toxic products, lax regulatory practices, global imbalances, and financial sector shortcomings are generally acknowledged as the contributory factors to the global financial crisis, its major impact was felt on the fisc. Yet, there is little evidence to suggest or assert a clear causal link between the global financial crisis and the fiscal health of countries. In dealing with the unprecedented fallout of the pandemic, similar but more massive fiscal and monetary stimuli were injected all over the world. While such stimuli have helped bring back the demand to some extent, given the supply disruptions they could also have contributed to inflationary pressure in some cases.

Chapter 3 ('Impact of the Crisis on Fiscal Positions') sets out how the various crises (viz., global financial crisis, euro area crisis, or the pandemic) tend to have adverse fiscal impacts through many channels and on many fronts, with both revenue and expenditure implications. Predictably, the revenue and expenditure impact of a financial crisis and its resultant economic recession is reflected in fiscal balances, revenue

---

[4] See Chapter 10 ('Fiscal Implications and Central Banking') for a discussion on new fiscal dominance.

balances, and primary balances, each of which is both important and significant. And obviously, these have an impact on public debt too. Drawing from International Monetary Fund (IMF) and other publicly available data, the chapter indicates how the fiscal and primary balances and public debt of global economies and G20 countries have been impacted by the crisis, and to what extent, if any, they have been able to retrace to pre-crisis levels. The chapter concludes by noting that at the best of times fiscal management is challenging; in an economic recession induced by the global financial crisis and the pandemic, the task could be daunting. It underscores the need to look beyond headline figures of fiscal deficits and public debt, and to delve into their composition at a disaggregated level; otherwise, it could lead to a misleading or incomplete appreciation of the real fiscal situation, without which appropriate policy responses may be elusive.

It notes that in a world dominated by global finance, fiscal management has to reckon with the reactions of financial markets to fiscal measures. Thus, fiscal management is hemmed in to some extent by uncertainties in financial markets and their reactions, thereby putting pressure on policy space.

Starting with the run-up to the crisis, Chapter 4 ('Response to the Crisis and Fiscal Implications') discusses the responses to the crises, monetary, and fiscal, and their implications. With the weakening of the 'umbilical link between the financial sector and the real economy', the world witnessed its severest economic crisis in nearly eight decades. All the countries (both developed and developing, including emerging economies) were affected by it. It is only in the timing and intensity of the impact that they might have differed.

The immediate response of monetary authorities in the seriously affected economies was to increase liquidity and enable a smooth flow of credit by reducing interest rates and taking other allied steps. However, to shore up and protect the stability of the financial system, action by monetary authorities alone was not sufficient. Government support to the banking sector was also essential, in some cases with attendant fiscal and quasi-fiscal costs, which could potentially devolve upon taxpayers.

With interest rates reduced to historic lows and hovering close to zero, central banks were left with few options and had to resort to unconventional monetary policies, like direct bailouts of banks, and the Troubled

Asset Relief Program (TARP) in the US with underlying fiscal implications, and quantitative easing. As serial doses of quantitative easing were possibly knocking against diminishing effectiveness, attention turned to more aggressive strategies of monetary easing, like money drops in the US.

Debates also centred on whether recession should best be countered by monetary or fiscal expansionary measures and, if by the latter, whether they should be by deficit spending resorting to further borrowings, or by monetizing the deficit. The chapter touches on the monetary and fiscal stimuli provided across nations and their implications, both of which in the final analysis have inevitable fiscal consequences. The effectiveness of fiscal stimulus programmes is also discussed with reference to multiplier effects, and the quality, structure, and sequencing of measures.

It then proceeds to highlight policy issues and lessons from the crisis, including the polemic debate: whether the contractionary and recessionary pressures in the economy be met with short-term fiscal spending within a medium-term fiscally sustainable framework or whether short-term pain induced by the crisis be subordinated to the larger goal of fiscal orthodoxy and sustainability. The importance of prudential countercyclical measures in the financial sector is mentioned as a salient lesson from the crisis.

In conclusion, the chapter underscores two points: that the financial sector has a complementary role to play alongside monetary, fiscal, and structural policies, a role that assumes importance and warrants serious review going forward; and that the various ramifications of the global financial crisis ultimately and inevitably have fiscal consequences, thus underscoring the centrality of fiscal issues, which is necessary to be addressed at a national level.

The General Government debt-to-GDP ratio for Advanced Economies is hovering around 120 per cent of GDP.[5] For the Emerging and Middle-Income Economies, the ratio is around 60 per cent. Though the debt-to-GDP ratio stabilized during the fiscal year 2021, IMF *Fiscal Monitor* (2021) observed that, 'The pandemic will leave a lasting mark on government finances, inequality, poverty, and the level of GDP in many

---

[5] General Government consists of all government units and nonmarket non-profit institutions that are controlled by government units (IMF Fiscal Monitor 2021).

countries'. It further noted that '(F)ollowing this one-time jump, debt in the coming years is expected to remain persistently higher than the levels projected before the pandemic—in advanced economies, it is projected to be almost 20 percentage points higher through 2026'.

Cross-Country Experience

Chapter 5 ('The Crises and the Global Economy in the Twenty-First Century') provides a synoptic view of the economic developments of the tumultuous years since 2007. The period witnessed various crises. To begin with, the sub-period 2007–9 saw the emergence of the sub-prime crisis in the US residential mortgage market, leading to the global financial crisis, which finally culminated in the great recession of 2009 (when global GDP growth, as well as the growth of both advanced economies and emerging and developing economies [EMDEs], registered a contraction). Countries all across the world have undertaken simultaneously coordinated monetary and fiscal stimulus—more so the bigger countries in the G20. Consequently, growth resurfaced during 2010 with a number of countries in developing Asia (led by China) emerging as growth poles. But this resurgence of growth was transitory, uneven, and fragile. And by the end of 2010, it was apparent that the euro area would be affected by a sovereign debt crisis. Admittedly, there are various dimensions of the euro area crisis transmitted through the cross-holding of sovereign debt of the affected countries (such as Greece, Ireland, Italy, Portugal, and Spain; often referred to as GIIPS countries) by the banking sector of the core euro area economies (such as Germany, France, Belgium, or Austria) and erosion of confidence. The fisc was dependent on the sovereign debt market in a big way and through it international financial players were affected. Finally, apart from probing into the US-China trade war and its ramifications, it looks into the economic implications of the pandemic and the Russia-Ukraine war.

Insofar as inflationary trends are concerned, the period from 2009–19 was rather uneventful in most of the geographies. Various factors could have played their roles in this phenomenon (Gopinath 2021).[6]

---

[6] Gopinath, Gita (2021), 'Structural Factors and Central Bank Credibility Limit Inflation Risks', https://blogs.imf.org/2021/02/19/structural-factors-and-central-bank-credibility-limit-inflation-risks/

First, due to globalization, inflation in traded goods could have been muted. Second, the spread of automation and artificial intelligence could have prevented wage pressures being translated to prices. Third, central bank independence and pursuit of anti-inflationary policies by the central banks could have anchored inflationary expectations.

Chapter 6 ('Euro Area Economies: The Crisis and Thereafter') gives an account of the genesis of the crisis in the euro area economies with emphasis on the crisis-ridden GIIPS countries, as well as the impact of the pandemic. While concentrating on the crisis-ridden euro area economies, it notes that apart from the crisis-ridden GIIPS countries, the crisis engulfed non-euro area but EU member countries like Iceland (initially) and the UK and Cyprus (of late). Among the GIIPS countries, the diagnosis was by no means uniform. The Greek tragedy can be primarily traced to fiscal profligacy fuelled by the private financial sector's myopia that chose to ignore the internal fundamental differences among the euro area countries in the hope of a bailout in the event of a crisis. Thus, fisc became both a cause and effect of the Greek crisis. The Irish problem, on the other hand, was quite different from that of Greece as it was essentially an issue related to its banking sector. While the global financial crisis exacerbated matters in Ireland, the banking crisis in Ireland was primarily a home-grown phenomenon. It stemmed from the collapse of the domestic property sector and the subsequent contraction in national output. In some sense, its root cause can be found in the inadequate risk management practices of the Irish banks and the failure of the financial regulator to supervise these practices effectively. While the global financial crisis had a marginal impact on Portugal, in an already deteriorating debt-deficit situation coupled with low productivity–low growth syndrome, such marginal impact was amplified. Italy, often described as the 'sick man of Europe', had one of the largest public debts in the EU (103 per cent of GDP in 2007) and ranked third in the world in 2007. Notwithstanding such debt configuration, Italy did not face any major debt crisis till about 2010, with a fairly long average maturity of Italian debt (at around seven years) and about half of it locally owned. However, as a result of the structural problems and political uncertainty, Italy was hit hard during the crisis with GDP contracting by more than 5 per cent in 2009 and 1.2 per cent in 2012. Of course, Italy being a wealthier country than Greece, Spain, or Portugal, has greater capacity to withstand the crisis. The Spanish crisis was in a sense a culmination of over-exposure of shadow banks (regional savings banks, called cajas de ahorros, accounting for half of the Spanish banking system) to the housing sector and pricking of the housing bubble. Among the non-euro area countries, Iceland was one of the initial victims of the crisis because its banking sector was over-leveraged and exposed to foreigners (primarily British citizens via the Icesave accounts). Finally, the economic situation in the UK seems to be not so exciting with the Brexit-related pangs with its elongated recovery process, dominant financial sector, and perhaps premature efforts at fiscal rectitude in line with the conservative philosophy.

The general patterns of the euro area crisis along with some proposed policy packages are also taken up in this chapter. What stands out is that the euro area faces not one but three interlocking crises: (a) a banking crisis (where banks are undercapitalized and face liquidity problems); (b) a sovereign debt crisis (when a number of countries are facing increasing sovereign bond yields and consequent funding challenges); and (c) a growth crisis (with a low aggregate growth in the area as well as unequal distribution across countries). Against the backdrop of a discussion on the optimum currency area, the chapter argues that the seeds of the current crisis among the euro area countries could have germinated in the very nature of the euro area currency union which, with incomplete adherence to the conditions of the Maastricht Treaty, brought into its fold very dissimilar economies. This was accentuated by a private-sector financial sector that tended to hold the government debt of these dissimilar economies without paying any heed to their fundamentals, implicitly assuming any funding difficulty would be bailed out by the stronger partners of the euro area. Thus, in many countries, it was both a case of irresponsible borrowing by the national government as well as irresponsible lending by the private agents. The crisis has attracted a rescue package both from the EU (in the form of the European Financial Stability Facility in May 2010 being transformed to a more permanent European Stability Mechanism) as well as from the IMF with countries such as Greece, Ireland, or Portugal already under IMF programmes. This was complemented by monetary policy actions by the European Central Bank, both in the form of interest rate cuts and quantitative easing. However, the contradictions within the currency union are much more fundamental in nature. Two sets of policy initiatives are currently active within the euro area countries: (a) formation of a banking union; and (b) formation of a fiscal union. The policy efforts are at an early stage and it will be premature to pass any judgment on their eventual effectiveness. To speculate, it may not be an exaggeration to say that in the days to come, there could be increasing tension between non-euro area EU countries (such as the UK) and euro area countries. What indubitably stands out is that whatever be the specific and proximate causes for the occurrence of the crisis in individual countries, in the ultimate analysis, the inexorable linkages between fiscal, monetary, and financial issues can no longer be ignored. Also, without fiscal union, the monetary union may not survive exogenous and asymmetric shocks unleashed by a financial crisis; and monetary and fiscal union may not be feasible without political union.

The pandemic has increased the macroeconomic vulnerability further. Rising debt and deficits in the eurozone area need to be revisited in terms of its impact on macro management. It is argued that

(T)he negative fiscal impacts of the pandemic will be exacerbated in 2021 by the need to maintain restrictions on the economy, at least until the second quarter. On the other hand, the cost of servicing public debt in euro area countries is still at near record lows. The reasons for this are the interventions of the Euro system, which consists of the ECB and the 19 national central banks of the Eurozone. For this purpose, a special purchase programme was launched, mainly for government bonds (the pandemic emergency purchase programme, PEPP). Can rising government debt nevertheless become a pressing problem for the Eurozone?[7]

Despite the near-zero exposure of Indian banks, given the extent of globalization, India was affected by the global financial crisis. Also during the pandemic Indian authorities have undertaken a substantial fiscal stimulus. Hence, given our interests and location, Chapter 7 ('India: Crisis and the Impact on Fiscal Space') delves into the implications of the ongoing global crisis for the Indian fiscal situation in terms of its crisis resilience and the impact on fiscal space. Documenting the

---

[7] Tokarski and Wiedman (2021).

monetary and fiscal elements of the Indian stimulus package, the chapter hints at the structural weaknesses of the Indian fiscal situation. It further argues that despite the small size of the Indian stimulus package (in comparison to other countries) the fiscal space in India was rather meagre. Furthermore, coupled with the problem of twin deficits, a major factor that did not expose India to the whims and fancies of the sovereign debt market was its avoidance of original sin, whereby India's public debt was primarily rupee denominated. However, in line with India's policy of calibrated financial and external sector liberalization, while households, governments, and even the financial sector had manageable exposure to foreign currency liabilities, the same is perhaps not true for the larger entities in the Indian corporate sector. Thus, in the days to come, issues relating to exposure to foreign currency liabilities and fiscal prudence may turn out to be more important than before.

This increase in the debt-to-GDP ratio across countries resulted in a reassessment of the conventional wisdom on fiscal rule and accumulation of public debt. In India, between 2020–21 (the first year of the COVID-19 pandemic) and 2022–23, the fiscal challenges have eased, but remain present as we navigate economic recovery in uncertain times. It is difficult to predict the impact of the ongoing war between Russia and Ukraine and the war in Gaza on the macro management and fiscal situation as we move during the fiscal year 2023–24. However, a medium-term view needs to focus on return to a sustainable debt and deficit path at the general government level.

The approach taken in the book is somewhat eclectic in nature. Nevertheless, at the end of the cross-country experience and before delving into the key emerging issues, for the sake of completeness, Chapter 8 ('Public Debt, National Income, and Growth: A Selective Review') presents a review of the major strands of the theoretical and empirical literature on public debt, national income, and growth. While the pre-Keynesian literature tended to view public debt almost with contempt, with the emergence of the Keynesian revolution, an activist fiscal policy came to be recognized as a standard policy tool in dealing with the recessionary situation in any economy. Over the years, however, a distinction is made between the short- and medium-term effects of incurring public debt, and it was demonstrated that under some conditions the medium-term effects could be less beneficial than the short-term effects.

Beneficial effects of incurring public debt have been questioned subsequently in this context of Barro-Ricardo equivalence wherein altruistic (but rational) households with a strong bequest motive fail to make any distinction between debt-financing and tax-financing. Consequently, the demand-generating (and income-augmenting) role of public debt could be redundant. While empirical verification of Barro-Ricardo equivalence produced dismal evidence, its spirit, in some sense, could give an inkling about the possible leakages from the expansionary impact of fiscal policy. From a holistic viewpoint, the chapter also looks into the contributions of some of the major non-mainstream schools (e.g., post-Keynesians) and notes that in such alternative paradigms, the scope of fiscal expansion could be far more. Summarizing the recent controversies concerning the evidence put forward by Reinhart and Rogoff (2011a) on the relationship between debt and growth, it has been noted that the fixation of a threshold level of debt, above which any further increase in debt becomes growth reducing, is extremely difficult. Against this background of the significant plurality of views, when we are unable to infer a cohesive set of lessons, the next few chapters explore the emerging issues.

The pandemic also renewed the debate on debt sustainability and fiscal rule. Since the COVID-19 pandemic resulted in a sharp increase in debt-to-GDP ratio across countries, there is a reassessment of the conventional wisdom on public debt. It has been argued in recent literature that if the multipliers of the fiscal stimulus due to COVID are high, then the higher debt will be sustainable.[8] Krugman (2020) also argued for a deficit-financed public investment programme on a continuing basis.

Emerging Issues

Against this backdrop, the subsequent chapters focus on five distinct but related emerging issues confronting the global economy.

Chapter 9 ('Crisis and Public Debt Management') is devoted to issues relating to public debt and points to several new dimensions of public debt. Illustratively, while in recent decades, till the onset of the crisis, a

---

[8] Codogno, Lorenzo, and Giancarlo Corsetti (2020), 'Post-pandemic debt sustainability in the EU/Euro area: This time may (and should) be different', VoxEU, 18 September 2020.

sovereign debt crisis was almost wholly confined to developing countries, the present crisis emanating from advanced economies. Besides, the growth of public debt has been significantly higher in advanced economies, unlike in the pre-crisis period. Consequently, fiscal sustainability has become an important consideration in monetary operations in view of the large supply of government securities. Further, as a consequence of quantitative easing, central banks' balance sheets in advanced economies contain government securities on a larger scale than before. It is also significant that a reserve currency area, the euro, is confronting sovereign debt issues and likelihood of lowered credit rating because of possible default or restructuring. The chapter flags several lessons for management of public debt. While reviewing the existing and evolving global financial architecture, the chapter notes the impressive role played by the G20 in enhancing cooperation at the global level and coordinating measures of policy stimulus. The recently concluded G20 summit in New Delhi observed that '(C)ascading crises have posed challenges to long-term growth.'[9] The G20 New Delhi declaration emphasized that 'Global economic growth is below its long-run average and remains uneven. The uncertainty around the outlook remains high. With notable tightening in global financial conditions, which could worsen debt vulnerabilities, persistent inflation and geoeconomic tensions, the balance of risks remains tilted to the downside. We, therefore, reiterate the need for well-calibrated monetary, fiscal, financial, and structural policies to promote growth, reduce inequalities and maintain macroeconomic and financial stability.'[10]

However, past experience shows that coordination of national policies relating to exit from stimulus measures during the global financial crisis has proved more contentious, due mainly to uneven recovery across nations and sectors. In sum, the chapter points out absence of any significant change in the global financial architecture insofar as public debt management is concerned. While from the macroeconomic viewpoint, large public debt burdens need to be managed through a combination of policy responses, such as (a) higher taxes and austerity; (b) financing through inflation; and (c) financial repression, going forward

---

[9] MEA, GoI (2023).
[10] http://www.g20.utoronto.ca/2023/230909-declaration.html

the linkages between the management of public debt and financial stability need to be better appreciated than ever before especially when there is a renewed pressure to monetize the deficit to finance government expenditure.

Recognizing that most operations of central banks have fiscal implications, Chapter 10 ('Fiscal Implications and Central Banking') looks into issues related to fiscal implications and central banking. Since central banks, particularly in advanced economies, permitted excess liquidity by adopting relatively loose monetary policy as they focused excessively on inflation or price stability and neglected credit booms and asset bubbles, they cannot be absolved of their role in the crisis. However, there are elements of the country-specificity in this regard. But in almost all the countries, central banks played the role of an activist in mitigating the fallout of the crises; those central banks which were in the forefront of managing the crisis had to assess whether they were taking serious risks by supporting insolvent institutions on the strength of market instruments of uncertain value as collaterals. During all these crises there followed an enormous bloating of the central bank balance sheets. Illustratively, after a sharp increase in the aftermath of the global financial crisis, the US Fed had reversed its policy of asset purchases but after the onslaught of the pandemic, an aggressive asset purchase programme was initiated since early 2020. Consequently, the size of its aggregate balance sheet increased from US$4.2 trillion as of January 2020 to nearly US$8.9 trillion as of 14 June 2022.

Admittedly, in their role in rescue operations, there was close coordination with the fiscal authorities. While there is a general consensus that in managing the crisis all central banks succeeded in avoiding the collapse of financial markets, there are allegations that in doing so, central banks in systemically important advanced economies undertook extraordinary monetary measures, involving significant fiscal costs. In the new normal, the role of central banks is expected to be different from that in the pre-crisis era. The mandate of central banks is being widened to formally include financial stability and this wider mandate may warrant several judgments and trade-offs, requiring a greater role for discretion in monetary policy. Finally, new fiscal dominance (whereby foreign financial market players, as the holders of the sovereign debt in an open capital account, play a major role) may emerge for central banks to reckon with alongside other sources of threat to financial instability.[11]

Debt restructuring is often conceived as one of the solutions to acute debt crises. It is in this context that Chapter 11 ('Sovereign Debt Restructuring') deals with issues relating to fiscal solvency and sovereign debt restructuring. Conceptually, sovereign debt restructuring is a far more complex issue than corporate debt restructuring. Though standard liquidity support mechanisms could come from central banks' swap lines or from an IMF programme, historically there were many abortive attempts towards sovereign debt restructuring. Sovereign debt restructuring is on the active agenda with the flaring up of the euro area debt crisis. The Greek debt restructuring programme has faced several roadblocks. In this context, the Stiglitz Commission (UN 2009) took a fresh look at this issue and pointed out the limitations (if not failure) of both the IMF and the International Centre for Settlement of Investment Disputes (ICSID) within the World Bank to act as the international bankruptcy court; it called for strengthening UNCTAD's (United Nations Conference on Trade and Development) advisory role in debt management. In specific terms, the commission called for the creation of an 'International Debt Restructuring Court', similar to national bankruptcy courts. The emergence of an effective mechanism for sovereign debt restructuring, however, seems a distant dream at the current juncture.

Recent IMF review (2020) of sovereign debt restructuring highlighted that there have been significant developments in sovereign debt restructuring involving private-sector creditors since the IMF's last stocktaking in 2014.[12] It has also been observed in this review that though the current contractual approach has been largely effective in resolving sovereign debt cases since 2014, it has gaps that could pose challenges in future restructurings. Literature on the subject shows that total sovereign debt as a percentage of GDP has increased and the creditor base has become diverse over the years posing major challenges to restructuring. China's bilateral lending to developing countries has increased sharply in recent

---

[11] See Chapter 10 ('Fiscal Implications and Central Banking') for a discussion on new fiscal dominance.

[12] IMF (2020), The International Architecture For Resolving Sovereign Debt Involving Private-Sector Creditors—Recent Developments, Challenges, and Reform Options, https://www.imf.org/-/media/Files/Publications/PP/2020/ English/PPEA2020043.ashx [07/12/2022]

years and the lending volumes far surpass those of other bilateral creditors and compare in scale only to World Bank lending practices. It is observed that, 'due to the extensive efforts of independent researchers and better reporting by official sources outside of China, it is increasingly clear that the Chinese government—through its major policy banks, state-owned commercial banks, and government agencies—now represents the largest official external creditor to developing country governments worldwide. By some estimates, it is larger than World Bank and IMF individually and all of the Paris Club creditors combined' (Horn, Reinhart, and Trebesch 2019).[13] The limited availability of information on Chinese debt to developing countries makes it difficult to make a detailed analysis of its long-run implication in terms of debt sustainability and development finance. Data that is available also show that Chinese debt is less concessional than many other lenders. The emergence of China as a major lender to the developing world has implications for long-term development finance, the role of multilateral and other bilateral institutions, the nature of aid flow and public policy, and sovereign debt management. Issues related to China's bilateral lending to developing countries have also been discussed in detail in this chapter with a special focus on emerging evidence of Chinese debt to low-income developing countries.

Chapter 12 ('Taxation and Regulation of the Financial Sector') deals with the specific issue of taxation and regulation of the financial sector. The links between fiscal management and regulation of the financial sector have varied over time. Specifically, the global financial crisis has led to the consideration of some new forms of taxes in the context of the crisis and its management and has also led to a re-examination of the links between regulation and taxation. There have been various proposals. For example, the European Commission supported the establishment of ex-ante resolution funds based on the polluter pays principle, outside the financial stability framework. There was also a proposal for levying of financial transactions tax at 0.1 per cent on the trading of stocks and bonds, and 0.01 per cent for derivatives contracts; the US has proposed a Financial Crisis Responsibility fee to recover intervention

---

[13] Horn, Sebastian, Carmen M. Reinhart, and Christoph Trebesch (2019), 'China's Overseas Lending', NBER Working Paper No. 26050.

costs. Tobin Tax was also considered on capital outflows from emerging markets. At an operational level, taxation of financial sector, in particular financial transactions may enhance regulatory effectiveness. While recognizing that taxation is no substitute for regulation, it is argued that both are related and that there are elements of the current tax system that may contribute to excessive financialization, including volatility in financial markets. Hence, the need to consider regulation and taxation in an integrated manner for policy purposes is advocated.

The downside risks to the financial stability has increased due to the pandemic and the Russia-Ukraine war. According to the IMF's (2022) Global Financial Stability Report, 'Repercussions of the war continue to reverberate globally and will test the resiliency of the financial system through various channels, including direct and indirect exposures of banks, nonbank financial intermediaries, and firms; market disruptions (including in commodity markets) and increased counterparty risk; acceleration of cryptoization in emerging markets; and possible cyber-related events'. There has also been a sharp rise in inequality. According to the World Inequality Report (2022), income inequality has sharply increased in recent years and global wealth inequalities are even more pronounced than income inequalities. The Report highlighted that '(T)he poorest half of the global population barely owns any wealth at all, possessing just 2% of the total. In contrast, the richest 10% of the global population own 76% of all wealth. On average, the poorest half of the population owns PPP €2,900 per adult, i.e. USD 4,100 and the top 10% own €550,900 (or USD 771,300) on average.' The Report suggested a progressive wealth taxation on global multimillionaires, which could generate up to 1.6 per cent of global income as taxes for redistribution.

The issue of sub-national finance is taken up in Chapter 13 ('Sub-national Finance and Crisis'). While a study of sub-national finance is made difficult by the incompleteness/limitation of data, there is some evidence that the current crisis has impacted sub-national finances as well (e.g., the north-eastern region of Catalonia in Spain). The results of a survey in the Organization for Economic Co-operation and Development (OECD) countries indicate that the most direct effect of the global economic slowdown on local governments has been on both the level and composition of revenue and expenditure of local government finances, but there are many nuances. While there could be a debate on the need to review the structures of fiscal relations between central and sub-national governments in view of the experience with the crisis, the evidence so far does not indicate high volatility or severe pro-cyclicality in the finances of sub-national governments. A related issue is the lack of adequate buffers against shocks in many sub-national governments. Though definitive answers in this area are few and far between, various questions (e.g., Will the space for fiscal management in sub-national levels increase?) remain unanswered. Sub-national governments continue to play a major role in dealing with the pandemic within the overall resource envelope available to them. This also requires rethinking on the role of sub-national fiscal space in managing a crisis like a pandemic. This book brings cross-country evidence on the issue and try to draw important policy lessons.

Finally, Chapter 14 ('Emerging Challenges') highlights the emerging challenges for public policies in general, in view of the confluence of health of financial and fiscal aspects of national economies.

The book is, no doubt, about some episodes of live history, and the happenings described could have had a short shelf life. However, the broad policy messages and issues identified have much more relevance across space and time. Thus, while the diagnosis of the ailments could contain large elements of conjecture rather than well-analysed empirical evidence, the debates are worthwhile. After all, Lord Keynes once said that it is worthwhile to be vaguely right than precisely wrong. This is particularly relevant when one is addressing evolving public policy issues in a rapidly changing global economic environment in the context of the twenty-first century.

2

Background

The Global Financial Crisis

As this book covers broadly the period, 2010–22, it may be apposite to delve into the history of what happened during the immediately preceding period. The first decade of the new millennium was marked by the onslaught of the global financial crisis. What started as a sub-prime crisis in the US residential mortgage market in 2007, impacted the global economy after the fall of the investment bank Lehman Brothers in September 2008 and emerged as a global financial crisis. The immediate solution to handling the crisis was in terms of an expansionary monetary and fiscal stimulus. Thus, in order to discuss the implications for financial and fiscal policies, this chapter looks into the global financial crisis, its genesis, and its solution package.

Specifically, this chapter seeks to give, by way of background, a broad overview of the causes of the crisis; its global fiscal impact; responses to the crisis and their fiscal implications, including the larger fiscal consequences on public debt. It concludes by stressing the importance of different dimensions of imbalances, the need for rebalancing them and reassessing fiscal, financial, and monetary linkages that may be necessary in distilling lessons from the crisis for the future. The global financial crisis originated in select advanced economies. Their financial sectors were severely affected and the linkages between financial and fiscal situations in such significantly affected countries are the main thrust of this chapter. No doubt several developing countries were also affected, but that was essentially through contagion. The background chapter, therefore, concentrates on the relevant advanced economies, in particular the US.

Financial and Fiscal Policies. Second Edition. Y. V. Reddy, Partha Ray, and Pinaki Chakraborty, Oxford University Press.
© Y. V. Reddy, Partha Ray, and Pinaki Chakraborty 2024. DOI: 10.1093/9780198934288.003.0002

The Global Financial Crisis and Its Aftermath

Causes of the Global Financial Crisis

Many analyses, discussions, and commentaries on the causes of the global financial crisis have appeared in the recent past. It may therefore be superfluous to recount, at length, the multiple and interrelated causes of the crisis. In short, as is generally acknowledged, the causes of the crisis could be attributed to the following, broadly classified under macroeconomic, financial sector-related, and institutional factors. Of course, these factors were not universally present in all countries; notable exceptions are Canada, Australia, China, India, etc.

The salient macroeconomic causes are primarily loose monetary policies in the advanced economies; increasing delinquency in the subprime US housing mortgage market and piercing of the property price bubble; and persistent large current account surpluses in some countries and regions such as China and Asia, with correspondingly large current account deficits in the US and other countries. Large current account surpluses in China and elsewhere created excess savings in the global economy; these savings sought higher yields in financial instruments abroad in the absence of developed financial markets and domestic avenues for profitable investment in their own countries. This spawned exotic (and often imperfectly understood) financial products whose risks were underpriced. Loose monetary policy and excess liquidity saw the build-up of asset bubbles, which monetary authorities were either ignorant of or chose to ignore as it was not falling within their express mandate. Widening inequalities resulting in volatility in aggregate demand were another factor.

Adding to the macroeconomic factors that contributed to the crisis were some striking failures ascribable to the financial sector. Notable among these were: excessive deregulation and misplaced faith in financial markets' ability to regulate themselves and inadequate skills of regulators to assess the lurking risks of innovative financial products. Compounding these shortcomings, institutions were allowed to grow as financial conglomerates comprising interconnected banking and non-banking entities to circumvent regulation. The net result had been 'too big to fail' institutions. Further muddying the waters were the skewed compensation packages of financial and bank executives, with their distorted incentive structures that gave rise to excessive risk taking.

In addition to these, there were infrastructure failures as well. These were: absence of competitive markets in global finance with the dominance of only two credit agencies, two financial news agencies, and two international financial centres; and infirmities in governance structures, including audit agencies, giving rise to conflicts of interest.

To dispel any mistaken impression that the causes of the crisis were entirely financial in nature, it needs to be mentioned that there were contributory factors in the real sector too. For instance, widening inequalities in income and wealth in the US; failure of the US government in undertaking effective health and education sector reforms; and conscious efforts by successive US governments to make cheap credit available to poor American households to achieve the American dream of owning a home (Rajan 2010), were also responsible.

These views are echoed in mainstream literature too. High levels of inequality in the US are said to be comparable to the trends before the Great Depression, casting a shadow on the modest recovery currently being experienced in the US. Stiglitz (2013) cites four major reasons for this dampening effect on the US economy: inability of the average US middle class to support consumer spending; their inability to invest in educating their offspring; dipping tax revenues since 'those at the top are so adroit in avoiding taxes and in getting Washington to give them tax breaks'; and correlation between increasing income inequalities and severity of boom-and-bust cycles. Krugman (2013), while concurring with the view that income and wealth inequalities could have played some role in the financial crisis in the US, differs from Stiglitz in that in the US, which does not have a very progressive tax structure, high income inequality may not depress tax receipts.

It is interesting to note that fiscal management or lack thereof is not cited in the mainstream analysis as a cause of the crisis; it finds mention only in the context of fiscal deficits contributing to the current account deficits in the US and, hence, indirectly to global imbalances. Developments in Iceland demonstrated that a financial crisis could be visited with deleterious fiscal consequences, but there was no suggestion of fiscal mismanagement having caused the crisis. The unfolding of the euro area crisis, however, presents a somewhat different picture because of its unique circumstances of a currency union with little fiscal cohesion. The persisting fiscal surpluses and deficits of large magnitudes within the region unravelled the linkages between fiscal management and the financial sector.[1] Suffice it to say here that prudent fiscal management was not viewed as integral to the health of the financial sector until the financial crisis erupted and the linkages became apparent, especially in the context of managing the crisis and reviving economies. It thus becomes necessary to explore the contours of the fiscal impact of the crisis to better comprehend the nature and complexity of their linkages for effective fiscal management during a financial crisis.

There is little evidence, therefore, to suggest or assert a clear link between the global financial crisis and fiscal health of countries. No doubt, countries with weak fiscal situations were more vulnerable to the crisis; at the same time, it would bear mention that countries with weak and fragile fiscal positions were not as severely affected, while some with relatively strong fiscal indicators were impacted heavily. There is little empirical evidence to suggest a causal link between the two.

Impact of the Global Financial Crisis on Fiscal Position

The global financial crisis had far-reaching ramifications, not the least of which is its fiscal impact on countries, further heightened by some of the policy responses to the crisis. Among other factors, a combination of falling revenues as a direct consequence of the financial crisis, operation of automatic stabilizers, declining asset values and commodity prices, direct support to the financial sector, and discretionary fiscal stimulus measures impacted severely on the fiscal balances of countries. While some of the measures taken did cushion the impact of the crisis, they nonetheless contributed to fiscal deterioration, exacerbating in some cases already high levels of debt and raising risks of contingent liabilities being realized.

---

[1] These aspects are dealt with in some detail in Chapter 6.

In the wake of the crisis, some estimates projected the fiscal balances of G20 advanced countries to dip by as much as 8 percentage points of GDP on an average, and government debt to rise by 20 percentage points of GDP in 2008 9, with most of the deterioration taking place in 2009. The same estimates indicated that the fiscal balances of G20 emerging market economies would worsen by 5 percentage points of GDP (IMF 2009). In the case of advanced countries, the contributing factors for the unprecedented increase in debt levels were said to be a support to the financial sector, fiscal stimulus action, and revenue losses resulting from the crisis. On the other hand, in some countries a considerable proportion of the projected fiscal slide was attributed to declining commodity prices. Shrinking asset prices were also said to have had an adverse impact on funded components of pension systems, which could pose risks for public accounts.

Falling revenues, higher public spending to combat deflationary tendencies in the economy, and rising unemployment result in increased fiscal deficit, which adds to the stock of public debt. Whereas the stock of debt is already high in relation to GDP, it could aggravate an already perilous fiscal situation. Further, resorting to larger borrowings on top of high public debt has the potential to push up interest rates and borrowing costs, subject to monetary conditions and state of financial markets. This additional cost often, in turn, leads to even larger fiscal deficit and public debt.

Ageing populations, particularly in the advanced economies, exacerbate downward pressures on their fiscal situation. This could arise from a combination of factors such as greater drawing on social security benefits, and increased healthcare costs, in addition to reduced income levels, and consequently low savings rate. Moreover, in a financial crisis collapsing asset prices could adversely impact on pension funds, thus further compounding the travails of an ageing population.

A major direct consequence of the crisis is the normal tendency for the cost of raising debt to increase. Exceptions to this may arise from special circumstances: for instance, if a country is considered to be a safe haven, global uncertainties increase the demand for public debt as in the case of the US; also, if financial markets perceive strong growth potential for a country despite increase in public debt. However, in assessing the impact on borrowing costs, the distinction between nominal and real interest rates would need to be kept in mind because of inflation dynamics during the crisis.

With high levels of debt to GDP, lenders may not only be averse to extending their commitments but may also factor in higher risk premiums, resulting in widening spreads. Lowering of sovereign credit ratings may, in many circumstances, add to the cost of raising debt. For example, in the wake of the euro crisis, it is not just the periphery countries of the eurozone like Greece and Ireland that are countenancing difficulties in raising debt even at higher spreads but also Spain and Italy.

With most of the major advanced economies reeling under the financial crisis and consequently with their fiscal manoeuvrability severely constrained, aid to less developed and developing countries is often impacted adversely. This has unfortunate consequences for the poorer nations, whose budgets depend significantly on foreign aid. Thus, these countries are often adversely affected by a combination of a drop in foreign aid and simultaneous choking off of commercial borrowings.

Response to the Global Financial Crisis and Fiscal Implications

In the context of a crisis, in order to avoid collapse of financial institutions and serious disruptions in markets, monetary authorities usually act by injecting liquidity in the markets and by supporting institutions that need liquidity. However, during a financial crisis, the boundaries between liquidity and solvency are thin, and hence, fiscal authorities are ready to backstop monetary authorities in case segments of institutions and markets eventually turn out to be less than solvent. In addition, if there are serious issues of solvency, fiscal authorities may need to act directly, through injection of equity or nationalization or other forms of financial support, including issue of guarantees. These measures could have monetary or fiscal implications or both. It also raises three questions: moral hazard, avoiding collapse of the edifice as a whole, and enforcing fiscal or financial discipline. In a crisis situation, each of these presents difficult choices where the primary concern is to ensure uninterrupted functioning of the system, which may have to be addressed separately as part of financial sector reform.

Moral hazard is inherent in a situation where an entity taking a risk does not bear the full consequences of its actions and thus may act carelessly or irresponsibly. According to some, ' "Too big to fail" is the cancer of moral hazard in the financial system' (Liu 2008). But if the survival or existence of even those who acted prudently is threatened because of the contagion effect, putting the whole edifice in danger of collapse, questions of moral hazard naturally yield to salvaging the system. The overriding concern in such a situation is preserving the integrity and stability of the financial system, and issues of moral hazard and fiscal and financial discipline become somewhat subservient.

Faced with a financial crisis, particularly of the magnitude and severity of the one witnessed in 2008, fiscal policy has to contend not only with avoiding disruption or collapse of the financial sector and markets but also with rescuing the economy from depression. But fiscal policy alone may not be able to achieve these twin objectives; it may need to act in concert with monetary policy. But most monetary policy measures do impinge on fiscal policy during extraordinary times and have implicit or latent fiscal implications.

Fiscal policy, since it deals with government revenue (taxation) and government spending, by definition, has to respond to current and emergent needs of the economy and macroeconomic situation. It would be a truism, therefore, to say that fiscal policy cannot be fixed or cast in stone; it has to, by its very own nature, be evolutionary and adaptive, based on experience and expediency. The onset of a financial crisis, therefore, signals the possible need for prompt effective fiscal strategy and action, though the first line of defence would be monetary measures. The latter have, as already mentioned, quasi fiscal implications.

The interplay between monetary and fiscal policy is thus brought into sharp relief during a financial crisis, including issues relating to debt and currency (not excluding the unique status of reserve currency countries). With the onset of a financial crisis the distinction between operations of the monetary authority and fiscal operations could get blurred, with both working in tandem towards common immediate and pressing objectives. It is well known that all monetary actions have fiscal implications, but in the context of a crisis, fiscal considerations and outcomes tend to assume importance.

When as a response to the crisis, stimulus measures are set in motion, the actions of the monetary authority could have substantial fiscal and quasi-fiscal implications. In the next stage of recovery from financial crisis, both monetary and fiscal authorities have complementary and supplementary roles to play. The overriding concern of fiscal authorities to stem the possible downward path of growth could impact the independence of monetary authorities to set interest rates and manage money supply and credit availability. Thus, not only do monetary and fiscal policy have to act in tandem and in concert but their distinctive roles also tend to get blurred during all the phases of a financial crisis.

The looming dangers of a financial crisis are severe contraction in demand because of the rising levels of unemployment and its consequent deflationary impact. With job losses causing substantial fall in incomes, the demand for goods and services declines noticeably. The immediate concern of public policy, therefore, is to counteract this deflationary impact by making up this loss of demand through measures designed to boost private purchasing power. This could take different forms: for example, transfer payments from the government enabling increased private consumption, as was done in India for instance; another method could be undertaking substantial public investment, say like in infrastructure projects, of which China is a prime example. Tax cuts on consumption and investment could be another instrument for giving a fillip to demand. The former would be an incentive to increase private consumption; the latter an inducement to greater private investment, leading to more employment, increased incomes, and greater purchasing power.

The impact of the crisis was widespread, owing to globalization and financial integration. However, its degree and timing varied across countries; not all the countries experienced the effects of the crisis at the same time; nor was its intensity the same in all the countries. Most advanced countries and, to some extent, many major emerging nations suffered considerable financial stress. They were sucked into the crisis through financial contagion, in particular, as a consequence of collapse of international trade. The emergence of financial crisis and resultant recession in advanced economies affected global economic activity. These developments have significant fiscal implications across nations.

Different countries adopted different measures or a combination of these in varying degrees to stimulate their economies. As in the case of most other economic indices, the metric generally used to assess the quantum of stimulus is its ratio in relation to GDP. Resort to fiscal stimulus results in higher fiscal deficits unless the country in question has a substantial fiscal surplus before the onset of the crisis to give it sufficient headroom to put in place stimulus measures without pushing the budgetary balance into the red. The substantial recourse to fiscal stimulus would be evident by comparing the pre- and post-crisis fiscal deficit of countries.

There are other allied aspects of stimulus that need to be kept in mind. For example, it is the quality of stimulus rather than its quantity that is important. The multiplier effects of stimulus measures determine the degree of effectiveness of the measures. For instance, fiscal stimulus measures that encourage consumption could have a larger multiplier effect than say bailouts per se. Further, investments undertaken as part of stimulus measures may have lower multiplier effect, but in the long run they enhance the output potential or productive capacity of the economy. Moreover, while stimulus measures may give a boost to domestic demand, an incidental fallout could have cross-border spillover effects. In other words, the additional demand and consumption so generated may not necessarily be directed to domestically produced goods and services but towards imported goods.

Also, discretionary stimulus measures taken in the wake of crises are generally of a cyclical nature; however, entrenched vested interests could coalesce around such measures. In the process, what starts out as a cyclical response in the fiscal management of the crisis, may impart a structural character to it, with enduring fiscal costs.

How long and to what extent stimulus measures should be continued is fraught with fiscal consequences too. Determining when stimulus should be rolled back is a knotty issue that will be discussed in Chapter 4: suffice it to say here that premature withdrawal of stimulus action could possibly lead to relapse into recessionary pressures on the economy; continuance of the measures beyond economic revival runs the risk of the measures becoming quasi-permanent or permanent as mentioned earlier with attendant fiscal consequences.

Fiscal Consequences of Crises Mitigating Package

A deep and widespread financial crisis brings in its wake substantial job losses, curtailed bonuses, and reduced incomes. Adverse macroeconomic conditions affect corporate profitability. The combined effect of these is to reduce tax revenues of governments, both direct and indirect, from individuals as well as corporates. This, in turn, leads to reduced spending and curtailed services, if not their scrapping altogether in some cases. Apart from this, transfers to lower tiers of government are also affected. This takes a heavy toll on social services to the populace. Poverty levels are heightened because of low growth; expenditure on education and health services declines; nutrition and health of children in poor households are at risk; all of which severely dent the nurturing of human capital. Automatic stabilizers, if any are in place, like unemployment benefits and other social safety nets, add to an already precarious fiscal situation.

Falling commodity prices owing to contraction in demand because of reduced growth impulses take a toll on the incomes of developing countries that depend on commodity exports, apart from their taking a knock from diminished international trade.

The deteriorating fiscal situation manifests itself in primary deficit, revenue deficit, fiscal deficit, and burgeoning public debt. The emergence of primary deficit would indicate that borrowings would need to be resorted to even to make interest payments. Fiscal deficit represents the amount of borrowing required to bridge the financing gap between revenues and expenditure. Fiscal deficit adds to the stock of public debt. If the rate of increase of fiscal deficit outstrips the rate of growth of the economy, it results in higher ratios of debt to GDP. An ineluctable fallout from high levels of debt is unwillingness of markets to lend, pushing up borrowing costs because of lowered credit ratings. This, in turn, leads to larger deficits, creating a vicious cycle of rising deficits, mounting debt, and higher interest costs contributing to even larger deficits, thus ensnaring the country in a debt trap as it were. Borrowing costs pushed up by a crisis of confidence may take a long time to retrace to earlier levels.

In the face of persistent fiscal deterioration, governments may often find it increasingly difficult to access money markets; interest spreads widen to factor in risk premiums, and even so, financial markets may be chary of lending. Higher interest rates aggravate an already dismal fiscal situation and add to the escalating debt burden. However, it is necessary to recognize that as long as private demand is subdued and monetary policy continues to be accommodative, the adverse consequences mentioned before may not materialize. Over the medium term too, significant pick-up in growth prospects may suppress upward pressures on the costs of borrowing.

In a situation where financial markets perceive that unsustainably high debt to GDP is occurring, there may be calls for fiscal consolidation and austerity. However, such measures in the face of rising unemployment and falling incomes could have given rise to widespread social unrest. Austerity measures in an already depressed economy could see curtailment of public spending, including caps on entitlement expenditures, thereby heightening social distress and discontent, apart from further deepening the downward spiral of the economy.

Two contrary views dominate the current debate on the role of fiscal policy to redress economies in recession. One view holds that in a depressed economy with high levels of unemployment and falling or stagnant economic growth, considerations of fiscal rectitude should take a back seat. The immediate concern should be to stimulate demand by substantial doses of public spending even if it means increasing the fiscal deficit and raising the level of debt. Once the economy is restored to health and economic growth resumes at acceptable levels, then fiscal deficit and debt will show a downward trend. What is needed, therefore, they assert, is fiscal stimulus in the immediate term combined with structural reforms as needed for medium to long-term financial or fiscal stability. In their view, fiscal consolidation and austerity in a climate of high unemployment levels and falling incomes would only exacerbate the depressed conditions in the economy.

The other view advocates fiscal consolidation and austerity measures to rein in fiscal deficit and to curb the rising graph of debt to GDP. They argue that only fiscal consolidation and fiscal rectitude will restore confidence in pulling the economy back to the path of growth; though this may have deleterious short-term effects, in the long run it would be beneficial for the economy. This is an argument that was being vigorously pushed in the euro area crisis in the context of Greece. It also finds support and many adherents amongst a section of eminent and influential economists and political luminaries on both sides of the Atlantic.

Belt tightening through austerity programmes could produce un-intended and undesirable consequences on the fiscal position itself. Higher taxes and reduced government spending constricting demand could squeeze growth, causing an anomalous situation of having to run harder just to stay in place. One may also have to contend with the back-lash of social and political unrest unleashed by expenditure cutbacks, as witnessed in Greece recently. On the other hand, larger government deficits may inhibit growth according to a study cited by The Economist, which postulates that each percentage point increase in government spending results in reducing growth by 12 to 13 basis points a year (The Economist, 26 June 2010). Further, increasing government deficits may induce fears of higher future taxes, engendering economic behaviour that may negate or crimp any benefits that are expected from stimulus spending.

Persuasive arguments can be advanced in support of each of these op-posing positions; and eminent economists can be found on both sides of the divide espousing these divergent stances. However, in the ultimate analysis, the raison d'être of public policy is to subserve public good. The challenge for public policy is to strike the right balance between short-term compulsions and medium- to long-term sustainability in a prag-matic manner, taking account of unique country contexts.

Public Debt

One of the major issues brought to the fore by the recent global finan-cial crisis is the issue of debt or rather excessive and looming unsustain-able levels of debt. Hitherto, unsustainable levels of sovereign debt were usually associated with developing or underdeveloped countries. But the financial crisis of the first decade of the twenty-first century has shown that developed countries too could face stress and forfeit their traditional status of being immune to sovereign defaults. To parody a statement of Michael Lewis,[2] lending is an act of faith and debt is sustainable only as long as the lender believes it is so.

---

[2] The original statement is: 'A banking system is an act of faith; it survives only as long as people believe it will' (Lewis 2011).

Without credit flow to the real economy, growth would remain stifled. Debt, used prudently and within limits, provides muscle and sinews—or leverage—for development and growth. But prudential limits are not easy to prescribe, nor are they absolute or immutable. Prudence is contextual and may be conditioned by contemporary circumstances, with economic logic, at times, yielding to social and political imperatives. But, it is widely recognized that runaway debt has large potential for serious adverse economic consequences, though reserve currency countries may have a different set of challenges. However, the adverse consequences of high debt make no distinction between advanced, emerging, and developing countries; they are mitigated only by prudent fiscal policies preceding financial crises. In fact, emerging economies that have weathered the recent global crisis better than advanced economies may hold sobering lessons for the latter. It is interesting that policymakers in advanced economies may have to draw from the experience of emerging markets or nations, given that about 50 or more sovereign restructurings in recent times have occurred in developing countries.[3]

It is well known that borrowing is sustainable only if the returns from the use of borrowed funds are higher than the cost of servicing the borrowing.[4] When private debt reaches unsustainable levels—to the point of threatening the survival of banks and the financial system—and is likely to hurtle the economy into recession, the public sector is drawn into its vortex. For, the government or public sector has willy-nilly to step into the breach to protect the edifice of growth, employment, and its own revenues with which to service debt. Reinhart and Reinhart point out that a recurring pattern from financial crises is that government debt swells from having to take over private debt obligations as part of rescue of the financial system (Financial Times, 4 November 2010). In this context, they point to Ireland running a budget surplus as recently as three years earlier and having a debt to GDP ratio of only 13 per cent, only to see

---

[3] It is ironic that, 'There are European policymakers in prominent positions who have sovereign debt restructuring experience gained in an emerging market context, and this experience will no doubt shape their views on how a future eurozone restructuring could or should evolve', says Sebastian Espinosa of White Oak, a sovereign advisory firm. (Financial Times, 'Sovereign Debt: Pointers from the Past', 30 January 2011).

[4] Returns, when broadly defined in the context of public policy, include avoidance of loss of output that would have occurred but for the borrowing undertaken to enhance effective demand.

it increased by 50 percentage points through having to assume private financial obligations. But moral hazard is latent in such backstopping by government, giving rise to objections of 'privatizing profits and socializing losses'. This raises the larger issue of 'too big to fail' because of inherent systemic risks, with lurking potential to bring down the whole financial structure.

Public debt, which is an accumulation of fiscal deficits over time, could reach disconcerting, if not alarming or unsustainable levels, even without the occurrence of a financial crisis. With the onset of a financial crisis, the fallout of mounting public debt could exacerbate an already perilous situation. It is generally accepted that public finances in advanced economies are today in worse shape than at any other time since the industrial revolution, barring wartimes and their surrounding years. Debt levels of advanced countries have reached unparalleled heights, following the financial crisis that brought about 'the Great Recession'. This is unprecedented outside the World Wars. The debt-to-GDP ratio of the G7 group of countries is said to be the highest in 60 years. Peace-time increases in debt generally prove more intractable to contain than debts incurred during wars as they finance expenditures around which entrenched vested interests develop. Consequently, cyclical deficits may in some cases transform into structural deficits.

Balance sheets of households, corporates including financial institutions, and countries alike take a severe knock in a financial crisis. This is because asset values decline while liabilities remain constant or even rise. Moreover, there is a transmission effect: the adverse effect on household balance sheets has inevitable consequences for financial institutions, which beyond a point tend to get shifted to national balance sheets, either in part or in full. And the larger the financial institutions, whose failure or collapse may have a domino effect threatening the system as a whole, the 'too big to fail' syndrome surfaces. Central monetary authorities and national governments are willy-nilly compelled to intervene to stem the resultant catastrophic effects. Thus, the drastic impact of a financial crisis on household balance sheets culminates in bloating public sector balance sheets through the transmission effect.

Ballooning private debt often entails or heralds banking crises. The precipitation of banking crises by the swelling of private debt suggests an inexorable link between the two; and banking crises plant the seeds of sovereign debt crises. The plunge to sovereign debt crises occurs through rapid acceleration of public borrowing, at times boosted by lurking hidden debts or unfunded contingent liabilities. The progression from surging private debt to banking crises to sovereign debt crises suggests a serial passing the buck or a financial play-out of the hot potato game: highly leveraged households transfer part or whole of their debt to creditors who are equally, if not more over-leveraged, who in turn unburden part of the debt on to the government. For example, the Ireland crisis was brought on by the government taking over or underwriting the liabilities of banks and financial institutions (in effect, transferring private and bank debt to the government). The case of Ireland is rather striking: private credit rose from 100 per cent of GDP in 2000 to 230 per cent in 2008; net foreign liabilities of domestic banks which was 20 per cent of GDP in 2003 increased to 70 per cent in early 2008; government debt which was 25 per cent of GDP in 2007 climbed to as high as 95 per cent in 2010; and unemployment steeped to 13.3 per cent of GDP in 2010 from a low of 4.6 per cent in 2007.[5] Ireland has seen its GDP dip by as much as 16 per cent in nominal terms. Historical instances abound of links between banking crises and sovereign default.

It may be facile to lay the blame on irresponsible and reckless borrowing by some but no borrowing is possible without the counterpart activity of lending. In boom times, lenders tend to loosen lending norms lulled into complacence by a sense of euphoria, which raises questions about rationality of lenders and adequacy of risk assessment and premiums. Irresponsible lending spurred by the questionable notion that sovereigns do not default[6] could lead to immoderately high debt levels. Hyman Minsky reportedly warned that 'an out of control financial sector creates self-fulfilling euphoria and then panic' (Financial Times, 23 February 2011). High levels of public debt arguably have the effect of dampening economic growth as a consequence of the combined effect of rising interest rates and crowding out private borrowing.

In general, governments have greater resilience in withstanding high levels of debt than banks or financial institutions because of their

---

[5] Martin Wolf in Financial Times, 23 February 2011.
[6] Former Citibank Chairman Walter Wriston (1967–84) is reported to have famously remarked: 'Countries don't go bust' (Reinhart 2010).

ability to raise taxes or print money, stoking inflation to moderate the real impact of debt on the fisc. However, there are limits to what they can do, which may vary across nations. For example, the option of printing money and devaluing currency is not open to Greece or other members of the euro currency. As alluded to earlier, there are two sides to the argument of reducing debt by stimulating growth. With higher growth, GDP rises, thereby pushing down the debt-to-GDP ratio; besides, higher growth will boost tax revenues and reduce expenditures arising from automatic stabilizers and discretionary spending, thus reducing the debt-to-GDP ratio. On the other hand, high levels of debt (incurred to stimulate growth) could, in some circumstances, dampen economic growth. Therefore, the challenge lies in determining at what level and in what circumstances adding to public debt ceases to be benign.

A possible fall-out from high levels of debt is unwillingness of markets to lend, pushing up borrowing costs because of lowered credit ratings. This, in turn, leads to larger deficits, creating a vicious cycle of rising deficits, mounting debt, higher interest costs, contributing to even larger deficits, ensnaring the country in a debt trap as it were. Borrowing costs pushed up by a crisis of confidence may take a long time to retrace to earlier levels. Escalating levels of government debt raise concerns about government creditworthiness. In fact, sovereign debt should normally be low risk and provide a benchmark for pricing other debt. But this yardstick is imperilled if sovereign debt rises to untenable levels.

Two factors could understate the severity of debt crises. First, analysis purely in terms of debt could be misleading since this would tend to gloss over or ignore contingent liabilities, which are, in a sense, concealed latent threats lurking in the penumbral shadows. Unfunded and contingent liabilities could pose a hidden risk to the already strained fiscal position of governments. Second, viewing the sustainability of debt purely in terms of current debt stock would be to ignore future fiscal deficits spawned by inherent structural fiscal imbalance. This could possibly be further compounded by crisis spending, leaving behind a residue of structural deficit elements, or what may be termed as the fiscal deficit debris of stimulus spending.

History suggests that debt reduction following a financial crisis could stretch over long periods of time. A variety of factors could contribute to this: profile of debt and its concentration by country and sectors, currency in which debt is incurred, debt owed to domestic and foreign lenders, maturity profile of debt, and so on. Faced with the stupendous task of confronting seemingly intractable debt levels the options available to a government are: growing one's way out, inflating away the debt, sovereign default, and austerity measures forced by fiscal tightening. Each of these has limitations and drawbacks. A McKinsey study (January 2010) finds that: 'Countries which defaulted or inflated their debt away saw bigger recessions at first, but had higher output growth than the belt-tighteners by the end' (quoted in The Economist, 16 January 2010). Sovereign default is not an easy option because its consequences could be severe. The ignominy of loss of reputation (reputation risk) could block or choke off access to debt markets and raise the cost of whatever borrowing may still be available. There could be ripple effects of sovereign default as well, including cross-border effects on creditors as well as others, depending on the degree of their economic relationship with the defaulting nation.

Since debt default can damage reputation, it is not a route that countries would tread lightly. Besides, as already mentioned, default carries with it inherent penalties in terms of shutting off or reduced access to debt markets and higher interest rates. Freezing of financial (and debt) markets can paralyse real economic activity. A knotty issue in the context of debt default or restructuring relates to odious debt. The circumstances under which debt is incurred may give rise to ethical questions regarding its fairness and hence moral justification in repudiating it. Lenders may also in such circumstances take a more indulgent view.

Debt default has many facets, ranging from outright default to restructuring or rescheduling, which is a euphemism for soft or partial default. In a partial default, lenders agree to take a haircut, by softening or relaxing the terms of debt, including reductions in the principal amount or rates of interest; in other words, a form of financial oppression[7] where creditors are willy-nilly forced to take haircuts.

---

[7] 'Financial Oppression—the fact of imposing on creditors real rates of return that are negative or artificially low' [Arnaud Mares (of Morgan Stanley)]: 'Ask not Whether Governments Will Default, But How', 26 August 2010 (Available at https://www.econlib.org/archives/2010/08/bond_bubble_wat.html; accessed in April 2024).

Global Imbalances and Rebalancing

Whether or not one agrees that global imbalances were the main or major contributory cause of the financial crisis, there is no gainsaying that it was a relevant factor. Low interest rates in the US over a prolonged period led to excessive borrowing and bubbles. Persistently high consumption levels in the US were facilitated by the current account surpluses and excess savings of some oil-producing nations and Asian countries, which not only provided the goods but also the financing to enable their consumption.

Imbalances arose, among other things, from one set of countries borrowing heavily from another group of countries, mostly to finance their increased consumption. As a result, borrowing countries ran up huge deficits and creditor countries accumulated large surpluses. When the resultant imbalances attained unsustainable levels it triggered a financial crisis. The dominant issue confronting the global polity, therefore, is what actions and sacrifices are needed both within and among countries to rebalance the global economy while at the same time reconciling conflicting domestic and national interests. At a national level, one would need to determine and resolve what sacrifices need to be made and by whom; across nations the burden of adjustment between surplus and deficit countries would call for a high degree of cooperative endeavour.

Borrowing countries may no longer be able to sustain large current account deficits, and may need to take measures to squeeze consumption, boost savings, raise revenues, and reduce government budget deficits. This may also entail structural changes calling for sectoral shifts, by switching from non-tradable to tradable goods industries in order to boost exports. Surplus creditor countries too may find themselves having to reduce their dependence on exports and encourage greater domestic consumption, which could be fraught with political and social problems.

Severely indebted countries (like Greece for instance) may have to seek restructuring of their debts, with consequent cross-border implications, both for the lending institutions and their host nations. Demands could also arise for revaluation and readjustment of exchange rates, which may have to be dealt with in an accommodative spirit instead of obdurate refusal to budge from entrenched positions.

Reduced consumption in the US (and other advanced countries) of goods and services from abroad because of recession in these countries will have an impact on aggregate global demand. This has a consequence for nations whose growth is largely dependent on exports; for reduced demand in the US and other advanced countries may not be fully compensated for by higher domestic demand in the export-dependent countries. Further, rebalancing efforts in recession-hit advanced countries could spark protectionist measures. Without cooperation on a global scale it would be difficult to manage shortfalls in aggregate demand, slower global growth, and militant protectionism.

As the impact of the crisis unfolds globally, one would need to reckon with: (a) the resultant structural shifts within economies that may be necessary; (b) divergences in regulatory frameworks across countries in the face of the tendency of global firms to seek regulatory arbitrage; and (c) public-private divide across nations. The magnitude of the likely difficulties in coordination of national policies at the global level can be gauged from the hesitant and halting steps towards consensus in resolving the euro crisis, within a much smaller arena than a global amphitheatre.

* * *

The severity and global spread of the financial crisis of 2008 was of a magnitude not experienced since the Great Depression of the 1930s. The functioning of the global financial system was on the brink of collapse. That total economic devastation was averted is owed in no small measure to timely and coordinated rescue measures taken across nations. Nonetheless, the bottling up of liquidity and credit lines did unleash what had come to be named the Great Recession.

The path to full recovery was long and arduous. We are going to argue in the book that while hitherto accepted notions of normalcy could have taken a knock, *new normal* called for reassessing linkages between fiscal, financial, and monetary stances and policies. In fact, subsequent crises like the euro area crisis or the economic fallout of the pandemic have demonstrated that fiscal policies tend to play a critical role in attaining and sustaining for economies a new normal that would minimize the possibility of severe financial crises in future and restore growth and employment.

3

Impact of the Crisis on Fiscal Positions

The adverse effects of macroeconomic uncertainties arising due to the ongoing war and the pandemic are still unfolding and manifesting themselves through many channels and are wide-ranging. These comprise falling revenues, both tax and non-tax, rising non-discretionary and discretionary expenditures, a one-time increase in health spending and curtailed social sector expenditures in other sectors. The cumulative upshot of buffeting from different directions can be serious. The adverse impact of the crisis on the rate of economic growth and rising unemployment could be socially unsettling. The combined effect has resulted in swelling fiscal deficits and escalating public debt.

However, the impact of the COVID-19 crisis and macroeconomic uncertainty vary across nations, depending on the conjuncture of their macroeconomic variables and their fiscal and economic conditions. Thus, not all countries have been affected in the same manner and to the same extent; besides, the various channels through which the effects of the crisis are transmitted could have differential impact too. This chapter explores in detail the manner in which the crisis, in the normal course, has revenue and expenditure implications and thus consequences for fiscal balances. Further, it presents the factual position with regard to the differential impact of the crisis on fiscal balances in select countries.

Revenue Implications

A financial crisis fuels economic recession by shrinking liquidity and tightening lines of credit. With recession and declining economic activity, public revenues dip sharply: falling incomes from rising unemployment dent tax payments by individuals; likewise, if corporate profits decline they pull down receipts from corporate taxes and also

Financial and Fiscal Policies. Second Edition. Y. V. Reddy, Partha Ray, and Pinaki Chakraborty, Oxford University Press.
© Y. V. Reddy, Partha Ray, and Pinaki Chakraborty 2024. DOI: 10.1093/9780198934288.003.0003

revenue from capital gains because of falling asset values. There are similar negative consequences on non-tax revenues like dividends, fees from public services, and tourism-related earnings. Moreover, measures undertaken to cushion the impact of the crisis like reductions in tax rates for individuals and corporates, and of indirect taxes, also further reduce tax revenues.

Flow of grants notably from advanced countries to less privileged economies could also suffer following a crisis. Strapped by falling revenues, advanced economies could cut back on their assistance to developing and underdeveloped economies. This could affect low-income countries that rely heavily on donor funds. The decline in the fund flow to the low-income developing countries is evident as more and more countries have seen a decline in their credit ratings, making it difficult to mobilize borrowing from external commercial sources.

In the contemporary and globalized world, economic recession in some nations impacts export-dependent economies that might otherwise have recovered faster. For example, China (and other export-dependent nations) witnessed a sharp reduction in exports to the US, a major export destination, following the recession in the US with resultant contraction of consumption. Consequently, factories in China (and elsewhere) closed down or drastically scaled down their operations. This, in turn, curtailed purchase of commodities and intermediate goods that are anterior in the supply chain, depressing the incomes of these nations. This chain of events inevitably has corresponding ripple effects on public finances, and is still unfolding.

Movements in prices of globally traded commodities, notably of primary products, the prices of which are set in world markets, are another channel through which the crisis affects economies, particularly of developing countries. During the pre-crisis years, some commodity prices peaked to unprecedented levels, often propelled by ample global liquidity in search of yields. In fact, trading in commodities markets took place as if they were financial assets, regardless of their underlying supply and demand. This boosted the economies of commodity-exporting nations but worked to the detriment of commodity and raw materials importing nations. With the onset of the crisis and advanced economies gripped in severe recession, this played out in reverse and more poignantly on the way down as demand for commodities shrank. Either way, public finances of countries took a severe hit from sharp movements in commodity and raw material prices consequent upon deceleration in economic activity and expansion in global liquidity as a result of the crisis. In brief, revenues of countries linked to commodities shrunk as a result of collapsing commodity prices.

The crisis impacts the fiscal position through earnings of migrant workers too. For example, during the boom years, particularly in the housing boom in the US and some advanced countries, migrant workers were drawn to these countries. The remittances to their home countries constituted a substantial portion of the incomes of these countries. With recession hitting some of the host nations of migrant labour, the earnings of migrant labour dipped, and the flow of remittances reduced, causing expenditures in their home countries to contract, with consequent effect on their economies, growth, and naturally public finances.

Expenditure Implications

In a financial crisis, expenditures have an inherent tendency to increase, though there may be policy-induced declines in expenditures dependent on the state of revenues and public debt. Non-discretionary expenditures in the shape of automatic stabilizers kick in, upping expenditures, and with entitlements generally not capped such expenditures are open ended. But in addition to automatic stabilizers, governments are often impelled to undertake discretionary spending too to soften the baleful effects of an economy in recession. These take many forms: enhanced subsidies including reductions in tax rates both to stimulate consumption and prod investment; stimulus measures by way of government spending to offset falling incomes and diminishing demand arising from growing unemployment; bailouts of sectors of the economy facing collapse or extinction or which could potentially threaten system-wide contagion; capital injections to shore up tottering financial institutions; contingent liabilities like extending lines of credit or guarantees with inherent and lurking risk of their devolving, for example to the financial sector to allay apprehensions of collapse. Also, tumbling asset values of pension funds could spark demands to compensate or provide succour to pensioners.

While in theory discretionary spending is conceived as a temporary expedient to alleviate the rigours of economic recession, in practice some of the expenditures may persist beyond the crisis: like, for instance, maintenance expenditures relating to infrastructure projects that may have been undertaken. Special interest groups and vested interests could bring pressure to continue with some of the spending measures even after the crisis has abated. Thus, some of the cyclical expenditures incurred primarily as interim measures may acquire a degree of permanence, blurring the distinction between cyclical and structural components.

Spending financed through additional borrowings carries the burden of additional interest payments. Besides, increased borrowings by government could push up interest rates, raising the cost of borrowing for government. At times, monetary responses to the crisis could transmute into fiscal liabilities. These quasi-fiscal effects could be transmitted not only through the interventions of the central bank but also by actions of the larger public sector.

On the other hand, inherent in depressed economic activity is also the prospect of cutbacks in expenditure, induced by austerity and belt-tightening measures necessitated by falling revenues because of slow-down in economic activity. These result in curtailment of social sector spending, notably in health, education, food security, and poverty alleviation programmes, adversely affecting human resource development that is essential for both long-term welfare and economic growth. A World Bank estimate in the early years of the financial crisis placed the number of people who would be pushed into extreme poverty (below $1.25 a day)[1] at the end of 2010 at 89 million (Ravallion and Chen 2009). In October 2020, using the growth forecasts from the Global Economic Prospects, the World Bank estimated that between 88 and 115 million people around the globe would be pushed into extreme poverty in 2020 due to the COVID-19 pandemic.[2]

---

[1] $ refers to US dollar unless stated otherwise.
[2] https://blogs.worldbank.org/opendata/updated-estimates-impact-covid-19-global-poverty-looking-back-2020-and-outlook-2021

Fiscal Balances

Understandably, the revenue and expenditure impact of a financial crisis and resultant economic recession would be reflected in fiscal balances: primary balance, revenue balance, and fiscal balance, each of which is both important and significant. Fiscal balance is the difference between the total receipts of government (tax, non-tax, and non-debt capital receipts) and the total expenditure of government. A fiscal deficit would imply that the government would need to borrow in order to balance its receipts and expenditure and is a measure of the borrowing needed to balance the books. The stock of public debt is the cumulative aggregate of fiscal deficits. However, if borrowings are utilized to build or acquire physical or financial assets by the government, there will be corresponding additions to the stock of capital assets of the government. The returns from such assets, direct and indirect, will contribute to and hence ease servicing of the stock of public debt.

Revenue balance represents the difference between the current receipts of government (tax, non-tax, and non-debt capital receipts) and current expenditures. In normal circumstances, a persisting revenue deficit is undesirable in that government would need to borrow even to meet current expenditures, in other words borrowing to meet consumption needs. The *golden rule* is that one should not borrow to meet consumption expenditures; applied to public finance that would mean that over the economic cycle government should not borrow to fund current spending but only to invest. In the short run, revenue deficit may be induced by shocks such as natural calamities, global price movements in commodities, or from other unexpected quarters. Revenue deficit may also be engendered by policies to stimulate the economy during the downward movement of a business cycle. The major issue for public policy is to design policies that generate revenue surpluses during the boom phase of the business cycle, as part of counter-cyclical fiscal policies. It must be recognized that fiscal policies should ideally encompass both revenue account and non-revenue components of the budget.

Primary balance represents the difference between the total receipts (tax and non-tax) of government and the total expenditure *before* meeting interest payments. A primary deficit is normally undesirable since it implies that government would need to borrow even to discharge interest payment obligations, either fully or partially. A primary deficit unrelated to the state of the business cycle points to the need for structural rebalancing.

Table 3.1 shows overall deterioration in fiscal balances across nations from the onset of the global financial crisis and during the pandemic. This deterioration is more pronounced in the case of advanced countries, and among advanced economies more so in the case of the US. The US was the epicentre of the global financial crisis. Although the country was severely affected by the pandemic, it also provided large-scale fiscal stimulus during the pandemic which resulted in the sharp increase of the debt ratio. According to the IMF, it is expected that the pandemic would leave a lasting mark on the fiscal balance in general and any significant improvement would only be visible by the end of the fiscal year 2025–26.

However, following 2020's historic surge in public debt to nearly 100 per cent of gross domestic product across the world, nearly three-quarters of countries tightened both fiscal and monetary policies in 2023, which resulted in the steepest decline in the global public debt in the last two years (Francesca et al. 2023).

If we consider individual countries, Canada showed a sharp deterioration in its fiscal balance immediately following the crisis and a repeat of the same situation was visible during the pandemic. The position of Japan and the UK is not very edifying or promising either, though that of the UK seems relatively better as it is expected to attain near or below pre-crisis levels in the next couple of years. Among euro area countries, Germany is seen to regain its pre-crisis level of more-or-less fiscal balance; and surprisingly, Greece shows remarkable rebound, with Ireland and Italy expected to show much improved fiscal balances as compared to their pre-crisis levels.

Emerging economies have been relatively less affected by the crisis in terms of their fiscal balances, due both to the state of their financial sector and the extent of their integration into the global financial system. Within Asia, it is noteworthy that China too exhibits a perceptible downtrend in its fiscal balances, though much less compared to advanced countries; further, it is not expected to return to its pre-crisis situation in the immediate future.

Table 3.1 Overall Fiscal Balances (% of GDP)

Country	2008	2009	2010	2011	2012	2013	2014	2015	2016	2017	2018	2019	2020	2021	2022
Advanced economies	-3.5	-8.6	-7.6	-6.2	-5.5	-3.7	-3.1	-2.6	-2.7	-2.4	-2.4	-3.0	-10.2	-7.5	-4.3
Euro area	-2.2	-6.2	-6.3	-4.3	-3.8	-2.9	-2.5	-1.9	-1.5	-0.9	-0.4	-0.6	-7.1	-5.4	-3.8
France	-3.3	-7.2	-6.9	-5.2	-5.0	-4.1	-3.9	-3.6	-3.6	-3.0	-2.3	-3.1	-9.0	-6.5	-4.9
Germany	-0.1	-3.2	-4.4	-0.9	0.0	0.0	0.6	1.0	1.2	1.3	2.0	1.5	-4.3	-3.7	-2.6
Greece	-10.3	-15.3	-11.4	-10.5	-6.8	-3.9	-4.2	-3.0	0.3	0.9	0.8	0.2	-10.7	-8.0	-4.0
Ireland	-7.0	-13.9	-32.1	-13.6	-8.5	-6.4	-3.6	-2.0	-0.8	-0.3	0.1	0.5	-5.0	-1.7	1.2
Italy	-2.6	-5.1	-4.2	-3.6	-2.9	-2.9	-3.0	-2.6	-2.4	-2.4	-2.2	-1.5	-9.7	-9.0	-8.0
Portugal	-3.7	-9.9	-11.4	-7.7	-6.2	-5.1	-7.3	-4.4	-1.9	-3.0	-0.3	0.1	-5.8	-2.8	-1.9
Spain	-4.6	-11.3	-9.5	-9.7	-11.6	-7.5	-6.1	-5.3	-4.3	-3.1	-2.6	-3.1	-10.1	-6.9	-4.5
Japan	-4.1	-9.7	-9.1	-9.0	-8.2	-7.6	-5.6	-3.7	-3.6	-3.1	-2.5	-3.0	-9.1	-6.2	-7.8
United Kingdom	-5.1	-10.0	-9.2	-7.5	-7.6	-5.5	-5.5	-4.5	-3.3	-2.4	-2.2	-2.2	-13.0	-8.3	-6.3
United States	-6.6	-13.2	-11.0	-9.7	-8.1	-4.5	-4.0	-3.5	-4.4	-4.8	-5.3	-5.7	-14.0	-11.6	-5.5
Canada	0.2	-3.9	-4.7	-3.3	-2.5	-1.5	0.2	-0.1	-0.5	-0.1	0.4	0.0	-10.9	-4.4	-0.7
Other advanced economies (excluding G7 and euro area)	2.0	-1.2	-0.4	0.2	0.2	0.1	0.2	0.0	0.5	1.2	1.2	-0.1	-4.8	-1.3	0.2
Major advanced economies (G7)	-4.5	-9.8	-8.8	-7.4	-6.4	-4.3	-3.6	-3.0	-3.3	-3.3	-3.3	-3.8	-11.6	-9.1	-5.4

(*continued*)

Table 3.1 Continued

Country	2008	2009	2010	2011	2012	2013	2014	2015	2016	2017	2018	2019	2020	2021	2022
Emerging markets and developing economies	0.6	-3.8	-2.2	-1.0	-1.0	-1.7	-2.4	-4.1	-4.5	-3.8	-3.5	-4.5	-8.6	-5.2	-5.2
Emerging and developing Asia	-1.6	-3.3	-2.2	-1.6	-1.7	-1.9	-1.8	-3.1	-3.7	-3.6	-4.2	-5.7	-9.4	-6.4	-7.3
China	0.0	-1.8	-0.4	-0.1	-0.3	-0.8	-0.7	-2.5	-3.4	-3.4	-4.3	-6.1	-9.7	-6.0	-7.5
India	-9.0	-9.5	-8.6	-8.3	-7.6	-7.0	-7.1	-7.2	-7.1	-6.2	-6.4	-7.7	-12.9	-9.6	-9.6
Emerging and developing Europe	0.3	-6.0	-4.1	-0.7	-1.1	-1.9	-1.8	-2.5	-2.8	-1.7	0.1	-0.7	-5.4	-1.8	-3.1
Russia	4.5	-5.9	-3.2	1.4	0.4	-1.2	-1.1	-3.4	-3.7	-1.5	2.9	1.9	-4.0	0.8	-2.2
Türkiye	-2.6	-5.8	-3.4	-0.7	-1.8	-1.5	-1.4	-1.3	-2.3	-2.2	-3.8	-4.8	-5.1	-4.0	-1.6
Latin America and the Caribbean	-1.0	-3.6	-2.7	-2.6	-2.7	-3.2	-4.8	-6.3	-5.7	-5.1	-5.0	-4.0	-8.8	-4.5	-3.9
Brazil	-2.0	-3.2	-2.4	-2.5	-2.3	-3.0	-6.0	-10.2	-9.0	-7.8	-7.0	-5.8	-13.3	-4.3	-4.6
Mexico	-0.7	-4.1	-4.0	-3.3	-3.7	-3.7	-4.5	-4.0	-2.8	-1.1	-2.2	-2.3	-4.4	-3.9	-4.4
Middle East and Central Asia	8.7	-2.7	0.8	3.4	4.3	2.0	-1.5	-7.1	-7.7	-4.8	-1.7	-2.7	-7.9	-2.5	1.4
Sub-Saharan Africa	1.2	-4.2	-3.3	-1.1	-1.7	-3.0	-3.5	-4.2	-4.3	-4.4	-3.5	-3.9	-6.4	-5.0	-4.4

Source: International Monetary Fund, World Economic Outlook Database (accessed in April 2023).

If one were to ignore the Middle East and North Africa, India was expected to register the highest fiscal deficit among all at 12.9 per cent of GDP in 2020. In relation to emerging market economies, India's fiscal deficit which was a little over double that of emerging market economies in 2009 was projected to be significantly higher than that of emerging market economies in 2020. The position was more or less identical while comparing India with G20 emerging market countries or with Asia as a group. Viewing the fiscal deficit over time, India was expected to reduce its fiscal deficit from 12.9 per cent of GDP in 2020 to 9.8 per cent of GDP by 2022. During the same period, emerging market economies were expected to reduce their fiscal deficit from 8.6 per cent of GDP to 5.2 per cent of GDP.

Table 3.2 presents the primary balances of countries from 2006 to 2022 (forecast). Again, unsurprisingly, the deterioration in the primary fiscal balances as a result of the pandemic is more pronounced in the case of advanced economies than those of developing countries.

Fiscal deficits need to be viewed in conjunction with and in the context of other macroeconomic data. An important factor in assessing fiscal deficits is the level of public debt. IMF studies indicate an inverse relationship between high levels of public debt and the effectiveness of fiscal policy, which is also evident intuitively. The crowding out effect is more likely at higher levels of public debt rather than at lower levels. Other factors that affect fiscal sustainability are the ability to service external debt (in foreign currencies) and holdings of foreign currency reserves. An obvious example is that of Japan, which has inherent financial strengths because of its strong export revenues and robust private sectors.

Public Debt

Public debt is the cumulative effect of fiscal deficits aggregated over the years. Even without the onset of a financial crisis, public debt can attain disconcerting and unsustainable levels. What a financial crisis with economic recession in tow does is to exacerbate an already parlous situation, particularly of those countries whose finances are already considerably strained. On the other hand, countries that have followed prudent fiscal policies, including counter-cyclical fiscal policies, are able to weather

Table 3.2 Primary Balance of G20 Countries (% of GDP)

Country	2006	2007	2008	2009	2010	2011	2012	2013	2014	2015	2016	2017	2018	2019	2020	2021	2022
Advanced countries																	
Australia	1.5	1.3	-1.1	-4.5	-4.9	-4.1	-2.9	-2.1	-2.1	-1.9	-1.5	-0.8	-0.4	-3.6	-7.8	-5.4	-2.3
Canada	2.4	2.4	0.5	-2.8	-3.9	-2.7	-1.8	-1.0	0.5	0.6	0.1	0.1	0.4	0.1	-10.5	-5.0	-1.3
France	-0.1	-0.2	-0.6	-4.9	-4.6	-2.7	-2.5	-1.9	-1.9	-1.8	-1.9	-1.3	-0.7	-1.7	-7.8	-5.2	-3.0
Germany	0.7	2.7	2.2	-0.8	-2.2	1.1	1.9	1.5	1.8	2.0	2.1	2.2	2.7	2.1	-3.9	-3.3	-2.1
Israel	3.2	3.7	1.2	-2.2	-0.2	0.0	-1.4	-1.1	-0.2	0.6	0.2	0.7	-1.4	-2.0	-9.0	-1.0	2.5
Italy	0.6	3.2	2.1	-0.9	-0.1	0.8	2.0	1.8	1.4	1.4	1.3	1.2	1.3	1.7	-6.4	-5.6	-3.8
Japan	-2.4	-2.2	-3.3	-8.7	-8.0	-7.8	-7.0	-6.5	-4.5	-2.6	-2.5	-2.2	-1.7	-2.4	-8.4	-5.6	-7.5
Korea	2.4	1.8	1.2	-0.4	0.9	1.1	1.3	0.4	0.2	0.2	1.4	1.8	2.1	-0.1	-2.7	-0.4	-1.2
United Kingdom	-1.2	-1.0	-3.6	-8.6	-6.8	-4.8	-5.3	-4.2	-3.7	-3.1	-1.8	-0.6	-0.5	-0.9	-12.0	-6.0	-2.7
United States	-0.1	-0.8	-4.6	-11.3	-9.0	-7.4	-5.9	-2.6	-2.1	-1.7	-2.4	-2.8	-3.1	-3.5	-11.9	-9.3	-3.4
Emerging economies																	
Argentina	3.3	2.6	1.9	-0.5	-0.5	-1.6	-1.7	-2.6	-3.5	-4.4	-4.8	-4.2	-2.2	-0.4	-6.2	-2.5	-1.8
Brazil	3.2	3.2	3.3	1.9	2.6	2.9	2.2	1.7	-0.6	-1.9	-2.5	-1.7	-1.5	-0.8	-9.2	0.7	1.3
China	-0.7	0.4	0.4	-1.3	0.1	0.4	0.2	-0.3	-0.1	-2.0	-2.7	-2.6	-3.5	-5.3	-8.8	-5.1	-6.6
India	-1.5	0.3	-4.3	-5.0	-4.4	-4.0	-3.2	-2.4	-2.6	-2.7	-2.5	-1.5	-1.7	-3.0	-7.3	-4.5	-4.4
Indonesia	2.6	0.9	1.7	-0.1	0.0	0.5	-0.4	-1.0	-0.9	-1.3	-1.0	-0.9	-0.1	-0.4	-4.1	-2.5	-0.4
Mexico	1.4	1.1	2.1	-1.0	-1.2	-0.7	-0.9	-0.9	-1.7	-1.2	0.4	2.6	1.6	1.4	-0.5	0.0	-0.1
Russia	8.3	5.6	4.7	-6.2	-3.1	1.7	0.7	-0.8	-0.7	-3.1	-3.2	-1.0	3.4	2.2	-3.7	1.1	-2.0
Saudi Arabia	21.3	10.8	28.6	-5.5	4.7	11.5	11.6	5.1	-4.2	-17.5	-16.5	-11.3	-6.0	-4.2	-12.5	-2.0	2.8
South Africa	3.3	3.4	1.6	-2.6	-2.3	-1.4	-1.6	-1.2	-1.2	-1.4	-0.6	-0.8	-0.4	-1.1	-5.5	-1.3	0.1
Türkiye	4.1	2.6	1.5	-1.5	0.1	1.8	0.7	0.8	0.5	0.6	-1.0	-0.9	-2.3	-2.9	-3.2	-2.3	-0.4

Source: International Monetary Fund, World Economic Outlook Database (accessed in April 2023).

the crisis better as they have sufficient *fiscal space* and *head room* with a greater degree of flexibility and manoeuvrability.

The financial crisis of 2008 witnessed unprecedented levels of debt in peace time and post-Second World War. Though debt levels during the war might have touched historical highs, one needs to distinguish them from peacetime episodes of towering debt levels. Besides, most war-time debts were financed from domestic (patriotism-inspired) sources. Peacetime spurts in public debt would tend to be more difficult to curb and pull back as they normally finance expenditures around which vested interests form. It must be noted that gross government debt figures may, to some extent, inflate the extent of indebtedness as they omit to take into account assets held by governments and financed from debt.

Table 3.3 shows that there were substantial increases in debt levels in the immediate aftermath of the global financial crisis and the pandemic. It is noteworthy that the deterioration is much more marked in advanced economies than in emerging economies. The same trend is also notice-able in the net debt of countries. Further, even four to five years after the crisis struck debt levels in almost all the advanced economies, without exception, both of gross and net debt, they are still not projected to show a downward trend.

This may be contrasted with emerging economies whose debt levels are projected to remain more or less steady or trend slightly downwards. In China, the level of gross debt rose sharply from 27.2 per cent of GDP in 2008 to 70.1 per cent in 2020, but thereafter increased further to 77.1 per cent in 2022. As for India, its gross debt-to-GDP ratio is expected to increase from a pre-pandemic level of 75 per cent in 2019 to 83.1 per cent in 2022. This could be misleading in that the debt-to-GDP ratio (which is based on nominal GDP) would be depressed because of the high rate of inflation in India. No doubt this would be true of other countries as well but the rate of inflation in India is significantly higher than those of other countries (as will be brought out in Chapter 7).

Net government debt would represent gross government debt re-duced by the value of assets created from debt (borrowings); hence, the lower net government debt in relation to gross debt, the higher the cre-ation of assets from borrowings. Net government debt figures for India are not available in Table 3.3; it would be interesting, however, to com-pare debt figures for India in relation to gross government debt of other

Table 3.3 General Government Debt (% of GDP)

	2008	2009	2010	2011	2012	2013	2014	2015	2016	2017	2018	2019	2020	2021	2022
Gross debt															
Australia	11.7	16.6	20.4	24.0	27.5	30.5	34.0	37.8	40.6	41.2	41.8	46.7	57.1	57.6	55.7
Canada	70.4	81.9	84.0	84.3	87.2	87.6	85.5	92.0	92.4	90.9	90.8	90.2	118.9	115.1	106.6
Germany	65.7	73.2	82.0	79.4	80.7	78.3	75.3	71.9	69.0	64.6	61.3	58.9	68.0	68.6	66.5
Italy	106.2	116.6	119.2	119.7	126.5	132.5	135.4	135.3	134.8	134.2	134.4	134.1	154.9	149.8	144.7
Korea	26.9	30.0	29.5	33.1	35.0	37.7	39.7	40.8	41.2	40.1	40.0	42.1	48.7	51.3	54.3
Portugal	75.6	87.8	100.2	114.4	129.0	131.4	132.9	131.2	131.5	126.1	121.5	116.6	134.9	125.4	116.0
United Kingdom	49.2	63.1	74.0	79.8	83.1	84.1	86.1	86.7	86.6	85.6	85.2	84.5	105.6	108.1	102.6
United States	73.4	86.6	95.1	99.5	103.0	104.5	104.5	105.1	107.2	106.2	107.4	108.7	133.5	126.4	121.7
Brazil	62.3	65.5	63.0	61.2	62.2	60.2	62.3	72.6	78.3	83.6	85.6	87.9	96.8	90.7	85.9
China	27.2	34.6	33.9	33.8	34.4	37.0	40.0	41.5	50.7	55.0	56.7	60.4	70.1	71.8	77.1
India	72.8	71.5	66.4	68.6	68.0	67.7	67.1	69.0	68.9	69.7	70.4	75.0	88.5	84.7	83.1
Mexico	42.5	43.7	42.0	42.9	42.7	45.9	48.9	52.8	56.7	54.0	53.6	53.3	60.1	58.7	56.0
South Africa	24.0	27.0	31.2	34.7	37.4	40.4	43.3	45.2	47.1	48.6	51.7	56.2	69.0	69.0	71.0
Net debt															
Australia	−5.3	1.2	6.3	10.6	13.8	16.0	19.1	22.1	23.4	23.3	24.1	27.9	34.5	33.3	32.4
Canada	22.4	26.8	28.3	28.9	28.6	26.6	21.7	18.5	18.0	12.5	11.6	8.5	15.7	15.4	13.9

Germany	53.2	60.0	62.0	60.1	59.4	58.4	54.9	52.2	49.3	45.0	42.2	40.1	45.4	45.6	45.1
Italy	97.2	106.4	108.2	109.5	114.1	119.2	121.4	122.2	121.6	121.3	121.8	121.7	141.4	137.3	133.0
Korea	25.7	28.7	28.0	31.5	2.3	5.8	7.5	9.5	9.7	9.6	9.6	11.7	18.3	20.9	23.9
Portugal	64.1	76.1	82.2	103.8	117.1	118.9	120.7	121.0	119.4	116.0	113.4	109.9	123.0	118.1	109.6
United Kingdom	43.4	56.4	66.9	71.6	74.6	75.8	77.9	78.2	77.6	76.2	75.4	74.6	94.5	96.7	91.9
United States	51.6	62.6	69.8	76.3	80.4	80.3	81.1	80.9	81.8	80.4	81.1	83.1	98.3	98.3	94.2
Brazil	37.6	40.9	38.0	34.5	32.2	30.5	32.6	35.6	46.1	51.4	52.8	54.7	61.4	55.8	57.1
Mexico	32.9	36.0	36.0	37.2	37.2	40.0	42.6	46.5	48.7	45.7	44.9	44.5	51.6	50.8	49.7
South Africa	20.1	23.5	26.4	29.1	32.4	35.2	38.1	41.1	42.1	43.8	46.7	50.7	62.2	63.2	66.3

Note: Data on Net Debt are not available for China and India.

Source: International Monetary Fund, World Economic Outlook Database (accessed in April 2023).

countries. Another point to be kept in mind is the frequency of issuance of debt. With shorter maturities of debt, the frequency of issuance of debt rises; this could pose difficulties for highly indebted and fiscally stressed countries.

The IMF cautions,[3] 'the focus on headline debt ratios may also overstate—in some cases, by sizable margins—the degree of short-term financial pressure faced by some governments'. The likely misreading of debt levels is ascribed to central banks pursuing expansionary monetary policy (for example, in the US, the UK, Japan, etc.) through quantitative easing and adding to their holdings of government securities and large-scale monetary expansion during the pandemic.

In 2011, central bank purchases accounted for 27 per cent of sovereign debt issues in the UK, 15 per cent in the US, and 6.1 per cent in Japan—with the stock of central bank claims on the government reaching 18.4, 11.1, and 19.4 per cent of GDP, respectively (see Table 3.4). If they are not sterilized,[4] these purchases reduce the *gross consolidated* government debt and the central bank debt by the same amount.

Perusal and contrasting of columns (1), (3), and (8) in Table 3.4 would reveal the sharp differentials invariably across all countries/regions between gross general government, net general government debt, and net consolidated government and central bank debt.

The difference between the gross general government debt and net general government debt would represent the amount of debt used for creating assets (financial and non-financial). (Net government general debt is defined above as: 'Gross general government debt minus financial assets, excluding shares and other equity and financial derivatives.') The larger the difference the greater is the creation of assets from government debt. For example, the net government debt of the US at 80.3 (per cent of GDP) against its gross debt of 102.9 (per cent of GDP) would suggest that the US has used only 22 per cent of its gross debt to create assets, whereas (calculations show) the corresponding figure for Japan is 45 per cent, that for Germany is 31 per cent, Australia 66 per cent, Canada 61 per cent,

---

[3] IMF *Fiscal Monitor*, April 2012, p. 17.
[4] Sterilization operations appear as an increase in the central bank's nonmonetary liabilities, off-setting the increase in central bank assets due to the purchases of government paper (IMF *Fiscal Monitor*, April 2012, footnote 8, p. 17).

Table 3.4 Components of Consolidated Government and Central Bank Debt, 2011[i]

Country/Region	Gross Cons. Govt. and Cent. Bank Debt[ii]	Net Gen. Govt. Debt[iii]	Cent. Bank Nonmonetary Liabilities	Cent. Bank Net Claims on Govt.	Cent. Bank Net Foreign Assets	Cent. Bank Claims on Other Sectors	Net consl. Govt. and Cent. Bank Debt
	(1)	(2)	(3)	(4)	(5)	(6)	(7)	(3)+(4)−(5)−(6)−(7)
United States	102.9	91.9	80.3	0.0	10.5	0.5	6.5	62.8
Japan[iv]	229.8	210.3	126.6	0.0	15.8	1.4	11.1	98.3
Euro Area	88.1	104.1	68.4	22.5	5.9	5.2	30.1	49.7
Austria[v]	72.2	86.1	52.5	19.6	5.1	4.5	22.5	39.9
Belgium[v]	98.5	112.7	83.2	20.0	5.2	4.6	31.8	61.6
France[v]	86.3	101.6	80.4	21.6	5.6	5.0	28.9	62.5
Germany[v]	81.5	97.4	56.1	22.4	5.6	5.2	22.6	44.8
Ireland[v]	105.0	120.3	95.9	21.6	5.6	5.0	86.6	20.3
Italy[v]	120.1	137.1	99.6	24.0	6.3	5.6	34.0	77.8
Netherlands[v]	66.2	80.4	31.8	20.0	5.2	4.6	18.2	23.7
Portugal[v]	106.8	128.7	100.4	30.9	8.1	7.2	41.5	74.6
Spain[v]	68.5	85.1	56.9	23.5	6.1	5.4	37.8	31.1
Australia	22.9	19.8	7.8	0.0	1.6	3.1	0.0	3.1

(*continued*)

Table 3.4 Continued

Country/Region	(1)	Gross Cons. Govt. and Cent. Bank Debt(ii) (2)	Net Gen. Govt. Debt(iii) (3)	Cent. Bank Nonmonetary Liabilities (4)	Cent. Bank Net Claims on Govt. (5)	Cent. Bank Net Foreign Assets (6)	Cent. Bank Claims on Other Sectors (7)	Net consl. Govt. and Cent. Bank Debt (3)+(4)−(5)−(6)−(7)
Canada	85.0	81.4	33.3	0.1	3.5	0.2	0.1	29.5
Denmark	46.4	54.8	2.6	8.4	−12.5	26.8	4.0	−7.3
Korea, Rep.	34.1	33.4	32.9	0.6	0.7	28.1	0.3	4.3
New Zealand	37.0	34.4	8.3	0.0	−7.3	13.4	0.4	1.9
Sweden	37.4	37.4	−21.4	0.0	−2.5	9.2	0.4	−28.1
Switzerland	48.6	56.3	6.4	7.9	0.2	55.9	2.9	−44.7
United Kingdom	82.5	63.8	78.3	0.0	18.7	−0.5	0.1	60.0

Source: IMF Fiscal Monitor April 2012, Table 6.

(i) General government (excluding Central Bank net claims on the government) plus nonmonetary liabilities of the Central Bank (excluding currency in circulation and reserve).

(ii) Excludes Central Bank gross claims on government and includes Central Bank nonmonetary liabilities, for example, deposits not part of base money or Central Bank securities.

(iii) Gross general government debt minus financial assets, excluding shares and other equity and financial derivatives.

(iv) Central Bank data based on latest available.

(v) In the euro system, profits and losses from most monetary policy operations are pooled and shared among national Central Banks according to their respective capital shares in the European Central Bank.

Table 3.4A Components of Consolidated Central Government and Central Bank Debt, 2020

Country	Central government debt, total (% of GDP)	Claims on central government (% of GDP)	Net foreign assets (% of GDP)
United States	126.2	53.0	1.3
Japan	216.1	153.4	17.2
Austria	99.9	20.1	36.9
Belgium	119.2	25.9	32.6
France	122.9	25.2	20.8
Germany	..	9.6	56.1
Ireland	71.3	14.0	61.7
Italy	..	71.4	−9.4
Netherlands	..	15.3	35.7
Portugal	..	33.6	−10.6
Spain	140.3	45.8	−7.1
Australia	69.2	8.9	−23.3
Canada	74.9	..	..
Denmark	..	−0.8	41.4
Korea, Rep.	46.4	−1.3	23.2
New Zealand	46.1	19.7	−30.5
Sweden	44.0	6.5	9.8
Switzerland	20.9	..	..
United Kingdom	195.9	42.9	10.3

Source: World Development Indicators Database, The World Bank World Development Indicators | DataBank (worldbank.org) (accessed in December 2022).

and New Zealand 78 per cent. At the other end, France comes in at a low 7 per cent, Ireland 9 per cent, and Italy and Spain at 17 per cent.

Column 4 in Table 3.4 shows central bank's net claims on government. Unwinding of central bank purchases of government securities as and when they take place would reflect in outstanding government debt. This phenomenon is more pronounced when we examine the data on net claims on central government for the year 2020 (see Table 3.4A).

* * *

At the best of times, fiscal management is challenging. In an economic recession induced by the global financial crisis and the change brought by the pandemic, the task could be daunting. Expenditure management in the face of inevitably falling revenues has to confront challenges on many fronts: (a) non-discretionary disbursements triggered by automatic stabilizers; (b) balancing the demands and need for discretionary spending to stimulate the economy in the face of conflicting pulls of fiscal rectitude and consolidation calling for austerity and spending cuts; (c) the imperative of alleviating social distress born of rising unemployment; (d) weighing the costs of short-term measures to boost the economy with medium- to long-term negative fallout unless dovetailed in a fiscally responsible medium-term financial and fiscal framework; and (e) the challenging task of determining when to retreat from stimulus action or reverse its course without jeopardizing what may well be a fragile or hesitant recovery.

It would bear mention that one would need to look beyond headline figures of fiscal deficits and public debt, and delve into their composition at a disaggregated level. Otherwise, it could lead to misreading or incomplete appreciation of the real fiscal situation, without which appropriate policy responses may be elusive.

In a world dominated by global finance, fiscal management has to keep in view the responses of financial markets to the fiscal measures undertaken during the global financial crisis and the pandemic. Financial markets tend to consider short-term interests and to view fiscal expansion with considerable scepticism, thus circumscribing fiscal pace. At the time, sound macroeconomic management may warrant expansionary fiscal policies. In brief, the policy space in fiscal management is often unduly constrained by the perspective of financial markets. Thus, fiscal management is hemmed in by uncertainties in financial markets induced by the crisis and the resultant constraints on policy space.

4

Response to the Crisis and
Fiscal Implications

Edwin M. Truman of the Peterson Institute for International Economics identified seven distinct phases of a severe financial crisis.[1] The first is the incipient stage of the crisis when one is either in ignorance or in denial; the second is when the crisis has struck and in hindsight one ascribes a particular event to have caused or triggered the crisis; the third is the management phase when one is trying to cope and come to terms with the turn of events; the fourth phase, attributed to Anna Gelpern (2009), is crisis containment when rules and norms may be subordinated to the immediate task of stopping the bleeding; the fifth phase is the mopping up phase when the bleeding has stopped; the sixth phase consists of distilling the lessons learnt (or not learnt) or only partially learnt; and, finally, the seventh phase consists of taking steps to prevent or minimize the severity of the next crisis. Truman adds that generally 'lessons are only partially learned and incompletely applied'.

This chapter concerns itself primarily with the third phase and beyond. It will present a broad canvas of the responses to the global financial crisis and the pandemic, both monetary and fiscal, its implications for public finances and the fisc, effectiveness of the measures, policy issues including exit strategies for retreating from them, and lessons from both the crises.

---

[1] Remarks made at the Ninth Annual International Seminar, 'Policy Challenges for the Financial Sector Emerging from the Crisis: Building a Stronger International Financial System', Board of Governors of the Federal Reserve System, World Bank, and IMF, 3 June 2009 (Available at http://www.piie.com/publications/papers/paper.cfm?ResearchID = 1225 [accessed on 2 March 2024])

Financial and Fiscal Policies. Second Edition. Y. V. Reddy, Partha Ray, and Pinaki Chakraborty, Oxford University Press.
© Y. V. Reddy, Partha Ray, and Pinaki Chakraborty 2024. DOI: 10.1093/9780198934288.003.0004

Run-up to the Crisis

Turmoil in the financial markets in the wake of systematic under-pricing of risk, particularly in the sub-prime housing mortgage market in the US, is generally perceived as being the trigger for the global financial crisis. The proximate cause for the financial upheaval was the default and collapse of Lehman Brothers in mid-September 2008. Uncertainty about solvency of financial institutions induced fear bordering on panic in the market. Consequently, liquidity dried up and flow of credit to the economy ebbed. The crumbling financial system and freezing of credit lines inevitably had deleterious effects on the real economy. With the weakening of the 'umbilical link between the financial sector and the real economy', the world witnessed its severest economic crisis in nearly eight decades. Almost all the countries were consumed by the conflagration, be they advanced or developing nations, including emerging economies. It is only in the timing, nature, and intensity of the adverse impact that they have differed.

On the other hand, in the case of the COVID-19 pandemic, though the impact and the spread of the pandemic differed across countries and region, the nature of response was widely different across countries (see Tables 4.2, 4.3, and 4.4). Both health and economic recovery were also different across countries. Unevenness in economic recovery and its implications on fiscal management would only be known in the medium term. Available evidence suggests that it would take some time for the debt ratio to decline to the pre-pandemic level. The global economy is faced with high inflation, high debt, a weak fisc, uncertainties due to the war between Russia and Ukraine and other geopolitical risks.

Responses to the Crisis

Realizing the gravity of the global financial crisis, monetary and fiscal authorities in some of the systemically important countries sprang into action. Initially, the financial rescue measures, both monetary and fiscal, appeared somewhat piecemeal and uncoordinated; but as the crisis seemed to threaten the global economy as a whole, it led to a more systematic and coordinated approach.

To stem the crisis and its contagion, ad hoc measures primarily safe-guarding one's national interests were taken; and later, even when countries seemed to act almost in concert, national interests were paramount. Two notable examples of national interest overriding global concerns were from the UK and Germany. Apprehending the imminent collapse of the Icelandic Bank, UK authorities sequestered the assets of its branches in the UK. This action was prompted by the fear that the bank branches might not be forthcoming in honouring their liabilities in the UK, since they were under the authority of Icelandic authorities. Remarkably, the UK supervisors resorted to the Anti-Terrorism, Crime, and Security Act! Germany too acted in a similar manner (though without resort to any terrorism legislation!). To forestall the assets of Lehman Brothers being appropriated to the parent body in the US in bankruptcy proceedings, it froze them to ensure that the demands of local depositors could be satisfied (Claessens et al. 2010).

The immediate response of monetary authorities in the seriously affected economies was to increase liquidity and enable smooth flow of credit by reducing interest rates and taking other allied steps. However, to shore up and protect the stability of the financial system action by monetary authorities alone was not sufficient. Government support to the banking sector was also essential, in some cases with attendant fiscal and quasi-fiscal costs, which could potentially devolve upon taxpayers.

In the case of the global financial crisis, government intercession had to go beyond propping up the financial sector and financial institutions. It had to forcefully contain the negative impact of the financial crisis on the real economy. Though automatic stabilizers would naturally come into play, they were clearly inadequate. Discretionary measures too were necessary. These included lowering of taxes, stepping up government spending to boost falling incomes to soften the impact of rising unemployment, and to counteract shrinking of aggregate demand. Prasad and Sorkin (2009) note that, 'the financial crisis turned into a broader macroeconomic crisis in the fall of 2008' with growth declining sharply in all major advanced countries and emerging economies. In the case of the pandemic, the crisis had three dimensions: protecting life, livelihood, and economic recovery. Unlike the global financial crisis, the pandemic required real sector response from the fiscal and monetary side.

Transfers to households through fiscal and monetary measures were a distinguishing feature of the response to the pandemic.

In absolute terms, designated in US dollars, the largest stimulus in 2009 was by the US followed by China, Japan, and Germany; in terms of GDP (of 2008) the highest amounts of stimulus were by China—2.1 per cent followed by the US—1.9 per cent, Germany—1.5 per cent, and Japan—1.4 per cent. Tax cut as a share of stimulus presents a more varied picture with some countries showing a marked preference for a higher share of tax cuts. For public confidence in government finances not to be eroded, crisis-mitigating measures, both monetary and fiscal, needed to be prompt, contextual, and effective in the short run. They also needed to instil faith in government's resolve to promote and preserve fiscal sustainability and economic growth in the medium-to-long term. Many measures were taken, both by way of monetary and fiscal stimulus to avoid collapse of financial markets and to stimulate the economies; the challenge facing most of the countries then was to generate confidence among its people that these policy responses would contribute to creating and sustaining stability, growth, and equity.

When we examine the response to the pandemic, countries across the world provided fiscal stimulus to deal with the crisis. Globally, the total support was estimated to be US$17,000 billion, of which government guarantees accounted for more than US$4000 billion—roughly one-fourth of the total. The downside fiscal risk cannot be ignored. If there is large default, it can weaken the fiscal balance sheet in the medium term for items that are below the line item at the moment and not reflecting in the budget. The quantum of stimulus varied across countries. It is evident that countries with great ability to spend, spent more and the quantum of stimulus was very low in low-income developing countries.

Monetary Policy Responses and Implications

During the global financial crisis, monetary stimulus to the financial sector comprised many measures varying in degree and across countries. Faced with instability in financial markets and persistent credit squeeze throttling the real economy, most of the countries resorted to substantial and progressive easing of monetary policy by reducing short-term interest rates, even to historic lows. Re-capitalization of banks was undertaken mostly by public authorities in advanced economies having systemically important banks which should they fail might pose a threat to the smooth functioning of the banking sector. In some instances, central banks extended substantial loans and purchased illiquid assets from financial institutions in order to shore up their balance sheets. There were also instances of central bank support, both with and without direct treasury funding, in the form of credit lines to financial institutions, purchase of assets-backed securities, etc. Notable among countries extending assistance with treasury support were the US, the UK, and Russia. Measures to allay misgivings about financial sector liabilities included guarantees for bank deposits, inter-bank loans and in some cases for bonds as well, and raising of limits for deposit insurance. Thus, even where support to the financial sector was mainly from the monetary authorities, there was an inherent element of latent fiscal underpinning, either direct or immediate or of contingent nature (IMF 2009a).

During the global financial crisis, with interest rates already at historic lows and hovering close to zero, central banks were left with few options. Digging deeper into the arsenal of stimulus measures to redress or at least arrest the economic slump ushered in by the crisis, and to further increase liquidity, they resorted to unconventional monetary policies. This consisted of direct bailout of banks and financial institutions like the TARP in the US with underlying fiscal implications, and of quantitative easing.

Quantitative easing, by way of central banks buying bonds from financial institutions, thus found itself added to the armoury of monetary stimulus measures of central banks, notably the Federal Reserve of the US, Bank of England, Bank of Japan, and more recently of the European Central Bank (ECB). Quantitative easing has a two-pronged effect: purchase of bonds by the central bank from financial institutions pushes up the value of the bonds and consequently depresses the underlying interest rate since bond prices and yields move inversely; second, it puts more money in the hands of the financial institutions, thereby injecting further liquidity into the system. An interesting example of innovation is what has been described as funding for lending, and focusing on credit to small industry. These are clearly in the nature of setting sector priorities for credit by central banks.

Like all stimulus measures, quantitative easing or QE as it is popularly referred to, is intended to be a temporary measure or should be so. The repeated resort to QE with less than expected impact on reviving the global economy gives rise to questions about its sustained efficacy.

At a conference convened by the Bank of England in November 2011 to discuss the lessons learnt from such unconventional monetary policies, unsurprisingly, there were divergent views. There appeared to be broad agreement that quantitative easing and other unconventional monetary measures did help soften the macroeconomic effects of the global financial crisis. But opinion was divided about the magnitude of the effects and the mechanisms through which they may have worked.

With serial doses of quantitative easing knocking against possibly diminishing effectiveness, attention is turning to more aggressive strategies of monetary easing, heralding talk of helicopter money drops following the Chairman of Federal Reserve, Ben Bernanke's utterances (at Jackson Hole, Wyoming Conference in August 2012). The term helicopter money—popularized by Milton Friedman—refers to increasing money supply by printing currency notes and distributing them to the public at large in order to encourage immediate short-term spending to boost aggregate demand. The economic argument favouring this stratagem is that it gives an impetus to sluggish aggregate demand. The success of the artifice would naturally depend on whether additional money so provided would be spent and how quickly. Apprehensions of the public holding on to such gratuitous dollops of money are easily dispelled since any suspicions about helicopter money would only impel speedy spending.

Fears that this would stoke inflation are countered by the argument that it is unlikely, considering that there is acute demand deficit in relation to potential output and underutilization of economic resources. Further, if inflationary pressures do manifest themselves they could be counteracted and restrained through timely and appropriate monetary and fiscal measures.

It is arguable that aggregate demand could be boosted by more conventional means like infrastructure spending. This brings up the ideology-laden issue of whether recession should be countered by monetary or fiscal expansionary measures. In the contemporary context of fierce opposition of financial markets to enlarge fiscal deficits and outstanding public debt, the monetary as opposed to fiscal approach may find greater favour, but it would amount to enlarging the balance sheet of central banks. This inclines to the view that expansionary measures are best financed by central banks rather than by the fisc resorting to market borrowings. But whatever the approach, there lurks an inherent risk of expectations that the measures would endure beyond the duration of recession, not to mention pressures to retain them. Unambiguous and explicit statements that these are temporary emergency measures and firm assurances that they would be dismantled once recession is seen to be abating could diminish the political risk (Brittan 2012).

Failure to pull back extraordinary monetary policy measures implemented to stem the tide of financial or economic downslide once the exigent circumstances are absent would exhaust the ammunition to deal with future crises, rendering monetary authorities impuissant. Determining the timing and pace of retreat of emergency measures may prove tricky, but indeterminate extension of support has to be weighed against the ability of monetary authorities to effectively intervene going forward. The policy challenges, therefore, revolve around the appropriate dynamic mix of monetary and fiscal measures, and the timing and sequencing of withdrawal to less unconventional set of measures. The challenges are particularly acute in respect of advanced economies, in view of the incomplete process of deleveraging in relevant balance sheets.

Fiscal Stimulus

Three 'T's could be said to characterize the general principles governing fiscal stimulus measures: first, their *timely* nature in order to be effective; second, being well *targeted* on areas and entities that need to be addressed since diffused focus could lead to diluted results; and, third, ensuring they are *temporary* and ready to be rolled back once the need for them ceases to exist.

Stimulus responses could be categorized as either stabilization or stimulation measures. Broadly speaking, stabilization signifies implicit acknowledgement of the inevitability of having to adjust to the crisis and hence seeks to lessen the pain and to bring about an orderly adjustment. On the other hand, stimulation attempts to shorten or eliminate the adjustment period and therefore involves a much larger financial response or stimulus package (Hannoun 2009). By and large, the response to the crisis so far, particularly in advanced economies, has been more in the nature of stimulation rather than stabilization. As pertinently observed by former US President Bill Clinton, stimulus does not restore the economy to normal levels but is designed to put a floor under the collapse and begin the recovery (Clinton 2011).

The global stimulus spending estimated at $1.98 trillion in 2009 in 32 countries (including G20 countries) accounted for about 1.7 per cent of their GDP, and 1.4 per cent of global GDP. Almost as high as 90 per cent of the global economic stimulus reportedly came from the G20 countries. According to Sameer Khatiwada (2009) (of the International Institute for Labour Studies), based on information available for 22 countries, tax cuts represented more than one-third of fiscal stimulus in advanced economies as against only 3 per cent in developing and emerging economies; in contrast, in developing and emerging economies, infrastructure spending of stimulus measures was three times higher than in advanced economies; spending on employment measures represented 3 per cent of total spending in advanced economies as opposed to only 0.2 per cent in developing and emerging economies; and social transfers to low-income households was relatively low in both groups, at 10.8 per cent and 6.8 per cent, respectively.

Further, by and large, financial measures reportedly outweighed fiscal measures by about five times (Khatiwada 2009). Table 4.1 presents a snapshot of the discretionary fiscal spending in G20 countries immediately after the global financial crisis. Tables 4.2, 4.3, and 4.4 show the quantum of fiscal stimulus provided by the Advanced Economies, Emerging Economies, and Low-Income Developing Economies during the pandemic. Fiscal stimulus measures undertaken in response to the crisis comprised both expenditure and revenue measures. On the expenditure side they encompassed infrastructure spending and protection to vulnerable groups, and in the case of some countries, support for small- and medium-sized enterprises; some countries extended support to specific sectors, for instance, the automobile industry in the US. On the revenue side, the attempt was to assist households through cuts in personal income and indirect taxes. Though the measures were in response to the crisis and, hence, both discretionary and apparently, or at least, in principle temporary, they could acquire some degree of permanence.

Table 4.1 Discretionary Fiscal Stimulus in G20
Countries During the Global Financial Crisis

	(as a per cent of GDP)		
Countries	2009	2010	2011
Argentina	4.7	1.4	...
Australia	2.7	1.7	1.3
Brazil	0.7	0.6	0.0
Canada	1.8	1.7	0.0
China	3.1	2.7	...
France	1.2	1.1	0.6
Germany	1.7	2.2	1.7
India	0.5	0.3	0.0
Indonesia	1.4	0.0	0.2
Italy	0.0	0.0	0.0
Japan	2.8	2.2	1.0
Korea	3.6	1.1	0.0
Mexico	1.5	1.0	0.0
Russia	4.5	5.3	4.7
Saudi Arabia	5.4	4 2	1.6
South Africa	3.0	2.1	0.0
Turkey	1.2	0.5	0.0
United Kingdom	1.6	0.0	0.0
United States	1.8	2.9	1.7
G20 Average	2.1	2.1	1.1

Note: '...' denotes data not available.

Source: International Monetary Fund, Fiscal Exit: From Strategy to
Implementation, Fiscal Monitor, November 2010, pp. 6–7.

Maintenance expenditures of newly started infrastructure projects with associated recurring costs have a benign impact, unless excess capacities were created in the first place like roads to nowhere. However, when vested interests coalesce around individual items of spending with concomitant pressures for their retention, they may not be harmless.

During the global financial crisis, debt incurred by government to acquire troubled or toxic assets could turn out to be only a temporary palliative to stabilize the banking system if fully covered by future sales of these

Table 4.2 Fiscal Stimulus During COVID-19: Advanced Economies

Country	(Estimates as of 5 June 2021) (as a % of GDP)	
	Additional Spending and Forgone Revenue	Equity, Loans, and Guarantees
Denmark	3.5	15.7
Sweden	4.2	5.3
Finland	4.3	7.5
Korea	4.5	10.1
Norway	7.4	4.5
Spain	7.6	14.4
Switzerland	7.8	6.2
Belgium	8.2	11.9
France	9.6	15.2
Czech Republic	9.6	15.5
The Netherlands	10.3	8.1
Italy	10.9	35.3
Germany	13.6	27.8
Canada	15.9	4.0
United Kingdom	16.2	16.7
Japan	16.5	28.3
Australia	18.4	1.8
Singapore	18.4	4.7
AEs	17.3	11.4
New Zealand	19.3	1.6
United States	25.4	2.4

Source: https://www.imf.org/en/Topics/imf-and-covid19/Fiscal-Policies-Database-in-Response-to-COVID-19 (Accessed in June 2021).

assets. In such an event, such operations may be fiscally neutral over the medium term. However, it is reported that favourable tax treatments are extended in some cases to enable the concerned financial entities to re-purchase such assets. These operations make it difficult to assess the fiscal costs and benefits of discretionary measures.

As previously mentioned, recessions have an inevitable impact on governments' fiscal position because of the operation of automatic stabilizers and discretionary fiscal measures aimed at softening the rigours

Table 4.3 Fiscal Stimulus During COVID-19: Emerging Economies

| Country | (Estimates as of 5 June 2021)
(as a % of GDP) | |
	Additional Spending and Forgone Revenue	Equity, Loans, and Guarantees
Mexico	0.7	1.2
Egypt	1.6	0.1
Pakistan	2.0	0.0
Saudi Arabia	2.2	0.8
Albania	2.3	1.6
United Arab Emirates	2.5	0.0
Tunisia	2.7	0.8
Turkey	2.7	9.5
Philippines	2.7	0.9
Romania	3.2	4.2
India	3.5	5.2
EMEs	4.1	2.6
Kazakhstan	4.4	2.9
Argentina	4.5	2.0
Indonesia	4.5	0.9
Russia	4.5	1.5
Colombia	4.7	5.7
China	4.8	1.3
Bulgaria	5.0	3.9
South Africa	5.9	4.1
Georgia	6.1	0.0
Poland	6.5	4.8
Peru	7.8	11.8
Brazil	9.2	6.2
Thailand	11.4	4.2
Chile	14.1	2.5

Source: https://www.imf.org/en/Topics/imf-and-covid19/Fiscal-Policies-Database-in-Response-to-COVID-19 (Accessed in June 2021).

of slackening economic activity. These are amenable to some quantification, despite the complexities mentioned. However, it is difficult to quantify or monitor the impact of the crisis with regard to quasi-fiscal costs. Quasi-fiscal effects are also likely by way of spillovers from monetary

Table 4.4 Fiscal Stimulus During COVID-19: Low-Income
Developing Economies (Estimates as of 5 June 2021)

Country	(as a % of GDP)	
	Additional Spending and Forgone Revenue	Equity, Loans, and Guarantees
Myanmar	0.7	0.3
Niger	0.7	1.3
Bangladesh	1.4	0.1
Vietnam	1.7	0.5
LIDCs	2.0	0.2
Zambia	2.1	0.3
Nigeria	2.4	0.0
Honduras	2.4	1.2
Ethiopia	2.5	0.6
Côte d'Ivoire	2.5	0.0
Kenya	2.5	0.0
Ghana	3.3	0.3
Senegal	4.3	0.2
Uzbekistan	4.4	1.3
Guinea-Bissau	6.7	1.8

Source: https://www.imf.org/en/Topics/imf-and-covid19/Fiscal-Policies-Database-in-Response-to-COVID-19 (Accessed in June 2021).

measures and actions by the larger public sector. Contingent liabilities arising from responses to the crisis, for example guarantees, could materialize over a period.

In general, experience and common sense indicate that the capacity of a country to countenance and weather a financial crisis with its accompanying economic downturn depends on the fiscal space that it continues to have, and the quality of fiscal management, and not merely quantitative indicators of fiscal health. Those that are perceived to be in a position to follow fiscally prudent policies, including counter-cyclical measures, would have greater headroom and financial manoeuvrability to undertake measures to exit without seriously undermining their financial stability. Financing fiscal stimulus from domestic funding resources, as was done by Malaysia in the 1990s, would impart a greater degree of resilience. Evidently, not all the countries and economies have the same capacity to sustain and finance fiscal deficits; much would depend on other attendant factors (Abidin 2010).

Implications and Effectiveness

Three issues came to the fore with the onset of the crisis, policy responses thereto, and their effectiveness or otherwise: namely, liquidity management, credit conditions, and restoration of confidence. To ease the liquidity crisis, central banks lowered short-term interest rates. But this did not necessarily ease the credit crunch because banks were unwilling to lend in view of the crisis of confidence. When short-term interest rates veered to near zero, central banks ran out of ammunition to ease liquidity through monetary measures. To further shore up the balance sheets of banks and financial institutions, central banks resorted to purchasing some of the illiquid assets of the banks. The Federal Reserve in the US went one step further by resorting to quantitative easing, which involved purchase by the central bank of long-term bonds. In essence, this meant intervening in long-term interest rates as well. To what extent this served the underlying objective of channelling funds to boost economic activity in the US is moot, in view of the temptation of banks and financial institutions to borrow at low rates from the central banks and invest elsewhere seeking higher returns. The reluctance of banks to lend to other financial institutions stemmed from apprehensions about their solvency, not being sure of the extent of toxic assets held by them. Overall, though immediate steps were taken with a view to increasing liquidity, the intended objective of easing the credit crunch does not seem to have been achieved for a long time.

Two questions that arise are: whether the steps taken were sufficient and capable of restoring confidence, and whether they would be effective. It has been argued that financial sector intervention and support would be more effective in the medium term for developed economies than fiscal stimulus (Zhang and Zhang 2009). The argument rests on the premise that correcting the fundamental weaknesses in the financial systems of advanced countries as evidenced by the recent crisis could lead to sustainably lower financing costs, promote capital accumulation, and also drive technological progress. On the other hand, fiscal stimulus being a one-time exercise could have inherent negative fallouts in the medium term, owing to fears of fiscal sustainability and possible inflationary impact. It therefore inclines towards policy on both sides of the Atlantic favouring financial reforms over government spending. It concedes that both fiscal stimulus and financial sector rehabilitation are important instruments in the short term, but adds that they could have differential impact in different regions. Financial sector rehabilitation, in its opinion, would seem more important for developed countries whose financial sectors were more badly affected.

Opinion is divided on the effectiveness of monetary policy during a financial crisis or recession. While in normal times monetary policy has traction, in a balance sheet recession following a financial crisis the private sector seeks to pay down debt. Hence, credit expansion, however low interest rates may be, has little impact because borrowers are not forthcoming; in other words it results in a liquidity trap. However, Mishkin (2009) counters this saying, 'more aggressive easing of monetary policy may be necessary to counter the contractionary effects of financial crises'.

On the question of whether stimulus has generated sufficient numbers of jobs, one view is that a more pertinent way of looking at the issue is not how many jobs have been created but whether the benefits of stimulus outweigh the costs or not. Opinion on this issue is said to be divided among those who believe benefits exceed costs, those who dispute this, and a third set who are uncertain. Some economists point to the need for comparing the deleterious effects of short-term collapse or contraction of the economy with the long-term fiscal damage engendered through heightened deficit spending and elevated debt. Others, though siding with those who see positive benefits flowing from stimulus spending, caution about likely or looming future crises brought on by high debt. What sometimes gets lost in this sharply divided debate, particularly by politicians or policymakers, is the distinction between short-term and long-term spending; in other words, one-off expenditures as opposed to recurrent outlays. The issues are further complicated by entitlement spending or kicking-in of automatic stabilizers (The Economist, 7 June 2012).

Multiplier effects of stimulus programmes are important indicators to judge the efficacy of such measures and programmes; the higher the figure, the greater the effectiveness of stimulus. But in the absence of definitive and incontrovertible figures, this is largely a matter of conjecture or informed guesses.

Economic stimulus, particularly in the US, is often criticized as having failed to deliver the expected economic benefits. The criticism levelled is that inflated claims had been made about the efficacy of the measures and that they failed to deliver on the lauded benefits. A counter-argument is that the severity of the recession was possibly underestimated to start with, and that the quantum of stimulus was inadequate to reverse the deep recession. Further, it can plausibly be argued that in the absence of the stimulus measures that were undertaken, the disastrous impact of the financial crisis could well have been worse. While it may be difficult to assess or quantify what the deleterious effects of the crisis would have been in the absence of stimulus measures, it should be possible, nonetheless, to take a view on the sequencing, extent, and timing of those measures.

The effectiveness of stimulus measures will depend on their quality and structure. Besides, they could also have unintended consequences. China is held out as an example of the effectiveness of fiscal stimulus programmes. The macroeconomic stimulus measures adopted in developed countries are said to have had mixed results. In contrast, China's stimulus is shown to have upped real GDP growth from a low annualized rate of 6.2 per cent in the first quarter of 2009 to as high as 11.9 per cent in the first quarter of 2010. According to one view, however, the apparently phenomenal achievement of China is owed entirely to state control over its banking system and corporate sector, with state-owned enterprises (SOEs) complying with centrally mandated dictates on how and where to invest. Thus, the apparently vaunted success of the macroeconomic stimulus package of China could well have resulted in costly misallocation of resources, as well as a lurking real estate bubble (Deng et al. 2011). That a good part of the investment largely financed by debt and mandated by state capitalism was misdirected (towards the property sector) also finds resonance in an article by Michael Schuman (Schuman 2012).

It would seem that the stimulus response of China to the global financial crisis is not the unqualified success that it was thought to be, considering China's mandate to its banks in February 2012 to rollover their loans to local governments and cities. It is estimated that the provinces and cities in China were burdened with debts of slightly under $2 trillion or about a quarter of the country's output, which, if defaulted, could dent the country's economic growth (Financial Times, 12 February 2012). No doubt it can be argued that China's fiscal position is strong enough to support the financial sector in case of weaknesses. China mainly used its state-controlled financial sector to respond to the crisis; thus, while most countries resorted to monetary and fiscal stimulus, or a combination of the two, China relied heavily on its public sector banking system. What this illustrates is that in addition to monetary and fiscal measures, it is also possible to press the financial sector into service. Hence, while assessing the efficacy of China's response to the crisis, one would need to take a comprehensive view of the totality of measures, namely monetary, fiscal, and financial.

Stimulus measures taken to compensate for a dip in demand induced by recession beget larger issues of cross-border spillover effects and global rebalancing of demand. With increasing globalization of trade and economic ties, stimulus measures taken at a national level to stimulate demand do have cross-border spillover effects. But for countries whose growth is largely propelled by exports, the additional demand created through spillover effects is not likely to be of sufficient magnitude to counterbalance reduced export earnings as a result of contraction in global demand. This will naturally have a negative impact on corporate and financial sector balance sheets in the export-dependent countries and consequently compress growth impulses in their economies. For example, about half or more of China's exports are to the US and eurozone countries. However much the stimulus measures taken in these countries create additional demand through spillover effects for the exporting countries, it would not be large enough to make up for the loss of export earnings because of global recession. Thus, structural reforms to rebalance demand, shifting it more towards domestic consumption, are desirable in the case of countries dependent on exports for their economic growth.

In brief, whether financial sector intervention and financial reforms or fiscal stimulus should be favoured in preference to the other will depend on the state of the economic cycle, individual circumstances of different nations, nature of inter-dependencies among sectors and economies, and may vary over time. The management of crisis should be viewed not only in terms of an appropriate package of monetary, fiscal, and financial sector policies, but also in the framework of structural reforms. Oversimplification of the costs, benefits, and effectiveness of various options is best eschewed.

Policy Issues and Lessons from the Crisis

The financial crisis has brought into pointed focus the sharp ideological divide, both among policymakers and economists. An unending and often polemic debate driven by seemingly irreconcilable ideological differences is about stimulus and austerity; and short-term palliative measures to boost incomes, demand, and employment versus fiscal rectitude, consolidation, and sustainability. To the former, immediate action by way of stimulus spending to prime the economy is a social and economic imperative. To the latter, short-term pain must necessarily yield to the long-term interests of fiscal and debt sustainability. In their view, austerity creates confidence in the market about long-run economic growth and financial health. Stimulus and austerity are two creeds clung to with religious fervour by their respective adherents. Some economists lean heavily in favour of stimulus spending to prime the economy by boosting aggregate demand. Other policymakers and economists are vehemently opposed to this approach that relies on spending financed by borrowings. They contend that it would exacerbate already high and unsustainable fiscal deficit and add to burgeoning debt that is spiralling out of control. They plump for a fiscally conservative, if not hawkish, stand calling for austerity and spending cuts, unmindful of any short-term pain it may cause and impair growth prospects.

The essence of this polemic ideological divide lies in whether one sees the policy response to the crisis from a short-term or a medium- to long-term perspective, and the extent of human suffering and burden sharing between different sections of society. They often ignore the socio-political dimensions of economic policy and its consequences. The former recognizes the immediate economic distress—manifested through falling incomes and rising unemployment—causing severe contraction in aggregate demand. The latter is more concerned with fiscal rectitude that is essential for long-term financial and economic health. Arguments on both sides are persuasive and not without validity. A pragmatic approach, without repudiating the basic tenets of either, would opt for short-term stimulus measures set against a medium- to long-term fiscally appropriate framework. The attempt would be to provide immediate succour and soften the rigours of economic recession without jettisoning long-term commitment to fiscal sustainability. In short, the response would be to relieve the immediate distress, push up aggregate demand to revive economic growth, and to return to the path of fiscal rectitude as soon as circumstances warrant. In other words, short-term public welfare is not sacrificed on the altar of fiscal propriety that is undeniably crucial for long-term growth and public welfare. While debating fiscal issues, it would be totally inappropriate to consider options without reference to structural elements of the economy concerned. It may be imprudent to incline heavily either towards fiscal activism or towards fiscal fundamentalism in the absence of a credible framework for structural reform.

Utterances by the Managing Director of the IMF at the annual meeting of the Fund and World Bank in Tokyo in October 2012 and observations in the World Economic Outlook 2012 revealed a notable shift in and softening of their stance with regard to fiscal austerity. Christine Lagarde, Managing Director of the IMF, 'cautioned against front-loading spending cuts and tax increases' and 'also urged countries more generally to refrain from new austerity measures amid signs that the IMF is becoming increasingly concerned about the impact of government cutbacks on growth' (Financial Times, 11 October 2012). She also further urged, 'accommodative monetary policy; the right pace of fiscal adjustment, mindful of not undercutting growth but with solid and realistic plans to bring debt down over the medium term; finishing the banking sector clean-up; and structural reforms to boost productivity and growth'.

Withdrawing from stimulus and other measures initiated in response to an economic crisis is fraught with striking a delicate and right balance between not upsetting the slow march towards economic recovery and the medium- to long-term goal of financial stability and health. As pointed out in the previous section (Implications and Effectiveness), the success or impact of stimulus programmes in stimulating demand depends on their multiplier effects. Multipliers are not easy to estimate and depend on the extent of openness; they are imprecise and vary across countries. By and large, infrastructure spending and international cooperation in setting in motion stimulus programmes may maximize benefit. With increasing interconnectedness of markets, trade, and financial systems a coordinated approach to stimulus programmes is likely to increase benefits. Besides, measures to stimulate demand in one country can have beneficial effects across its borders, underlining the spillover effect or cross-border effect of stimulus programmes.

It would be also pertinent to see to what extent short-term stimulus measures have a positive impact on economic growth; that is to say, whether the effects are temporary and confined to the short term or extend beyond the short term, producing more durable benefits, that is, a double dividend.

If public faith in the adherence to long-term fiscally prudent policies is not to be shaken, stimulus programmes should begin to unwind once recovery is seen to be firmly on course. This brings into play the thorny issue of exit policy. An exit strategy is a delicate operation, involving rolling back stimulus measures taken in the immediate aftermath of a crisis, ensuring, however, that their withdrawal would not harm the recovery. Withdrawing too soon might unsettle a recovery that is still fragile. Persevering with stimulus programmes even after recovery takes firm root may compromise long-term fiscal health. Besides, entrenched interests may hinder their dismantling. Thus, temporary cyclical expenditures might transmute into structural elements. If stimulus measures adopted in the wake of a crisis are not rolled back as early as it is deemed prudent to do so, monetary and fiscal authorities might be lacking in ammunition to tackle future crises. Determining precisely when recession has turned course and economic recovery has struck firm roots is a matter of judgement. Done too early, one runs the risk of economic relapse; put off until too late, one may lay the seeds of vested interests perpetuating a cyclical measure into a structural issue.

Laying down absolute principles about when retreat from stimulus should begin is not easy. However, the guideposts could be discernible uptick in economic growth, observable and sustained pick-up in employment levels, and breaching of debt sustainability capacity. Also, how soon or how fast the pull-back can be put into effect would depend on the fiscal space available to nations. The larger the fiscal space available to a country, the more its flexibility in attuning the near-term imperative of not deflecting the path towards recovery to the goal of long-term adjustment plans. For long-term sustainability is essential to provide a cushion to meet future economic downturns should they arise. Policy outcome will depend on political processes though technical analysis and judgements will enable better informed decisions.

As countries begin to push back and recover from the ravages of economic recession, they may reformulate their fiscal rules to better weather future episodes of economic cataclysms. But fiscal rules alone offer no guarantee against future recurrences of economic slumps; at best, if adhered to, they provide a buffer to fend off future economic onslaughts. This underscores the importance of counter-cyclical policies.

A salient lesson from the crisis is the importance of adopting counter-cyclical policies. Essentially, it means setting aside reserves to draw upon during periods of adversity; a fiscal granary to draw from during times of scarcity, as it were. Good economic times, if prudently managed, provide a fiscal cushion to soften the baleful impact of economic downturns. In the absence of judicious fiscal measures, the room for manoeuvrability during periods of crisis is circumscribed. What better illustration of this than the fact that countries with relatively stronger fiscal balances were able to better withstand the onslaught of the crisis, and also undertake corrective fiscal measures because of the buffer they enjoyed.

Fortunately or unfortunately, credit rating agencies do play a role in influencing, though not determining, fiscal sustainability and credit worthiness. An important lesson from the global financial crisis is that short-term fixes without medium-term commitment to fiscal rectitude would undermine the confidence of financial markets. This is illustrated by the downgrading of the credit rating of the US and other major economies like France and the UK. It is noteworthy, however, that financial markets reacted differently to changes in credit ratings of different countries.

It is generally easier to achieve coordination on a global scale when a crisis is at its peak rather than later during the recovery phase. The ingredients for sustainable recovery are: meaningful fiscal consolidation in countries with large deficits accompanied by rebalancing of global demand (as was mentioned in Chapter 2); strengthening of banking systems together with financial regulation, preferably coordinated global financial regulation, though regulation is normally at a national level; and structural reforms aimed at improving economic performance (in developed countries). Successful rebalancing of global demand will also depend on progress in global trade negotiations. It would be unrealistic to assume that these would not call for tough decisions on spending, entitlements, and taxes. Given the social turmoil and hardships that fiscal consolidation might bring in its wake—elevated unemployment and falling incomes—fiscal policies that do not alleviate unemployment (through training to upgrade skills) and improve the climate for enhanced private investment are unlikely to succeed or be popular. Considering that the global financial crisis had its origins in the US and global recovery is imperilled by the eurozone crisis, the pandemic and various geo-political risks, both the US and the eurozone countries have not only an important role to play but also a leading one.

* * *

The depth and spread of the financial crisis was of such magnitude that most of the nations plunged into action with conventional and unconventional globally coordinated measures, not only to contain the damage but also to prevent the total collapse of global finance and its institutions. Remedial stimulus measures were both monetary and fiscal, by central banks and national governments, respectively, recognizing that monetary or fiscal actions alone might not suffice. To begin with, the actions were at a national level but soon converged to globally concerted and coordinated action. With traditional monetary easing of lowering interest rates knocking against the zero-bound limit, some monetary authorities even resorted to extraordinary monetary actions like quantitative easing and the like.

Stimulus measures inevitably have fiscal consequences, even monetary stimulus action because of latent quasi-fiscal implications. Equally inevitably, debates arise about the need for stimulus and its effectiveness on the one hand, and adequacy of stimulus on the other. Opinion is also sharply divided on ideological lines: whether the response to the crisis should more appropriately be through monetary action alone, jettisoning short-term fiscal measures to boost demand in favour of the larger goal of fiscal orthodoxy and rectitude or whether fiscal stimulus should be embraced in the short term to alleviate economic distress but within a medium- to long-term framework of fiscal sustainability.

Post-COVID fiscal consolidation is emerging as a major issue as countries deal with large deficits and debt, high inflation, and uneven economic recovery. Though in the short run, necessary flexibility for the creation of fiscal space needs to be provided through higher borrowing, there is a need to return to a sustainable fiscal management for macro stability and growth when we take a medium-term view. This rising debt has the potential to reduce fiscal space for development spending. Fiscal policies need to achieve a fine balance between the fiscal expansion and stability. What would emerge will depend on the way the global economy handles macro uncertainties, the actual quantum of fiscal shock due to COVID and the fiscal need required for COVID response and recovery.

Unlike COVID, during the global financial crisis the whole debate relating to responses to the crisis was also about the role of the financial sector. The financial sector had considerably benefitted from the rescue measures in response to the crisis, having been saved from collapse (in many advanced countries). In a sense, it was also an arbiter of monetary and fiscal measures, since these had to reckon with the reactions of financial markets. Yet, it is fiercely opposed to regulation of financial markets, an incongruously insular approach. What the financial crisis has brought to the fore is that the financial sector has a complementary role to play alongside monetary, fiscal, and structural policies; a role that assumes importance and hence warrants serious review, going forward.

What emerges from the foregoing discussion is that the various ramifications of the global financial crisis and the pandemic ultimately and inevitably have fiscal consequences, thus underscoring the centrality of fiscal issues, which are to be addressed at a national level.

5

The Crises and the Global Economy in the Twenty-First Century

The preceding chapters have focused on the background of the various crises, policy response to these crises, and their fiscal implications. Against this backdrop, the next three chapters will focus on the country-specific details. In particular, this chapter gives a synoptic account of the global economic development during 2001–22 with a view to providing the milieu for the currently unfolding euro area fiscal/debt crisis and the pandemic later.

The period has been marked by three major crises, namely, (a) the global financial crisis of 2008–9; (b) the euro area crisis of 2011–13; and (c) the pandemic of 2020–22. These apart, events like Brexit, whereby the British people gave a verdict for exiting the EU on 23 June 2016 (that, after a few years of uncertainty, finally came into effect on 1 February 2020), or the US-China trade war, since January 2018, when US President Donald Trump began imposing tariff and trade restrictions on China, or the ongoing Russia-Ukraine military conflict that began on 24 February 2022, also added to the volatile global economic situation.

The period of time beginning from 2007 onwards is often compared with the Great Depression of the 1930s, and in order to emphasize the metaphor, the period is often termed as the Great Recession. Subsequently, the year 2020 is described as the year of the great lockdown, coinciding with the first wave of the pandemic. Thus, this chapter examines the salient features of the period 2007–22. As the next chapter will be fully devoted to the euro area, developments related to the euro area are consciously not discussed in this chapter.

Financial and Fiscal Policies. Second Edition. Y. V. Reddy, Partha Ray, and Pinaki Chakraborty, Oxford University Press.

The rest of the chapter is organized as follows. To begin with, an overview of the period preceding the global financial crisis is presented. This is followed by the global trends during the crisis. The developments before and during the pandemic are analysed next. This is followed by a discussion of the economic developments of the G20 economies and the big three (i.e., the US, the EU, and China). Before offering the concluding observations, experience of some of the advanced economies is discussed.

Growth

The Lull before the Storm: 2001–6

After the crash of the dot-com bubble in 2001, the global economy has done extremely well during the first decade of the twenty-first century till the occurrence of the crisis. The average global growth during 2001–6 was around 4 per cent. Subdividing the global population of countries adopting the standard IMF grouping, several broad patterns emerge (Appendix 6B gives the details of country groupings). First, this optimism was shared by both the advanced economies as well as the emerging markets. Emerging markets grew at a faster rate than the advanced economies in consonance with the newfound dynamism as well as low base in these economies. Second, the period also witnessed emergence of developing Asia in general and China and India in particular as the global growth pole(s). Third, with their share in global GDP at nearly 50 per cent, the emerging market and developing economies have supported the global growth in a big way. Fourth, this is not to mean that these emerging market and developing economies (EMDEs) have decoupled from the advanced economies. In fact, if there is any evidence, it is one of increased synchronicity between the growth of the advanced economies and that of the EMDEs. Thus, with the brewing of the subprime crisis in the US economy since 2007, when the global economy was pushed to a recession in 2009, growth of both these two groups of countries suffered (Chart 5.1).

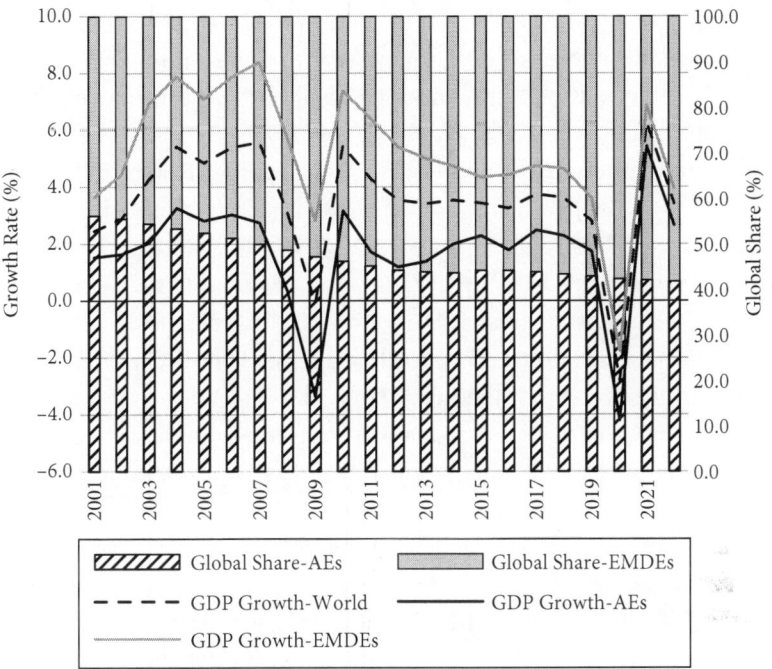

Chart 5.1 Real GDP Growth and Share in Global GDP (at PPP)
Source: Constructed by authors from *World Economic Outlook* Database, April 2023, IMF.

The Great Recession and the After Shocks: 2007–13

The Great Recession: 2007–9

It may not be melodramatic to say that the scenario changed 2007 on-wards like wildfire—first in bits and pieces and later in an all-out manner. By late 2007, the US sub-prime crisis and the consequent turbulent financial conditions seemed to have clouded the prospects of global growth. These uncertainties got accentuated day by day and distress of newer financial institutions started coming to light each day—the situation reached its peak in September 2008 with the fall of the iconic investment bank Lehman Brothers and the subsequent partial nationalization of the financial sector in the leading economies like the US and the UK.

There was huge deleveraging on the part of the financial institutions accompanied by increased counterparty risks, and deflationary tendencies. All the major equity indices dropped by about 25 per cent in October 2008 and credit spreads spiked to distress levels. Sovereign debt of the emerging markets also came under more severe pressure and spreads on sovereign debt of the emerging markets nearly doubled, returning to 2002 levels. Emerging equity markets lost about more than a third of their value (in local currency terms). This was clearly not good times and despite its normal optimistic stance, the IMF in its October 2008 *World Economic Outlook* noted: 'The world economy is now entering a major downturn in the face of the most dangerous shock in mature financial markets since the 1930s ... the major advanced economies are already in or close to recession, and, although a recovery is projected to take hold progressively in 2009, the pickup is likely to be unusually gradual, held back by continued financial market deleveraging.'

The genesis of the global financial crisis, by now, is well known (Desai 2011; Lybeck 2011; Reddy 2011). While it originated in the sub-prime segment of the US mortgage market with increasing delinquency and bursting of the property price bubble, practice of securitization (whereby mortgage-related products were bundled into some structured investment vehicles) accelerated its impact. The exposure of the US government-sponsored enterprises like Fannie Mae or Freddie Mac to the US mortgage products also increased the momentum of the crisis. Alongside, factors like lax regulation of the US financial sector, proliferation of shadow banking activities which did not come under the regulatory oversight, skewed incentive structure in the financial sector along with pro-cyclical behaviour of the rating agencies played a role in the genesis of the crisis. In macro terms, loose monetary policy of the US as well as prevalence of global imbalance wherein oil producing and a number of Asian economies had current account surplus and the US had current account deficit for quite a number of years, could have contributed to the global financial crisis. While the financial sector started having initial cases of failures during 2007 to mid-2008, with the failure of Lehman Brothers in September 2008, there arose a serious crisis of confidence and accentuation of counterparty risks. Thus, what started as a purely mortgage market crisis slowly permeated into other segments of financial markets like the money market, the credit market, and the commercial paper market, and culminated in a global financial crisis. With uncertainties in the market and huge increase in counterparty risks, credit channels of the banking sector became effectively choked. Consequently, trade credit suffered substantially, which affected trade adversely. All these took a toll on global growth, which turned into the Great Recession whereby global GDP shrank by 0.6 per cent during 2009 (see Chart 5.1).

Uneven and Fragile Recovery: 2010

With such widespread monetary and fiscal stimulus, by the end of 2009 there were indications that growth could turn positive in 2010. The IMF, in its October 2009 *World Economic Outlook*, projected 2010 global growth at 3.1 per cent. Expectedly, the recovery turned out to be uneven and fragile; for example, while the advanced economies were projected to grow at 1.3 per cent, the growth for the emerging markets was projected at 5.1 per cent. There were at least three major risks to this outlook. First, the resolution of the toxic assets of the US banking sector remained unfinished and financial systems continued to remain impaired. Second, the recovery was essentially an offshoot of the monetary and fiscal stimulus, many of which had to be withdrawn shortly, particularly in countries with limited fiscal space. Third, with asset prices busts, household savings suffered losses in a number of countries. Things continued to brighten up till mid-2010 and the projected global growth for that year was revised upwards in April 2010 by a full 1 percentage point to 4.2 per cent.

From Uneven Recovery to Another Crisis: End 2010–14

Despite such growth optimism, financial stability received a setback with the brewing of the euro area debt crisis in the second quarter of 2010. In fact, two things happened in the euro area. First, a few of the euro area economies, like Ireland, whose banking sector had large real estate exposure, either domestically or to sub-prime toxic assets of US origin, started facing some difficulties. Second, international investors, who for long treated the sovereign debt of all the euro area economies on par, suddenly became conscious of country-specific circumstances, having been bitten by the global financial crisis. They started to factor in such differences in calculating sovereign yields as well as credit default swaps. Countries where fisc happened to be a concern, like Greece, became the worst affected in this process. Thus, by the end of 2010, there was substantial increase in financial market volatility and decline in risk appetite triggered by heavy selling of sovereign debt of the vulnerable euro area economies. This also sent shockwaves to the banking systems of a number of otherwise strong euro area economies which were holders of such debt.

Furthermore, many of these countries which also had current account deficit, financed heavily through subscription of sovereign debt by international investors, found this source drying up and effectively faced bankruptcy issues with their sovereign papers. Additionally, since these countries were members of currency union, they did not have the flexibility of devaluing their currency.

Thus, with a slower growth in advanced economies and increase in financial and fiscal uncertainties, global growth decreased in 2011. The IMF's October 2011 *World Economic Outlook* painted quite a bleak picture of the world economy and went on to say:

> The global economy is in a dangerous new phase. Global activity has weakened and become more uneven, confidence has fallen sharply recently, and downside risks are growing. Against a backdrop of unresolved structural fragilities, a barrage of shocks hit the international economy this year ... At the same time, the handover from public to private demand in the US economy stalled, the euro area encountered major financial turbulence, global markets suffered a major sell-off of risky assets, and there are growing signs of spillovers to the real economy ... Prospects for emerging market economies have become more uncertain again, although growth is expected to remain fairly robust, especially in economies that can counter the effect on output of weaker foreign demand with less policy tightening. (p. xv)

By mid-2012, the depth and breadth of the euro area expanded considerably. The sovereign debt crisis in the euro area caused sharp increases in the bond rates of a number of economies in the euro area. As a result of the depleted confidence and increasing financial stress, as of April 2012, the euro area was projected to be experiencing a contraction of 0.3 per cent in 2012. By the end of 2012, despite a number of policy actions, the conditions of the euro area continued to deteriorate further and the crisis from the euro area periphery (like Greece and Ireland) spread to the core of the euro area. Spanish sovereign spreads hit record highs and there was sharp upward movement in Italian spreads.

Thus, through a complex process of interrelation between the financial and fiscal sectors, the initial global financial crisis which turned into a global recession (2007–9) culminated in a full-fledged euro area debt crisis in 2010.

The Uncertain Recovery: 2014–19

While the euro area crisis peaked between 2010 and 2012, its impact continued at least for a year. In the January 2014 update of its World Economic Outlook, the IMF noted three upsides in the global economy, namely, strengthened global activity during the second half of 2013; the euro area moving from recession to recovery; and higher export demand in emerging markets. However, this recovery did not last long. The first shock came from the result of the British referendum whereby in response to a referendum held on 23 June 2016, 52 per cent of the British voters voted to leave the EU. After a protracted period of policy confusion regarding the process of exit, Brexit finally came into effect on 1 February 2020 with an adverse economic impact on the British economy. An assessment from the OECD (2016, p. 5) noted:

Membership of the European Union has contributed to the economic prosperity of the United Kingdom. Uncertainty about the outcome of the referendum has already started to weaken growth in the United Kingdom. A UK exit (Brexit) would be a major negative shock to the UK economy, with economic fallout in the rest of the OECD, particularly other European countries. In some respects, Brexit would be akin to a tax on GDP, imposing a persistent and rising cost on the economy that would not be incurred if the UK remained in the EU. The shock would be transmitted through several channels that would change depending on the time horizon. In the near term, the UK economy would be hit by tighter financial conditions and weaker confidence and, after formal exit from the European Union, higher trade barriers and an early impact of restrictions on labour mobility. By 2020, GDP would be over 3% smaller than otherwise (with continued EU membership), equivalent to a cost per household of GBP 2200 (in today's prices).

Meanwhile, across the Atlantic, Donald Trump became President of the US on 20 January 2017 and on 14 August 2017, President Trump instructed the US Trade Representative to begin the Section 301 process against China. It is important to note that Section 301 of the US Trade Act of 1974 grants 'the Office of the United States Trade Representative (USTR) a range of responsibilities and authorities to investigate and take action to enforce US rights under trade agreements and respond to certain foreign trade practices' (CRS 2023). In a detailed 200-page report the USTR found that China has been engaging in restrictive trade practices involving 'the transfer and theft of intellectual property and technology to the detriment of' the US economy and the future of US workers and businesses. Following such findings, the US raised the tariff on imports from China in 2018 and 2019, mainly in machinery and metals. China retaliated and imposed tariffs on imports from the US and it also lowered tariffs on imports from the rest of the world. Such tariff increases were a major departure from long-run trends towards tariff reductions across the globe (Fajgelbaum et al. 2021). Effectively bilateral tariffs between the US and China have increased on average to 17%; the trade conflict has led to a sizeable reduction in trade between the US and China in 2019 and is accompanied by considerable trade diversion to imports from other regions. Admittedly, this could have led to a reorganization of value chains in (East) Asia—a strategy often known as 'China plus one'.

All these affected global growth adversely and in its October 2019 edition of *World Economic Outlook* the IMF noted, 'The global economy is in a synchronized slowdown, with growth for 2019 downgraded again—to 3 percent—its slowest pace since the global financial crisis . . . This subdued growth is a consequence of rising trade barriers; elevated uncertainty surrounding trade and geopolitics; idiosyncratic factors causing macroeconomic strain in several emerging market economies; and structural factors, such as low productivity growth and aging demographics in advanced economies.'

The Pandemic and the Great Lockdown: 2020–2

When the first case of coronavirus was reported at Wuhan City in China in early December 2019 no one had any idea that humanity was about to face one of the biggest public health crises of the last 100 years or so. The infecting virus was designated as 'Severe Acute Respiratory Syndrome Coronavirus 2' (SARS-CoV-2). Subsequently, the World Health Organization coined the term COVID-19 and declared this novel coronavirus disease as a pandemic on 11 March 2020. The virus turned out to be highly contagious. While many infected were either asymptomatic or developed mild fever and respiratory illness, the effect on people with comorbidity conditions was severe including mortality. Also, during 2020 and 2021 there were a number of variants of the virus giving rise to at least four major waves of the pandemic. With a total death toll of around 7 million and the death toll in the US surpassing one million, it turned out to be a major human tragedy. Also, the spread of the pandemic was global with both developing and advanced countries being affected almost uniformly (Table 5.1). However, with the invention of a number of coronavirus vaccines within less than a year of the outbreak of the pandemic, the incidence of the pandemic was in check. In fact, there are estimates that vaccinations could have prevented 14.4 million deaths from COVID-19 in 185 countries and territories between 8 December 2020 and 8 December 2021 (Watson et al. 2022).

The economic impact of the pandemic was transmitted both in terms of a demand shock and a supply shock. With the pandemic spreading globally, there were lockdowns of different intensities in most of the geographies. Naturally, with broken global and even national supply chains, the supply shock played havoc in the production process. With lower labour demand, the resultant unemployment (longer-term or temporary) and income loss have also led to lower demand. The 4.2 per cent contraction of global growth in 2020 turned out to be the most severe of the

Table 5.1 Incidence of the COVID-19 Pandemic in the 25 Most-Affected Countries

	Country	Total Cases	Total Deaths	Total Cases per million population	Deaths per million population	Tests per million population
		(in terms of total infected cases) (as of September 2023)				
1	US	108,670,700	1,176,595	324,579	3,514	3,542,866
2	India	44,998,650	531,930	31,990	378	661,721
3	France	40,138,560	167,642	612,013	2,556	4,139,547
4	Germany	38,490,086	176,031	458,851	2,099	1,458,359
5	Brazil	37,796,956	705,775	175,511	3,277	296,146
6	Korea	34,571,873	35,934	673,523	700	307,892
7	Japan	33,803,572	74,694	269,169	595	799,578
8	Italy	26,043,870	191,586	432,172	3,179	4,567,139
9	UK	24,704,113	229,089	360,655	3,344	7,628,357
10	Russia	23,029,404	400,047	157,946	2,744	1,875,095
11	Turkey	17,232,066	102,174	201,399	1,194	1,902,052
12	Spain	13,914,811	121,760	297,840	2,606	10,082,298
13	Australia	11,768,585	22,754	451,443	873	3,142,326
14	Vietnam	11,623,649	43,206	117,466	437	867,342
15	Taiwan	10,241,523	19,005	428,720	796	1,286,903
16	Argentina	10,070,247	130,608	218,870	2,839	776,264
17	Netherlands	8,617,412	22,992	500,679	1,336	1,509,718
18	Mexico	7,649,199	334,472	58,141	2,542	152,124
19	Iran	7,615,822	146,364	88,533	1,701	666,338
20	Indonesia	6,813,429	161,918	24,409	580	408,975
21	Poland	6,522,506	119,650	172,828	3,170	1,029,248
22	Colombia	6,378,000	142,961	123,814	2,775	717,327
23	Greece	6,101,379	37,089	591,412	3,595	9,909,078
24	Austria	6,081,287	22,542	670,727	2,486	23,302,116
25	Portugal	5,621,390	27,437	554,347	2,706	4,549,993
26	*World*	*695,871,945*	*6,920,665*	*38,063*	*89,274*	

Source: World Health Organization. Available at https://data.who.int/dashboards/covid19/cases (accessed in May 2024).

last 50 years. With near-universal vaccination all over the world and aggressive usage of monetary and fiscal stimulus, growth recovered in 2021. However, with the triggering and escalation of the Russia-Ukraine war since 24 February 2022, growth decelerated in 2022.

A Period of Marked Volatility and Uncertainty: 2000–22

The first 22 years of the twenty-first century are marked by great volatility. Is there a standard way to characterize this period? Towards this end, Table 5.2 below reports the subtitles of the IMF's *World Economic Outlook* (WEO) updates since 2008. A look at the table makes one discern words like stress, weakening prospects, crisis, setbacks, dangers,

Table 5.2 Subtitles of IMF's World Economic Outlook (WEO), 2008–2022

Time	Subtitle of WEO Update
Oct 2008	Financial Stress, Downturns, and Recoveries
Nov 2008	Rapidly Weakening Prospects Call for New Policy Stimulus
Jan 2009	Global Economic Slump Challenges Policies
Apr 2009	Crisis and Recovery
Jul 2009	Contractionary Forces Receding But Weak Recovery Ahead
Oct 2009	Sustaining the Recovery
Jan 2010	A Policy-Driven, Multispeed Recovery
Apr 2010	Rebalancing Growth
Jul 2010	Restoring Confidence without Harming Recovery
Oct 2010	Recovery, Risk, and Rebalancing
Jan 2011	Global Recovery Advances but Remains Uneven
Apr 2011	Tensions from the Two-Speed Recovery: Unemployment, Commodities, and Capital Flows
Jun 2011	Mild Slowdown of the Global Expansion, and Increasing Risks
Sep 2011	Slowing Growth, Rising Risks
Jan 2012	Global Recovery Stalls, Downside Risks Intensify
Apr 2012	Growth Resuming, Dangers Remain
Jul 2012	New Setbacks, Further Policy Action Needed
Oct 2012	Coping with High Debt and Sluggish Growth
Jan 2013	Gradual Upturn in Global Growth During 2013
Apr 2013	Hopes, Realities, Risks
Jul 2013	Growing Pains
Oct 2013	Transitions and Tensions
Jan 2014	Is the Tide Rising?
Apr 2014	Recovery Strengthens, Remains Uneven
Jul 2014	An Uneven Global Recovery Continues

(continued)

Table 5.2 Continued

Time	Subtitle of WEO Update
Oct 2014	Legacies, Clouds, Uncertainties
Jan 2015	Cross Currents
Apr 2015	Uneven Growth: Short- and Long-Term Factors
Jul 2015	Slower Growth in Emerging Markets, a Gradual Pickup in Advanced Economies
Sep 2015	Adjusting to Lower Commodity Prices
Apr 2016	Too Slow for Too Long
Jul 2016	Uncertainty in the Aftermath of the UK Referendum
Oct 2016	Subdued Demand: Symptoms and Remedies
Jan 2017	A Shifting Global Economic Landscape
Apr 2017	Gaining Momentum?
Jul 2017	A Firming Recovery
Oct 2017	Seeking Sustainable Growth: Short-Term Recovery, Long-Term Challenges
Jan 2018	Brighter Prospects, Optimistic Markets, Challenges Ahead
Apr 2018	Cyclical Upswing, Structural Change
July 2018	Less Even Expansion, Rising Trade Tensions
Oct 2018	Challenges to Steady Growth
Jan 2019	A Weakening Global Expansion
Apr 2019	Growth Slowdown, Precarious Recovery
Jul 2019	Still Sluggish Global Growth
Oct 2019	Global Manufacturing Downturn, Rising Trade Barriers
Jan 2020	Tentative Stabilization, Sluggish Recovery?
Apr 2020	The Great Lockdown
Jun 2020	A Crisis Like No Other, An Uncertain Recovery
Oct 2020	A Long and Difficult Ascent
Jan 2021	Policy Support and Vaccines Expected to Lift Activity
Mar 2021	Managing Divergent Recoveries
Jul 2021	Fault Lines Widen in the Global Recovery
Oct 2021	Recovery During a Pandemic
Jan 2022	Rising Caseloads, A Disrupted Recovery, and Higher Inflation
Apr 2022	War Sets Back the Global Recovery
Jul 2022	Gloomy and More Uncertain
Oct 2022	Inflation and uncertainty

Source: Authors' compilation from World Economic Outlook, IMF, various issues.

slowdown, sluggish, or uncertain in the subtitles of WEO updates. This gives an indication that the twenty-two-year period, 2000–22, could be one of the most volatile periods, in the assessment of IMF.

Stimulus Package

Perhaps because the experience of the Great Depression of the 1930s was in the global consciousness, public authorities all over the world went all-out for stimulus packages. The G20, which was a forum of the finance ministers and central bank governors of 19 member countries and the EU since 1999, effectively graduated to a country leaders' summit in 2008. After the first summit meeting on 14–15 November 2008 in Washington DC, the G20 leaders, while claiming to have reached a common understanding of the root causes of the global crisis, agreed on common principles for reforming their financial markets and launched an action plan to implement those principles. In fact, the Final Declaration of the Washington Summit of November 2008 vowed to 'use fiscal measures to stimulate domestic demand to rapid effect, as appropriate, while maintaining a policy framework conducive to fiscal sustainability'. Consequently, despite the differences in economic conditions across the G20 countries, most of the countries undertook heavy fiscal stimulus. Similar fiscal stimulus was initiated during the pandemic as well.

It is well known that multiplier effects have leakages depending upon the extent of crowding out mechanisms. Recent research indicates that there have been significant variations in the value of multipliers, which did vary from 0.2 to 2.2, depending on the fiscal instrument, the extent of monetary accommodation, and the presence of a financial accelerator mechanism. For example, a permanent 10 percentage point increase in the US debt to GDP ratio was seen to be raising the US tax burden and world real interest rates in the long run, thereby reducing US and rest of the world output by 0.3 to 0.6 per cent and 0.2 to 0.3 per cent, respectively (Freedman et al. 2011).

The fiscal stimulus was complemented by monetary accommodation. Many of the emerging markets reduced policy interest rates substantially and tried to inject domestic liquidity. Since, in the advanced countries, interest rates were already at near-zero levels, many of these countries resorted to heavy dosages of quantitative easing in monetary policy and chose to work at the long end of the yield curve of government securities. Consequently, there was a quantum jump in the balance sheets of the advanced countries' central banks. The size of the US Fed's balance sheet which was around $800 billion in January 2007 touched nearly $4 trillion by the end of 2013. Similar expansion is evident in the balance sheets of the Bank of England or the ECB. Such balance sheet expansion and policies of quantitative easing continued during the pandemic as well. Illustratively, total assets (less elimination from consolidation) of the US Fed went up from US$4.2 trillion on 25 December 2019 to USD 8.5 trillion on 28 December 2022—an expansion of USD 4.3 trillion over a span of three years.

Inflation

Inflation was also under reasonable control during the initial period, i.e., 2000–7, in most of the countries except the commonwealth of independent states (mostly breakaway nations from the erstwhile USSR) and countries in Central and Eastern Europe. Control of inflation during this period is often cited as the positive offshoot of adoption of inflation targeting by a large number of central banks, both in advanced economies and emerging markets. However, emergence of China as a cheap channel of outsourcing along with reduced trade union pressure and consequent fall in input costs in many of the advanced countries may not be ruled out. Inflation, however, started rearing its ugly head towards the end of this period, reflecting higher commodity prices and possibly increasing financialization of commodities around that time. Simmering trends of global imbalances were visible. In particular, the Middle East and North African region were seen to have sizeable current account as well as fiscal surplus; this was of course reflective of their hydrocarbon-rich status and buoyant oil prices during the period. From a vantage point, it is interesting to note that the IMF in its April 2006 *World Economic Outlook* noted: 'Notwithstanding higher oil prices and natural disasters, global growth has continued to exceed expectations, aided by benign financial market conditions and continued accommodative macroeconomic policies' (p. 1). Thus, in some sense, the situation as it existed in 2006 was like a Goldilocks scenario.

In discussing any recessionary period, inflation often rightly takes a back seat. After all, with the sole exception of a stagflationary situation, any recessionary condition is typically associated with demand constraint where inflation may not turn out to be a problem. While accepting these general tendencies, in discussing the inflationary trends during 2001–13 two caveats are in order.

First, as already noted, during 2005–6 inflation has turned out to be a concern. Buoyant growth during the last few years could have depleted the excess capacity and could have given rise to inflationary spirals. This was true both for advanced economies as well as EMDEs. Additionally, exchange rate depreciation in EMDEs could have added to inflationary pressures in these countries. In fact, against this backdrop, central banks in many of the advanced economies and EMDEs took measures to tighten monetary conditions.

Second, the dichotomy between the advanced economies and EMDEs is reflected quite glaringly in inflation numbers till 2019 (Chart 5.2). With growth having been affected severely in advanced economies, inflation is hardly a concern in these countries; on the contrary, in the EMDEs, with growth being less affected, inflation has turned out to be much more of a worry. This has implications for any

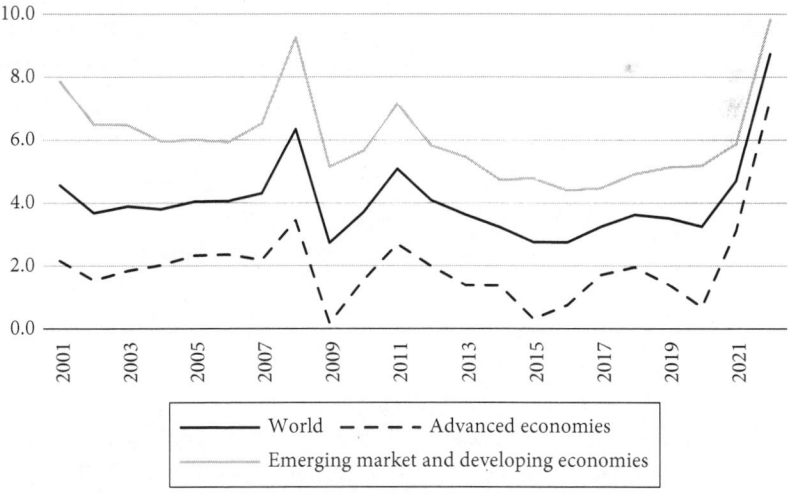

Chart 5.2 Global Inflation (%)

Source: Constructed by authors from *World Economic Outlook* database, IMF, April 2014.

one-size-fits-all application of uniform sets of policies across all countries in the world.

In the aftermath of the global financial crisis, initially global inflation eased considerably. However, subsequently, inflation experienced some surge during 2010 and 2011. According to the IMF, world inflation went up from 2.2 per cent in 2009 to 3.3 per cent and 4.4 per cent in 2010 and 2011 respectively. Within this, average inflation in the advanced economies rose from 0.1 per cent in 2009 to 1.5 per cent in 2010 and 2.7 per cent in 2011, while the corresponding figures in developing Asia were notably higher, at 3.1 per cent, 5.9 per cent, and 6.6 per cent, respectively.

Four factors can be discerned in this connection. First, there has been some surge in international commodity prices—particularly food and oil; and the role of resurfacing of financialization of commodities cannot be ruled out either. Second, in their pursuit of quantitative easing, a huge amount of liquidity was made available around the globe by the advanced economies' central banks—in all likelihood, it could have found its way in terms of capital inflow to a number of EMDEs and added to inflationary pressure. Third, there was a number of adverse supply shocks. Fourth, generalized strong demand in large developing economies arising out of rising incomes and wages in these economies could also have added to price pressures.

In the more recent period, during 2021–2, there has been a steep spurt in global inflation, increasing from 3.2 per cent in 2020 to 8.7 per cent in 2022; in advanced countries, the spurt is sharper with inflation shooting up from 0.7 per cent in 2020 to 7.8 per cent in 2022 (Chart 5.2). Apart from local factors, various global factors seem to be responsible. These include extra-lax fiscal and monetary policies and the resultant excess liquidity; the presence of supply-side restrictions and associated global value chain bottlenecks; and the war-induced spurt of energy and food prices.

Imbalances: Fiscal and External

In the context of the twin crises over 2007–13, it is widely believed that global imbalances and public debt played their due roles. Thus, the huge current account surplus of Japan, a number of countries in developing Asia (led by China) and the oil exporting countries in the Middle East and North Africa are largely believed to have supplied cheap funds to the US, much of which was placed in the huge securitized market for sub-prime assets and led to mispricing of risks. On the other hand, researchers found that over the last 15 years or so there has been a huge increase in global public debt, so much so that if unchecked, it has the potential to touch the public debt level experienced in the post-Great Depression years of late 1930s.

Fiscal stimuli were resorted to during at least two of the crises during the period, namely, the global financial crisis and the pandemic. In fact, in 2020, the net borrowing of the general governments of the advanced economies surpassed 10 per cent of their total GDP and stood at an all-time high. Similar trends are noticeable in gross debt levels (as a percentage of total GDP). Perhaps, because of the paucity of fiscal space, lack of capability to have loans from the global financial markets, and absence of universally accepted currencies, the debt-to-GDP ratios of the emerging market economies were a bit lower.

In this context, the role of flows of budget balances in the build-up of public debt is of paramount importance. Chart 5.3 depicts: (a) the net lending/borrowing position of the government sector (fiscal balance); and (b) the extent of imbalance in external accounts, as measured by current account balances.

Some interesting stylized facts emerge. First, the advanced economies seem to have lower fiscal deficits than those of the EMDEs till about 2014. Second, the fiscal deficits of euro area economies do not seem to be that high; of course, this could be indicative of the fiscal deficit-related heterogeneity within euro area economies. Third, Middle East and North African (MENA) economies is the only group which had a budget surplus reflecting their hydrocarbon-rich status.

In terms of current account balance, a key stylized fact needs mention. Till about 2014, the dichotomy between the advanced economies and EMDEs remains in the sense that advanced economies are in deficit and EMDEs are in surplus. This could be reflective of the Lucas Paradox of capital going uphill from poor to rich countries. However, the extent of current account surplus from the developing Asia have come down in recent years, reflecting weakening of the forces behind global imbalances, initiation of the US-China trade war, and reduced export growth to developed countries from Asia.

Fiscal Balance (% of GDP)

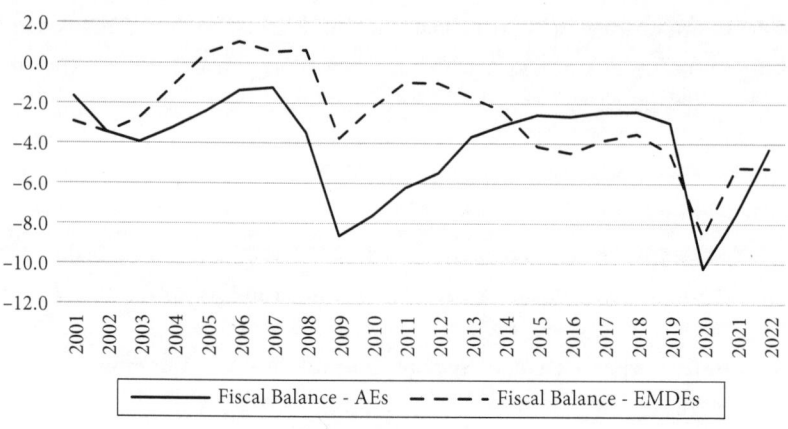

Current Account Balance (% of GDP)

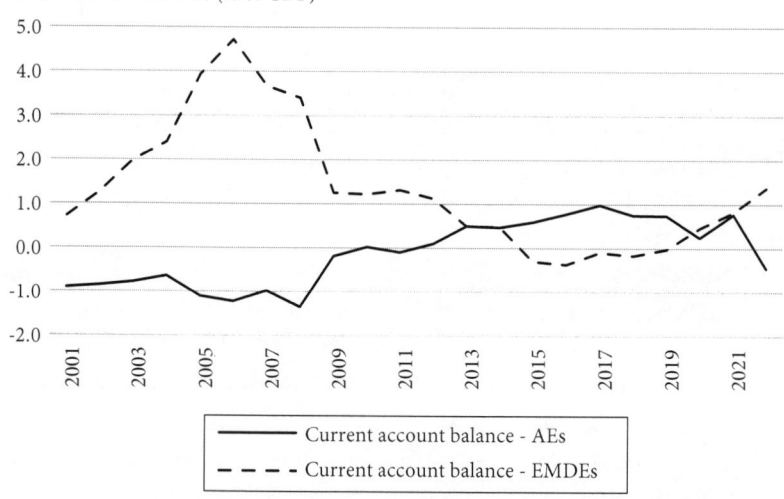

Chart 5.3 Fiscal Balance and Current Account Balance (Percentage of GDP)
Source: Constructed by authors from *World Economic Outlook* database, IMF, April 2023

Trends in G20 Economies

The narrative so far was in broad aggregative terms, essentially dividing the globe into bi-polar groups of advanced economies and EMDEs. But what happened in terms of economic realities at the ground level of countries? As already indicated, the Great Recession has witnessed the emergence of the G20 as an effective global decision making forum.

Appendix Table 5A.1 to Appendix Table 5A.4 depicts GDP growth rates, inflation, fiscal balance, and current account balance of the G20 nations, respectively.[1] These are further subdivided into advanced economies and emerging market economies. Some interesting patterns emerge.

Growth

As far as the GDP growth during the global financial crisis is concerned, the following regularities deserve special mention (Appendix Table 5A.1). First, during the 2009 Great Recession, there are only seven countries that experienced positive growth, namely, Australia and Korea (two advanced economies), Argentina, China, India, Indonesia, and Saudi Arabia. Second, in terms of a double dip, three G20 members registered a contraction in 2012, namely, the UK, Italy, and the EU. Third, going by a small post-2009 sample, it seems that global growth could have taken a semi-permanent hit so that there is no indication whether the global economy will be back to the Goldilocks scenario of pre-crisis years. Fourth, looking at the growth experience of Australia and Canada, which showed agility among the advanced economies, one may, with ample reason, be sceptical about the financial sector-led growth in many of the advanced economies. Finally, notwithstanding the fact that China and India have turned out to be islands of solid growth supporting global growth, of late, growth in these two economies is yet to return to the pre-crisis trajectory. In particular, Indian growth seemed to have suffered quite a bit in the recent period.

Interestingly, in 2020, the first year of the pandemic, there has been an all-around contraction of GDP across all 19 countries (Appendix Table 5A.1). With a contraction of 11 per cent, the UK has been hit the most (perhaps coupled with the impact of Brexit as well) among all the countries; Italy and France have also been affected significantly. Among the EMDEs, Mexico was hit most. While growth recovered in 2021,

---

[1] -20 comprises these 19 countries and the euro area.

coupled with inflationary shock and reeling under the Russia-Ukraine war, growth took a hit in some geographies, particularly Russia and Germany.

Inflation

Interestingly, the dichotomy between the advanced economies and emerging market economies is prominent in inflation numbers during 2001–14 (Appendix Table 5A.2). First, the Indian inflation record stands out in terms of high magnitude in the world, which makes the relevance of monetary and fiscal stimulus much more nuanced than elsewhere. Second, Russia has managed to tackle its inflation in recent times. Third, as of now, there are no deflationary tendencies in the advanced economies, making them less prone to a depression-like situation. Finally, apart from India there are at least two other economies, namely, Argentina and Turkey where inflation has turned out to be a concern. Poor supply response, high-income growth leading to higher demand for proteins, the partial dismantling of administered price mechanisms, delayed policy response, all have been seen to be the major responsible factors.

As already indicated, more recently in 2022, there has been a sharp spurt in inflation across all geographies—both in developed as well as EMDEs. Illustratively, the annual inflation rate of 8 per cent in the US was the highest since the early 1980s. The 70 per cent plus inflation rates in Argentina and Turkey, were more in the nature of outliers.

Fiscal Balance

How did these countries do in terms of fiscal balance (Appendix Table 5A.3)? First, while all the advanced G20 economies (except Korea) have fiscal deficit, three countries, namely, the UK, the US, and Japan stand out. Of course, this possibly reflects their status as safe havens of funds as well as their reserve currency status. Second, fiscal deficit is small in almost all the south and south-east Asian nations, such as Thailand, Indonesia, or China. Third, Russia and Saudi Arabia are seen to have registered fiscal surplus; this could be due to their oil-exporting status. Fourth, despite a 7 per cent plus fiscal deficit, near absence of sovereign debt in India, limited capital account convertibility could have insulated the country from possible speculative attacks from outside thereby engendering a crisis-like situation. Finally, as we already indicated, in all the G20 countries there has been a significant increase in fiscal deficit in the first year of the pandemic, i.e., 2020. This is in sync with the statement of the Extraordinary G20 Leaders' Summit by videoconference from Riyadh, Saudi Arabia, on 26 March 2020, which stated, 'We are injecting over $5 trillion into the global economy, as part of targeted fiscal policy, economic measures, and guarantee schemes to counteract the social, economic and financial impacts of the pandemic'.

Current Account Balance

A look at the current account balance position of these G20 countries, reveals some interesting features (Appendix Table 5A.4). First, among the advanced G20 countries, three countries have a current account surplus, namely, Germany, Japan, and Korea. Second, both within the EU and the euro area, there is a mild surplus, indicating heterogeneity among these groupings. Third, temporally, within the advanced economies, the extent of the current account deficit seemed to have gone up at least for two countries—the UK and Australia. Fourth, the surplus position of Saudi Arabia and Russia could be due to their hydrocarbon-rich status. Fifth, India stood second in terms of the highest current account deficit among the emerging market economies, just next to Turkey. Finally, the current account surpluses of China have narrowed significantly, contributing to some resolution of global imbalance. Illustratively, China registered a current account surplus of 0.2 per cent in 2018, dropping from a high of around 10 per cent of GDP in 2007.

How Did the Big Three (US, China, and EU) Do?

Over the last decade, the world economy turned out to be more like a two-legged stool with their combined GDP share exceeding half of global

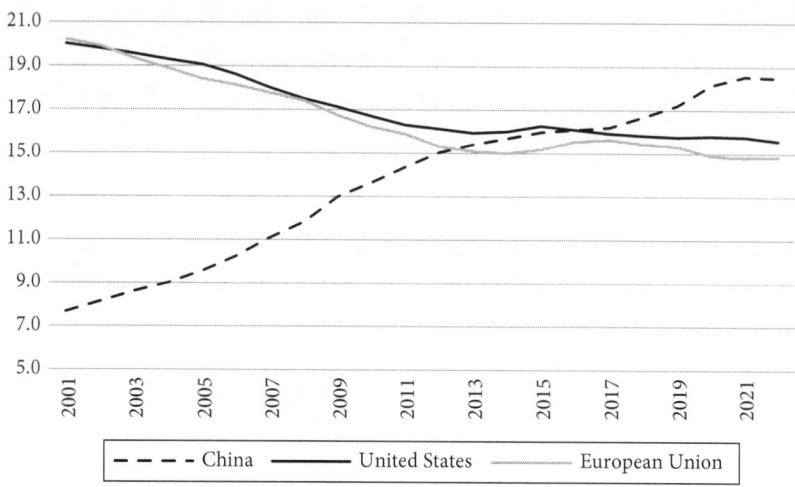

Chart 5.4 Share of the US, the EU, and China in World GDP (Based on Purchasing Power Parity, Percentage)

Source: Constructed by authors from *World Economic Outlook* database, IMF, April 2023.

GDP. In terms of their shares in global GDP (at PPP), while both the US and the EU account for nearly one-fifth at the beginning of the millennium there have been steady declines in their shares, hovering around 15 per cent now. The share of China has registered a steady and sharp increase to a little over 18 per cent (Chart 5.4).

Before proceeding further, some comments on the composition of the EU and the euro area are in order. First, till the operationalization of Brexit on 1 February 2020, the EU, as is well known, used to refer to 27 economies that have joined in a trade and customs union. The euro area, on the other hand, is a currency union and refers to 14 countries that have given up their individual currencies and have adopted the euro as their currency. Needless to say, the euro area is a subset of the larger group called the EU (Appendix 6B). While Chapter 6 is devoted to euro area economies, in the present chapter, economic development of some of the EU countries is taken up briefly.

Thanks to the substantial monetary and fiscal stimuli, the US economy came out from the Great Recession of 2009 within a year (Appendix Table 5A.1). The growth in the US economy, during the decade of 2010s, was, however, modest. Interestingly, the legacy of an expanding economy during the Obama administration continued during the first three years of the Trump presidency. Things went bad with the advent of the pandemic in the US; US GDP contracted by nearly 9 per cent in the second quarter of 2020, the largest single-quarter contraction in more than 70 years.

A few features about China are worth emphasizing. First, given its share at around 15 per cent and average growth of 10 per cent plus during the period 2001–13, China has really become the growth pole of the world economy, which has pulled global growth during the Great Recession. Second, in between, Chinese inflation has become a concern, and during 2011 this was coupled with some asset price Central Bank increased reserve requirements, and raised policy interest rates several times in the recent past. Third, till 2007, Chinese current account surplus showed secular increase; this is often attributed to limited flexibility or conscious undervaluation of the Chinese currency. The extent of Chinese current account surplus has started waning since 2007, reflecting some degree of effort on the part of the Chinese authorities for appreciating the Chinese currency, limited impact on Chinese imports which suffered during the Great Recession, as well as higher inflation causing some erosion in its competitiveness via real exchange rate effects. Notwithstanding the fact that the COVID-19 pandemic started from China, it turned out to be one of the countries with rare positive growth in 2020! Things, of late, have started deteriorating in China. In a recent commentary on China the World Bank has pointed out, 'China's high growth based on investment, low-cost manufacturing, and exports has largely reached its limits and has led to economic, social, and environmental imbalances. Over the past few years, growth has moderated in the face of structural constraints, including declining labor force growth, diminishing returns to investment, and slowing productivity growth' (World Bank 2023).[2]

There has been a significant reduction in the large current account deficit in the US in recent times. Admittedly, the US could afford to have huge government deficit as well as current account deficit profiting from its reserve currency issuing status, which has been described as an *exorbitant privilege*.[3] Interestingly, fiscal deficit in the EU is much more

---

[2] https://www.worldbank.org/en/country/china/overview
[3] The term was coined in the 1960s by the then French Minister of Finance, Valéry Giscard d'Estaing.

manageable in aggregate; the issue, therefore, is perhaps one of intra-EU discrepancies. In particular, while the core euro area economies have surplus in their external current account, countries in the periphery (and in particular the crisis economies like Greece or Ireland) do have substantial current account deficit.

Some Other Advanced Economies

Non-Euro Area Advanced European Economies

What has been the impact on the non-euro area advanced countries? With non-Atlantic and Scandinavian countries as some outliers, growth in most of the non-euro area advanced economies had taken a hit during 2011 and a similar trend continued in 2012 as well. Among the non-euro area EU economies, while Iceland had been one of the initial crisis countries, the UK was seen as a late entrant to the crisis club as of 2012. Most of these countries came out of the collateral impact of the euro area crisis since 2013 (Appendix Table 5A.5). The pandemic, however, hit all these countries badly.

UK: A New Entrant to the Crisis Club?

The UK economy seemed to have been hit hard by the global financial crisis, with 2012 experiencing feeble growth. Since then, however, the UK economy experienced a turnaround. The scenario is summed up in the May 2012 Article IV report of the UK by the IMF as follows:

> Recovery has stalled. Post-crisis repair and rebalancing of the UK economy is likely to be more prolonged than initially envisaged. Confidence is weak and uncertainty is high. Looking ahead, the economy is expected to grow modestly, but with current policy settings the pace will be insufficient to absorb significant slack in the economy, raising the risk of a permanent loss of productive capacity. (IMF 2012b, p. 1)

How did it happen? It may be useful to go back a little into Britain's experience during the global financial crisis. To begin with, there was a run on Northern Rock's retail deposits on 11 September 2007 and around £4.6 billion in deposits was withdrawn. After an extensive search for a buyer, Northern Rock was nationalized in February 2008. Subsequently, after the fall of Lehman Brothers and consequent freezing of the credit markets, Halifax Bank of Scotland faced bankruptcy, and was bought by Lloyds Bank in September 2008. Meanwhile, the UK economy had to deal with the collapse of three Icelandic banks and its impact on UK depositors. There was quite a bit of bad blood on this issue between the UK and Iceland, so much so that UK assets of Landsbanki were frozen. In fact, there were serious issues with the capital position of the British banks and in October 2009, the UK government announced £37 billion of capital support for UK banks.

British economic development since 2016 has been dominated by the UK referendum on continuing membership of the European Union (EU) in June 2016. The result indicated a 51.9% to 48.1% victory for Brexit voters. Prime Minister David Cameron accepted it as a defeat and resigned. In March 2017, the British government under Prime Minister Theresa May invoked Article 50 of the Treaty on the European Union and began the negotiation for official process of withdrawal of the UK from the EU. The process took nearly three and a half years to complete.

But why did Brexit happen? Is it an outcome of the triumph of nationalistic feelings over the benefits of a common market? It is interesting to note that the UK's relationship with the EU has always been turbulent. It is instructive to recount the history:

The UK government refused to engage with the 1950 Schuman Declaration for integration of the coal and steel industries. In November 1955 it withdrew from the Spaak Committee preparing the eventual European Economic Community. Britain considered itself a world power and Europe only one of its spheres of influence. Prime Minister Harold Macmillan's effort to undertake a post-Suez policy shift by applying for membership of the European Communities (EC) failed in cabinet due to ministerial divisions ... When it was presented to cabinet again in April 1961—after a re-shuffle—it succeeded ... However, the French President, Charles de Gaulle, rejected the application in January

1963. While accession negotiations had been under way in Brussels the Labour leader, Hugh Gaitskell, declared his opposition at the October 1962 party conference. Membership would mean 'the end of Britain as an independent state' and 'the end of a thousand years of British history' . . . Hugo Young (1998: 161) dubbed Gaitskell the first 'Euro-sceptic'. These events set the tone for what followed. (Bulmera and Quaglia 2018)

Thus, while the seeds of an unhappy union between the UK and the EU could have been sown by the forces of history, a more important question at the current juncture would be: What will be the impact of Brexit? There have been many studies to capture the macroeconomic impact of Brexit; most of these predict that there would be a long-term loss to the UK economy (Begg and Mushovel 2019). The extent of loss of GDP, however, varies widely according to different estimates (Table 5.3).

Non-European Advanced Economies

How were the other bigger countries among advanced economies outside Europe doing? Experiences of select economies are worth noting (Appendix Table 5A.5).

Table 5.3 Different Estimates of the Impact of Brexit on the GDP Growth of the UK Economy

(all outcomes are relative to a projected annual growth of 2.1 per cent per annum up to 2030)	
HM Treasury	−7.5 to −3.8
Centre for Economic Performance (CEP)	−9.5 to −6.3
Open Europe	−2.2 to + 1.6
Oxford Economics	−4.0 to −0.1
PricewaterhouseCoopers (PwC)	−3.5 to −1.2
National Institute of Economic and Social Research (NIESR)	−9.2 to −2.4
CEP commentary on Minford	−2.6 to −2.3
Lyons, G.	−0.5 to + 0.6
Minford, P.	+4.0

Source: Based on Begg and Mushovel's (2019) compilation from various public sources.

First, while the global financial crisis led Canada into deep recession, it came back to the pre-crisis trajectory with remarkable agility and performed far better than the US and most of the European countries. The timely and appropriate macroeconomic policy response, backed by solid fundamentals that included a sturdy banking sector (with sub-prime mortgages accounting for only 5 per cent of total mortgages) and a strong fiscal position (with public debt at 28 per cent of net GDP, compared to 101 per cent in the US) have enabled the economy to come out of the crisis fast and to support the growth momentum. Apart from policy stimulus and strong fundamentals, high commodity prices seem to have helped the country in coming out of the global financial crisis. However, the economy suffered during 2015–16 on account of the wildfires in Northern Alberta, coupled with the uncertainties in the energy sector. After experiencing a contraction during 2020 on account of COVID-19, the economy, however, made a turnaround.

Second, the Japanese economy continued to be plagued by the longer-term challenges such as high public debt, rapidly aging population, low growth, and deflation. However, Japan bounced back reasonably well in recovering from the March 2011 Great East Japan earthquake. Thus, the economy experienced a growth rate of around 1.5 per cent during the next two years (i.e., 2012 and 2013). However, the possibility of Japan facing a fiscal problem in the near future seems real. Its net public debt has increased nearly tenfold over the last two decades and stood at more than 125 per cent of GDP. An ageing population, consequent rising social security spending, and persistently weak growth and deflation have depressed tax revenues. Thus, Japan continues to be fiscally vulnerable.

Third, the Australian economy has been affected by the global financial crisis. The most immediate effect of the crisis in Australia was the collapse of the Australian dollar from US$0.98 in July 2008 to $0.60 in October 2008. Unemployment increased from 4.1 per cent in February 2008 to 5.8 per cent in August 2009; however, it declined to 5.3 per cent in February 2010. Nonetheless, the Australian economy bounced back fairly fast and as a commodity exporter, the strong demand from China has contributed to Australia's resilience during the crisis. The contraction of the Australian economy during 2020 was, however, modest.

Finally, in line with the global trend, all these economies experienced high inflation in recent years (Appendix Table 5A.6).

* * *

Against the backdrop of the Goldilocks scenario in the global economy during 2001–6, the chapter provides a synoptic view of the economic developments of the period 2007–20. This period witnessed various crises. To begin with, the sub-period 2007–9 saw emergence of the sub-prime crisis in the US residential mortgage market, leading to a global financial crisis finally culminating in the Great Recession of 2009 (when global GDP growth as well as growth of both advanced economies and EMDEs registered a contraction). Countries all across the world have undertaken simultaneously coordinated monetary and fiscal stimulus—more so the bigger countries in G20. Consequently, growth resurfaced during 2010 with a number of countries in developing Asia (led by China) emerging as growth poles. But this resurgence of growth was transitory, uneven, and fragile. Thus, the recovery was seriously punctured in the subsequent period of 2011–12 with the emergence of a euro area debt crisis. A number of reasons may be identified behind the emergence of the euro area crisis, such as unsustainable fiscal position and high current account deficit in some of these economies. Besides, in some countries bursting of property price bubbles and banking sector exposure to the property market played a crucial role in the emergence and propagation of the crisis. Productivity growth also seemed to be an issue in a few countries. Interestingly, to begin with, players in the sovereign debt market were myopic and treated all the countries in the euro area equally without any reference to their differences in fundamentals. However, in the post-crisis world of 2009, these market players became cautious and started punishing the sovereign debts of select peripheral economies of the euro area on account of their poor and deteriorating fundamentals. This was reflected in a phenomenal rise in credit default swaps (CDS) spreads of these economies. The crisis was transmitted through cross holding of sovereign debt of these affected countries by the banking sector of the core euro area economies and erosion of confidence. Besides, there was considerable difference between the advanced economies and EMDEs insofar as the growth and inflation dynamics are concerned. Later, country-specific developments like Brexit or the US-China trade war affected these economies. Finally, while the pandemic has affected most of the countries in the world adversely, the developed countries were also affected to a great extent.

In all these, the fiscal situation played a key role in a number of ways. First, pursuit of fiscal stimulus in the absence of fiscal space to deal with the fallout of the global financial crisis could have cost some countries dearly and made the fiscal situation further vulnerable. Second, the fisc was dependent on sovereign debt market in a big way and through it on the international financial players. Third, apart from the severely affected countries in the euro area like Greece or Ireland, core euro area economies with sound macroeconomic fundamentals like Germany or France were exposed to these economies via their banking sectors' holding of sovereign debt of the affected countries.

Going forward, how do we see the world economy today? The continued pursuit of monetary and fiscal stimulus as crisis management measures has created some degree of fragility across the world—with the developed countries having their share as well. Following the pandemic, increasing debt levels, higher inflation, and subdued growth performance have made the global economy a somewhat fragile place. It remains to be seen how far these fault lines are repaired in the days to come.

Appendix Table 5A.1 GDP Growth (%) across the G20 Economies

	Country	2006	2007	2008	2009	2010	2011	2012	2013	2014	2015	2016	2017	2018	2019	2020	2021	2022
1	Australia	2.6	4.4	2.5	1.9	2.4	2.8	3.8	2.2	2.6	2.3	2.7	2.4	2.8	1.9	-1.8	5.2	3.7
2	Canada	2.6	2.1	1.0	-2.9	3.1	3.1	1.8	2.3	2.9	0.7	1.0	3.0	2.8	1.9	-5.1	5.0	3.4
3	France	2.6	2.4	0.2	-2.8	1.8	2.2	0.4	0.7	1.0	1.1	1.0	2.4	1.8	1.9	-7.9	6.8	2.6
4	Germany	3.8	3.0	1.0	-5.7	4.2	3.9	0.4	0.4	2.2	1.5	2.2	2.7	1.0	1.1	-3.7	2.6	1.8
5	Italy	1.8	1.5	-1.0	-5.3	1.7	0.7	-3.0	-1.8	0.0	0.8	1.3	1.7	0.9	0.5	-9.0	7.0	3.7
6	Japan	1.4	1.5	-1.2	-5.7	4.1	0.0	1.4	2.0	0.3	1.6	0.8	1.7	0.6	-0.4	-4.3	2.1	1.1
7	Korea	5.3	5.8	3.0	0.8	6.8	3.7	2.4	3.2	3.2	2.8	2.9	3.2	2.9	2.2	-0.7	4.1	2.6
8	United Kingdom	2.2	2.6	-0.2	-4.5	2.4	1.1	1.4	1.8	3.2	2.4	2.2	2.4	1.7	1.6	-11.0	7.6	4.0
9	United States	2.8	2.0	0.1	-2.6	2.7	1.6	2.3	1.8	2.3	2.7	1.7	2.2	2.9	2.3	-2.8	5.9	2.1
10	Argentina	8.0	9.0	4.1	-5.9	10.1	6.0	-1.0	2.4	-2.5	2.7	-2.1	2.8	-2.6	-2.0	-9.9	10.4	5.2
11	Brazil	4.0	6.1	5.1	-0.1	7.5	4.0	1.9	3.0	0.5	-3.5	-3.3	1.3	1.8	1.2	-3.3	5.0	2.9
12	China	12.7	14.2	9.6	9.4	10.6	9.6	7.8	7.8	7.4	7.0	6.9	6.9	6.8	6.0	2.2	8.5	3.0
13	India	9.3	9.8	3.9	8.5	10.3	6.6	5.5	6.4	7.4	8.0	8.3	6.8	6.5	3.9	-5.8	9.1	6.8
14	Indonesia	5.5	6.3	7.4	4.7	6.4	6.2	6.0	5.6	5.0	4.9	5.0	5.1	5.2	5.0	-2.1	3.7	5.3
15	Mexico	4.5	2.3	1.1	-5.3	5.1	3.7	3.6	1.4	2.9	3.3	2.6	2.1	2.2	-0.2	-8.0	4.7	3.1
16	Russia	8.2	8.5	5.2	-7.8	4.5	5.1	4.0	1.8	0.7	-2.0	0.2	1.8	2.8	2.2	-2.7	5.6	-2.1
17	Saudi Arabia	2.8	1.8	6.3	-2.1	5.0	11.0	5.4	2.9	4.0	4.7	2.4	-0.1	2.8	0.8	-4.3	3.9	8.7
18	South Africa	5.6	5.4	3.2	-1.5	3.0	3.2	2.4	2.5	1.4	1.3	0.7	1.2	1.5	0.3	-6.3	4.9	2.0
19	Türkiye	6.9	5.0	0.8	-4.8	8.4	11.2	4.8	8.5	4.9	6.1	3.3	7.5	3.0	0.8	1.9	11.4	5.6

Advanced Countries (rows 1–9); Emerging & Developing Countries (rows 10–19)

Source: International Monetary Fund, *World Economic Outlook* database, April 2023.

Appendix Table 5A.2 Inflation (%) across the G20 Economies

	Country	2006	2007	2008	2009	2010	2011	2012	2013	2014	2015	2016	2017	2018	2019	2020	2021	2022
1	Australia	3.6	2.4	4.3	1.8	2.9	3.4	1.7	2.5	2.5	1.5	1.3	2.0	1.9	1.6	0.9	2.8	6.6
2	Canada	2.0	2.1	2.4	0.3	1.8	2.9	1.5	0.9	1.9	1.1	1.4	1.6	2.3	1.9	0.7	3.4	6.8
3	France	1.9	1.6	3.2	0.1	1.7	2.3	2.2	1.0	0.6	0.1	0.3	1.2	2.1	1.3	0.5	2.1	5.9
4	Germany	1.8	2.3	2.8	0.2	1.1	2.5	2.2	1.6	0.8	0.7	0.4	1.7	1.9	1.4	0.4	3.2	8.7
Advanced Countries 5	Italy	2.2	2.0	3.5	0.8	1.6	2.9	3.3	1.2	0.2	0.1	-0.1	1.3	1.2	0.6	-0.1	1.9	8.7
6	Japan	0.3	0.0	1.4	-1.3	-0.7	-0.3	0.0	0.3	2.8	0.8	-0.1	0.5	1.0	0.5	0.0	-0.2	2.5
7	Korea	2.2	2.5	4.7	2.8	2.9	4.0	2.2	1.3	1.3	0.7	1.0	1.9	1.5	0.4	0.5	2.5	5.1
8	United Kingdom	2.3	2.3	3.6	2.2	3.3	4.5	2.8	2.6	1.5	0.0	0.7	2.7	2.5	1.8	0.9	2.6	9.1
9	United States	3.2	2.9	3.8	-0.3	1.6	3.1	2.1	1.5	1.6	0.1	1.3	2.1	2.4	1.8	1.3	4.7	8.0
10	Argentina	10.9	8.8	8.6	6.3	10.5	9.8	10.0	10.6	n/a	n/a	n/a	25.7	34.3	53.5	42.0	48.4	72.4
11	Brazil	4.2	3.6	5.7	4.9	5.0	6.6	5.4	6.2	6.3	9.0	8.7	3.4	3.7	3.7	3.2	8.3	9.3
12	China	1.6	4.8	5.9	-0.7	3.2	5.5	2.6	2.6	2.1	1.5	2.1	1.5	1.9	2.9	2.5	0.9	1.9
Emerging & 13	India	6.7	6.2	9.1	12.3	10.5	9.5	10.0	9.4	5.8	4.9	4.5	3.6	3.4	4.8	6.2	5.5	6.7
Developing 14	Indonesia	13.1	6.3	9.9	4.8	5.1	5.3	4.0	6.4	6.4	6.4	3.5	3.8	3.3	2.8	2.0	1.6	4.2
Countries 15	Mexico	3.6	4.0	5.1	5.3	4.2	3.4	4.1	3.8	4.0	2.7	2.8	6.0	4.9	3.6	3.4	5.7	7.9
16	Russia	9.7	9.0	14.1	11.6	6.8	8.4	5.1	6.8	7.8	15.5	7.0	3.7	2.9	4.5	3.4	6.7	13.8
17	Saudi Arabia	1.9	5.0	6.1	4.3	3.7	3.7	2.9	3.5	2.2	1.2	2.1	-0.8	2.5	-2.1	3.4	3.1	2.5
18	South Africa	4.7	7.1	11.0	7.2	4.2	5.0	5.6	5.7	6.1	4.6	6.3	5.3	4.6	4.1	3.3	4.6	6.9
19	Turkey	9.6	8.8	10.4	6.3	8.6	6.5	8.9	7.5	8.9	7.7	7.8	11.1	16.3	15.2	12.3	19.6	72.3

Source: International Monetary Fund, *World Economic Outlook* database, April 2023.

Appendix Table 5A.3 Fiscal Balance (% of GDP) across the G20 Economies

	Country	2006	2007	2008	2009	2010	2011	2012	2013	2014	2015	2016	2017	2018	2019	2020	2021	2022
1	Australia	1.8	1.5	-1.1	-4.6	-5.1	-4.5	-3.5	-2.8	-2.9	-2.8	-2.4	-1.7	-1.3	-4.4	-8.7	-6.3	-3.3
2	Canada	1.8	1.8	0.2	-3.9	-4.7	-3.3	-2.5	-1.5	0.2	-0.1	-0.5	-0.1	0.4	0.0	-10.9	-4.4	-0.7
3	France	-2.4	-2.6	-3.3	-7.2	-6.9	-5.2	-5.0	-4.1	-3.9	-3.6	-3.6	-3.0	-2.3	-3.1	-9.0	-6.5	-4.9
4	Germany	-1.7	0.3	-0.1	-3.2	-4.4	-0.9	0.0	0.0	0.6	1.0	1.2	1.3	2.0	1.5	-4.3	-3.7	-2.6
5	Italy	-3.6	-1.3	-2.6	-5.1	-4.2	-3.6	-2.9	-2.9	-3.0	-2.6	-2.4	-2.4	-2.2	-1.5	-9.7	-9.0	-8.0
6	Japan	-3.0	-2.9	-4.1	-9.7	-9.1	-9.0	-8.2	-7.6	-5.6	-3.7	-3.6	-3.1	-2.5	-3.0	-9.1	-6.2	-7.8
7	Korea	1.2	2.6	1.6	0.2	1.7	1.8	1.7	0.8	0.6	0.5	1.6	2.2	2.6	0.4	-2.2	0.0	-0.9
8	United Kingdom	-2.8	-2.6	-5.1	-10.0	-9.2	-7.5	-7.6	-5.5	-5.5	-4.5	-3.3	-2.4	-2.2	-2.2	-13.0	-8.3	-6.3
9	United States	-2.0	-2.9	-6.6	-13.2	-11.0	-9.7	-8.1	-4.5	-4.0	-3.5	-4.4	-4.8	-5.3	-5.7	-14.0	-11.6	-5.5
10	Argentina	1.7	0.8	0.4	-1.8	-1.4	-2.7	-3.0	-3.3	-4.3	-6.0	-6.7	-6.7	-5.4	-4.4	-8.6	-4.3	-3.9
11	Brazil	-3.6	-2.7	-2.0	-3.2	-2.4	-2.5	-2.3	-3.0	-6.0	-10.2	-9.0	-7.8	-7.0	-5.8	-13.3	-4.3	-4.6
12	China	-1.1	0.1	0.0	-1.8	-0.4	-0.1	-0.3	-0.8	-0.7	-2.5	-3.4	-3.4	-4.3	-6.1	-9.7	-6.0	-7.5
13	India	-6.3	-4.5	-9.0	-9.5	-8.6	-8.3	-7.6	-7.0	-7.1	-7.2	-7.1	-6.2	-6.4	-7.7	-12.9	-9.6	-9.6
14	Indonesia	0.5	-1.0	0.1	-1.6	-1.2	-0.7	-1.6	-2.2	-2.1	-2.6	-2.5	-2.5	-1.8	-2.2	-6.1	-4.5	-2.3
15	Mexico	-1.3	-1.5	-0.7	-4.1	-4.0	-3.3	-3.7	-3.7	-4.5	-4.0	-2.8	-1.1	-2.2	-2.3	-4.4	-3.9	-4.4
16	Russia	7.8	5.6	4.5	-5.9	-3.2	1.4	0.4	-1.2	-1.1	-3.4	-3.7	-1.5	2.9	1.9	-4.0	0.8	-2.2
17	Saudi Arabia	20.8	11.8	29.8	-5.4	4.4	11.5	11.8	5.6	-3.5	-15.5	-13.7	-8.9	-5.5	-4.2	-10.7	-2.3	2.5
18	South Africa	0.8	1.2	-0.5	-4.7	-4.5	-3.7	-4.0	-3.9	-3.9	-4.4	-3.7	-4.0	-3.7	-4.7	-9.6	-5.6	-4.5
19	Turkey	-0.7	-1.9	-2.6	-5.8	-3.4	-0.7	-1.8	-1.5	-1.4	-1.3	-2.3	-2.2	-3.8	-4.8	-5.1	-4.0	-1.6

Rows 1–9 grouped as **Advanced Countries**; rows 10–19 grouped as **Emerging & Developing Countries**.

Source: International Monetary Fund, *World Economic Outlook* database, April 2023.

Appendix **Table 5A.4** Current Account Balance (% of GDP) across the G20 Economies

		Country	2006	2007	2008	2009	2010	2011	2012	2013	2014	2015	2016	2017	2018	2019	2020	2021	2022
	1	Australia	-5.9	-6.7	-4.8	-4.5	-3.6	-3.0	-4.3	-3.4	-3.0	-4.6	-3.3	-2.6	-2.2	0.4	2.2	3.0	1.2
	2	Canada	1.4	0.8	0.1	-2.9	-3.6	-2.7	-3.5	-3.1	-2.3	-3.5	-3.1	-2.8	-2.4	-2.0	-2.2	-0.3	-0.4
	3	France	0.3	-0.1	-0.7	-0.6	-0.6	-0.9	-1.0	-0.5	-1.0	-0.4	-0.5	-0.8	-0.8	0.5	-1.8	0.4	-1.7
	4	Germany	5.8	6.9	5.7	5.8	5.7	6.2	7.1	6.6	7.2	8.6	8.6	7.8	8.0	8.2	7.-	7.7	4.2
Advanced Countries	5	Italy	-1.5	-1.4	-2.8	-1.9	-3.3	-2.8	-0.2	1.1	1.9	1.4	2.6	2.7	2.6	3.3	3.9	3.0	-0.7
	6	Japan	3.8	4.6	2.8	2.7	3.8	2.1	1.0	0.9	0.8	3.1	4.0	4.1	3.5	3.4	2.9	3.9	2.1
	7	Korea	0.2	0.9	0.2	3.5	2.4	1.3	3.8	5.6	5.6	7.2	6.5	4.6	4.5	3.6	4.6	4.7	1.8
	8	United Kingdom	-3.2	-3.8	-4.0	-3.2	-2.9	-1.8	-3.3	-4.8	-5.2	-5.1	-5.5	-3.6	-4.1	-2.8	-3.2	-1.5	-5.6
	9	United States	-5.9	-5.1	-4.7	-2.6	-2.9	-2.9	-2.6	-2.0	-2.1	-2.2	-2.1	-1.9	-2.1	-2.1	-2.9	-3.6	-3.6
	10	Argentina	2.8	2.1	1.5	2.2	-0.4	-1.0	-0.4	-2.1	-1.6	-2.7	-2.7	-4.8	-5.2	-0.8	0.3	1.4	-0.7
	11	Brazil	1.0	-0.2	-2.1	-1.8	-3.9	-3.2	-3.8	-3.6	-4.5	-3.5	-1.7	-1.2	-2.9	-3.6	-1.9	-2.8	-2.9
	12	China	8.4	9.9	9.2	4.8	3.9	1.8	2.5	1.5	2.2	2.6	1.7	1.5	0.2	0.7	1.7	1.8	2.3
Emerging & Developing Countries	13	India	-1.0	-1.3	-2.3	-2.8	-2.8	-4.3	-4.8	-1.7	-1.3	-1.1	-0.6	-1.8	-2.1	-0.9	0.9	-1.2	-2.6
	14	Indonesia	2.4	1.4	0.0	1.8	0.7	0.2	-2.7	-3.2	-3.1	-2.0	-1.8	-1.6	-2.9	-2.7	-0.4	0.3	1.0
	15	Mexico	-0.3	-0.9	-1.6	-0.8	-0.4	-0.9	-1.5	-2.5	-2.0	-2.8	-2.4	-1.9	-2.1	-0.4	2.1	-0.6	-0.9
	16	Russia	8.7	5.2	5.8	3.9	4.1	4.8	3.3	1.5	2.8	5.0	1.9	2.0	7.0	3.9	2.4	6.7	10.3
	17	Saudi Arabia	26.3	22.5	25.5	4.9	12.6	23.4	22.2	18.0	9.6	-8.5	-3.6	1.5	8.5	4.6	-3.1	5.1	13.8
	18	South Africa	-4.0	-4.8	-5.0	-2.4	-1.3	-2.0	-4.7	-5.3	-4.8	-4.3	-2.7	-2.4	-2.9	-2.6	2.0	3.7	-0.5
	19	Turkey	-5.6	-5.4	-5.1	-1.8	-5.7	-8.9	-5.4	-5.8	-4.1	-3.1	-3.1	-4.7	-2.6	1.4	-4.4	-0.9	-5.4

Source: International Monetary Fund, *World Economic Outlook* database, April 2023.

Appendix Table 5A.5 Growth in Some Non-Euro Area Advanced Economies (%)

	Country	2006	2007	2008	2009	2010	2011	2012	2013	2014	2015	2016	2017	2018	2019	2020	2021	2022
Non-Euro Area European AEs	Denmark	3.9	0.9	-0.5	-4.9	1.9	1.3	0.2	0.9	1.6	2.3	3.2	2.8	2.0	1.5	-2.0	4.9	3.6
	Norway	2.5	2.9	0.5	-1.9	0.8	1.1	2.7	1.0	2.0	1.9	1.2	2.5	0.8	1.1	-1.3	3.9	3.3
	Sweden	4.7	3.4	-0.5	-4.3	6.0	3.2	-0.6	1.2	2.7	4.5	2.1	2.6	2.0	2.0	-2.2	5.4	2.6
	Switzerland	4.2	3.9	2.7	-2.3	3.2	1.9	1.2	1.8	2.3	1.6	2.1	1.4	2.9	1.2	-2.5	4.2	2.1
	United Kingdom	2.2	2.6	-0.2	-4.5	2.4	1.1	1.4	1.8	3.2	2.4	2.2	2.4	1.7	1.6	-11.0	7.6	4.0
	Iceland	6.3	8.5	2.2	-7.7	-2.8	1.8	1.1	4.6	1.7	4.4	6.3	4.2	4.9	1.8	-7.2	4.3	6.4
Non-European AEs	Australia	2.6	4.4	2.5	1.9	2.4	2.8	3.8	2.2	2.6	2.3	2.7	2.4	2.8	1.9	-1.8	5.2	3.7
	Canada	2.6	2.1	1.0	-2.9	3.1	3.1	1.8	2.3	2.9	0.7	1.0	3.0	2.8	1.9	-5.1	5.0	3.4
	Japan	1.4	1.5	-1.2	-5.7	4.1	0.0	1.4	2.0	0.3	1.6	0.8	1.7	0.6	-0.4	-4.3	2.1	1.1
	New Zealand	2.8	3.5	-0.3	-1.1	1.8	1.8	2.5	2.3	3.8	3.7	3.9	3.5	3.5	3.1	-1.5	6.1	2.4
	Hong Kong	7.0	6.5	2.1	-2.5	6.8	4.8	1.7	3.1	2.8	2.4	2.2	3.8	2.8	-1.7	-6.5	6.4	-3.5
	Singapore	9.0	9.0	1.9	0.1	14.5	6.2	4.4	4.8	3.9	3.0	3.6	4.5	3.6	1.3	-3.9	8.9	3.6

Source: International Monetary Fund, *World Economic Outlook* database, April 2023.

Appendix Table 5A.6 Inflation in Some Non-Euro Area Advanced Economies (%)

Country	2006	2007	2008	2009	2010	2011	2012	2013	2014	2015	2016	2017	2018	2019	2020	2021	2022
Non-Euro Area European AEs																	
Denmark	1.8	1.7	3.6	1.0	2.2	2.7	2.4	0.5	0.4	0.2	0.0	1.1	0.7	0.7	0.3	1.9	8.5
Norway	2.3	0.7	3.8	2.2	2.4	1.3	0.7	2.1	2.0	2.2	3.6	1.9	2.8	2.2	1.3	3.5	5.8
Sweden	1.5	1.7	3.3	1.9	1.9	1.4	0.9	0.4	0.2	0.7	1.1	1.9	2.0	1.7	0.7	2.7	8.1
Switzerland	1.1	0.7	2.4	-0.5	0.7	0.2	-0.7	-0.2	0.0	-1.1	-0.4	0.5	0.9	0.4	-0.7	0.6	2.8
United Kingdom	2.3	2.3	3.6	2.2	3.3	4.5	2.8	2.6	1.5	0.0	0.7	2.7	2.5	1.8	0.9	2.6	9.1
Iceland	6.7	5.1	12.7	12.0	5.4	4.0	5.2	3.9	2.0	1.6	1.7	1.8	2.7	3.0	2.8	4.5	8.3
Non-European AEs																	
Australia	3.6	2.4	4.3	1.8	2.9	3.4	1.7	2.5	2.5	1.5	1.3	2.0	1.9	1.6	0.9	2.8	6.6
Canada	2.0	2.1	2.4	0.3	1.8	2.9	1.5	0.9	1.9	1.1	1.4	1.6	2.3	1.9	0.7	3.4	6.8
Japan	0.3	0.0	1.4	-1.3	-0.7	-0.3	0.0	0.3	2.8	0.8	-0.1	0.5	1.0	0.5	0.0	-0.2	2.5
New Zealand	3.4	2.4	4.0	2.1	2.3	4.0	1.1	1.1	1.2	0.3	0.6	1.9	1.6	1.6	1.7	3.9	7.2
Hong Kong	2.0	2.0	4.3	0.6	2.3	5.3	4.1	4.3	4.4	3.0	2.4	1.5	2.4	2.9	0.3	1.6	1.9
Singapore	1.0	2.1	6.6	0.6	2.8	5.2	4.6	2.4	1.0	-0.5	-0.5	0.6	0.4	0.6	-0.2	2.3	6.1

Source: International Monetary Fund, *World Economic Outlook* database, April 2023.

6

Euro Area Economies

The Crisis and Thereafter

When the euro was first introduced in 1999, as 'book' money, the euro area comprised 11 of the then 15 EU member states. Various other countries joined subsequently, Greece in 2001, followed by Slovenia in 2007, Cyprus and Malta in 2008, Slovakia in 2009, Estonia in 2011, Latvia in 2014, Lithuania in 2015, and Croatia in 2023.[1] At present the euro area numbers 20 EU member states (Appendix 6.A). The experience of the euro area in some sense depicts the rollercoaster movement of the growth trajectory.

In particular, the crisis in the euro area economies, broadly spanning 2009–15, is somewhat unique in many respects. It erupted well after the global financial crisis, which originated in the US and, to some extent, in the UK. The crisis manifested itself not so much as a financial crisis but as a sovereign debt crisis in some countries. It brought to the fore several issues relating to the currency union. Further, though the balances of the euro economies in relation to those of the rest of the world were not much affected, economists considered that the current account surplus and current account deficit of China and the US, respectively, could potentially cause a crisis. But very few analysts expected the current account imbalances within the euro area economies could be a trigger for a crisis in the area. The intra-eurozone fiscal and financial linkages have come to the fore in a most telling fashion. What distinguished the euro area crisis

---

[1] Of the member states outside the euro area, Denmark has an 'opt-out' from joining. Also there are EU members who did not meet the necessary conditions for entry to the euro area, but have committed to joining as and when they meet them. Finally, there are non-EU member countries such as Sweden, Andorra, Monaco, San Marino, and the Vatican City who have adopted the euro as their national currency (https://economy-finance.ec.europa.eu/euro/what-euro-area_en, accessed in November 2023).

Financial and Fiscal Policies. Second Edition. Y. V. Reddy, Partha Ray, and Pinaki Chakraborty, Oxford University Press.
© Y. V. Reddy, Partha Ray, and Pinaki Chakraborty 2024. DOI: 10.1093/9780198934288.003.0006

from others was that the resolution of the crisis did call for significant institutional changes that included banking and fiscal union among sovereign entities within the euro area.

The chapter proceeds as follows. After noting the importance of euro area economies in the global context in the next section, the chapter turns to economic developments in the euro area economies in general and bigger economies in the euro area in particular. The chapter then focuses on the five euro area countries that were severely hit by the crisis, namely, Greece, Ireland, Italy, Portugal, and Spain (popularly referred to by the acronym 'GIIPS'). Iceland is also discussed in this context; though it is not a part of the euro area, it is a potential member where the crisis had hit rather early. Later, the chapter discusses the possible channels of contagion of the euro area crisis and possible solutions. Finally, the chapter discusses the rescue and solution packages.

Euro Area Economies in the Global Economy

To begin with, it is useful to have a sense of the economic weight of these countries in the global GDP. As a group, the euro area crisis has led to a reduction of their share in world GDP from 17.3 per cent to 12 per cent; notwithstanding this reduction, the share of the EU is higher than that of the US (Table 6.1). As far as the euro area is concerned, five countries—namely, Germany, France, Italy, Spain, and the Netherlands—are the big economic powers, with each country's GDP share being higher than 1 per cent of the global GDP—interestingly, out of these big five, two major countries, namely Spain and Italy, have been engulfed by the crisis. In terms of its share in the global GDP, the euro area roughly accounts for one-fifth of global output and is second to the US economy.

Of course, there are interesting similarities among these countries. First, among the bigger countries, Germany, Austria, the Netherlands, and Belgium have a current account surplus (France has a current account deficit, however). Almost all the crisis countries have current account deficits (with the sole exception of Ireland, since the Irish programme under the IMF has already started). Second, with the exception of Spain, all the crisis countries have a high debt-to-GDP ratio. Thus,

Table 6.1 Euro Area Countries' Share in World GDP at PPP; Percentage

	Country Group	2001	2011	2021
1	Germany	4.7	3.6	3.3
2	France	3.3	2.6	2.3
3	Italy	3.3	2.3	1.9
4	Spain	1.9	1.6	1.4
5	Netherlands	1.1	0.8	0.8
6	Belgium	0.6	0.5	0.4
7	Ireland	0.2	0.2	0.4
8	Austria	0.5	0.4	0.4
9	Portugal	0.4	0.3	0.3
10	Greece	0.4	0.3	0.2
11	Finland	0.3	0.2	0.2
12	Slovak Republic	0.1	0.1	0.1
13	Croatia	0.1	0.1	0.1
14	Lithuania	0.1	0.1	0.1
15	Slovenia	0.1	0.1	0.1
16	Luxembourg	0.1	0.1	0.1
17	Latvia	0.04	0.04	0.05
18	Estonia	0.04	0.03	0.04
19	Cyprus	0.03	0.03	0.03
20	Malta	0.01	0.01	0.02
	Memo Items			
21	*European Union*	*20.2*	*15.9*	*14.8*
22	*Euro Area*	*17.3*	*13.2*	*12.0*

Source: *World Economic Outlook* database, IMF, October 2023.

the crisis countries, in general, have been borrowing both domestically as well as externally. After a point, the advantage of the currency union could not camouflage the lack of strong macroeconomic fundamentals. In this sense, bigger countries (Germany primarily and France, to a lesser extent) with strong macroeconomic fundamentals (namely, with low fiscal deficit, low current account deficit or preferably with a current account surplus, low inflation, high growth, and low unemployment) have the wherewithal to bear the onerous responsibility of bailing out the crisis countries. Issues like how such bailouts take place (if at all) are more complex matters of both pan-European as well as global political economy.

At the risk of oversimplification, at the current juncture one can further subdivide the euro area economies into three groups: (a) the Centre (or core) euro area countries (namely, the bigger countries comprising Austria, Belgium, France, Germany, and the Netherlands); (b) smaller economies (like Malta or Slovenia); and (c) those euro area countries that are severely hit by the crisis (namely, the GIIPS countries). Notwithstanding the usual distinction between Centre and periphery economies in the euro area, it is pertinent to note that almost all the euro area economies have been affected adversely in 2012. Despite their size, the Centre economies have all been hit by the euro area crisis, admittedly less than the five GIIPS economies; after all, in none of the five countries (Austria, Belgium, France, Germany, or the Netherlands), the growth rate crossed 1 per cent in 2012. The euro area contracted by 0.5 per cent in 2013; there were improvements in most of the economies in the euro area in 2014.

With this backdrop, specifically, the chapter focuses on the Centre economies and those hit severely by the crisis in the euro area in greater detail.

Macro Performance of the Euro Area

In terms of aggregate behaviour, during the period 2011–22, the euro area had experienced three distinct crises, namely, (1) the global financial crisis (2009); (2) the euro area crisis (2012–13); and (3) the pandemic (2020). While the impact of the global financial crisis and the pandemic is along expected lines, the genesis and transmission of the euro area crisis during 2012–13 is completely unique to the area (Table 6.2). A number of features of the euro area countries can be noted. First, with the sole of exception of 2022, inflation has not been much of a problem in the euro area; inflation of course shot up 8.4 per cent during 2022, following a generalized price pressure across the world, issues regarding post-pandemic global supply chains, and the Russia-Ukraine conflict. Second, while at an aggregate level the fisc has not posed much of a problem, the situation in specific countries has been different. Following the pandemic, expectedly the fiscal deficit went up. Third, the current account balance in the

Table 6.2 Major Macroeconomic Variables of the Euro Area

	GDP Growth (%)	Inflation (%)	General government primary net lending / borrowing (% of GDP)	General government gross debt (% of GDP)	Current account balance (% of GDP)
2001	2.2	2.3	1.3	67.9	−0.4
2002	0.9	2.3	0.4	67.9	0.6
2003	0.7	2.1	−0.2	69.2	0.2
2004	2.3	2.1	−0.1	69.5	0.7
2005	1.7	2.2	0.0	70.2	0.1
2006	3.2	2.2	1.0	68.2	−0.2
2007	3.0	2.1	1.9	65.7	0.0
2008	0.4	3.3	0.4	69.4	−1.8
2009	−4.5	0.3	−3.8	79.9	−0.3
2010	2.1	1.6	−3.8	85.3	−0.3
2011	1.7	2.7	−1.7	87.2	−0.4
2012	−0.9	2.5	−1.1	90.6	1.0
2013	−0.2	1.4	−0.5	92.6	2.1
2014	1.4	0.4	−0.2	92.8	2.3
2015	2.0	0.2	0.1	90.9	2.7
2016	1.9	0.2	0.4	90.1	3.0
2017	2.6	1.5	0.8	87.7	3.1
2018	1.8	1.8	1.2	85.7	2.8
2019	1.6	1.2	0.8	83.7	2.4
2020	−6.1	0.3	−5.7	96.8	1.8
2021	5.6	2.6	−4.0	94.8	2.8
2022	3.3	8.4	−2.1	91.0	−0.7

Source: World Economic Outlook database, IMF, October 2023.

euro area has been, by and large, manageable. Finally, the fluctuation of the exchange rate between the euro and the US dollar has been range bound (Chart 6.1).

By 2017, it appeared that the euro area was finally out of its crisis. However, as elsewhere in the world, the euro area too was affected deeply by the pandemic. In fact, while indicating that 'economic activity in the euro area is forecast to drop sharply in 2020, before starting to

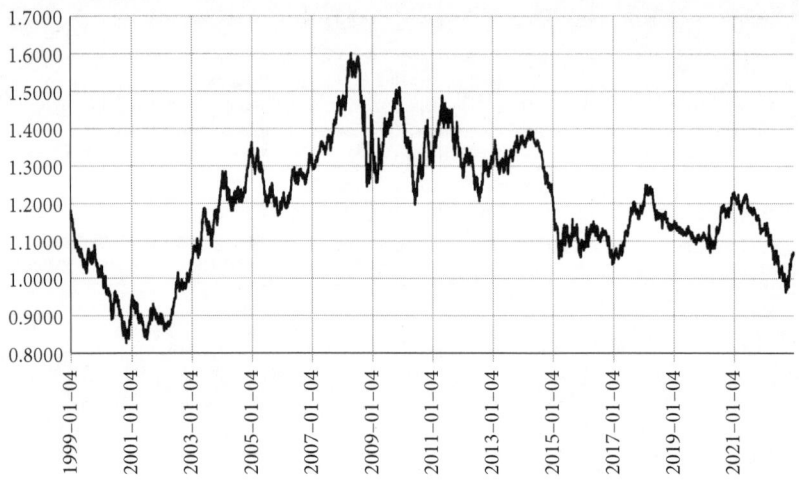

Chart 6.1 USD to Euro Spot Exchange Rate

Source: Board of Governors of the Federal Reserve System (US), US Dollars to Euro Spot Exchange Rate [DEXUSEU], retrieved from FRED, Federal Reserve Bank of St Louis; https://fred.stlouisfed.org/series/DEXUSEU, April 2024

rebound in 2021', the IMF projection showed that despite the projected recovery, the euro area is expected to suffer permanent output losses from the crisis.[2] By some unfortunate coincidence, by the time the euro area economy began to recover, the Russia-Ukraine conflict started and has begun to affect the euro area and significantly increased uncertainties. Analysis of the European Central Bank indicated, 'While the very high energy prices and renewed supply shortages resulting from the war are key observable factors affecting economic activity, a third unobservable factor—the associated rise in uncertainty—is also playing a major role.'[3]

However, such an aggregative story camouflages the inter-country differences within the euro area. Hence, in order to understand, we look at the features of Centre countries and the crisis countries of the euro area separately.

---

[2] https://www.imf.org/en/News/Articles/2020/12/21/na122220five-charts-on-the-euro-areas-postcovid19-recovery-and-growth (accessed in March 2024)

[3] https://www.ecb.europa.eu/pub/economic-bulletin/focus/2022/html/ecb.ebbox202204_02~b5e18e967d.en.html (accessed in March 2024)

The Centre Countries of the Euro Area

Select macro variables of the five large euro area economies are presented in Table 6.3.[4]

Some features emerge out of the data. First, inflation, despite its low levels, has been on an increasing trend in 2014. Second, apart from Germany, all other countries have significant fiscal deficits; Germany's fiscal deficit over 2011–12 has been modest (at less than 1 per cent of GDP). Third, among the bigger countries, while Germany has been experiencing a current account surplus, France has been incurring a current account deficit; Austria and the Netherlands have also experienced a current account deficit.

As far as the Centre euro area economy is concerned, Germany and France are two economies that are important by most criteria and hence there is a need for more focused attention on these two economies.

The German economy is the strongest (accounting for nearly 4 per cent of global GDP at PPP) in the area. The global financial crisis badly hit Germany and in 2009 the economy contracted by 3.7 per cent. Apart from the trade channel, the banking sector in Germany was the first place where the financial crisis surfaced (Hoffmann 2011). The economy of course rebounded fast and both in 2009 as well as in 2010 growth was impressive. But the shadows of the euro area crisis loomed large and the German economy grew at a modest 0.9 per cent in 2012 and 0.5 per cent in 2013.

The financial sector of Germany during the euro area crisis exhibited its vulnerability because of its risky investments. Banks like Deutsche Bank, Commerzbank, or Dresdner Bank, all were affected by varying degrees. In order to maintain solvency of its banking sector, the German state intervened and became a shareholder with 25 per cent ownership. Also a federal agency was set up for financial market stabilization and the transfer of some institutions' risky assets to bad banks. This raised government debt in 2010 significantly. Furthermore, due to its high leverage, the German banking sector continued to be

---

[4] Note that in view of their crisis-hit status, economies like Italy or Portugal, despite their size, are discussed in the next section.

Table 6.3 Select Indicators in Centre Euro Area Economies

	Growth (%)					Inflation (%)				
	Austria	Belgium	France	Germany	Netherlands	Austria	Belgium	France	Germany	Netherlands
2001	1.3	1.1	1.9	1.7	2.3	2.3	2.4	1.8	1.9	5.1
2002	1.7	1.7	1.2	−0.2	0.2	1.7	1.6	1.9	1.3	3.9
2003	0.9	1.0	0.8	−0.7	0.2	1.3	1.5	2.2	1.1	2.2
2004	2.7	3.6	2.5	1.2	2.0	2.0	1.9	2.3	1.8	1.4
2005	2.2	2.3	1.7	0.7	2.0	2.1	2.5	1.9	1.9	1.5
2006	3.5	2.6	2.7	3.8	3.5	1.7	2.3	1.9	1.8	1.7
2007	3.7	3.7	2.4	3.0	3.8	2.2	1.8	1.6	2.3	1.6
2008	1.5	0.4	0.1	1.0	2.2	3.2	4.5	3.2	2.8	2.2
2009	−3.8	−2.0	−2.8	−5.7	−3.7	0.4	0.0	0.1	0.2	1.0
2010	1.8	2.9	1.8	4.2	1.3	1.7	2.3	1.7	1.1	0.9
2011	2.9	1.7	2.2	3.9	1.6	3.5	3.3	2.3	2.5	2.5
2012	0.7	0.7	0.4	0.4	−1.0	2.6	2.6	2.2	2.2	2.8
2013	0.0	0.5	0.7	0.4	−0.1	2.1	1.2	1.0	1.6	2.6
2014	0.7	1.6	1.0	2.2	1.4	1.5	0.5	0.6	0.8	0.3
2015	1.0	2.0	1.0	1.5	2.0	0.8	0.6	0.1	0.7	0.2
2016	2.0	1.3	1.0	2.2	2.2	1.0	1.8	0.3	0.4	0.1
2017	2.3	1.6	2.5	2.7	2.9	2.2	2.2	1.2	1.7	1.3
2018	2.4	1.8	1.8	1.0	2.4	2.1	2.3	2.1	1.9	1.6
2019	1.5	2.3	1.9	1.1	2.0	1.5	1.3	1.3	1.4	2.7
2020	−6.5	−5.4	−7.7	−3.8	−3.9	1.4	0.4	0.5	0.4	1.1
2021	4.6	6.3	6.4	3.2	6.2	2.8	3.2	2.1	3.2	2.8
2022	4.8	3.2	2.5	1.8	4.3	8.6	10.3	5.9	8.7	11.6

Source: *World Economic Outlook* database, IMF, October 2023.

General Government Net Lending / Borrowing (% of GDP)					Current Account Balance (% of GDP)				
Austria	Bel-gium	France	Ger-many	Nether-lands	Austria	Bel-gium	France	Ger-many	Nether-lands
−0.7	0.2	−1.4	−3.0	−0.4	−0.8	3.3	1.6	−0.4	2.3
−1.9	0.0	−3.2	−3.9	−2.0	2.1	4.5	1.1	1.9	2.3
−1.4	−1.9	−4.0	−3.7	−3.1	1.5	3.4	0.8	1.4	5.2
−4.8	−0.2	−3.6	−3.3	−1.8	2.1	3.1	0.5	4.5	7.6
−2.5	−2.7	−3.4	−3.3	−0.5	2.3	2.0	0.1	4.7	7.0
−2.6	0.2	−2.4	−1.7	0.0	3.3	1.9	0.3	5.8	9.1
−1.4	0.1	−2.6	0.3	−0.2	3.8	1.5	−0.1	6.9	6.9
−1.5	−1.1	−3.3	−0.1	0.1	4.5	−1.0	−0.7	5.7	5.0
−5.4	−5.4	−7.2	−3.2	−5.2	2.6	1.7	−0.6	5.8	5.4
−4.5	−4.1	−6.9	−4.4	−5.3	2.9	1.6	−0.6	5.7	6.9
−2.6	−4.3	−5.2	−0.9	−4.4	1.6	−1.9	−0.9	6.2	8.5
−2.2	−4.3	−5.0	0.0	−3.9	1.5	−0.1	−1.0	7.1	10.2
−2.0	−3.1	−4.1	0.0	−3.0	1.9	1.0	−0.5	6.6	9.8
−2.7	−3.1	−3.9	0.6	−2.3	2.5	0.8	−1.0	7.2	8.2
−1.0	−2.4	−3.6	1.0	−1.9	1.7	1.4	−0.4	8.6	5.2
−1.5	−2.4	−3.6	1.2	0.1	2.7	0.6	−0.5	8.6	7.1
−0.8	−0.7	−3.0	1.3	1.4	1.4	0.7	−0.8	7.8	8.9
0.2	−0.9	−2.3	2.0	1.5	0.9	−0.9	−0.8	8.0	9.3
0.6	−2.0	−3.1	1.5	1.8	2.4	0.1	0.5	8.2	6.9
−8.0	−9.0	−9.0	−4.3	−3.7	3.0	1.1	−1.6	7.1	5.1
−5.8	−5.5	−6.5	−3.6	−2.3	0.4	0.4	0.4	7.7	12.1
−3.2	−3.9	−4.8	−2.5	−0.1	0.7	−3.6	−2.0	4.2	9.2

vulnerable. In fact, the 2011 OECD Economic Survey for Germany commented:

[T]he (non-risk weighted) capital to total asset ratio was 4.3 per cent in 2010, the lowest among European countries; the ratio has decreased slightly in recent years, whereas in most other euro area countries it has increased. The difference between this leverage ratio and the ratio of regulatory capital to risk-weighted assets is among the highest in the euro area. This indicates a high vulnerability of the German banking system to financial market stress in case risk has not been appropriately assessed.

How did the euro area crisis affect Germany? There are three competing views on the impact of the euro area crisis on Germany. First, many believe that the burden of the crisis in the GIIPS countries could lead to increased burden on German taxpayers. Second, there is an influential opinion that 'the euro crisis is dragging Germany to the brink of a recession' (Broyer et al. 2012). Third, there is a contrary view that the German government is actually benefiting from the euro crisis by way of the low interest rates making it easier for the German government to borrow and create more demand for loans from the household sector. Interestingly, the possible recession argument in Germany cuts both ways. On the one hand, German exports to the euro area (in volume terms) are down with German incoming orders from European Monetary Union (EMU) countries in Q2 2012 decreasing by more than 10 per cent in Q2 2011; on the other hand, a depreciated euro could make German exports more competitive. The combined effect of the European debt crisis on German exports, consumption, and investment has been estimated to affect German GDP by possibly as much as 1 percentage point (Broyer et al. 2012).

In a caricatured world of opposites, France and Germany are often seen as poles apart within the euro area. This is reflected in social norms, mores, and attitudes as well as in the economic sphere. France, accounting for nearly 3 per cent of world GDP, had significant fiscal and current account deficit in the recent period, unlike Germany. Interestingly, thanks to a large social safety net via timely government intervention, the French economy registered a lower contraction of around 3 per cent in 2009. The economy recovered in 2010 and the momentum continued in 2011 as well; this was largely driven by healthy consumption growth. Unemployment, hovering around 8–9 per cent, continues to remain an issue in France. Furthermore, in line with international trends, energy prices in France have surged and there are, thus, inflationary risks. The earlier uncertainty in the sovereign debt market has subsided for France; while in 2010 France's sovereign CDS spread and its 10-year government bond yield spread (relative to the German Bund) have increased, in most of 2011, French and German spreads have moved in a different direction than those of GIIPS economies. Nevertheless, in 2012, France narrowly averted recession with a slight uptick in GDP growth in the third quarter and GDP growth was stationary for 2012 as a whole and reached 0.3 per cent in 2013.

Insofar as the impact of the pandemic on the Centre euro area countries is concerned, all these five countries experienced contraction. But as elsewhere, thanks to widespread vaccination and substantial monetary and fiscal stimuli these economies hit back swiftly. However, the Russia-Ukraine conflict has affected the euro area adversely through several channels. First, the rise in energy prices has added to the inflationary pressures and expectations. Second, for select countries the conflict has added to immigration costs and refugee crisis. Third, the fisc also came under substantial strain as a result of mitigating policies about the war.

The Crisis Countries in the Euro Area

This section will focus on five euro area countries that have been affected by the crisis, namely, Greece, Ireland, Italy, Portugal, and Spain (GIIPS), as well as one potential euro area country, namely, Iceland.

Greece: Public Sector as the Villain

Greece's association with the euro area dates long back. While an Association Agreement with the European Economic Community (EEC) was signed by Greece as early as 1961, it froze during 1967–74—a period of dictatorship in Greece; it was reactivated when democracy was restored in Greece in July 1974. Greece finally became a full-fledged member of the EU in 1981 and entered the euro area in 2001. Greece's entry to the euro area was marred by controversy even at the beginning. In 2004, it was revealed that the budget numbers that Greece used to gain euro area membership were fudged. We will see in the following lines that this spectre of accounting irregularities did not leave Greece![5]

Before we proceed to diagnose the nature of Greece's current problems, to set the context, it may be useful to have a quick review of the developments in Greece immediately preceding the crisis.[6]

Without any claim to being exhaustive, the treatment that follows is highly selective—after all, with present-day information overflow there is no dearth of material on the Greek crisis.

The first sign of the crisis may perhaps be traced to April 2009, when the EU ordered a number of countries including Greece (apart from France, Spain, Ireland) to reduce their budget deficits. Subsequently, in December 2009, when Greek debts reached €300 bn or 113 per cent of GDP, the market showed the first signs of concern. In January 2010, an EU report unearthed several irregularities in Greek accounting procedures and Greece's budget deficit in 2009 was revised upwards from 3.7 per cent to 12.7 per cent. Subsequently, in March 2010, the euro area and IMF agreed to a safety net of €22 bn to help Greece and in April, following worsening financial markets and protests, euro area countries agreed to provide up to €30 bn in emergency loans.[7]

Meanwhile, Greek borrowing costs reached further record highs. In July 2011, the Greek parliament voted in favour of a fresh round of drastic austerity measures, following which the EU approved the latest tranche of the Greek loan, worth €12 bn. Despite various political posturing and differences of opinion within and outside Greece about the nature of the package, on 21 October 2011, euro area finance ministers approved the next €8 bn tranche of Greek bailout loans, potentially saving the country from default.

---

[5] British newspaper *The Independent* reported on 16 November 2004, 'Greece admitted yesterday that the budget figures it used to gain entry to the euro three years ago were fudged. The Finance Minister, George Alogoskoufis, said the true scale of Greece's budget deficit was massively understated enabling Athens to dip below the qualification bar and into the EU's single currency' (available at http:// www.independent.co.uk).

[6] This account depends heavily on the developments and the chronology given in the *New York Times*.

[7] The EU report found evidence of 'severe irregularities in the Excessive Deficit Procedure (EDP) notifications of April and October 2009, including submission of incorrect data, and non-respect of accounting rules and of the timing of the notification; ... an institutional setting and a public accounting system inappropriate for a correct reporting of EDP statistics, especially non-transparent or improperly documented bookkeeping, which has lead to several, in some cases significant, revisions of data by the Greek authorities over an extended period of time ...'; see http:// epp.eurostat.ec.europa.eu/portal/page/ portal/product_details/publication? p_product_code = COM_2010_report_greek for details.

However, as time progressed it soon became clear that Greece needed much more substantial assistance from the international community including, but not necessarily confined only to, a large debt relief package.

Later, euro area finance ministers in March 2012 approved financing of the second Greek economic adjustment programme for an amount of up to €130 bn until 2014, including an IMF contribution of €28 bn. Euro area member states also authorized the European Financial Stability Facility (EFSF) to release the first instalment of a total amount of €39.4 bn, which will be disbursed in several tranches. Also in March 2012, the Greek authorities completed a debt-swap deal, covering: (a) €177 bn of Greek law bonds (GGBs); (b) €.8 bn of foreign law bonds; and (c) €9.5 bn of performing state enterprise debt guaranteed by the Greek government. There were, thus, deep write-downs for bondholders involving haircut amounting to 53.5 per cent (in nominal terms).[8] The debt exchange attracted near-universal participation, surpassing the targeted improvement in debt dynamics under the programme.

How did Greece reach this monumental height of crisis proportion? To appreciate this, it is useful to go back a little bit in time. Greece experienced a significant drop in its borrowing cost in the 1990s as it prepared to adopt the euro. Interest rates on 10-year Greek bonds dropped from 24.5 per cent to 6.5 per cent between 1993 and 1999. Subsequently, as Greece entered the euro area, the global financial market by and large chose to ignore Greek fundamentals and treated it as almost indistinguishable from euro area core countries like France and Germany with the nominal interest rate on 10-year Greek government bonds declining to less than 3.5 per cent in early 2005. Thus, Greece got the undeserved benefit of joining the euro area without necessarily going through the fiscal discipline required by the convergence criteria of the Maastricht Treaty.[9] In fact, it was noted in 1998, while discussing the performance

---

[8] In NPV terms the losses range from 70 to 75 per cent (relative to par, and given exit yields in the 9–12 per cent range).

[9] In broad terms, the convergence criteria were as follows: (a) Inflation rate: no more than 1.5 percentage points higher than the average of the three best-performing member states of the EU; (b) Government finance: the annual deficit-GDP ratio must not exceed 3 per cent at the end of the preceding fiscal year; (c) Government debt: the ratio of debt-GDP must not exceed 60 per cent at the end of the preceding fiscal year; (d) Exchange rate: applicant countries should have joined the Exchange Rate Mechanism II (ERM II) for two consecutive years and should not have devalued its currency during the period; and (e) Long-term interest rates: the nominal long-term interest rate must not be more than 2 percentage points higher than in the three lowest inflation member states.

Table 6.4 Greece: Select Macroeconomic Indicators

	GDP Growth (%)	Inflation (%)	Government Net Lending / Borrowing (% of GDP)	Government Gross Debt (% of GDP)	Current Account Balance (% of GDP)
2001	4.1	3.6	−5.5	107.1	−6.9
2002	3.9	3.9	−6.0	104.9	−6.3
2003	5.8	3.5	−7.8	101.5	−6.3
2004	5.1	3.0	−8.8	102.9	−5.5
2005	0.6	3.5	−6.2	107.4	−7.3
2006	5.7	3.3	−5.9	103.6	−10.9
2007	3.3	3.0	−6.7	103.1	−13.9
2008	−0.3	4.2	−10.2	109.4	−14.5
2009	−4.3	1.3	−15.2	126.7	−10.9
2010	−5.5	4.7	−11.4	147.5	−10.0
2011	−10.1	3.1	−10.5	175.2	−10.1
2012	−7.1	1.0	−6.8	162.1	−2.6
2013	−2.5	−0.9	−3.9	178.8	−2.6
2014	0.5	−1.4	−4.2	181.8	−2.5
2015	−0.2	−1.1	−3.0	179.1	−1.5
2016	−0.5	0.0	0.3	183.7	−2.4
2017	1.1	1.1	0.9	183.2	−2.6
2018	1.7	0.8	0.8	190.7	−3.6
2019	1.9	0.5	0.0	185.5	−2.2
2020	−9.0	−1.3	−10.5	212.4	−7.3
2021	8.4	0.6	−7.7	200.7	−7.1
2022	5.9	9.3	−2.3	178.1	−10.1

Source: *World Economic Outlook* database, IMF, October 2023.

of different euro area countries that without relaxation of entry criteria, more than half the present member states would have been denied euro area membership (Grauwe 2009). For instance, Greece would have been disqualified as its debt-GDP ratio exceeded 60 per cent in the year before entry and was increasing (from 111.6 per cent to 113.2 per cent). However, Greece had impressive growth till 2007 (Table 6.4).

How did the international financial markets perceive the Greek sovereign debt scenario? The entry of Greece into the euro area in 2001 led to a sharp reduction in interest rates (Gibson et al. 2012). Illustratively, the nominal interest rate on 10-year Greek government bonds declined from about 20 per cent in 1994, to less than 3.5 per cent in early 2005; with the crisis in late 2009, however, the 10-year government bond yield increased to almost 10 per cent at the end of 2010.

Another standard way to measure market perception about sovereign paper is to observe the behaviour of CDS, which are nothing but some sort of insurance premium in the event of default by the debt issuing authority. Normally, it is expressed as a difference from a safe counterpart. The initial bursts of increase in CDS spreads showed high volatility between May 2010 and July 2011. Since August 2011, the Greek CDS spread exhibited stratospheric levels of as much as 5,000 basis points, indicating a rise in market perception of a default by the Greek sovereign (perhaps associated with a fall in market perception about the probability of a complete euro area bailout)!

How did the Greek crisis germinate? Gourinchas, Philippon, and Vayanos (2017, p. 2) summarized the role of the global financial crisis in the Greek crisis as follows:

The global financial crisis that began in 2007 in the US hit Greece through three interlinked shocks. The first shock was a sovereign debt crisis: investors began to perceive the debt of the Greek government as unsustainable, and were no longer willing to finance the government deficit. The second shock was a banking crisis: Greek banks had difficulty financing themselves in the interbank market, and their solvency was put in doubt because of projected losses to the value of their assets. The third shock was a sudden stop: foreign investors were no longer willing to lend to Greece as a whole (government, banks, and firms), and so the country could not finance its current account deficit.

In some sense, the Greek crisis is symptomatic of the classical problems of countries within a currency union that face asymmetric shocks. In fact, at the time of its inclusion in the euro area, Greece did not fulfil the requisite criteria for the formation of an optimum currency area (OCA). Further, since joining the euro, Greece has had higher inflation than other euro area members. Besides, Greece was fiscally quite irresponsible and had generous public sector pay, welfare, and retirement benefits, while collecting a lower share in taxes due to widespread tax evasion. As a result, Greek goods have become increasingly expensive and uncompetitive, causing loss of market share thus further reducing revenues. Greece was well known for its lack of structural reforms (including labour reform)—so much so that it continued to remain the worst EU and OECD performing country in terms of the World Bank Doing Business indicators. Besides, the deadly combination of high current account as well as fiscal deficit made the Greek economy all the more vulnerable.

In fact, before the spread of the global financial crisis, Greece borrowed heavily from abroad to fund its large budget and current account deficits. There is an influential view that the roots of 'Greece's fiscal calamity lie in prolonged deficit spending, economic mismanagement, government misreporting, and tax evasion'.[10] So, naturally the corollary is: Greece had to pay the price for being an imperfect member in a currency union thereby losing the crucial tool of exchange rate management. To sum up, being a member of an OCA cannot mask the innate inefficiencies of any economy reflected in lack of productivity; further, access to cheap money from the market in the presence of the twin deficits could only be temporary, with heavy penalties to pay later. Also, the action of the market actors of ignoring Greece's fiscal and external payments problem was essentially myopic and based on the expectation that in case the Greek economy failed, the euro area and the EU would come to its rescue. All these expectations were belied in the recent crisis!

By 2017, the Greek economy started stabilizing—a process that continued till 2020. The Greek economy recovered fairly fast from the severe COVID-19-induced recession aided by a strong fiscal response, accommodative monetary policy and prudential policies, and sizable EU support. While it may be symbolic, on 20 October 2023 the Standard & Poor's (S&P) rating agency upgraded Greece's rating from BB+ to BBB-. Thus, 13 years after being downgraded to junk bond status Greece is now officially back in the investment grade category.[11]

---

[10] When pressed on where Greece had gone wrong, Prime Minister George Papandreou answered: 'Corruption, cronyism, clientalistic politics; a lot of money was wasted basically through these types of practices.'
[11] 'Greece painfully rebuilds its economy after 15 years of depression', Report by Eric Albert and Marina Rafenberg (Athens (Greece) correspondent), Published on 29 October 2023 in *Le Monde*, available at https://www.lemonde.fr/en/economy/article/2023/10/29/greece-painfully-rebuilds-its-economy-after-15-years-of-depression_6211022_19.html#:~:text = First%2C%20 there%20was%20the%20crisis,has%20fallen%20back%20to%2011%25 (accessed in March 2024)

Ireland: Domestic Banks and Property Price Bubble

The Irish problem was quite different from that of Greece as it was essentially related to its banking sector. While the global financial crisis exacerbated matters in Ireland, the banking crisis in Ireland was primarily a home-grown phenomenon. It stemmed from the collapse of the domestic property sector and the subsequent contraction in national output. In some sense, its root cause can be found in the inadequate risk management practices of the Irish banks and the failure of the financial regulator to supervise these practices effectively.

Interestingly, as in the case of a classic boom-bust cycle, for more than a decade (during 1995–2007) Ireland had been growing at a robust rate with 6.3 per cent average annual real GDP growth. Further, Irish debt-GDP ratio hovered below 30 per cent till 2007 and hence within some perceived safe limits (see Table 6.5).[12]

However, in all fairness, despite the well-known myopia of the IMF in anticipating the roots of the crisis in the US in 2007, the IMF was right in inferring the shape of things to come in Ireland. Noting that this remarkable performance in Ireland reflected both good policies and fortunate circumstances and that rapid credit growth was a vulnerability, the IMF's Article IV report on Ireland of June 2006 (2006, p. 2) observed candidly.

But rising real estate prices and a boom in mortgage lending were laying the groundwork for a recession. Economic activity has become reliant on building investment and competitiveness has eroded. The share of the construction sector in economic activity has increased and is now one of the highest in Europe. Bank credit to property-related sectors has grown rapidly and now accounts for more than half of total bank lending. Household debt as a share of household disposable income rose to about 130 per cent in 2005, among the highest in Europe.

A few features of the Irish financial sector may be noted. First, annual credit growth, at 25 per cent plus since 2005, was indeed high. Second,

---

[12] The IMF in its 2006 Article IV consultation report for Ireland in June 2006 noted: 'Ireland's economic performance remains strong . . . In recent years, real GNP growth was one of the highest among industrial countries; the unemployment rate was among the lowest; and HICP inflation declined to close to the Euro Area average. Employment growth was rapid, reflecting strong immigration and rising labour force participation.'

Table 6.5 Ireland: Select Macroeconomic Indicators

	GDP Growth (%)	Inflation (%)	Government Net Lending / Borrowing (% of GDP)	Government Gross Debt (% of GDP)	Current Account Balance (% of GDP)
2001	5.3	4.0	1.0	33.6	0.2
2002	5.9	4.7	−0.5	30.9	0.2
2003	3.0	4.0	0.3	29.8	0.5
2004	6.8	2.3	1.3	28.1	−0.1
2005	5.7	2.2	1.6	26.1	−3.5
2006	5.0	2.7	2.8	23.6	−5.4
2007	5.3	2.9	0.3	23.9	−6.5
2008	−4.5	3.1	−7.0	42.5	−6.3
2009	−5.1	−1.7	−13.9	61.8	−4.7
2010	1.7	−1.6	−32.1	86.2	−1.3
2011	1.3	1.2	−13.6	110.4	−1.7
2012	−0.1	1.9	−8.5	119.9	−3.4
2013	1.2	0.5	−6.4	120.1	1.6
2014	8.8	0.3	−3.6	104.0	1.1
2015	24.5	−0.1	−2.0	76.5	4.4
2016	1.8	−0.2	−0.8	74.4	−4.2
2017	9.3	0.3	−0.3	67.4	0.5
2018	8.5	0.7	0.1	62.9	4.9
2019	5.3	0.9	0.5	57.1	−19.9
2020	6.6	−0.5	−5.0	58.1	−6.5
2021	15.1	2.4	−1.6	54.4	13.7
2022	9.4	8.1	1.6	44.4	10.8

Source: *World Economic Outlook* database, IMF, October 2023.

personal lending and within it mortgage finance was high as well. Third, foreign currency denominated financial assets was high at 30 per cent plus. Fourth, foreign banks accounted for more than one-third of total banking sector assets. Fifth, non-performing loans experienced a sharp hike since 2008.

Thus, in September 2008, Ireland became the first euro area economy to fall into recession. In October 2008, apprehensions about a run on its domestic banks led to all the debt of its top six financial institutions being guaranteed. A Credit Institutions Financial Support Scheme (CIFS) was introduced on 30 September 2008, covering all deposits, senior debt, covered bonds, and dated subordinated debt of participating Irish banks.[13] Besides, there was a Credit Institutions Eligible Liabilities Guarantee Scheme (ELG Scheme) which commenced its operations in December 2009 and moved away from the blanket nature of the CIFS. The scheme was subsequently extended till December 2012 in various stages. The ELG Scheme covers deposits (more than €100,000) and eligible debt securities (senior unsecured CP, CD, and other senior unsecured notes and bonds) up to a maximum maturity of five years.[14] Besides, in order to handle the onslaught of the crisis, there were massive cuts in public spending. By March 2009, Ireland's credit rating was being downgraded by various credit agencies—a process which continued till July 2011 when ratings agency Moody's downgraded Ireland's debt rating to junk status.

Financial integration played a major role in the Irish crisis. A Preliminary Report on the sources of Ireland's Banking Crisis of the Government of Ireland in 2011 emphasized two aspects of the financial integration that made the Irish economy vulnerable. First, after the adoption of the euro, there was a quantum change in the availability of cross-border bank funding without foreign exchange exposure which facilitated the lending boom in Ireland. Second, there was competition among foreign (especially UK-based) banks to lend to the real estate sector.

How was the current situation in Ireland post crisis? The March 2012 issue of the Macro-Financial Review of the Central Bank of Ireland noted: 'Two principal dimensions of domestic macro-financial risk stand out. The first relates to domestic credit risk driven by property price declines, continued economic weakness and over-indebted private and

---

[13] The CIFS expired on 29 September 2010.

[14] However, the scheme does not guarantee covered bonds, dated subordinated debt or any senior term debt. To be eligible under this scheme, deposits and debt securities must be placed/issued during the extended issuance window. Furthermore, the ELG Scheme is irrevocable and overnight/on-call deposits/current accounts are guaranteed until the ELG Scheme issuance window closes. Participating Institutions in the ELG Scheme have the flexibility to issue un-guaranteed debt securities, but cannot place un-guaranteed deposits. See Bank of Ireland's Irish Government Guarantee: Factsheet for details (available at http://www.bankofireland.com/fs/doc).

public sectors. The second risk concerns threats to sovereign solvency due to crisis-related bank debt and the sovereign's capacity to service that debt, which depends on economic growth and repayment terms.'

While sovereign spreads for Ireland have declined, its credit rating after the crisis remained a matter of concern. The Fifth Review of Ireland's IMF loan (the Extended Arrangement program) of March 2012 had noted that significant reduction of Irish spreads relative to German bunds and remarked: 'The growth outlook has deteriorated as export prospects are dampened by the projected euro area recession, and a somewhat larger decline in consumption is anticipated in view of more rapid house price declines against the background of high household debt burdens.' Since then, things have improved in Ireland and the Twelfth and Final Review of the IMF loan for Ireland noted in December 2013: 'Ireland has pulled back from an exceptionally deep banking crisis, significantly improved its fiscal position, and regained its access to the international financial markets. Growth, though slower than initially projected, has exceeded the euro area average.'

Ireland came out of the euro area crisis quite early and with remarkable agility. Interestingly, within two years of the crisis, Irish growth rate turned out to be 24.5 per cent in 2015! This unusually high growth of 2015 was driven by Ireland's easy tax regime that attracted many American companies in the US to move their headquarters to Dublin, starting with Accenture in 2009.

In more recent times, the Irish economy weathered the COVID-19 pandemic well and showed remarkable stability in its growth and macro conditions in post-pandemic years.

Portugal: Low Growth and High Twin Deficits

The experience of Portugal in some sense was different from that of other crisis countries in the euro area. Unlike Greece, Ireland, or Spain, where economic growth had been high before the crisis, Portugal experienced low growth since 2002. In fact, during the years before the financial crisis (2001–8), average annual real GDP growth was only 1 per cent and in 2003 Portugal experienced a recession (–0.9 per cent) and did not really come out greatly (see Table 6.6).

Table 6.6 Portugal: Select Macroeconomic Indicators

	GDP Growth (%)	Inflation (%)	Government Net Lending / Borrowing (% of GDP)	Government Gross Debt (% of GDP)	Current Account Balance (% of GDP)
2001	1.9	4.4	−4.8	57.4	−10.4
2002	0.8	3.7	−3.8	60.0	−8.4
2003	−0.9	3.2	−5.6	63.9	−6.6
2004	1.8	2.5	−6.0	67.1	−8.0
2005	0.8	2.1	−6.1	72.2	−9.6
2006	1.6	3.0	−4.1	73.7	−10.3
2007	2.5	2.4	−2.9	72.7	−9.6
2008	0.3	2.7	−3.7	75.6	−11.8
2009	−3.1	−0.9	−9.9	87.8	−10.3
2010	1.7	1.4	−11.4	100.2	−10.3
2011	−1.7	3.6	−7.7	114.4	−6.0
2012	−4.1	2.8	−6.2	129.0	−1.6
2013	−0.9	0.4	−5.1	131.4	1.6
2014	0.8	−0.2	−7.3	132.9	0.2
2015	1.8	0.5	−4.3	131.2	0.2
2016	2.0	0.6	−1.9	131.5	1.2
2017	3.5	1.6	−3.0	126.1	1.3
2018	2.8	1.2	−0.3	121.5	0.6
2019	2.7	0.3	0.1	116.6	0.4
2020	−8.3	−0.1	−5.8	134.9	−1.0
2021	5.5	0.9	−2.9	125.4	−0.8
2022	6.7	8.1	−0.4	113.9	−1.2

Source: *World Economic Outlook* database, IMF, October 2023.

Estimates of the EU revealed that potential output growth has been on a downward trend in Portugal since the late 1990s and that structural problems have caused a major loss of competitiveness in Portugal. In fact, the competitiveness gap was estimated at 13–14 per cent as of 2010 by the IMF. On the other hand, while Portugal did not witness a property bubble, nor were Portuguese banks exposed to toxic assets, Portuguese banks have started suffering from funding pressures. Olivier Blanchard in an article in 2006 (i.e., before the crisis) diagnosed the symptoms of the impending crisis in Portugal in terms of (a) anaemic productivity growth, (b) high unemployment, (c) large budget, and (d) current account deficit. In order to trace the roots of the Portuguese ailment, Blanchard went on to say:

> Triggered by the commitment by Portugal to join the euro, a sharp drop in interest rates and expectations of faster growth both led to a decrease in private saving and an increase in investment. The result was high output growth, decreasing unemployment, increasing wages, and fast increasing current account deficits. The future however turned disappointing. Productivity growth went from bad to worse. The investment boom came to an end, and, with disappointed expectations, private saving increased. Fiscal deficits partly offset the increase in private saving, but not by enough to avoid a slump. Overvaluation, the result of earlier pressure on wages during the boom, implied that current account deficits remained large. (Blanchard 2006, p. 2)

While the global financial crisis had marginal impact on Portugal, in an already deteriorating debt-deficit situation, such marginal impact appeared magnified. By December 2009, the EU Council recommended that Portugal bring an end to the situation of an excessive government deficit by 2013. There were a number of austerity measures during 2010 and in February 2011, the Portuguese government announced that the 2010 fiscal deficit turned out to be 7.3 per cent of GDP. Events in the subsequent period were somewhat dramatic. On 24 March 2011, the Portuguese government resigned, and on 29 March 2011, Portugal's statistical office reported a government deficit of 8.6 per cent of GDP for 2010—above the previously claimed 7.3 per cent—as a result of the statistical rulings on the booking of two feasance structures.[15] By end-March 2011, the S&P downgraded Portugal's credit rating to BBB (European Commission 2011).

In order to tide over the crisis, Portugal approached the EC and the IMF for financial assistance. On 7 April 2011, following a request by Portugal, the EC, ECB, and IMF negotiated an Economic Adjustment Programme, which was agreed by the European Council on 30 May 2011

---

[15] A guarantee that was called and the inclusion of three state-owned enterprises in the government accounts.

and the IMF board on 20 May 2011. Covering the period 2011–14, its financial package extended up to €78 billion for possible fiscal financing needs and support to the banking system.[16]

Recent evaluation by the IMF revealed that there are signs of progress in Portugal along the programme's four main pillars: (a) competitiveness and growth, (b) financial stability and deleveraging, (c) fiscal solvency, and (d) budget financing (IMF 2012c).

Aided by such policies and the strong growth of exports, Portugal came out of the crisis and started experiencing robust growth by 2015. Another main driver had been the shift to a more accommodative fiscal policy stance in recent years. Recent increases in wages and in private investments—especially in tradables—are sustaining domestic demand and the restored profitability of the domestic banking system.

Italy: Private Sector and Governance Issues

Italy, despite its niche luxury products, has of late been described as the 'sick man of Europe', reflecting its economic stagnation, political instability, and slow pace of reforms. Even before the crisis, Italy had the largest public debt in the EU (103 per cent of the GDP in 2007) and ranked third in the world in 2007. Notwithstanding such debt configuration, Italy did not face any major debt crisis till about 2010; after all, the average maturity of Italian debt was around seven years and about a half was locally owned. However, as a result of the structural problems and political uncertainty Italy was hit hard during the crisis with the GDP contraction at more than 5 per cent in 2009 (see Table 6.7). The IMF in its 2011 Article IV report on Italy (20 June 2011, p. 4) noted:

> Italy suffered one of the largest output contractions in the Euro Area during the global financial crisis and is experiencing one of the slowest

---

[16] One-third (up to €26 billion) will be financed by the EU under the European Financial Stabilisation Mechanism (EFSM), another third by the European Financial Stability Facility (EFSF), and the final third by the IMF under an Extended Fund Facility. The programme centred around three major planks: (a) a fiscal consolidation strategy; (b) safeguarding the financial sector through market-based mechanisms supported by back-up facilities; and (c) frontloaded structural reforms to boost potential growth, create jobs, and improve competitiveness (see European Commission (2011) for details).

Table 6.7 Italy: Select Macroeconomic Indicators

	GDP Growth (%)	Inflation (%)	Government Net Lending / Borrowing (% of GDP)	Government Gross Debt (% of GDP)	Current Account Balance (% of GDP)
2001	2.0	2.3	−3.2	108.9	0.2
2002	0.3	2.6	−2.9	106.4	−0.5
2003	0.1	2.8	−3.2	105.5	−0.8
2004	1.4	2.3	−3.5	105.1	−0.5
2005	0.8	2.2	−4.1	106.6	−0.9
2006	1.8	2.2	−3.6	106.7	−1.5
2007	1.5	2.0	−1.3	103.9	−1.4
2008	−1.0	3.5	−2.6	106.2	−2.8
2009	−5.3	0.8	−5.1	116.6	−1.9
2010	1.7	1.6	−4.2	119.2	−3.3
2011	0.7	2.9	−3.6	119.7	−2.8
2012	−3.0	3.3	−2.9	126.5	−0.2
2013	−1.8	1.2	−2.9	132.5	1.1
2014	0.0	0.2	−3.0	135.4	1.9
2015	0.8	0.1	−2.6	135.3	1.4
2016	1.3	−0.1	−2.4	134.8	2.6
2017	1.7	1.3	−2.4	134.2	2.7
2018	0.9	1.2	−2.2	134.4	2.6
2019	0.5	0.6	−1.5	134.2	3.3
2020	−9.0	−0.1	−9.7	154.9	3.9
2021	7.0	1.9	−9.0	149.9	3.1
2022	3.7	8.7	−8.0	144.4	−1.2

Source: World Economic Outlook database, IMF, October 2023.

recoveries. The downturn started earlier and lasted longer than in most of the Euro Area (EA) countries. It was exacerbated by the economy's long-standing structural problems and reliance on international trade. Per capita GDP and productivity in 2010 were lower than in 2000, with Italy experiencing the largest per capita GDP contraction among OECD member countries over a decade.

It was not that the Italian authorities were unaware of the seriousness of their debt problem. In fact, in September 2007, the then Finance Minister

Tommaso Padoa-Schioppa made a statement that Italy is 'strongly indebted' and pledged to cut government expenditure. Subsequently, in October 2007, when the draft budget for 2008 was approved, it called for a reduction in the deficit from 2.4 to 2.2 per cent of GDP on the back of economic growth forecast at 1.3 to 1.6 per cent. In May 2008, Silvio Berlusconi began his third term as the prime minister of Italy and despite the low exposure of Italian banks to toxic assets, a credit crunch engulfed Italy as a result of the fallout of the global financial crisis. In November 2008, Berlusconi announced an €80 billion stimulus package and €30 billion was set aside for banks to encourage them to lend to private businesses.[17]

Meanwhile political uncertainties were brewing in Italy. Note that when the global financial crisis was brewing in 2008, Prodi's government collapsed in Italy and a Berlusconi-led right-wing coalition came to power. In July 2010, while Berlusconi's government survived a confidence vote on an austerity package, there was a split within the ruling coalition and the speaker of the Parliament, Gianfranco Fini set up a rival rightist party, 'Future and Freedom for Italy'. Within two months of approval of a €54 bn austerity package in September 2011, Berlusconi resigned after his government failed to gain a full majority during a budget vote in November 2011. A former EU Commissioner Mario Monti was nominated as the new Prime Minister by the Italian President. Monti chose himself to be the Finance Minister. By January 2012, despite approval of Monti's austerity measures of €33 bn of spending cuts by the Italian parliament, the rating agency Fitch downgraded Italy's credit rating by two notches to A. In terms of market perception, all these developments were reflected in CDS spreads of Italy (over Germany)—which had a rollercoaster ride— from 140 basis points (bps) in January 2009 to nearly 200 bps in June 2010 and finally to 300 bps in August 2011.

As a result of the double-dip recession in Italy during the period 2008–19, namely, the global financial crisis and the euro area crisis, the vulnerability of the Italian economy was manifested in two unexpected spheres, namely, public debt and 'non-performing loans' held by banks (Banca D'Italia, Annual Report, 2016, p. 9). The public debt situation

---

[17] Small- and medium-sized banks in Italy reacted to the liquidity crisis by reducing credit to clients and consumers and raising the amount of collateral required for new loans.

deteriorated further in the aftermath of a substantial fiscal stimulus during the pandemic with the debt-GDP ratio crossing the 150 per cent mark in 2020. Interestingly, despite surging energy prices during the pandemic, Italy registered robust output growth in 2022.

Another major dimension of the Italian crisis is the lack of structural reforms in the economy. Admittedly, the post-war model of Italian development was based on 'an export-oriented economy and the autonomous ability of SMEs to create jobs and growth, while the state supported larger firms with funds and other kinds of aid' (Di Quirico 2010). In some sense, this model of development reached a crisis point in the 1980s when privatization started and the small firms had to be taxed at a higher rate to meet the resource crunch of the government. Besides, there was competition from Asian and East European countries where wages made select segments of Italian industry unviable.[18] In terms of the World Bank's Doing Business indicators, among 183 economies, Italy's rank was 87 in 2012. These developments led to poor growth performance over the long run—real GDP growth averaged 1.6 per cent during the period 1995–2007, down from over 2 per cent in the earlier decade. Breaking down GDP growth into labour, capital, and total factor productivity (TFP) contributions, a recent IMF study showed that the Italian economy's dismal growth performance is mostly explained by the declining TFP with TFP contributions decreasing substantially over the period 1995–2005 (Morsy and Sgherri 2010). Seen against this backdrop, the introduction of reforms in the Italian pension system and labour market by Italian Prime Minister Mario Monti are steps in the right direction.

How do we see the Italian experience of the euro area crisis? Several pointers could be noted. First, while Italy's vulnerabilities (such as its high debt-GDP ratio, large gross financing requirements, and dismal growth performance) should not be underestimated, Italy's sound household balance sheets, the absence of housing bubbles, traditionally high private savings, low current account deficits and relatively favourable net

---

[18] It had been noted: 'In certain sectors such as metallurgy or cheap textiles, the number of factories and employees and the scale of production have fallen dramatically, while some of the sectors identified since the 1960s as the drivers of growth (e.g., chemicals) have been beset by crisis after crisis with many large firms such as Ilva, Montedison, and Parmalat losing their leading role in the Italian economy. Today, there are almost no large firms in Italy apart from Fiat (Di Quirico 2010).'

foreign asset position are its main points of strength (IMF 2011). Second, from this standpoint, Italy's problems are less serious as compared with those of Greece, Spain, or Portugal. Third, the fact that a large chunk of Italy's debt (at 119 per cent of GDP) has a silver lining in that its debt is largely held by Italians. Fourth, Italy being a wealthier country than Greece, Spain, or Portugal (with its per capita GDP nearly at $35,000, being higher than that of Spain, Greece, and Portugal) could have had greater capacity to withstand the crisis.

Spain: Current Account Deficit and Shadow Banking

The Spanish economy experienced a high growth cycle and registered an annual real GDP growth between 1 and 1.5 percentage points higher than the euro area over 1997–2007. But since 2007, the Spanish economy continued to be hit by three interrelated shocks—(a) global financial crisis, (b) busting of Spain's domestic housing boom, and (c) the euro area debt crisis. While its debt-deficit configuration was quite manageable (and in fact comparable to Germany's) current account deficit started burgeoning since 2005. In essence, the Spanish crisis was fuelled by busting of the housing sector and huge quantity of bank-financed housing credit going bad. Paul Krugman in his op-ed in the *New York Times* of 15 April 2012 commented: 'What happened to Spain was a housing bubble—fuelled, to an important degree, by lending by German banks.'

A major factor of the decade-long Spanish boom was the housing boom when the average annual growth in the construction sector was higher than 5 per cent and accounted for nearly 15 per cent of Spanish GDP. The demand for housing was stimulated by factors such as economic expansion, immigration-led population growth, and housing purchase by non-residents (Carballo-Cruz 2011). The extraordinary growth in housing demand led to an increase in housing investment (from 4.7 per cent of GDP in 1997 to 9.7 per cent in 2007). The supply response to this strong demand for housing was fairly quick and during the period 1997–2007 almost 5.3 million dwellings were finished in Spain.

Reduced interest rate on housing loans after the euro integration played a major inspiring factor in boosting housing demand. Illustratively, the reference rate for housing loans decreased from 9.6 per cent in 1997 to

3.3 per cent in 2007. This massive housing demand led to an amazing demand for credit, with housing loans as a percentage of GDP increasing from a little less than 30 per cent in 1997 to more than 100 per cent in 2007. Using more recent data, one gets a more accurate view of the credit expansion. In 2007, loans to both construction (around 15 per cent of GDP) and real estate sectors (around 30 per cent of GDP) accounted for almost 45 per cent of the Spanish GDP. All these resulted in huge expansion of household debt.[19] While in hindsight such numbers tend to give an early warning of a housing bubble waiting to burst, there was a general sense of euphoria all around. This euphoria was shared by international institutions as well. Illustratively, in 2006, the IMF did a Financial Sector Assessment Programme (FSAP) for Spain; in a background technical note to the Spanish FSAP, titled 'Housing Prices, Household Debt, and Financial Stability', the IMF noted:

> The Spanish financial system seems to be resilient to a downturn in the housing market. Large credit institutions appear solidly positioned to absorb an increase in mortgage-loan delinquency rates that could emerge from a fall in housing prices, increase in interest rates, or a downturn in the macro-economic cycle. The resilience of credit institutions is underpinned by (a) prudent LTV ratios on the outstanding loan portfolio; (b) a moderate DTI ratio for the average household; (c) a low proportion of households with DTI ratios above 50 percent; (d) good level of capitalization; and (e) very high provisioning.

All these symptoms of resilience faded away over the next three years and housing credit became the means of transmitting the housing crisis to the banking sector. Apart from the big Spanish banks, regional savings banks, called *cajas de ahorros* (accounting for half of the Spanish banking system) played a major role in the propagation of the crisis.[20]

---

[19] Carballo-Cruz (2011) noted: 'This debt rose from 52.7% of disposable income in 1997 to a maximum of 132.1% in 2007. As a result, the effort of individuals to acquire a dwelling rose from 4.3 years of salary at the beginning of the cycle to 9.1 years at the end of it.'

[20] Cajas are not publicly traded, and usually regional politicians control the cajas. Harrington (2011) noted: 'The majority of cajas' clients are families, small and medium-sized business, and non-governmental organizations such as health care facilities, environmental groups, and cultural groups.'

Cajas often extended housing loans to non-prime borrowers of Spain including those who were turned away by larger banks. Cajas were relatively unregulated, and disclosure of information on cajas was far from complete—as a result the Spanish authorities were unaware of the depth of cajas' investment in the real estate market. 'When Spain's two largest banks, Santander and BBVA, slowed lending in 2007, the cajas continued to lend heavily into the cooling housing market . . . by 2009, cajas owned 56 per cent of the country's mortgages, and loan payments from property developers accounted for one-fifth of the cajas' assets' (Harrington 2011). All these led to huge delinquency.[21] When in March 2009, the Spanish government announced its first bailout of a caja, it was seen as an indicator of the unhealthy status of the Spanish financial sector. Following the bailout, investor confidence in Spanish banks plummeted and bank share prices nosedived. These were reflected in CDS spreads as well.

As part of their early crisis response, the Spanish authorities adopted a number of measures. These included: (a) creation of the Financial Assets Acquisition Fund (FAAF) in October 2008; (b) approval of a series of government guarantees by the Spanish government, starting in early 2009; (c) provision of financial support to small and medium-sized enterprises and the self-employed; (d) introduction of more stringent loan loss provisioning requirements for credit institutions; and (e) increase in the deposit insurance guarantee threshold in October 2008 (from €20,000 to €100,000 per depositor). Besides, as the IMF's recent FSAP report of Spain (April 2012) has revealed, reforms to the savings banks' legal framework together with financial support from the state-owned recapitalization vehicle (FROB) have initiated the banking sector restructuring process in Spain; as a result, the number of banking institutions has been reduced from 45 to 11 (through actions including interventions, mergers, and takeovers). Also, new capital requirements have induced many savings banks to transfer their banking operations to commercial banks.

During 2015–18, Spanish GDP growth was decent at 3 per cent or higher. However, growth suffered during the pre-pandemic period and

---

[21] The Bank of Spain estimated the amount of potential troubled loan exposure in the Spanish banking system in the real estate market was around €180.8 billion in mid-2010.

Table 6.8 Spain: Select Macroeconomic Indicators

	GDP Growth (%)	Inflation (%)	Government Net Lending / Borrowing (% of GDP)	Government Gross Debt (% of GDP)	Current Account Balance (% of GDP)
2001	3.9	2.8	−0.5	54.1	−4.4
2002	2.7	3.6	−0.3	51.3	−3.7
2003	3.0	3.1	−0.4	47.7	−3.9
2004	3.1	3.1	−0.1	45.4	−5.5
2005	3.7	3.4	1.2	42.4	−7.3
2006	4.1	3.6	2.1	39.1	−8.9
2007	3.6	2.8	1.9	35.8	−9.4
2008	0.9	4.1	−4.6	39.7	−8.9
2009	−3.8	−0.2	−11.3	53.3	−4.1
2010	0.2	2.0	−9.5	60.5	−3.7
2011	−0.8	3.1	−9.7	69.9	−2.7
2012	−3.0	2.4	−11.6	90.0	0.1
2013	−1.4	1.5	−7.5	100.5	2.0
2014	1.4	−0.2	−6.1	105.1	1.7
2015	3.8	−0.6	−5.3	103.3	2.0
2016	3.0	−0.3	−4.3	102.7	3.2
2017	3.0	2.0	−3.1	101.8	2.8
2018	2.3	1.7	−2.6	100.4	1.9
2019	2.0	0.8	−3.1	98.2	2.1
2020	−11.2	−0.3	−10.1	120.3	0.6
2021	6.4	3.0	−6.8	116.8	0.8
2022	5.8	8.3	−4.7	111.6	0.6

Source: *World Economic Outlook* database, IMF, October 2023.

among the euro area economies the Spanish economy was hit hard during the pandemic with a contraction in GDP growth of 11 per cent. However, despite the new headwinds posed by Russia's invasion of Ukraine, the economy rebounded strongly during 2021 and 2022, with a buoyant tourism sector. With possibilities of elevated energy prices and inflation having shot up at 8 per cent plus during 2022, the economy is expected to face further headwinds in the near future.

Iceland: An Overleveraged Banking Sector Exposed to Foreigners

Iceland is not a member of the euro area, but considering that it was one of the earliest countries affected by the global financial crisis and that it was a candidate due for consideration for entry to the euro area (along with other countries like Turkey or Croatia) we choose to consider it. To set the context, a quick review of a few select economic developments in Iceland is in order. Iceland deregulated its financial markets in the 1990s (after Iceland joined the EEA); this was followed by privatization of banks in the early 2000s. Subsequently, Icelandic business and banks invested heavily abroad, often by leveraged buyouts and stock market prices in Iceland quadrupled in five years. A number of huge government-sponsored investment projects were launched during the 2000s—these included hydro-energy and aluminium melting plants.

In fact, at the beginning of the crisis it appeared that 'a long home-grown, foreign-funded boom led to large macroeconomic imbalances, overstretched private sector balance sheets, and high dependence on foreign financing' (IMF 2008). The current account deficit exceeded 15 per cent of GDP during 2005–8 and the Icelandic króna became overvalued. Furthermore, domestic credit growth reached new peaks and house prices shot up to record levels. One of the basic problems of Iceland has been an oversized financial sector which has expanded to over 1,000 per cent of GDP. The gross external indebtedness reached 550 per cent of GDP at the end of 2007, largely on account of the banking sector. The balance sheets of all the economic agents, namely, households and corporations also expanded. The basic features of the Icelandic banking system were summarized in the IMF's *Financial System Stability Assessment* update of August 2008 (2008, p. 11) as:

> The Icelandic financial system is dominated by three large banking groups (Glitnir, Kaupthing, and Landsbanki). In 2004, these banks began a period of expansion, with consolidated assets of the banks expanding from 100 percent of Icelandic GDP in 2004 to almost 900 percent at end-2007. By end-2007, over 50 percent of the banks' assets were held abroad in branches and subsidiaries, principally in the Nordic countries and the UK. This expansion was funded in global wholesale

markets, allowing banks to overcome domestic resource constraints but doubling their foreign debt. This dependence on wholesale market funding became a source of concern at the onset of the global turbulence in mid-2007, and caused banks' counterparty risk, as evidenced by CDS spreads, to increase sharply.

With the onslaught of the global financial crisis, Iceland faced severe financial turbulence in early 2008. In March, the CDS spreads of the three main commercial banks rose to over 1,000 basis points. Two factors can

Table 6.9 Iceland: Select Macroeconomic Indicators

	GDP Growth (%)	Inflation (%)	Government Net Lending / Borrowing (% of GDP)	Government Gross Debt (% of GDP)	Current Account Balance (% of GDP)
2001	4.0	6.4	−0.3	83.4	−4.3
2002	0.6	5.2	−2.3	82.2	1.2
2003	2.1	2.1	−2.3	85.1	−4.9
2004	7.8	3.2	0.3	80.9	−10.0
2005	6.1	4.0	5.0	68.9	−15.7
2006	6.3	6.7	6.4	70.7	−22.7
2007	8.5	5.1	5.6	68.4	−13.6
2008	2.2	12.7	−12.1	110.4	−20.8
2009	−7.7	12.0	−8.6	128.8	−8.9
2010	−2.8	5.4	−6.7	133.1	−6.1
2011	1.8	4.0	−6.5	138.2	−4.7
2012	1.1	5.2	−2.6	133.9	−3.6
2013	4.6	3.9	−1.2	122.0	6.3
2014	1.7	2.0	0.3	115.3	4.4
2015	4.4	1.6	−0.4	97.3	5.6
2016	6.3	1.7	12.5	82.5	8.1
2017	4.2	1.8	1.0	71.7	4.2
2018	4.9	2.7	1.0	63.2	4.3
2019	1.9	3.0	−1.6	66.5	6.5
2020	−7.2	2.8	−8.9	77.7	0.9
2021	4.5	4.5	−8.5	75.4	−3.0
2022	7.2	8.3	−4.1	68.9	−2.0

Source: World Economic Outlook database, IMF, October 2023.

be held responsible: (a) investors' concerns about large funding needs, and (b) high dependence on wholesale funding.

The króna depreciated by about 30 per cent in December 2007–March 2008. Apart from the traditional tools like tightening the policy rate and increasing liquidity, Iceland entered into currency swap arrangements with the central banks of Denmark, Norway, and Sweden, providing access to €1.5 billion.

However, Iceland's government and central bank were unable to support the overgrown banking sector in surmounting its difficulties. The banks had grown too big for Iceland. The high degree of foreign currency denominated lending made the economy susceptible to fluctuations in the external value of the Icelandic króna. The FME (Iceland's financial regulator) was too small to supervise a complex banking system like that in Iceland.

At the beginning of the crisis, a diplomatic dispute broke out in 2008 between Iceland on the one hand and the UK and the Netherlands on the other about the liquidation of Icesave accounts. A leading Icelandic bank, Landsbanki, offered online savings accounts under the brand of 'Icesave'. As Landsbanki faced serious liquidity problems, the bank was placed into receivership in October 2008 and more than 400,000 depositors with Icesave accounts in the UK and the Netherlands were unable to access their money for nearly two months. The matter became somewhat murky as the UK resorted to anti-terrorism legislation against Iceland. Subsequently, a referendum was held in Iceland on 6 March 2010 to approve the terms of a state guarantee on the obligation of a €3.8 billion loan from the governments of the UK and the Netherlands to cover deposit insurance obligations in those countries. The referendum was defeated, with 93 per cent voting against and less than 2 per cent in favour. Subsequently, another agreement was reached in December 2010 and in April 2011, another referendum was held and the agreement was again rejected by the Icelandic public. Subsequently, the Icesave dispute was brought to the EFTA (European Free Trade Association) court and in late January 2013, Iceland won the legal battle in the court of the EFTA and 'could avoid being forced to pay back the British and Dutch governments for not honouring deposit guarantees for savers in failed online banking operation Icesave' (Financial Times, 28 January 2013). How does Iceland stand now? In terms of broad macroeconomic outturns, the Icelandic economy grew by 3 per cent in 2011. Unemployment currently at 7 per cent too declined steadily. The financial markets, led by the government bond market, became more active, banks reported strong profits, high capital, and liquidity buffers. As part of their reserve management strategy, Iceland in March 2012 made early repayments of the IMF loan.

In most recent times, despite being affected by the pandemic, the Icelandic economy seemed to have done well with a much less financialized economy. What does the Icelandic experience teach us? Why did the crisis occur? Benediktsdóttir et al. (2017, p. 271) summarize it well:

> The banks grew too fast and became too large on the back of implicit and explicit guarantees. Their funding was funneled into loans to a large extent to the same groups of related parties and to insiders, i.e. the owners of the banks. In hindsight, the evidence ... suggest[s] that universal large exposure rules, that are meant to limit concentration risk and are crucial to banks['] viability, were broken for years before the failure of the banks. Owners of the banks had disproportionate access to the banks['] funds, despite rules on insider borrowing. How could this happen? While we have already pointed to one cause, namely complacency by supervisors and a general view that 'the banks are in the best position to regulate themselves', it is worth highlighting another potential reason. Nobody in [a] position of power knew, or in any event had the full picture what the banks were doing. Firm ownership in most western democracies is opaque. The only reason we know how much lending was channeled to groups of related parties and to insiders in Iceland is because of the crash, because ...
>
> investigation commission staffed with among others economist[s], lawyers and accountants who over a period of almost two years tracked down who received the money, and due to the establishment of a special prosecutor of the failed banks that prosecuted the bankers.

Channels of Contagion of the Euro Area Crisis

Having described both the core economies as well as crisis countries in the euro area, this section asks the question: How did the crisis spread? The answer is: contagion. The concept of contagion is borrowed from the epidemiology literature. In his epidemiology textbook, Gertsman (1998) argues that contagion is present when 'any disease or event occurs in clear excess of normal expectancy'. Thus, in order to define contagion one can distinguish between three mechanisms through which economic shocks spread across countries: (a) global disturbances that affect all (or most) countries in the world; (b) shocks coming from a related country; and (c) a situation where the extent and magnitude of the international transmission of shocks exceeds what was expected by market participants (Edwards 2000). Viewed against this taxonomy the current crisis perhaps embraced all these three aspects. As already mentioned in the beginning, at a general level, the channels of propagation of the crisis and contagion across countries can happen at three distinct levels, namely, (a) contagion of the crisis from country A to country B; (b) spreading of the crisis from one sector to another within a country (due to sectoral linkages within a country); and (c) centrality of fisc both in (a) and (b). Interestingly, there is an element of circularity of the fisc and the crisis in the sense that the fisc can both be a cause and a victim of the crisis. In specific terms, the contagion of the crisis may occur through a number of interconnected channels, namely, (a) trade, (b) financial flows, and (c) confidence channels.

In terms of these indicators, the important channels of contagion across the world would be through trade and banking, while within the euro area fiscal issues could be predominant. In particular, the financial spillovers from the euro area could intensify sharply if the sovereign debt difficulties in the EA were to intensify (IMF 2011). In terms of spreading, the spillover from the euro area to the world over, three factors could turn out to be of paramount importance: (a) high asset price correlations, (b) shocks to financial risk premia, and (c) limited policy space (IMF 2012). After all, in a tail risk scenario, euro area stress could become combined with fiscal policy concerns in the US and Japan as well as quantitative easing from a number of advanced countries' central banks (which could lead to increased volatility in the emerging countries' asset prices). While the probability of such a doomsday scenario could be small its occurrence cannot be ruled out and that could lead to what is formally called a double dip recession. Geographically the spillover could be varied across four levels:

1. within the periphery euro area (namely, affected countries like Greece, Portugal, Italy, Ireland, and Spain),

2. across the Centre euro area (economies like France or Germany),
3. across the non-euro EU economies (like the UK), and
4. across the rest of the world with its various layers.

Interestingly, there may be a phenomenon, where banks that lose money in their home markets withdraw from otherwise profitable activities abroad. Based on an analysis covering quarterly cross-border bank lending data for 40 emerging market economies between the third quarter of 2005 and the second quarter of 2012, the Bank of International Settlement (BIS) in its December 2012 Quarterly Review confirmed this phenomenon (see Chart 6.3). This phenomenon, which has been termed as reverse contagion by *The Economist*, is most pronounced in case of the East European countries.

Apart from banking and other financial channels, the trade channel is the usual route through which the crisis can spread or can get ameliorated. Research in the ECB has indicated that at constant prices, intra-euro area trade rose by around 50 per cent between 1999 and 2011.

A number of features are discernible in intra-euro area trade. First, intra-euro area trade accounts for almost half of total euro area trade. Second, however, there is considerable country specificity in this regard. In the sense that 'Countries that only share borders with other euro area countries, such as Luxembourg and Portugal, tend to have higher shares of intra-euro area trade compared with countries that also share borders with non-euro area countries, such as Finland, Greece and Ireland' (ECB 2013, p. 60). Third, Germany has the lowest share of intra-euro area trade, reflecting partly its trade with neighbouring eastern European countries and emerging markets in Asia. In this sense, it is less likely that a contagion from the smaller crisis euro area economies will permeate larger/core euro area economies or elsewhere.

Finally, while the contagion through confidence/sentiment channel is difficult to measure, there is narrative evidence. Illustratively, when the sovereign crisis again became more severe and Moody's downgraded Portugal on 5 July 2011, it cited developments in Greece as one of the major factors (Constâncio 2012). It may be pertinent to note what an article in *The Economist* (19 May 2012) has commented: 'Greece may account for only 2% of eurozone GDP but it is shaking everybody by calling into doubt the currency's supposed irrevocability.'

The IMF Financial Sector Assessment Program (FSAP) Report of the EU during that period pointed out the following vulnerabilities, namely, (a) stresses and dislocations in wholesale funding markets, (b) a loss of market confidence in sovereign debt, (c) further downward movements in asset prices, and (d) downward shocks to growth. The report noted: 'These vulnerabilities are exacerbated by the high degree of concentration in the banking sector; regulatory and policy uncertainty; and the major gaps in the policy framework that still need to be filled.' Going forward, these vulnerabilities will determine the extent and speed of contagion of the euro area crisis.

How do we sum up the origination of the crisis in the euro area? Paoul Thomsen, Director of the IMF's European Department has succinctly commented in a speech in 2019:

> The Euro Crisis originated in the mis-management of the monetary windfall enjoyed by countries in the periphery when they adopted the euro. In Ireland and Spain—and to some extent Portugal—this windfall fueled an unsustainable demand boom mainly through the private credit channel. In Greece, it took place . . . through a surge in public pensions, but also in other transfers and wages.[22]

Exploring Patterns and Solution Packages of the Euro Area Crisis

The previous discussion described how the debt crisis that broke out in the spring of 2009, while initially being limited to Greece, later spread involving five euro area member states, accounting for one third of the euro area's output. The crisis was indeed a maze, which Professor Buiter described as 'a syndrome of multiple interdependent crises' and went on to say:

> It is a sovereign insolvency crisis for a number of countries in the so-called euro area periphery, most notably Greece, Portugal and Ireland.

---

[22] 'The IMF and the Greek Crisis: Myths and Realities', Speech by Paoul Thomsen, Director of the European Department of the International Monetary Fund, at the London School of Economics, 30 September 2019, available at https://www.imf.org/en/News/Articles/2019/10/01/sp093019-The-IMF-and-the-Greek-Crisis-Myths-and-Realities (accessed in March 2024)

It is a sovereign liquidity crisis to other countries in what may be called the broader periphery—countries that one hopes and assumes are most likely solvent, as far as the sovereign is concerned, but at risk of being frozen out of the funding markets by markets panicking and refusing access to the sovereign. That is, Italy and Spain. We also have a banking crisis throughout the EU, not just the euro area ... So we have this triple crisis: sovereign insolvency, sovereign illiquidity and bank under-capitalisation, which is significant enough among the three of them to pose a global challenge. (Buiter 2012)

Characteristics of the Crisis Countries

As a broad generalization, the crisis countries in the euro area may be grouped under four categories.

First, countries (notably Greece and Italy) where the advantages of a common currency, namely the euro, and a single monetary authority lulled market players to ignore country-specific realities. This led to a fall in interest rates on domestic debt, which in turn encouraged fiscal profligacy. Over time, this manifested as high deficits and ballooning debt. Foreign ownership of debt further aggravated the issue. To compound matters further, political instability hindered quick and easy resolution of the crisis and formulation of a consensus rescue package.

The second group of countries are those that witnessed a bursting of the property bubble, which was transmitted to the banking sector by their exposure to the property market and consequently led to build-up of non-performing assets. Ireland and Spain fall into this category. Portugal falls in the third group that experienced no significant debt or deficit pressure, nor did it suffer from a property bubble; in its case, the crisis occurred primarily because of sustained low productivity. The advantage of a common currency shielded it from the adverse effects of low productivity for some time and thus the crisis was slow in coming in its case.

Fourth, Iceland (not formally a member of the euro area) did not enjoy the benefits of a common currency but the crisis that occurred there primarily stemmed from the banking sector, which was overly exposed to foreigners and debt denominated in foreign currency. Figure 6.1 depicts the broad taxonomy of these four groups of countries.

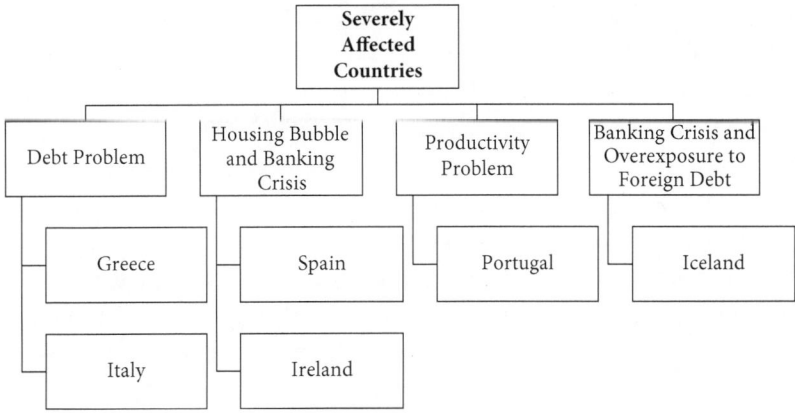

Figure 6.1 Nature of Crises in Euro Area Countries that are Severely Affected

Source: Authors' own.

Country-specific stories may not, however, be very helpful to draw general lessons about the euro area crisis. In fact, according to one view, the seeds of the crisis were inherent in the very nature of the formation of the euro area. As a starting point, in order to understand the basic features of the euro area as a currency union, a slight digressionary discussion on the optimum currency area (OCA) would be in order.

Optimum Currency Area: A Relevant Digression

The euro area is a currency union but neither a political nor fiscal union; the constituent countries have a common currency and a common monetary policy but distinct fiscal policies and structures. On whether this creates a conflict, one would need to refer to the relevant literature that talks of an OCA.[23] We owe the original discussion to Nobel Laureate Robert Mundell, who in an article in 1961 argued under what conditions two countries possibly could benefit by sacrificing their national

---

[23] There is a large literature on Optimal Currency Areas. See Lafrance and St-Amant (1999), Horvath (2003) for synoptic views.

currencies and forging a currency union.[24] Mundell showed that the benefits of an OCA are three: (a) lower transaction costs, (b) disappearance of currency risks, and (c) cross-country credit possibilities. On the negative side, the cost of an OCA is the inability of national governments and central banks to pursue independent monetary policies to stabilize their economies and financial sectors.

When do two central banks need independent monetary policies? If the nature of the shocks across the countries forming the currency union differs, then there is indeed a problem. In the classic version of Mundell's 1961 model, in a two-economy world (A and B) if there is a decline in aggregate demand in A and an increase in aggregate demand in B, there will be additional unemployment in A and a decline of unemployment in B. As a result, both countries will have an adjustment problem: A is plagued with unemployment and a current account deficit, while B experiences a boom and a current account surplus. Mundell posed the following question: Is there a mechanism that leads to automatic equilibration, without the countries having to resort to devaluations and revaluations? Mundell (1961) showed that in an OCA, wage flexibility and labour mobility can act as equilibrators in the absence of any exchange rate adjustment, as explained in the following lines.

The workers of country A who are unemployed will reduce their wage claims. Consequently, the aggregate supply curve moves downwards. In country B, on the other hand, the excess demand for labour will push up the wage rate and the aggregate curve of country B shifts upwards. In country A, the price of output declines, making A's products more competitive, stimulating demand. The opposite occurs in B. Finally, this adjustment improves the current account of A and reduces the current account surplus of B.

Mundell's analysis suggests that if the impact of shocks is asymmetric, high labour mobility and/or wage flexibility (more particularly in a downward direction) are the main prerequisites for an OCA.

Replacing countries A and B with Greece and Germany, respectively, may bestow verisimilitude to Mundell's hypothesis.

---

[24] The Nobel Committee in their citation for Mundell, who received the 1999 Nobel Prize for Economics, mentioned, 'his analysis of monetary and fiscal policy under different exchange rate regimes and his analysis of optimum currency areas'.

The formation of an OCA deprives national authorities of a critical tool of economic adjustment, namely exchange rate autonomy. In fact, all the previous economic crises in Europe led to large devaluations of currencies. However, within the euro area, the single currency prevents devaluation and provides automatic financial support through capital markets. It is noteworthy that non-euro currencies depreciated sharply in 2008.

But availability of geographical labour mobility and wage-price flexibility are not the only criteria for nations to join the OCA area. Subsequent literature emphasized a number of other features. Various properties of an OCA have been discussed in the literature, such as financial integration, degree of economic openness or inter-industrial factor mobility, and diversification in production and consumption. Other features mentioned are similarity in inflation rates and inflation rate preferences; fiscal integration and fiscal transfers between regions; effectiveness and credibility of common monetary policy, as also similarity in labour market institutions and business cycle synchronization. The absence of one or more of these features could hamper the smooth functioning of an OCA.

While it is difficult to prescribe a menu-based approach to adoption of a currency union, suffice it to say, various preconditions could go a long way to determine the potential success or otherwise of a currency union. Many of these conditions were perhaps not present within the euro area, which will come up while discussing the crisis in each of these countries.

No doubt, there are counter arguments too. It would be simplistic to ignore political forces (e.g., calls for rekindling euro-wide nationalistic spirits) that bind an OCA. Historically, there were enough euro enthusiasts to drive the initial formation of the euro area. It is instructive, in this context, to turn to Otmar Issing, a founding member of the executive board of the ECB, who commented:

The criteria developed under the theory of optimum currency area are, in any case, neither definitive nor complete. Conditions such as necessary market flexibility can also be created after entry into monetary union. To that extent, criteria are endogenous, that is, dependent on the process itself. Optimists were confident that with a single monetary policy the need for reforms to increase flexibility would become so obvious that policy makers would be bound to react . . . The theoretical criteria for an optimum currency area are incomplete because they exclude the political aspect of monetary union. (Issing 2008; pp. 50–1; emphasis in original)

A similar argument but supporting an opposite conclusion was put forth by Martin Feldstein. After the Maastricht Treaty was signed, Martin Feldstein, while supporting the creation of a free trade area, strongly opposed a common currency on the ground that euro area countries would lose control over their exchange rates and that the existence of a common currency is neither necessary nor sufficient for a successful trade relationship. In the context of the present euro crisis, the questions that arise are whether the essential features of an OCA were absent or whether there were political contradictions which led to the crisis. A dominant view emerging in recent times is the inherent differences between the constituent countries of the euro area. Martin Feldstein rightly noted:

The creation of the euro should now be recognized as an experiment that has had a number of substantial economic costs. The emergence of sovereign debt crises just a dozen years after its creation in 1999 was not an accident or the result of bureaucratic mismanagement but the inevitable consequence of imposing a single currency on a very heterogeneous group of countries, a heterogeneity that includes not only economic structures but also fiscal traditions and social attitudes. (Feldstein 2011, p. 1)

In a similar vein, the IMF's 2012 Article IV Report for the euro area commented: 'The euro area is in an uncomfortable and unsustainable halfway point; while it is sufficiently integrated to allow escalating problems in one country to spill over to others, it lacks the economic flexibility or policy tools to deal with these spillovers' (p. 10). This issue will be revisited at the end of the chapter.

The difficulty in writing about live events such as the euro area is the ever-changing economic reality and scenario. One lacks the support of pseudo-definitive evidence; neither does one have the luxury of post facto rationalization. Given these limitations, a discussion of some of the common features of euro area countries is presented in the further sections.

How does the euro area fare as an optimum currency area? In terms of the various criteria for an OCA one tends to get a mixed answer. Illustratively, soft measures of an OCA like financial market integration, diversification of production, trade openness, or similarity of inflation rates are valid for the euro area. On the contrary, the euro area fails to satisfy more demanding criteria like labour mobility, price and wage flexibility, fiscal integration, and political integration. Thus, by most of the demanding accounts, the euro area fails to emerge as an optimum currency area. Paul Krugman in a recent op-ed in the *New York Times* probed into this question. Terming the current crisis in the euro area as a 'revenge of the Optimum Currency Area', it is worth noting what he went on to say:

> The advantages of a common currency are obvious . . . reduced trans-action costs, elimination of currency risk, greater transparency and possibly greater competition . . . The disadvantages of a single currency come from loss of flexibility. It's not just that a currency area is limited to a one-size-fits-all monetary policy; even more important is the loss of a mechanism for adjustment . . . optimum currency area theory suggested two big things to look at—labour mobility and fiscal integration. And on both counts it was obvious that Europe fell far short of the US example, with limited labour mobility and virtually no fiscal integration. This should have given European leaders pause—but they had their hearts set on the single currency. (Krugman 2012, emphasis ours)

Euro Area Crisis: Some Common Features

The Maastricht Treaty was intended to be the gatekeeper for regulating entry into the euro area. However, rigid adherence to the principles of the Maastricht Treaty was never made a strict or inviolable condition of entry into the euro area. Rules were relaxed, at the entry stage, and even later as countries began to function within the euro area. Penalties for non-compliance of the rules were practically either non-existent or mild at best; and there was little transparency in the functioning of some of the member countries. It is in this background that the high levels of debt run up by some member countries are to be viewed.

Table 6.10 presents the various indicators of indebtedness and leverage of selected euro area countries in 2012. In regard to government debt, Greece is clearly the most indebted followed by Italy, Ireland, and Portugal. As for non-financial corporate debt and financial institutions' gross debt, Ireland is by far the worst indebted. What is most telling, however, is that Greece is the most exposed economy in terms of its gross external liabilities, indicating that a colossal amount of its debt is held by overseas entities, which does not augur well.

Table 6.10 Indebtedness and Leverage in Selected Euro Area Economies, 2012

	(Percentage of GDP)							
	Euro Area	France	Germany	Greece	Ireland	Italy	Portugal	Spain
Government Debt								
Gross Debt	90	89	79	153	113	123	112	79
Net Debt	70	83	54	n.a.	103	102	111	67
Primary Balance	−0.5	−2.2	1.0	−1.0	−4.4	3.0	0.1	−3.6
Household Debt								
Gross Debt	70	63	59	70	120	51	105	89
Net Debt	−123	−127	−118	−48	−68	−171	−124	−72
Nonfinancial Corporate Debt								
Gross Debt	138	152	63	75	244	112	154	196
Debt over Equity (%)	106	85	107	264	84	139	144	149
Financial Institutions								
Gross Debt	142	169	97	33	691	97	63	109
Bank Leverage	23	24	28	15	24	19	16	20
Bank Claims on Public Sector	n.a.	17	21	29	27	32	19	26
External Liabilities								
Gross	191	255	219	207	1,717	142	286	221
Net	14	9	−33	97	93	23	107	93
Government Debt Held Abroad	25	56	48	87	66	49	62	28

Source: Global Financial Stability Report, IMF, April 2012.

The crisis countries also turned out to be vulnerable in terms of their immediate financing need (i.e., gross government debt maturing plus budget deficit in 2012). With regard to government debt held abroad (external funding), that of Greece is the highest at 87.5 per cent of GDP. Barring the credit ratings of Germany and France, which are shown as stable, all the GIIPS countries have negative ratings; that of Greece is the worst at eight notches below speculative grade, while that of Portugal is just at speculative grade. Though the outlook for Spain and Italy are shown as negative, they are a few notches above speculative grade.

The behaviour of market participants in the euro area reveals that they blithely ignored the fundamental differences between euro area countries. To illustrate, interest rates on 10-year Greek government bonds dropped from 24.5 per cent to 6.5 per cent between 1993 and 1999, and from 1999 until 2013, they averaged 6.5 per cent with a record low of 3.2 per cent in June 2005. But since mid-2009 once market participants apprehended fiscal irregularities, the interest rate on Greek government bonds started climbing and reached an all-time high of 48.6 per cent in March 2012.

It has already been mentioned that before the global financial crisis compliance of the Maastricht Treaty fiscal rules was lackadaisical at best. Secure in the comfort of low interest rates afforded by their having embraced the common currency, the euro, some countries indulged in fiscally irresponsible behaviour. This was compounded by equally irresponsible actions of financial markets that chose to turn a blind eye to the fundamentals of these countries and priced all sovereign debt paper more or less on par.

Another point worthy of note is the extent of interdependence of euro area countries. Both German and French banks have large exposures to Greek assets, including both public and private debt. And there is a marked and observable reluctance on the part of Germany, the major and dominant economic power in the euro area, to bailout member countries like Greece or Spain without wresting promises of hard reforms, both fiscal and structural.

If, therefore, prior to the global financial crisis, the urgent need was to fix the fiscal slippages, shortcomings, and infirmities, what the crisis underscores is that in the post-crisis scenario, it is imperative to urgently address not just fiscal but also financial issues. Its urgent and ineluctable need is reinforced by the contagion effect of fiscal and financial linkages.

Euro Area Rescue Package

Expectedly, the package to address the recession on account of the euro area crisis and the subsequent pandemic had elements of fiscal and monetary stimulus.

Fiscal Package

After what was best described as 'months of uncoordinated, fragmented, and acrimonious recriminations against Greece and its culture of fiscal profligacy and Germany's resistance to turn the euro area from a monetary into a transfer union' (Brigitte and Semmler 2011), a rescue package to deal with the crisis was formulated. On 10 May 2011 the Council of the Finance Ministers of the 27 EU member states (popularly known as Ecofin), together with the ECB and the European Community, came out with a financial rescue package for the euro area member states. The three elements of the rescue package were: (a) a supranational €60 billion EU fund administered by the EC; (b) a €440 billion intergovernmental facility, the European Financial Stability Facility (EFSF) (which is a special purpose vehicle incorporated in Luxembourg), and (c) €250 billion from the IMF. The inclusion of the IMF along with EU and ECB in this troika arrangement raised some concerns. After all, the euro area crisis did not so far reveal any balance of payments ramifications to warrant the IMF's association.

Assistance from Europe

The EFSF was created by the euro area member states in May 2010. Its mandate was to safeguard financial stability in Europe by providing financial assistance to euro area member states within the framework of a macroeconomic adjustment programme. Towards this end, EFSF issued bonds or other debt instruments in capital markets and intervened in the primary and secondary bond markets. The EFSF took part in the rescue package of Ireland, Portugal, and Germany.

While the EFSF was created as a temporary rescue mechanism, in October 2010, it was decided to create a permanent rescue mechanism, the European Stability Mechanism (ESM). The ESM came into force on 8 October 2012. It was envisaged that the ESM would be globally the largest international financial institution with a strong capital base of €700 billion, of which €80 billion would be paid in by early 2014. While ESM would issue bonds in the global financial marketplace, the capital would be provided by the euro area governments. Germany is expected to provide 27 per cent of the capital, while the shares of France and Italy would be 20 per cent and 18 per cent, respectively. Meanwhile, the EFSF is envisaged to remain active only in financing programmes that started before the ESM Treaty was signed. As of 1 July 2013, the EFSF is no longer engaged in new financing programmes and the ESM is now the sole and permanent mechanism for responding to new requests for financial assistance by euro area member states.

IMF Programmes

The IMF was involved in the rescue actions of the euro area crisis countries and participated in the programmes for Greece, Ireland, and Portugal.[25] The arrangement was operationalized through an arrangement of troika, where the IMF along with the EC and the ECB was involved with the rescue package.

Technically, all these loans were approved under the extended fund facility of the IMF, which is disbursed to a country when it 'faces

---

[25] In fact, when the crisis started, the IMF was involved with a number of non-eurozone European countries. In October 2008, Hungary requested a Stand-By Arrangement (SBA) from the IMF. The EU and the IMF joined together and the IMF provided financial support to Hungary through its Balance of Payments (BoP) Assistance Facility. The total financing package amounted to €20 billion (IMF: €12.3 billion, EU: €6.5 billion, World Bank: €1.0 billion). Interestingly, the UK in 1976 was the last EU (then European Economic Community, EEC) member that had received IMF assistance.

serious medium-term balance of payments problems because of structural weaknesses that require time to address' (IMF, Factsheet on EFF).
Unlike the assistance under the more common stand-by arrangement
(in which Greece was initially provided assistance), assistance under an
EFF involves longer programme engagement (to help countries implement medium-term structural reforms) and a longer repayment period.
Whatever the technicalities or modalities of this assistance, one may le-
gitimately raise several questions about why the IMF was involved with
the assistance programme for these euro area countries, considering that
there was no immediate threat of any balance of payments crisis in these
countries.

First, the unprecedented scale of operations of the IMF in the euro
area is noteworthy. In the past, the typical loan-to-quota ratio averaged
300 per cent, reaching an exceptional high of about 2,000 per cent for
South Korea in the late 1990s during the Asian crisis. In contrast, the first
IMF loan to Greece was equivalent to 3,200 per cent of Greece's quota
(Jost and Seitz 2012).

Second, even within Europe, opinion is divided. Early in March 2010,
the then President of the ECB Mr Trichet denied the need for IMF help
and referred to the balance of payments financing mechanisms and the
deficit rules of the Stability and Growth Pact. On the other hand, IMF involvement was a precondition dictated by German Chancellor Merkel to
agree to financial assistance for Greece.

Third, given the nature of the debt crisis in the euro area, it has been
argued that 'it is not the task of the IMF to finance national public debt
in domestic currency', and that 'the IMF does not have strong experience
of how to solve such debt crises' (Jost and Seitz 2012). This view is reinforced by the Deutsche Bundesbank in an article as late as in March
2010, titled 'Financing and Representation in the International Monetary
Fund' (p. 60) that stated:

In line with its mandate, it (the IMF) may use the provided foreign reserves only to help overcome short-term balance of payments difficulties and thus cover temporary need for foreign currency. By contrast,
any financial contribution by the Fund to solve structural problems that
do not imply a need for foreign currency—such as the direct financing

of budget deficits or financing of a bank recapitalisation—would be incompatible with its monetary mandate.

Fourth, the IMF is now supporting countries in a currency union where the domestic currency is also a reserve currency (next in importance only to the US dollar). 'Since they are both denominated in the same reserve currency, the divide between fiscal and balance of payments problems of euro area countries is blurred in terms of Article 1 (v) of the IMF's Articles of Agreement, which envisages IMF liquidity provision only on balance of payments grounds' (Sheel 2012). Further, the IMF is already seen to have unusually large exposure and concentration risk in Europe. Besides, the IMF's financial involvement 'can seriously cripple its capacity to firewall its traditional developing country clients'.

Fifth, it is ironic that poor countries with large developmental needs of their own are, indirectly through the IMF, being called upon to go to the rescue of richer countries either unable or unwilling to adjust. Of course, it could be argued that stabilizing the euro area is in the interests of developing countries as any meltdown there would have deleterious consequences for them (Sheel 2012).

Thus, the criticism that the IMF possibly overstepped its mandate by its active involvement in the euro area package is not without merit.

An important question is what the cost of insolvency of the crisis countries would be. While a detailed global assessment could be difficult, IFO Institute of the University of Munich had released some ball-park numbers. According to these estimates, if Greece becomes insolvent and exits the euro area, Germany and France would face losses of up to €82 billion or €62 billion, respectively (Table 6.10). If, however, Greece were to become insolvent but remain in the eurozone, Germany and France must reckon with losses of up to €89 billion and €67 billion, respectively. Thus, departure of Greece from the eurozone would be quite expensive for the Centre eurozone economies like Germany and France.

Thus, bold actions by the European Central Bank (ECB) and major architectural projects—creating the European Stability Mechanism (ESM), the Single Supervisory Mechanism (SSM), and the Single Resolution Mechanism (SRM)—demonstrated resolve and cohesion under duress.

Intervention by the ECB

As elsewhere, in order to counter liquidity shortage in various crises episodes, increase in counterparty risk and associated confidence problems, the ECB responded with a series of measures. These included, 'series of interest rate reductions, the expansion of liquidity provision to banks at longer maturities and under fixed rate full allotment (FRFA), expanded the collateral framework and set up a covered bond purchase program (CBPP) for 60 billion Euros' till 2011.[26]

At the height of the global financial crisis in October 2008, the ECB established temporary swap lines with the US Fed to counter pressures in the global funding market. While the ECB discontinued these temporary swap lines in February 2010, it reactivated them in May 2010.

When the crisis hit the euro area, the ECB initially tweaked its three key interest rates, namely, (a) the interest rate on the main refinancing operations, which provides the bulk of liquidity to the banking system; (b) the rate on the deposit facility, which banks may use to make overnight deposits with the euro system; and (c) the rate on the marginal lending facility, which offers overnight credit to banks from the euro system. But, by mid-2012, most of these interest rates hit near zero lower bounds. It is only after being affected by a spurt in inflation since mid-2022 that monetary policy rates started increasing from July 2022 (Chart 6.2).

As elsewhere, the ECB also resorted to specific forms of quantitative easing. During May–June 2010, it established the securities market programme (SMP) to purchase government bonds in secondary markets, and introduced long-term refinancing operations (LTROs) initially on 6 May 2009 by announcing one-year LTRO under FRFA; these one-year LTROs continued for some time. Subsequently, through two three-year LTROs the ECB allotted nearly €1 trillion to the euro area over the period December 2011–March 2012.

The ECB's asset purchase programme (APP) started as part of a package of non-standard monetary policy measures that also included targeted longer-term refinancing operations, and which was initiated in October 2014 to support the monetary policy transmission mechanism

---

[26] IMF 2011 Euro Area Article IV Report, available at http://www.imf.org/external/pubs/ft/scr/2011/cr11186.pdf (accessed in March 2024)

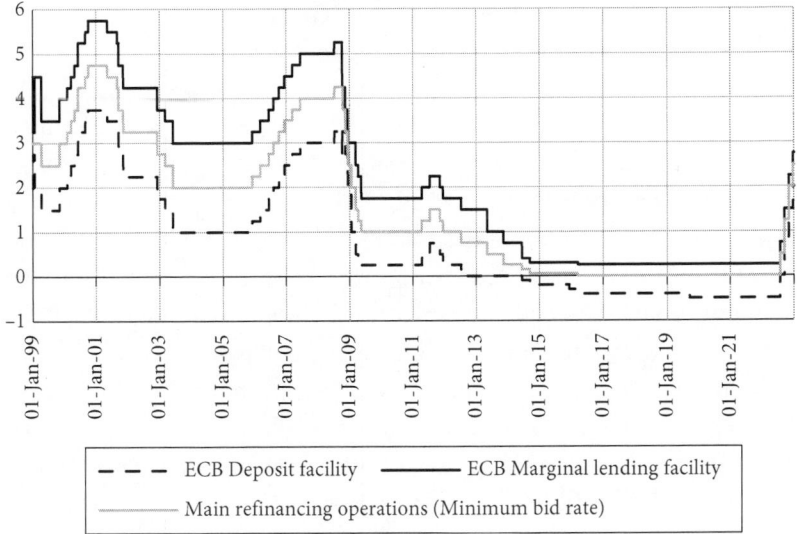

Chart 6.2 ECB's Monetary Policy Rates

Source: European Central Bank. https://www.ecb.europa.eu/stats/policy_and_exchange_ra
tes/key_ecb_interest_rates/html/index.en.html (accessed on 4 May 2024)

and provide the amount of policy accommodation needed to ensure price stability. The APP consists of the following four programmes: (a) corporate sector purchase programme (CSPP); (b) public sector purchase programme (PSPP); (c) asset-backed securities purchase programme (ABSPP); and (d) third covered bond purchase programme (CBPP3). It is only after 2022, that the asset purchases programmes of the ECB started unwinding. More recently, since 15 June 2023, the ECB announced that it would discontinue reinvestments under the APP. Thus, going forward, it is expected that the APP portfolio is going to decrease as assets reach maturity.[27]

---

[27] The Governing Council of the ECB recalibrated the overall net purchases under these APP as follows: '€60 billion of net purchases from March 2015 to March 2016; €80 billion of net purchases from April 2016 to March 2017; €60 billion of net purchases from April to December 2017; €30 billion of net purchases from January to September 2018; €15 billion of net purchases from October to December 2018; no net purchases, only reinvestments of redemptions, from January to October 2019; €20 billion of net purchases from November 2019 to March 2022 (a temporary €120 billion envelope of net asset purchases was added from March to December 2020); €40 billion of net purchases in April 2022; €30 billion of net purchases in May 2022; €20 billion of net purchases in June 2022; no net purchases, but full reinvestments of redemptions between July 2022 and February 2023; no net purchases and only partial reinvestments of redemptions from

Why Did the Pandemic Not Accentuate a Crisis in the Euro Area?

It is important to recognize that the pandemic and the associated fiscal stimulus did not lead to a new sovereign debt crisis in the euro area. Why? There is an influential view that having learnt from the 2012 eurozone crisis, European authorities used new instruments of stabilization more effectively (De Grauwe, 2022). Illustratively, unlike the earlier monetary stimulus, ECB's Pandemic Emergency Purchase Programme (PEPP) of large-scale government bond purchases in 2020 was marked by the absence of conditionality. Even in the fiscal front, half of the proceeds from the NextGeneration EU (NGEU) plan of 2020 was supposed to be used as transfers to those countries most hit by the pandemic. Nevertheless, the surge in inflation poses newer sources of fragility in the euro area. This is all the more true in 2021 when supply shocks, like a surge in energy and commodity prices, increased the cost of production, thereby leading to elevated inflation. Besides, the differential impact of the bond purchases on bonds of different countries exposed the ECB to the earlier dilemma of an optimum currency area.

Fiscal and Financial Linkages: Structural Characteristics

The economic area of a nation (even in a federation with disparate units) is characterized by unified currency, near-common fiscal policy, similar banking, and financial sector regime. An optimum currency union can try to mimic these features but since it embraces different nations, states lack some of these features. It is often argued whether this incompleteness of an optimum currency area could be mitigated via formation of a banking and/or fiscal union. With a view to bringing about greater cohesion in the euro area, the ideas of banking union and fiscal union are being mooted, both in the context of the present crisis and with a view to minimizing the extent of economic heterogeneity across euro area nations.

March 2023 to June 2023; no reinvestments of redemptions as of July 2023' (https://www.ecb.eur opa.eu/mopo/implement/app/html/index.en.html (accessed in April 2022))

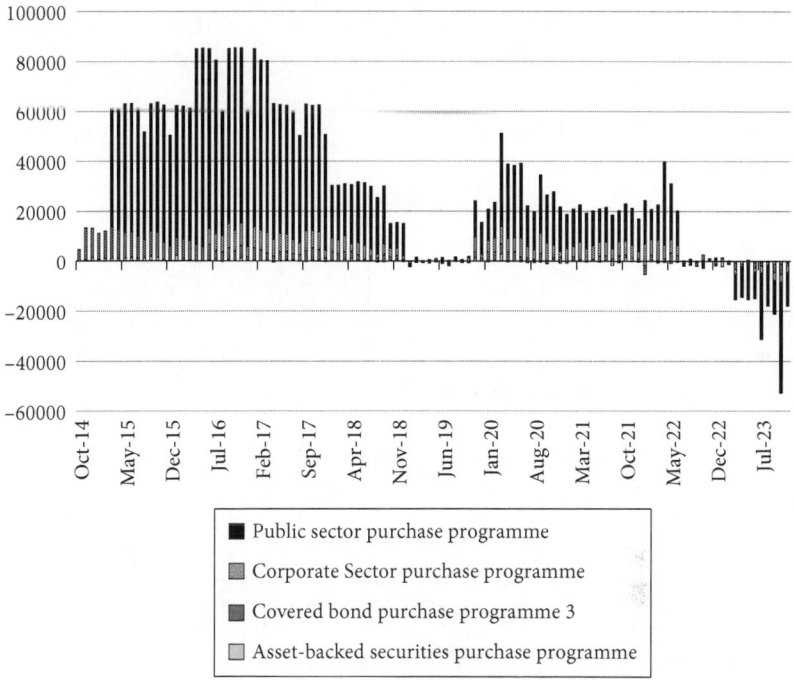

Chart 6.3 ECB's Net Asset Purchases by Programme under APP

Source: ECB (https://www.ecb.europa.eu/mopo/implement/app/html/index.en.html (accessed on 4 May 2024)

Banking Union

Considering the close negative feedback loop between banks and sovereign bond markets and possibility of cross-border contagion owing to a common currency, the idea of a banking union has attracted the attention of the EU. Thus, while the banks in the EU area (including the euro area) come under their national supervisors, the European Banking Authority (EBA) was established in January 2011[28] to act as some sort of a hub-and-spoke network of EU and national bodies safeguarding the stability of the financial system. Its power over the national

---

[28] Two other institutions, namely, the European Securities and Markets Authority (ESMA), which deals with the supervision of capital markets, and the European Insurance and Occupational Pensions Authority (EIOPA), which deals with insurance supervision, also came into existence in January 2011.

authorities is somewhat loose; this has affected its capacity to function as an effective regulator in a number of euro area countries, during the banking crisis.

The idea of a banking union evoked support both from the IMF as well as the ECB. Benoît Cœuré, Member of the Executive Board of the ECB, stated categorically: 'The establishment of a banking union is a key factor in the completion of monetary union, and probably a turning point in the current crisis, with profound repercussions for the financial sector and the real economy alike' (2012). The IMF too endorsed the notion of a banking union, and in its 2012 Article IV Report on Euro Area Policies the IMF was candid enough to say:

> The creation of a 'Banking Union' is critical for the viability of the Economic and Monetary Union. It will help break the adverse feedback loops between sovereigns, banks and the real economy by creating an institutional framework that provides common backstops to restructure failed banks and enhance confidence in safety nets. Taking steps towards a Banking Union will contribute in ending the ongoing financial fragmentation of the euro area by reducing incentives to cut cross-border exposures. In the medium-term, it will help minimize the probability of bank failures and the cost of resolution borne by taxpayers. (IMF 2012)

To this end, the European Commission on 12 September 2012 proposed new ECB powers for banking supervision as part of a banking union.[29] Under the new proposed mechanism, the common banking regulator for the 27 EU states would continue to be the EBA. But banks in the euro area would come under a wing of the ECB called the Single Supervisory Mechanism (SSM), to be operative from November 2014, 12 months after the SSM regulation creating the supervisor enters into force.

Besides the EBA, another institution that came to the spotlight in recent times is the European Systemic Risk Board (ESRB). The de Larosière Group in 2009, recommended, inter alia, that a union-level body be established with a mandate to oversee risk in the financial system as a

---

[29] European Commission (2012), 'Banking Union: Commission Proposals for a Single Supervisory Mechanism', available at http://ec.europa.eu/internal_market/finances/

whole.[30] In this spirit, the ESRB was established in December 2010. The ESRB is part of the European System of Financial Supervision (ESFS), the purpose of which is to ensure supervision of the Union's financial system. While identifying and prioritizing systemic risks, the ESRB is expected to issue warnings where such systemic risks are significant and recommend remedial action in response to the risks so identified.

Three cornerstones have been highlighted as the major planks in such a banking union, in particular: (a) a single supervisory mechanism, (b) a common resolution structure, and (c) a common deposit insurance (Cœuré 2012). In such a scenario, the ECB along with the EBA, national supervisors, governments, and ESRB would define the contours of banking union (Eijffinger and Nijskens 2012).

Finally, the banking union was created in 2014 as a key component of the EU's economic and monetary union, with the following major objectives:

- to make the banks robust so as to make the banks withstand any future financial crises
- to make the non-viable banks resolved without recourse to taxpayers' money and with minimal impact on the real economy
- to reduce market fragmentation by harmonized financial sector rules.

All euro area member states are now part of the banking union.[31] Non-euro area EU member states can join the banking union by entering into close cooperation with the European Central Bank. The banking union is currently based on two fully operational pillars: (a) Single Supervisory Mechanism (SSM); and (b) Single Resolution Mechanism (SRM).[32] To

---

[30] The de Larosière Group Report (Chairman: Jacques de Larosière), Report of the High Level Expert Group on Financial Supervision in the EU, available at http://ec.europa.eu/internal_market/finances/docs/de_larosiere_report_en.pdf

[31] Croatia and Bulgaria being the latest countries to join on 1 October 2020.

[32] The three European supervisory authorities (ESA) (viz., the European Banking Authority (EBA), the European Insurance and Occupational Pensions Authority (EIOPA), the European Securities and Markets Authority (ESMA)), while being independent regulatory agencies, each responsible for supervision in a particular industry. But contrary to the ECB-linked Banking Union, each ESA primarily has 'soft' powers, meaning that its role is mainly to provide coordination.

strengthen the banking union further, the European Commission put forward in 2015 a proposal to establish a common system for deposit protection—the European deposit insurance scheme.

More recently, the Eurogroup issued a statement on the future of the banking union in June 2022. While this statement highlighted the creation of banking union as a powerful response to the financial crisis, it also noted that the banking union remains incomplete. It emphasized that a major requirement to strengthen the common framework would be to create an effective framework for bank crisis management and national deposit guarantee schemes (CMDI framework). Later in April 2023, the European Commission put forward a proposal for a reform of the CMDI framework with a focus on medium-sized and smaller banks.

Fiscal Union

The euro area, as stated earlier, is essentially a monetary union while fiscal policies are under the control of national authorities. This is a key challenge as well as a limitation of the eurozone; in fact, lack of fiscal union turned out to be an essential ingredient of the euro area crisis. The core logic has been succinctly put forth in a recent report of the 'Tommaso Padoa-Schioppa Group', which observed:

> EMU was also deficient in the area of fiscal policy coordination and fiscal surveillance. In fact, as the crisis later revealed, internal imbalances only became a matter of euro area concern when the mechanism of a 'self- fulfilling solvency crisis' set in and EMU lacked the appropriate instruments to respond. As EMU member states issue their debt in a currency over which they do not have full control, a liquidity crisis in these countries cannot be solved through devaluation, but increases the likelihood of default. Investors anticipate this logic and act accordingly: when an EMU country experiences budget difficulty, there is an over-reaction in the risk attached to the government bonds of the respective country. This in turn increases the interest rates of the country's bonds, aggravating the problems of liquidity and leading to even higher budget deficits. The result is that the EMU countries can be forced by financial markets into a bad equilibrium (characterized by

deflation, high interest rates, high budget deficits and a banking crisis) and into a 'self-fulfilling solvency crisis': the country becomes insolvent because investors fear insolvency. (Notre Europe 2012)

In fact, there is no denying the fact that these euro area economies are essentially heterogeneous in terms of their political and economic structures. But is it markedly different from a federation with strong bias in favour of constituent states? For instance, how different is the extent of heterogeneity between West Bengal and Maharashtra on the one hand and between Greece and Germany on the other? Admittedly, West Bengal and Maharashtra are under the same political union of India, but just to drive home the point, let us, for the time being, assume away political boundaries. The discussion on the optimum currency area indicates that the likelihood of facing asymmetric economic shocks is far less in the case of constituent states within a political boundary (and hence having both similar monetary and fiscal policies) than in the case of two states under a currency union.[33] In that case, one can even make a distinction between structural versus cyclical heterogeneity and argue that in the absence of freedom to use exchange rate as an adjustment variable (as in case of a currency union), cyclical heterogeneity could matter more for the constituent states in a currency union in handling the fallout of a shock. One of the solutions in this case is creation of a fiscal union.

To answer the question of what a fiscal union is, it is pertinent to turn to Bordo, Markiewicz, and Jonung (2011) who have argued that the concept of a fiscal union, 'entails fiscal federalism among its members, which could be either subnational (sub-central or regional) political units or nation states' and 'is based on a cooperative arrangement between the members of the fiscal union regarding the design and distribution of taxes and public expenditures' (p. 3). But the idea of fiscal union in the euro area has to be seen in the context of the specific issue of fiscal union within a currency union. There have been theoretical developments in this area.

---

[33] Labour mobility in that case can definitely act as an equilibrator. While de jure there are no issues with labour mobility in the euro area, there are de facto impediments. In fact, the 2012 OECD Economic Survey of the EU pointed out five factors in this regard: (a) the lack of portability of supplementary pension rights, (b) scarce cross-country information about job vacancies, (c) the difficult recognition of professional qualifications, (d) housing market policies that raise the costs of moving, and (e) the difficulty in accessing public sector jobs as non-nationals.

It has been shown that if monetary and fiscal authorities have different ideal output and inflation targets, Nash equilibrium output or inflation or both are suboptimal (Dixit and Lambertini 2001). A major conclusion that emanates from these studies is that coexistence of a single monetary authority and numerous fiscal authorities requires binding fiscal policy constraints to avoid excessive deficits at the sub-central level. Thus, default by a subnational government can impose a negative externality upon other subnational governments—which is known as a common pool problem. In historical context, looking into the fiscal federalism in Argentina, Brazil, Germany, and the US, Bordo, Markiewicz, and Jonung (2011) concluded: 'A main problem of fiscal policy making in the euro area, undermining budgetary discipline and the workings of the Stability and Growth Pact, is found in the lack of efficient fiscal governance in a number of member countries.'

How to ensure efficient fiscal governance then? The 2012 Tommaso Padoa-Schioppa Group report examined this issue and has suggested 'a sui generis fiscal federalism approach for the euro area'. The report argues that a fiscal framework for the euro area in a minimal form needs to achieve three main functional tasks: '(a) allow for a sufficient degree of macroeconomic stabilization to react to internal imbalances in the euro area (this was discussed in the previous section); (b) present a workable solution to the problem of fiscal discipline; (c) make the euro area resilient to self-fulfilling solvency crises' (Notre Europe 2012). In this spirit, the report recommended the establishment of a European Debt Agency (EDA), which could be guaranteed by all euro area countries.[34]

But fiscal union extends beyond establishing a common debt office. In fact, Lane (2012) observed: 'Europe might seek a deeper level of fiscal union, agreeing to share certain tax streams or spending programs in a way that would be delinked from fluctuations in national-level output. In related fashion, *enhanced coordination of national fiscal policies* would also be helpful, thereby enabling the collective fiscal position of the euro area to be appropriately calibrated in relation to the prevailing macroeconomic conditions' (p. 64, emphasis in original).

---

[34] The report notes: 'Such an agency would be less than a fully-fledged finance ministry or a treasury, but it would be more than a simple European Monetary Fund providing emergency assistance against strict conditionality.'

It is good to see some early indications in this regard. On 26 June 2012, an EU report by the President of the European Council, Herman Van Rompuy, entitled 'Towards a Genuine Economic and Monetary Union', was released.[35] It highlighted four building blocks: (a) an integrated financial framework to 'ensure financial stability in particular in the euro area and minimise the cost of bank failures to European citizens'; (b) an integrated budgetary framework to ensure sound fiscal policy making at the national and European levels;[36] (c) an integrated economic policy framework for ensuring national and European policies for promoting 'sustainable growth, employment and competitiveness'; and (d) ensuring the necessary democratic legitimacy and accountability of decision-making within the EMU, based on the joint exercise of sovereignty for common policies and solidarity. However, in recent times, the proposed scheme was much less ambitious.

But political reality is far from making it a reality. Consequently, can one be a little cynical and agree with an assessment which states: 'The euro area has not yet reached a point where a discussion can be begun on the overall fiscal stance of the euro area and the way it could be aligned to the situation of the euro area as a whole' (Darvas 2012)? Later, an IMF policy paper argues, 'The euro area needs to build elements of a common fiscal policy, including more fiscal risk sharing, to preserve financial and economic integration and stability. Without some degree of fiscal union, the region will continue to face existential risks that policymakers should not ignore' (Berger et al. 2018).

More recently, in an invited article in *The Economist* (6 September 2023), Mario Draghi, former Italian Prime Minister and ECB President remarked, 'paradoxically, the prospects for fiscal union in the euro zone are improving—because the nature of the needed fiscal integration is changing.'[37] Draghi argued that since the euro area crisis the eurozone has evolved in two ways that are 'opening up a different, and potentially more acceptable, road to fiscal union'. First, since 2012, the ECB developed policy

---

[35] Available at http://www.consilium.europa.eu/uedocs/ cms_data/docs/pressdata /en/ec/ 131201.pdf (accessed in July 2013)

[36] This would encompass coordination, joint decision-making, greater enforcement, and commensurate steps towards common debt issuance. This framework could include also different forms of fiscal solidarity.

[37] https://www.economist.com/by-invitation/2023/09/06/mario-draghi-on-the-path-to-fiscal-union-in-the-euro-zone

tools to contain unwarranted divergence between stronger and weaker countries' borrowing costs, and tried to use them. Second, 'Europe is no longer mainly facing crises caused by unsound policies in particular countries. Instead, it has to confront common, imported shocks like the pandemic, the energy crisis and the war in Ukraine.' In Draghi's opinion, the ECB has two options. First is to relax its fiscal and state-aid rules, allowing member states to shoulder the full burden of the necessary investment. The second option is to redefine the EU's fiscal framework and decision-making process to make them commensurate with our shared challenges.

In April 2023, based on two high-level principles of (a) fiscal sustainability, and (b) national ownership, the European Commission came out with new proposals on reform of European Union fiscal governance. The major elements of the new rules are given in Table 6.11. It remains to be seen how far these new rules enhance the movements towards a more effective fiscal union within the EU.

Table 6.11 EU's New Fiscal Rules

Element	Proposal
(1) Debt sustainability analysis	Classification of countries by risk level based on a debt sustainability analysis (DSA) with a transparent methodology agreed with Member States.
(2) Fiscal adjustment path	Customized and negotiated between the EU Commission and each Member State and approved by the EU Council. To be implemented within a maximum period of 4 years (extendable to 7 years with justified cause).
(3) Long-term objective	3% deficit and 60% of GDP.
(4) Medium-term objective (4–7 years)	Sustainable deficit and debt levels.
(a) Control variable: expenditure rule	Cap on net primary expenditure (excluding discretionary measures and European funds, debt interest and cyclical unemployment expenditure). Investments financed by EU funds in green and digital transition or other authorized investments will not be considered expenditure.
(b) Rate of reduction	The 1/20 rule is suppressed, but an annual structural deficit adjustment of 0.5% will be required for Member States with a deficit above 3% (whether they are in the excessive deficit procedure or not).

Table 6.11 Continued

Element	Proposal
(4) Corrective mechanism in case of non-compliance	Excessive deficit procedure, with smaller fines but stricter enforcement. Reputational sanctions such as bringing ministers before the European Parliament in case of non-compliance ('comply or explain'). Possibility of freezing EU funds and macroeconomic conditionality.
Other elements	
Institutional framework	Greater role for independent national fiscal institutions. Their assessment of debt reduction programmes must be considered by the EU Commission and Council, but recommendations will be non-binding.
Transparency	The Commission will make public the debt sustainability analysis, the multi-annual adjustment path, and the corresponding level of the structural primary balance at the end of the 4-year adjustment period.
Other issues	Possibility of an escape clause in 'exceptional circumstances'. Revision of the Macroeconomic Imbalances Procedure with a similar approach to the fiscal rules.

Source: Feas, Enrique (2023): 'An insufficient reform of the EU's fiscal rules', ARI 53/2023 - 19/6/2023 - Elcano Royal Institute Working Paper, available at https://media.realinstitutoelc ano.org/wp-content/uploads/2023/06/an-insufficient-reform-of-the-eus-fiscal-rules-elcano-royal-institute.pdf

Political Union

In the ultimate analysis, the importance of a possible political union, both for handling the current crisis and for tackling the inherent contradiction in an optimum currency area cannot be understated. As the former President of the ECB Jean-Claude Trichet mentioned, 'In this new global constellation, European integration—both economic and political—is central to achieving prosperity and influence' (Trichet 2012, p. 21). Does Europe then need a 'supra-national decision-making authority' where with the European Parliament it could play a crucial role and have the final say on different matters? How will such an institution have a strong democratic anchoring? Trichet made an emotional appeal for creating some surrogate of a political union; it is worth quoting him in detail.

The creation of Europe's economic and monetary union is unique in the history of sovereign states. The Euro area constitutes a 'society of states' of a completely new type. We have created progressively a concept which goes far beyond the Westphalian concept of sovereign states. Like individuals in a society, Euro area countries are both independent and interdependent. They can affect each other both positively and negatively ... The acronym EMU—Economic and Monetary Union—is made of three letters E, M and U which means that we must have, and have indeed, two Unions: a monetary union MU, and an economic Union EU. (Trichet 2012, p. 22)

What is the future of the euro area? Draghi (2023) argued passionately: 'The strategies that ensured Europe's prosperity and security in the past—reliance on America for security, on China for exports and on Russia for energy—have become insufficient, uncertain or unacceptable. In this new world, paralysis is clearly untenable for citizens, whereas the radical option of exiting the EU has delivered decidedly mixed results. Forging a closer union will ultimately prove to be the only way to deliver the security and prosperity that European citizens crave.'[38]

* * *

How can one sum up the broad conclusions of the country-specific details of the euro area? Insofar as the euro area crisis is concerned, it needs to be noted that like Tolstoy's proverbial unhappy families in *Anna Karenina*, the severely hit crisis countries of the euro area were different and crisis-ridden in their own different ways. While both Greece and Italy have been affected by fiscal problems, in the cases of Ireland or Spain the mortgage market turned out to be the main issue. Thus, more interestingly, these crisis countries differed in terms of their fiscal problem, fragility of their banking sector, or the extent of asset price bubble.

What stands out is that during 2012–15, the euro area faced not one but three interlocking crises: (a) a banking crisis (where banks are undercapitalized and face liquidity problems), (b) a sovereign debt crisis (when a number of countries are facing increasing sovereign bond yields and consequent funding challenges), and (c) a growth crisis (with a low

---

[38] https://www.economist.com/by-invitation/2023/09/06/mario-draghi-on-the-path-to-fiscal-union-in-the-euro-zone (accessed in March 2024)

aggregate growth in the area as well as unequal distribution across countries) (Shambaugh 2012).

As a broad generalization, it may not be incorrect to infer that these country studies illustrate the fragility of an optimum currency area in the absence of various preconditions like fiscal convergence. Beyond a point, no amount of financial opening up and no uniform currency can shield a country from fiscally irresponsible behaviour, bursting of property price bubble, or productivity inadequacies and deficiencies! The impact of fiscal irresponsibility on the part of select euro area countries was amplified by the irresponsibility of market participants. They took more than five years to come out of the euphoria induced by a common currency and to take cognizance of the deeply flawed fundamentals of a group of countries. Thus, irresponsible borrowing by select countries was compounded by irresponsible lending behaviour of market participants.

Whether the euro area crisis would have occurred even without the global financial crisis and the great recession is moot since counterfactuals are difficult to establish. But there is no gainsaying the fact that the global financial crisis would have provided the immediate trigger for the crisis and enhanced its severity. With hindsight, it is apparent that the combination of fiscal and current account deficits of a number of euro area countries, abetted by financial market participants who ignored their underlying fundamentals, was a sure recipe for a crisis!

What indubitably stands out is that whatever be the specific and proximate causes for the occurrence of the crisis in individual countries, in the ultimate analysis, the inexorable linkages between fiscal, monetary, and financial issues can no longer be ignored. Also, without fiscal union, monetary union may not survive exogenous and asymmetric shocks unleashed by a financial crisis; and monetary and fiscal union may not be feasible without political union.

At the current juncture, the euro area is in the midst of another crisis out of the Russia-Ukraine military conflict and the associated energy prices driven by the inflationary situation in the post-pandemic years. With the appropriate stabilization policy tools, so far, the euro area has been able to withstand the shocks. Also, since the existence of the euro area is an experiment without much precedence, going forward the area, on its own, needs to chalk out plans to face various eventualities. Establishment of a banking union and movement towards a fiscal union are steps in the right direction.

APPENDIX 6A

IMF Country Groupings

1. Advanced Economies (37 Countries)
Australia, Austria, Belgium, Canada, Cyprus, Czech Republic, Denmark, Estonia, Finland, France, Germany, Greece, Hong Kong SAR, Iceland, Ireland, Israel, Italy, Japan, Korea, Luxembourg, Malta, the Netherlands, New Zealand, Norway, Portugal, San Marino, Singapore, Slovak Republic, Slovenia, Spain, Sweden, Switzerland, Taiwan Province of China, the UK, and the US.

2. Euro Area (20 Countries)
Austria, Belgium, Croatia, Cyprus, Estonia, Finland, France, Germany, Greece, Ireland, Italy, Latvia, Lithuania, Luxembourg, Malta, the Netherlands, Portugal, Slovak Republic, Slovenia, and Spain.

3. Major Advanced Economies (G7)
Canada, France, Germany, Italy, Japan, the UK, and the US.

4. Newly Industrialized Asian Economies (Four Countries)
Hong Kong SAR, Korea, Singapore, and Taiwan Province of China.

5. Other Advanced Economies (Advanced Economies Excluding G7 and Euro Area—Composed of 17 Countries)
Andorra, Australia, Czech Republic, Denmark, Hong Kong SAR, Iceland, Israel, Korea, Macao SAR, New Zealand, Norway, Puerto Rico, San Marino, Singapore, Sweden, Switzerland, and Taiwan Province of China.

6. European Union (27 Countries)
Austria, Belgium, Bulgaria, Croatia, Cyprus, Czech Republic, Denmark, Estonia, Finland, France, Germany, Greece, Hungary, Ireland, Italy, Latvia, Lithuania, Luxembourg, Malta, the Netherlands, Poland, Portugal, Romania, Slovak Republic, Slovenia, Spain, Sweden.

7. Emerging Market and Developing Economies (151 Countries)
Afghanistan, Albania, Algeria, Angola, Antigua and Barbuda, Argentina, Armenia, Azerbaijan, the Bahamas, Bahrain, Bangladesh, Barbados, Belarus, Belize, Benin, Bhutan, Bolivia, Bosnia and Herzegovina, Botswana, Brazil, Brunei Darussalam, Bulgaria, Burkina Faso, Burundi, Cambodia, Cameroon, Cape Verde, Central African Republic, Chad, Chile, China, Colombia, Comoros, the Democratic Republic of the Congo, the Republic of the Congo, Costa Rica, Côte d'Ivoire, Croatia, Djibouti, Dominica, Dominican Republic, Ecuador, Egypt, El Salvador, Equatorial Guinea, Eritrea, Ethiopia, Fiji, Gabon, the Gambia, Georgia, Ghana, Grenada, Guatemala, Guinea, Guinea-Bissau, Guyana, Haiti, Honduras, Hungary, India, Indonesia, Iran, Iraq, Jamaica, Jordan, Kazakhstan, Kenya, Kiribati, Kosovo, Kuwait, the Kyrgyz Republic, Lao P.D.R., Latvia, Lebanon, Lesotho, Liberia, Libya, Lithuania, FYR Macedonia, Madagascar, Malawi, Malaysia, the Maldives, Mali, Mauritania, Mauritius, Mexico, Moldova, Mongolia, Montenegro, Morocco, Mozambique, Myanmar, Namibia, Nepal, Nicaragua, Niger, Nigeria, Oman, Pakistan, Panama, Papua New Guinea, Paraguay, Peru, the Philippines, Poland, Qatar, Romania, Russia,

Rwanda, Samoa, São Tomé and Príncipe, Saudi Arabia, Senegal, Serbia, Seychelles, Sierra Leone, Solomon Islands, South Africa, South Sudan, Sri Lanka, St. Kitts and Nevis, St. Lucia, St. Vincent and the Grenadines, Sudan, Suriname, Swaziland, Syria, Tajikistan, Tanzania, Thailand, Democratic Republic of Timor-Leste, Togo, Tonga, Trinidad and Tobago, Tunisia, Turkey, Turkmenistan, Tuvalu, Uganda, Ukraine, the United Arab Emirates, Uruguay, Uzbekistan, Vanuatu, Venezuela, Vietnam, Yemen, Zambia, and Zimbabwe.

10. Developing Asia (27 Countries)
Afghanistan, Bangladesh, Bhutan, Brunei Darussalam, Cambodia, China, Fiji, India, Indonesia, Kiribati, Lao PDR, Malaysia, Maldives, Myanmar, Nepal, Pakistan, Papua New Guinea, the Philippines, Samoa, the Solomon Islands, Sri Lanka, Thailand, Timor-Leste, Tonga, Tuvalu, Vanuatu, and Vietnam.

11. ASEAN-5
Indonesia, Malaysia, Philippines, Thailand, and Vietnam.

12. Latin America and the Caribbean (32 Countries)
Antigua and Barbuda, Argentina, the Bahamas, Barbados, Belize, Bolivia, Brazil, Chile, Colombia, Costa Rica, Dominica, the Dominican Republic, Ecuador, El Salvador, Grenada, Guatemala, Guyana, Haiti, Honduras, Jamaica, Mexico, Nicaragua, Panama, Paraguay, Peru, St. Kitts and Nevis, St. Lucia, St. Vincent and the Grenadines, Suriname, Trinidad and Tobago, Uruguay, and Venezuela.

13. Middle East and North Africa (20 Countries)
Algeria, Bahrain, Djibouti, Egypt, Iran, Iraq, Jordan, Kuwait, Lebanon, Libya, Mauritania, Morocco, Oman, Qatar, Saudi Arabia, Sudan, Syria, Tunisia, the United Arab Emirates, and Yemen.

14. Sub-Saharan Africa (45 Countries)
Angola, Benin, Botswana, Burkina Faso, Burundi, Cameroon, Cape Verde, Central African Republic, Chad, Comoros, the Democratic Republic of the Congo, the Republic of the Congo, Côte d'Ivoire, Equatorial Guinea, Eritrea, Ethiopia, Gabon, the Gambia, Ghana, Guinea, Guinea-Bissau, Kenya, Lesotho, Liberia, Madagascar, Malawi, Mali, Mauritius, Mozambique, Namibia, Niger, Nigeria, Rwanda, São Tomé and Príncipe, Senegal, Seychelles, Sierra Leone, South Africa, South Sudan, Swaziland, Tanzania, Togo, Uganda, Zambia, and Zimbabwe.

Source: www.imf.org (accessed in October 2023).

APPENDIX 6B

The European Union and the Euro Area

In order to put the country-specific discussion in context, it is useful to go a little bit into the history of the EU and the euro area. The foundation of the EU may be traced to as early as 1952 when the Treaty of Paris was signed, establishing the European Coal and Steel Community (ECSC). The six founding states were Belgium, France, Germany, Italy, Luxembourg, and the Netherlands. Subsequently, in 1957, the Treaties of Rome were signed by the six member states, forming the EEC and the European Atomic Energy Community (EUROATOM). In 1967, three organizations, namely, ECSC, EEC, and EUROATOM were merged to form the basis of the European Community (EC). Subsequently, various European countries joined the EC, namely, the UK, Denmark, and Ireland in 1973; Greece in 1981; Spain and Portugal in 1986; and Finland, Sweden, and Austria in 1995. Finally, in 1992, the Maastricht Treaty was ratified, which rechartered the EC as the EU.[39] With the fall of the Soviet Union and the Berlin Wall, a number of erstwhile East European countries entered the EU and its current membership has 27 countries. On 1 January 2014, Latvia became the 18th country to join the euro area.

It is important to recognize that the Maastricht Treaty (1991) set out a blueprint for the transition process for the member countries to adopt a single currency and, in doing so, prescribed a set of convergence criteria that the member countries have to meet before moving to a single currency. Three criteria were specified in terms of maximum inflation rate, exchange rate stability, and budget discipline.[40] Subsequently, a Stability and Growth Pact (SGP) in 1997 set up the medium-term budgetary objective of positions close to balance or in surplus.

The period from the Maastricht Treaty to actual operationalization of the euro can be divided into three stages.[41] In stage one, with Europe-wide liberalization of capital markets, a single market was established by January 1994. In stage two, a wide variety of activities were initiated to set the preparation. These included activities such as establishment of the European Monetary Institute (EMI) in 1994; agreement in Madrid by the European Council in 1995 on the name for the new currency (called the euro) and the date of starting the single currency (1 January 1999); establishment of the ECB and the European System of Central Banks (ESCB) in 1998. On 31 December 1998, the conversion rates between the euro and the currencies of the

---

[39] Currently the EU is run by five distinct institutions: European Parliament, Council of the Union, European Commission, Court of Justice, and Court of Auditors.

[40] In broad terms, the convergence criteria were as follows: (a) Inflation rate: no more than 1.5 percentage points higher than the average of the three best-performing member states of the EU; (b) Government finance: the annual deficit-GDP ratio must not exceed three per cent at the end of the preceding fiscal year; (c) Government debt: the ratio of debt-GDP must not exceed 60 per cent at the end of the preceding fiscal year; (d) Exchange rate: applicant countries should have joined the ERM II for two consecutive years and should not have devalued its currency during the period; and (e) Long-term interest rates: the nominal long-term interest rate must not be more than 2 percentage points higher than in the three lowest inflation member states.

[41] This discussion follows the material available at http://ec.europa.eu/economy_fina nce/euro.

participating member countries were fixed irrevocably and the euro was introduced on 1 January 1999. For the first three years the euro fundamentally was, 'an invisible currency, only used for accounting purposes, e.g., in electronic payments'.[42] Euro cash was finally introduced on 1 January 2002, when it replaced, at fixed conversion rates, the banknotes and coins of the national currencies.[43]

A major blow to the concept of the EU in recent times has been the long-drawn out process of Brexit that officially took place at 23:00 GMT on 31 January 2020.

In broad terms, European countries can be subdivided into three groups: (a) member of the EU (27 countries), (b) countries whose candidature is being considered for the EU, and (c) non-member EU countries.

---

[42] Available at http://www.ecb.int/euro/intro/html/index.en.html

[43] The conversion to old national currency to €1 were as follows: Belgian franc (0.33990), German mark (1.95583), Irish pound (0.78756), Greek drachma (340.75000), Spanish peseta (166.38600), French franc (6.55957), Italian lira (1936.27000), Cyprus pound (0.58527), Luxembourg franc (40.33990), Maltese lira (0.42930), Dutch guilder (2.20371), Austrian schilling (13.76030), Portuguese escudo (200.48200), Slovenian tolar (239.64000), Slovak koruna (30.12600), Finnish markka (5.94573), Estonian kroon (15.64660). These irrevocable conversion rates in euro were broadly set at the central rate observed for the national currencies within the ERM II. Participation in ERM II for at least two years without severe tensions was one of the preconditions of a Member State for adopting the euro.

7

India

Crisis and the Economic Stimuli

The discussion has so far focused on the various aspects of the ongoing crisis both globally as well as in the euro area. This chapter presents an overview of the state of the Indian fisc and its relationship with the global crisis. The aim of the chapter is to place the monetary and fiscal stimulus in the larger context of fiscal consolidation (both at the centre and the states) and macro-financial developments. The treatment is synoptic since the fiscal situation in India is an important issue in its own right and not necessarily in relation to the global financial crisis and the COVID-19 pandemic.

The chapter is organized as follows. To begin with, in order to get a sense of perspective, a brief discussion of Indian macroeconomic trends is attempted. This is followed by a discussion about the transmission of the global financial crisis to India and its impact. An account of monetary and fiscal stimulus in India and recovery and exit policies are taken up next. This is followed up by a discussion of placing the monetary and fiscal stimulus in a larger context—first, against the fiscal trends (both at the central and states' level) since the 1990s, and then against major macro-financial developments in growth, inflation, financial stability, and external sector stability. Before concluding the chapter, the implication of fiscal dominance on monetary, financial, and external sectors is explored.

Indian Macroeconomy: Trends during 2000–22

During the period 2000 through 2022, the Indian economy was marked by two distinct crisis years, namely, 2008 and 2020. We will take up these crises separately.

Financial and Fiscal Policies. Second Edition. Y. V. Reddy, Partha Ray, and Pinaki Chakraborty, Oxford University Press.
© Y. V. Reddy, Partha Ray, and Pinaki Chakraborty 2024. DOI: 10.1093/9780198934288.003.0007

It is useful to recall that despite the near-zero exposure of the Indian banking sector to the US sub-prime mortgage market-originated toxic assets, the Indian economy was also affected by the global financial crisis—particularly after the fall of Lehman Brothers in September 2008 and the subsequent increase in global uncertainty (Reddy 2009). Given the globalization of the Indian financial sector as well as of the corporates, various sectors of the Indian economy were affected to some extent. Furthermore, even if the primary drivers of growth in India were domestic consumption and investment, Indian growth was affected through some channels. But thanks to the prudent (*conservative* in some views) regulatory practices the extent of the negative impact of the US subprime crisis on the Indian economy was rather limited. In fact, characterizing the state of an economy as *resilient* or *contagious* is not a binary choice and the Indian story can be painted in tempera with contrasting colours of both its resilience as well as contagion.

In 2009, at the peak of the crisis, Indian growth was 8.5 per cent, which, though low by recent trends (and also in comparison with peers like China), was respectable by global standards. Both savings and investments were not affected. Volumes of exports and imports also bounced back within a year. Admittedly, a large chunk of this speedy recovery could be traced to a sizeable and prompt fiscal stimulus and this is reflected in a sharp rise in net government borrowing; this increase, however, did not contribute to government gross debt (see Table 7.1).

Real Economy: Growth and Inflation Trends (2000–8)

As far as growth is concerned, the five years before the crisis (i.e., 2003–4 through 2007–8) was sort of a golden period with average growth during this period being 8.7 per cent. Inflation too did not emerge as a major problem with an average inflation rate during this period being 5.6 per cent. However, a comparison between growth (and sectoral growth) and inflation between the pre-crisis and post-crisis period brings out a number of interesting features.

First, average growth during 2000–1 to 2007–8 at 7.2 per cent is, in fact, the same as the average growth experienced during 2008–9 to 2012–13. Second, the composition of growth raises some issues. In the two years

(2008–9 and 2009–10) the major impetus seems to have come from com-munity, social, and personal services which grew at 10 per cent plus rates. Considering the fact that for national accounting, community, social, and personal services would include government expenditure, growth during these two years is clearly stimulus-driven. Third, by all accounts growths in 2012–13 and 2012–13 seemed to have slowed down, indicating a complex interaction of various global factors (e.g., euro area crisis and the slowdown in growth in advanced economies) and domestic factors (structural as well as macroeconomic) (Ministry of Finance, Government of India 2012, *Mid-Year Economic Analysis: 2012–13*).

On the contrary, comparison of inflation rates during the two periods (i.e., before and after the crisis) clearly indicates that inflation rate at 7.0 per cent during 2008–9 through 2012–13 is much higher than that of 5.0 per cent experienced during the pre-crisis period. In fact, except for 2009–10, in all the years after 2008–9 inflation was significantly high. Several reasons are given for a rise in inflation rate, such as, higher international prices of crude, change in dietary patterns leading to structural demand-supply mis-match for protein-rich items, revision in MSP prices for some of the essen-tial commodities, or revision in petroleum prices (Ministry of Finance, Government of India 2012, *Mid-Year Economic Analysis: 2012–13*).

A number of conclusions can be drawn from the account of fiscal de-velopments and course of monetary stimulus and exit consequent upon the crisis. First, the fiscal and monetary policies reinforce each other, ar-guably excessively as an immediate response to the crisis. Second, the situation in India during 2010–11 through 2012–13 is characterized by an expansionary fiscal policy and, perhaps, a contractionary monetary policy. There is a view that the stance of monetary policy should be de-termined with reference to the policy interest rate in real terms in judging whether it is expansionary or contractionary! The implications of such a configuration can indeed be debated.[1]

---

[1] It is interesting to refer to Blinder (1982), who in a theoretical context, traced lack of co-ordination between monetary and fiscal policy in terms of the following three causes: (1) The fiscal and monetary authorities might have different objectives; (2) The two authorities might have different opinions about the likely effects of fiscal and/or monetary policy actions on the economy; (3) The two authorities might make different forecasts of the likely state of the economy in the absence of policy intervention. In this set-up, Blinder (1982) went on say: 'In each case, if we were certain about which of the two authorities was correct, then we would know what to do about the coordination problem. We would simply put all the policy levers in the hands of the authority with the proper objective or correct theory or accurate forecast, just

The nature of elevated inflation could technically be justified if the nature of inflation has actually undergone a radical transformation in recent years in India. Or, to put it differently, 'Is There a New Normal for Inflation?' (Subbarao 2013b). Several arguments have been put forward, such as, wage-price spiral could be a permanent shock to inflation, persistence of global commodity price inflation, quantitative easing in the advanced world, convergence of the Indian economy with the global economy. Former RBI Governor D. Subbarao in a speech has examined each of these factors for India and arrived at the following conclusion:

> Admittedly, the average inflation rate in India over the last three years has trended up. Nevertheless, the context presents neither a necessary nor a sufficient condition for the Reserve Bank to revise its inflation goal. Not a necessary condition because, as indicated earlier, much of our inflation is driven by supply constraints which can be corrected by appropriate policies and their effective implementation. Accepting a new normal for inflation not only has no theoretical or empirical support, but entails the moral hazard of policy inaction in dealing with supply constraints. Not a sufficient condition because there is no empirical evidence to establish that the benefits of higher growth outweigh the costs of welfare loss associated with higher inflation. (Subbarao 2013b)

The Pandemic and the Indian Economy

The macro trends of the Indian economy over the 22-year period (2000–22) reveals a number of interesting features (Table 7.1). First, there were two major crises, namely, 2008 (corresponding to the global financial crisis) and 2020 (corresponding to the pandemic).[2] Second, insofar as the

---

as we would want the instructor, not the student, to have ultimate control over the learn-to-drive car. But, in fact, we rarely know this in any particular case. And we certainly have no basis for setting out a general, constitutional rule predicated on one or the other authority "always" being right. As a consequence, we may conclude, as in the student driver example that the best strategy is to give some power to each authority, but at the same time to give each some ability to cancel out the actions of the other.'

[2] Interestingly, the growth rate during 2019 and the crisis year of 2008 were both the same at 3.9 per cent.

Table 7.1 India: Select Macro Indicators

	GDP Growth	Investment	Savings	Inflation	Growth in imports of goods and services	Growth in exports of goods and services	Government Borrowing	Government Gross Debt	Current account balance	GDP (current prices)
	%	% of GDP	% of GDP	%	%	%	% of GDP	% of GDP	% of GDP	Trillion
2000	4.0	24.3	23.7	3.8	2.2	11.4	-8.3	73.6	-0.6	0.5
2001	4.9	24.2	24.9	4.3	-0.9	2.4	-10.8	78.7	0.7	0.5
2002	3.9	24.8	26.0	4.0	12.4	17.7	-10.9	82.9	1.2	0.5
2003	7.9	26.8	29.1	3.9	8.5	16.2	-11.2	84.4	2.3	0.6
2004	7.8	32.8	32.5	3.8	35.8	27.0	-9.1	83.4	-0.3	0.7
2005	9.3	34.7	33.5	4.4	16.6	17.9	-7.4	81.0	-1.2	0.8
2006	9.3	35.7	34.7	6.7	11.5	16.0	-6.3	77.2	-1.0	0.9
2007	9.8	38.1	36.8	6.2	18.8	18.5	-4.5	74.1	-1.3	1.2
2008	3.9	34.3	32.0	9.1	3.5	7.1	-9.0	72.8	-2.3	1.2
2009	8.5	36.5	33.7	12.3	6.7	-5.5	-9.5	71.5	-2.8	1.4
2010	10.3	36.5	33.7	10.5	16.2	27.3	-8.6	66.4	-2.8	1.7
2011	6.6	39.6	35.4	9.5	10.6	12.9	-8.3	68.6	-4.3	1.8
2012	5.5	38.3	33.5	10.0	1.5	0.1	-7.6	68.0	-4.8	1.8
2013	6.4	34.0	32.3	9.4	-3.5	4.8	-7.0	67.7	-1.7	1.9
2014	7.4	34.3	33.0	5.8	5.9	4.2	-7.1	67.1	-1.3	2.0

(continued)

Table 7.1 Continued

	GDP Growth	Investment	Savings	Inflation	Growth in imports of goods and services	Growth in exports of goods and services	Government Borrowing	Government Gross Debt	Current account balance	GDP (current prices)
	%	% of GDP	% of GDP	%	%	%	% of GDP	% of GDP	% of GDP	Trillion
2015	8.0	32.1	31.1	4.9	0.8	-5.1	-7.2	69.0	-1.1	2.1
2016	8.3	30.2	29.5	4.5	4.4	6.7	-7.1	68.9	-0.6	2.3
2017	6.8	31.0	29.1	3.6	13.6	10.2	-6.2	69.7	-1.8	2.7
2018	6.5	32.3	30.2	3.4	4.1	4.9	-6.4	70.4	-2.1	2.7
2019	3.9	30.1	29.2	4.8	-4.0	-2.3	-7.7	75.0	-0.9	2.8
2020	-5.8	28.8	29.7	6.2	-13.9	-6.6	-12.9	88.5	0.9	2.7
2021	9.1	31.2	30.0	5.5	20.3	20.0	-9.6	83.8	-1.2	3.2
2022	7.2	31.0	29.1	6.7	10.1	9.7	-9.2	81.0	-2.0	3.4

Source: World Economic Outlook database, IMF, October 2023.

pandemic-related fiscal stimulus is concerned, there was substantial in-crease in fiscal deficit in 2020. Third, while there was an improvement in inflation outcomes after the adoption of the regime of flexible inflation targeting (FIT), inflation shot up following the pandemic-related supply side distortions. Fourth, public debt was under reasonable control. Fifth, India has been traditionally a current account deficit economy; the sur-plus in current account during the year of pandemic was more to do with import compression on account of depressed economic activity and im-pairment in the global supply chain.

Resilience of the Indian Economy During the Global Financial Crisis[3]

The resilience of the Indian economy stemmed broadly from Indian pur-suit of prudential financial stability and can be traced to a number of regulatory practices (Reddy 2009). First, India with its embryonic credit derivatives market as well as limited pursuit of the *originate to distribute* models, had near-zero exposure to the toxic assets that originated in the US sub-prime mortgage market. Second, the investment portfolios of Indian commercial banks were insulated by prudent regulatory practices such as, building up of an investment fluctuation reserve (within a period of five years, announced in 2002); progressive relaxation of investment under the *held-to-maturity* (HTM) category; or restricted investment in non-government securities. Third, regulators were careful enough to contain banks' exposure to risky assets and accordingly adjusted the risk weights of certain class of risky assets (e.g., real estate) for maintaining capital adequacy. Fourth, even within the standard assets, loans, and ad-vances to select assets were subject to preassigned limits; these included personal loans, capital market, real estate, and systemically important non-deposit accepting non-banking finance companies. Fifth, prudential limits were placed on the extent of inter-bank liabilities for the banking

---

[3] There is a sizeable literature on the impact of the global financial crisis on India; see Reddy (2009, 2011), RBI (2010), Bajpai (2011), Mohan (2011), Kishore et al. (2011), Mundle et al. (2011), Acharya (2012), and Subbarao (2013a), among others. Also, see the anthology of papers published in 2009 in *Economic and Political Weekly,* namely, *Global Economic and Financial Crisis: Essays from Economic and Political Weekly*, New Delhi: Orient Blackswan.

sector, thereby nipping the problem of too-interconnected-to-fail in the bud. Finally, under the Indian accounting practices, mark-to-market valuation is applied in a non-symmetric manner whereby banks are required to value their investments under held-for-trading (HFT) and available for-sale (AFS) categories at fair value at periodic intervals so as to provide for net losses but ignore net gains.

Besides, monetary policy during the years preceding the crisis was also countercyclical. Further, in consonance with the practices adopted by many other Asian economies, foreign exchange reserves were expanded during the boom while constraining external debt.

Contagion

But given such resilience, why was the Indian economy affected? The answer typically lies in the extent of globalization of the Indian economy, which is often misconceived as being relatively closed and the extent of its openness underestimated.

The most traditional metric of a country's openness is its exports and imports. In terms of India's exports and imports as a percentage of its GDP, openness has increased from nearly 20 per cent in the 1990s to close to 40 per cent in recent times. If this measure is extended to include all current receipts and payments, then it has more than doubled at 61 per cent in 2008–9. Finally, if an expanded measure of globalization were to be considered, comprising all items in the balance of payments accounts, as the ratio of total external transactions (gross current account plus account flows) to GDP, then this ratio is seen to have more than doubled from 46.8 per cent in 1997–8 to 117.4 per cent in 2007–8 (Subbarao 2009). Besides, Indian business cycles have over the years synchronized more and more with the global economy in general and emerging economies in particular.[4]

Hence, given the extent of globalization, India cannot be an island of tranquillity and it is no surprise that the Indian economy too was affected

---

[4] It has been observed that correlation coefficient between Indian growth and global growth has increased from 0.43 during the 1980s to 0.59 during the 1990s and finally to 0.92 during 2001–8 (RBI 2010).

by the global financial crisis, which turned into the great recession. The contagion of the crisis spread to India through all the channels—the financial channel, the real economy channel, and importantly, the confidence channel, though the countercyclical monetary, prudential, and external sector policies moderated its impact and provided policy headroom for countercyclical measures at the time of the crisis.

Thus, despite the near-zero exposure to US mortgage market-related toxic assets, the Indian financial sector was affected as well through various channels. Some segments of the financial system, particularly non-banking financial companies, faced severe liquidity pressures due to reduced foreign funding and the subdued domestic capital market. There were instances of capital flow reversals and drying up of funding from external markets for banks and corporates. Reversal of portfolio flows reflected unwinding of stock positions by foreign institutional investors (FIIs) to replenish cash balances abroad. All these created liquidity pressure on mutual funds during 2008–9 (RBI 2010). However, the range of policy tools, including unconventional measures such as market stabilization schemes, at the disposal of monetary authorities enabled them to minimize the adverse impact of the crisis.

Financial Channels

It is well known that given the nature of trading in financial markets, the speed of transmission of any crisis is normally faster in financial markets than in the real economy. India is no exception to this general rule. India's financial markets (comprising equity market, money market, foreign exchange market, and credit market) all came under pressure during the peak of the crisis, particularly following the Lehman crash.

The first impact fell on the Indian money market. In fact, while Lehman Brothers filed for bankruptcy on 15 September (Monday), financial markets were quite jittery during the week before. After 15 September, there was great instability in the call money market in India which had overshot the RBI's informal corridor defined by the repo and reverse repo rate. Moreover, the money market quickly transformed from a surplus to a deficit mode so much so that the net amount under liquidity adjustment facility (LAF) registered a quantum leap from around Rs 1,000 crore on 8

September 2008 to around Rs 20,000 crore on 8 October (see Chart 7.1).[5] However, by the end of October, the money market stabilized and called money rates came back within the corridor.

Downward sentiment was noticeable in the stock market as well. With increased uncertainty in the stock market, there was a lull in the primary market during the second half of 2008–9 with the number of initial public offerings (IPOs) as well as the amount mobilized through American Depository Receipts/Global Depository Receipts (ADR/ GDR) nose-diving during the second half of 2008–9. Activities in the secondary market too suffered through lack of interest from the FIIs and mutual funds.

External Sector Channels

Expectedly, the crisis was transmitted through the external channels. This was manifested in a number of ways. First, the crisis led to a sharp shrinkage in the demand for exports along with moderation in domestic demand especially during the second half of 2008–9. The impact of the global financial crisis was mostly felt in the exports sector. While during 2008–9, growth in exports was robust till August 2008, in September 2008, immediately after the fall of Lehman Brothers, export growth registered a sharp dip and turned negative in October 2008. It remained negative till the end of 2008–9. Though export of services was less affected than merchandise exports, in both the third and fourth quarter of 2008, the current account deficit was phenomenally high and crossed the $10 billion mark.

Second, during the crisis, there were outflows on account of foreign investment. While foreign direct investment slowed down, there were

---

[5] Aziz et al. (2008) traced the pressure on money market to two factors. First, prior to the financial crisis, a number of Indian multinationals (both financial and non-financial) established global treasury operations in London primarily for fund raising and when the London Interbank Offered Rate (LIBOR) rose sharply, cost of borrowing for these firms went up that prompted them to borrow in the Indian short-term money market. Second, with the increasing tightness of the Indian money market, there was redemption pressure on the mutual funds in which a number of local firms placed a significant amount of short-term funds (both debt and equity) because of their tax advantage status. This pressure was felt mostly on some of the non-bank finance companies and real estate companies.

(a) Call Rate, Repo, and Reverse Repo Rate

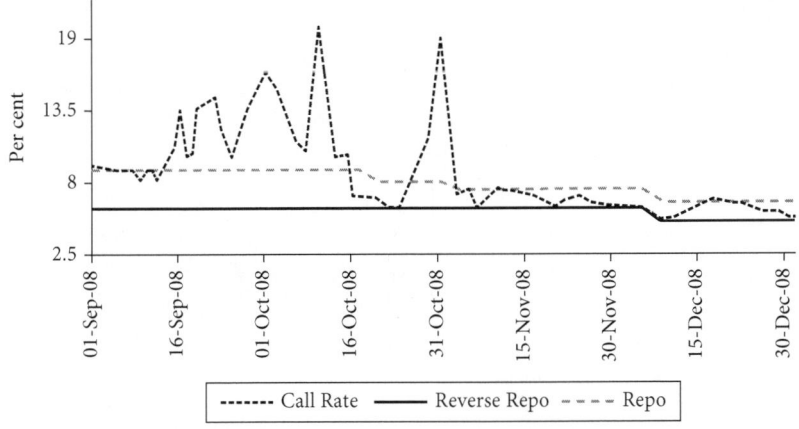

(b) Net LAF

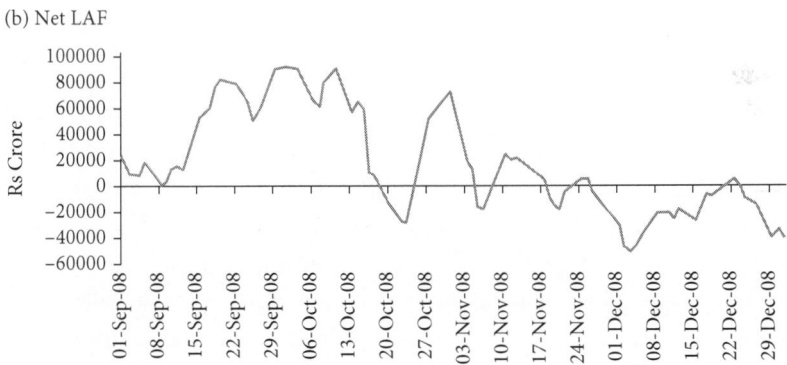

Chart 7.1 Impact on the Money Market

Source: World Economic Outlook database, IMF, October 2023.

substantial outflows in foreign portfolio investment amounting to nearly $6 billion during the fourth quarter of 2008, reflecting the usual syndrome of *flight to familiarity*. The withdrawal of FIIs also impacted the stock market adversely.

Third, over the years, Indian corporates began accessing global credit markets and hence there was a substantial increase in loans—both on account of external commercial borrowing as well as trade credit. The financial crisis affected capital flows on both these counts. In fact, as a result of the increase in counterparty risks and erosion of faith within the financial sector worldwide, trade credit suffered. In India too, it registered a massive contraction of more than $4.2 billion during the fourth quarter of 2008—this trend continued during the first half of 2009 as well. Trade credit, in fact, emerged as one of the key channels through which trade flows got affected worldwide. External commercial borrowing started receding with a lag. By the second quarter of 2009 it started experiencing a contraction.

Impact on the Real Sector

Growth was affected ultimately. Illustratively, while GDP growth during the first half of 2008–9 was 7.8 per cent, in the second half of 2008–9 it decelerated to 5.8 per cent. In fact, during 2008–9 the Indian economy grew at 6.7 per cent, which was way below the 9 per cent plus growth rate experienced during the previous three years (2005–6 through 2007–8).

Industrial growth decelerated significantly in the first half of 2008–9 from a high level during the past three years as a result of spillover effects of the global crisis penetrating through trade and financial channels. The decline in industrial growth was higher than the deceleration in overall growth and, accordingly, the relative contribution of the industrial sector in GDP also declined considerably during 2008–9. On the other hand, the services sector experienced moderate slowdown in growth compared to industry during 2008–9 and its relative contribution in GDP improved.

The impact on the industrial and services sectors was amplified in the second half of 2008–9 with overall contraction in merchandise exports and deceleration in the growth of services exports along with shattered confidence reinforcing the adverse effects stemming from the financial channel. During this period again, the deceleration in growth was more severe in the industrial sector than the services sector, as manufacturing exports, which contribute a large part to industrial sector demand, contracted sharply on the back of a sharp fall in the spending of the advanced economies on consumer durables. It may, however, be mentioned that services sector growth continued to decelerate during 2009–10, whereas industrial growth revived significantly.

Corporate Performance

The impact on private sector corporates became more pronounced from the third quarter of 2008–9 on the back of accentuating disruptions in international financial markets that eventually mutated into a world recession or economic slowdown. Tight domestic and foreign liquidity resulted in steep escalation in the cost of funds as well as reduced accessibility. On the other hand, the recession in advanced economies pulled down the demand for Indian corporates as manifested by contracting exports since October 2008. The uncertainty prevailing in the world economy also dampened investor confidence and, hence, private corporates were hesitant to undertake fresh investments. All these factors dampened both domestic and external demand, availability of funds, and investment prospects and were reflected in the subdued performance of private sector corporates during the second half of 2008–9.

Faced with such a situation, India, like other countries, undertook policy intervention on multiple fronts, spanning primarily over monetary and fiscal stimulus. The next two sections deal with the nature, composition, and quantum of these stimulus packages.[6]

Monetary Responses during the Global Financial Crisis

It is useful to recall that when the global financial crisis hit India, the RBI was pursuing a contractionary monetary policy for inflation control. Non-food inflation for both 2007–8 and 2008–9 crossed the 10 per cent mark and the RBI was increasing the repo rate steadily from 6.25 per cent in October 2005 to 9 per cent in October 2008. Thus, with the fallout of the global financial crisis, the RBI had to change its monetary policy stance midway. In fact, the Annual Report for 2008–9 (p. 6) of the RBI noted categorically:

> The high growth in credit and broad money in 2004–8 was taken cognisance of by the Reserve Bank and its policy response gradually turned

---

[6] See Subbarao (2008) and RBI (2010) for details on monetary stimulus in India.

Table 7.2 Liquidity Injection/Availability during September 2008–9

Measure/Facility	Amount (Rs crore)	Percentage of GDP (2008–9)
1. CRR Reduction	1,60,000	2.9
2. Unwinding/Buyback/De-sequestering of MSS Securities	1,59,044	2.9
3. Open Market Operations (Purchases) *	1,04,128	1.9
4. Term Repo Facility	60,000	1.1
5. Increase in Export Credit Refinance	22,328	0.4
6. Special Refinance Facility for SCBs (Non-RRBs)	38,500	0.7
7. Refinance Facility for SIDBI/ NHB/EXIM Bank	16,000	0.3
8. Liquidity Facility for NBFCs through SPV**	25,000	0.4
9. Total (1 to 8)	**5,85,000**	**10.5**
Memo: Statutory Liquidity Ratio (SLR) Reduction	40,000	0.7

Source: Report on Currency and Finance, RBI 2010, p. 237.

Note: * Includes Rs 57,487 crore of open market operations (OMO) purchases against the proposed OMO purchases of Rs 80,000 crore during the first half of 2009–10.

** Includes an option of Rs 5,000 crore.

to modulating the monetary overhang, without restricting the growth in credit and money that was necessary for sustaining the high growth. Reflecting the cautious monetary stance, the *repo* and *reverse repo* rates were raised gradually since September 2004, along with higher reserve requirements. The tightening stance had to be pursued more aggressively in the first half of 2008–9 to contain the building inflationary pressures. *Reflecting the moderation in growth in the second half and the contraction in aggregate demand, non-food bank credit ... fell to 17.5 per cent by end-March 2009. Part of the high growth in credit up to October 2008 reflected the shift in the pattern of resource mobilisation by the corporates in the face of emerging global credit squeeze.*

The external funding was partly substituted by resort to domestic credit ... Credit extended by private and foreign banks exhibited much sharper deceleration in growth in relation to the nationalised banks. More importantly, flow of resources from non-banking avenues (such as from the capital market, non-banking finance companies, ECBs, FCCBs, ADRs/GDRs and FDI) also fell by about 20 per cent over the level in the previous year. *Relaxing all constraints on the expansion in credit at lower cost without dilution of the emphasis on asset quality emerged as a major challenge for the Reserve Bank* ... The Reserve Bank ensured ample surplus liquidity in the system to ensure flow of credit to productive sectors, within the prudence necessary for preserving the asset quality of the banks. (*Annual Report 2008–9, RBI*; para 1.12; emphasis ours)

The essence of the monetary stimulus was initiation of measures for 'infusing rupee as well as foreign exchange liquidity' as well as maintaining 'credit flow to productive sectors of the economy' (Subbarao 2008).

First, under pure monetary measures, the policy repo rate was reduced by 425 basis points from 9 per cent to 4.75 per cent and the reverse repo cut by 275 basis points from 6 per cent to 3.25 per cent during December 2008–April 2009. Since the period witnessed a change of liquidity conditions from a surplus mode to a deficit situation, in effective terms the policy rate witnessed a cut of 575 basis points from 9 per cent in mid-September 2008 to 3.25 per cent in April 2009 (RBI 2010).

Second, as far as domestic liquidity condition is concerned, the cash reserve ratio (CRR) was reduced from 9 per cent (September 2008) to 5 per cent by early January 2009, injecting nearly Rs 1,60,000 crore of primary liquidity in the system. The statutory liquidity ratio (SLR) too was cut by 1 percentage point from 25 to 24 per cent in November 2008. Besides, special refinance facility was introduced for all commercial banks for extending finance to small and medium enterprises on 24 October 2008, which was discontinued in October 2009. As far as mutual funds and housing finance companies were concerned, a term repo facility for Rs 60,000 crore under the LAF was introduced to enable commercial banks to on-lend to these sectors; this facility was discontinued in October 2009. Fresh issuances of securities under the Market

Stabilisation Scheme (MSS) were stopped and buy-back of existing MSS securities was also used to inject liquidity into the system.

As a result of all these measures, nearly Rs 5,85,000 crore of liquidity was injected into the system during the period September 2008–9; this was slightly more than 10 per cent of GDP of 2008–9 (see Table 7.2). This is, however, a measure of *potential* liquidity injection. In actuality, the amount of liquidity injection was lower. In fact, as a consequence of the monetary stimulus, 'the banking system has been awash with liquidity since November 2008' (RBI, *Second Quarter Review of Monetary Policy for the Year 2009–10*, 27 October 2009). The LAF window moved to an absorption mode of a daily average of almost Rs 1,20,000 crore and the utilization of the several refinance facilities (such as Term Repo Facility, Special Refinance Facility for banks, refinance facility for SIDBI/NHB/ EXIM Bank, and liquidity facility for Non-Banking Financial Companies [NBFCs] through Special Purpose Vehicles [SPVs]) instituted by the RBI too has been low. Of course, it is well known that assurance of liquidity tends to help moderate the actual demand for liquidity—the fact that the Central Bank's assurance is there is sufficient to stabilize the market. This is the standard communication/confidence channel of monetary transmission.

As far as the measures to augment forex liquidity are concerned, a number of measures were initiated (RBI 2010). First, interest rate ceilings on non-resident deposits [namely, Foreign Currency Non-Resident (Bank) or FCNR(B) and Non-Resident (External) Rupee Account or NR(E)RA] were increased by 175 basis points each from 16 September 2008. Second, the policy regime for external commercial borrowings were relaxed through various means, such as enhancing all-in-cost ceilings for ECBs;[7] permitting ECBs up to $500 million per borrower per financial year under the automatic route; and expansion of the definition of infrastructure sector for availing ECB to include the mining, exploration, and refinery sectors. Third, access to short-term trade credit was facilitated by increasing the all-in-cost ceiling to six-month LIBOR plus 200 basis points for less than three years' tenor. Fourth, systemically

---

[7] The revised ceilings were as follows: 300 basis points above LIBOR (for average maturity periods of three to five years) and 500 basis points above LIBOR (for over five years).

important NBFCs were permitted to raise short-term foreign borrowings. Fifth, interest rate ceiling on export credit in foreign currency was increased to LIBOR plus 350 basis points.

The culmination of all these measures boosted the domestic and forex liquidity in the Indian financial system and stabilized various segments of the financial system. In fact, by March 2010, the RBI was back to inflation control mode and started pursuing a tight money policy by increasing its repo rate and reverse repo by 50 basis points each.

There are some key differences between the monetary stimulus measures undertaken in India vis-à-vis those of many advanced countries (Mohanty 2011). First, unlike the mortgage securities and commercial papers in the advanced economies, the range of collaterals was not expanded beyond government securities. Second, the RBI's balance sheet did not show unusual increase because of release of earlier sterilized liquidity. Third, pro-cyclical provisioning norms and countercyclical regulations helped safeguard financial stability. Finally, fiscal stimulus was geared to address deficiency in aggregate demand rather than supporting the financial sector as was the case in the advanced economies.

Monetary Stimulus and the Pandemic

In the wake of the pandemic, the RBI deployed both conventional and unconventional policy instruments for fostering three objectives of (a) providing liquidity, (b) promoting growth, and (c) ensuring financial stability. The measures effectively expanded liquidity 'in the system to ensure that financial markets and institutions can function normally in the face of COVID-related dislocations' (RBI 2022).[8] Various liquidity measures were initiated, the total of the availed measures amounted to 6 per cent of GDP.

---

[8] Reserve Bank of India, 2022. 'Monetary and Fiscal Policy Interactions in the Wake of the Pandemic', BIS Papers chapters, in: Bank for International Settlements (ed.), 'The Monetary-fiscal Policy Nexus in the Wake of the Pandemic', volume 122, pp. 149–157, Bank for International Settlements.

Table 7.3 Pandemic-related Liquidity Measures (INR Billion)

	(During February 2020 to March 2022)		
No.	Liquidity Facility	Announced	Availed
1	LTRO	2,000	1,251
2	Variable rate repo	2,250	900
3	SLF for PDs	72	60
4	CRR cut	1,370	1,370
5	MSF (dip by additional 1% in SLR)	1,370	-
6	TLTRO	1,000	1,001
7	TLTRO (2.0)	500	129
8	Net OMO purchases + G-SAP	3,700	5,703
9	Special liquidity facility for mutual funds	500	24
10	Refinance to NABARD, SIDBI and NHB, and EXIM Bank	1,410	1,298
11	Special liquidity scheme for NBFCs	300	71
12	56-day term repo	1,000	10
13	On tap TLTRO	1,000	90
14	SLTRO for small finance banks	100	31
15	On tap liquidity for emergency health services	500	–
16	On tap liquidity window for contact-intensive sectors	150	–
17	Total	17,222	11,937
18	*As percentage of nominal GDP for 2020–21*	*8.7*	*6.0*

Legends: LTRO: Long-term Repo Operation; SLF: Special Liquidity Facility; CRR: Cash Reserve Ratio; TLTRO: Targeted Long-term Repo Operations; MSF: Marginal Standing Facility; OMO: Open Market Operation; SLTRO: Special Long-term Repo Operations (SLTRO).

* Maximum during the period.

Source: Patra and Bhattacharyya (2022).

Fiscal Stimulus

It is worth noting that 2009 was an election year for India and hence, initially on 16 February 2009 the interim Budget for 2009–10 was placed; subsequently, the regular budget was presented on 6 July 2009. Following the intensification of the global crisis after the fall of Lehman Brothers in September 2008, India undertook three quick successive fiscal stimuli and three Supplementary Demands for Grants were approved by the

Parliament in October 2008, December 2008, and February 2009, respectively. These stimulus packages were primarily tax relief and increased expenditure on public projects to create employment and public assets (Government of India, *Economic Survey, 2008–9*). Generically, these measures can be subdivided under three broad heads: (a) revenue, (b) expenditure, and (c) unconventional measures.

First, in terms of revenue measures, central value added tax (CENVAT) was cut by 4 percentage points (excluding petroleum products) amounting to Rs 8,700 crore loss for the government (0.2 per cent of GDP). Besides, import duties on selected products were reinstated and accelerated depreciation of 50 per cent was introduced for vehicles purchased in January–March 2009.

Second, as far as expenditure is concerned, spending was enhanced on various items, such as housing, infrastructure, irrigation, textiles, rural employment, and social assistance schemes (0.4 per cent of GDP); for example, a Rs 4,000 crore refinance facility was introduced for National Housing Bank. Besides, a limit on market borrowing by states to finance capital expenditure was raised. Finally, for export promotion interest, a subsidy of 2 per cent was introduced for export credit for labour intensive exports (until March 2009). Duty drawback benefits were enhanced.

Third, a number of unconventional measures were adopted, for example, public sector banks were sought to be recapitalized by an additional 0.4 per cent of GDP over the next two years. Besides, there were off-budgetary measures in the form of allowing the India Infrastructure Finance Company Limited (IIFCL) to raise Rs 4,000 crore (0.8 per cent of GDP) over the next 18 months (IMF 2009b).

Interestingly, apart from these three stimulus packages, two other developments took place which had significant fiscal implications. First, a scheme of agricultural debt waiver and debt relief for farmers was announced in the Union Budget for 2008–9 before the crisis hit India.[9] The amounts under the debt waiver scheme were reimbursed in instalments with the central government releasing Rs 40,000 crore under this scheme. Second, the Sixth Pay Commission constituted by the

---

[9] The limits for debt waiver were as follows: the total estimated value of overdue loans being waived at Rs 50,000 crore and a one-time settlement (OTS) relief on the overdue loans at Rs 10,000 crore, for implementation by all scheduled commercial banks, local area banks, regional rural banks, and cooperative credit institutions.

Government of India for central government employees submitted its report on 24 March 2008; a number of states announced their decision to follow the recommendations of the Sixth Pay Commission. Thus, pay commission awards had implications for both central and states' fiscal health.[10] Interestingly, both these developments took place in the first half of 2008, that is, before the fall of Lehman Brothers. A recent working paper from the Ministry of Finance had put it succinctly, '*Somewhat serendipitously*, the government already had an expansionary fiscal stance in view of a rural farm loan waiver scheme, the expansion of social security schemes under the National Rural Employment Guarantee Act (NREGA) and the implementation of revised salaries and compensations for the central public servants as per the recommendations of the Sixth Pay Commission' (De 2012; emphasis ours). Furthermore, the 2009 parliamentary elections could have resulted in further government expenditures, as has been pointed out: 'The huge increase in public expenditure in 2008–2009 of 31.2 per cent that followed a 27.4 per cent in 2007–2008 was driven by the electoral cycle with parliamentary elections scheduled within a year of the announcement of the budget' (Kumar and Soumya 2010).

What was the fiscal implication of all these schemes? It is pertinent to turn to the *Economic Survey* of 2008–9 which noted:

To counter the negative fallout of the global slowdown on the Indian economy, the Government responded by providing a substantial fiscal expansion . . . The net result was an increase in fiscal deficit from 2.7 per cent in 2007–08 to 6.2 per cent of GDP in 2008–09. The difference between the actuals of 2007–08 and 2008–09 constituted the total fiscal stimulus, notwithstanding the fact that some expenditure was on account of the implementation of the Sixth Pay Commission award and the agriculture debt relief scheme (small farmers' debt waiver) announced in the Union Budget 2008–09. *Together about 0.5 per cent of*

---

[10] This apart, the National Rural Employment Guarantee Act (NREGA), enacted in 2005 to provide a minimum guaranteed wage employment of 100 days in every fiscal year to rural households with unemployed adult members prepared to do unskilled manual work could have added some fiscal strain. See Chakraborty (2007) for a contrary view.

the GDP was committed prior to the dramatic deterioration of the international financial markets in September 2008. (Economic Survey 2008–9, p. 21; emphasis ours)

Due to the sharp revenue contraction because of prolonged lockdown in order to combat the spread of COVID-19 and various expenditure-side stimulus measures, the fiscal deficits for the centre and states have recently soared.

Recovery and Exit Policies of the Monetary and Fiscal Stimuli during the Global Financial Crisis

The issue of exit is intimately interlinked with any stimulus package. What has been the experience of Indian fiscal and monetary stimulus in this regard?

The conduct of monetary policy during 2009–10 shifted gear from 'managing the crisis' to 'managing the recovery' (RBI 2010). Illustratively, the SLR was restored to 25 per cent with effect from 7 November 2009. Besides, the limit for export credit refinance facility, which was raised to 50 per cent of eligible outstanding export credit, was returned to the pre-crisis level of 15 per cent. Effectively, by early 2010, the RBI was back to inflation control with active pursuit of a contractionary monetary policy whereby the repo rate was raised by 25 basis points from 5 per cent to 5.25 per cent on 10 April 2010 and the CRR was increased by 75 basis points from 5 per cent to 5.75 per cent in two stages in February 2010. The exit path of fiscal policy was somewhat different from that of monetary policy mentioned above. The year 2008–9 witnessed gross fiscal deficit (GFD) of 6 per cent of GDP against the budgeted deficit of 2.5 per cent. The net market borrowings turned out to be Rs 2.34 trillion against the budgeted level of Rs 1 trillion; consequently, the 10-year benchmark yield on G-Sec rose from 5 per cent at end-December 2008 to 7 per cent by end March 2009. While fiscal marksmanship was better both in 2009–10 and 2010–11 (primarily on the account of a one-off revenue windfall through spectrum auctions and divestments), fiscal policy slipped during 2011–12. In fact, the RBI *Report on Currency and Finance, 2009–12* noted candidly:

The fiscal-monetary co-ordination in the aftermath of the global financial crisis was accompanied by less co-ordination on how the fallout
of the stimulus might be handled. As a result, there were some uncoordinated responses during the period of exit from the stimulus. An
underfunded budget and the fiscal stimulus of 2008–09 left awry the
budgeting mathematics during the year. (RBI 2013)

Thus, unlike the observed coordination between monetary and fiscal
policies for stimulus as a response to the onset of the crisis, as far as exit
from stimulus is concerned, there are elements of asymmetry between
monetary and fiscal policy. While monetary policy (either by design
or by compulsion, that is, dictated by the demands of inflation control)
made conscious efforts towards exiting from stimulus measures, the path
of the exit from fiscal stimulus has been hesitant, delayed and, perhaps,
incomplete. It is conceivable that the fisc was less than transparent at the
relevant time and fiscal performance fell short of fiscal assumptions. In
order to appreciate the extent and the path of fiscal slippage in recent
years, a brief narration of the process of fiscal consolidation on the eve of
the crisis is in order.

Subsequently, in 2010–11, the monetary policy stance changed course
from 'calibrated normalisation to tightening driven by inflation concerns'
(RBI, Annual Report, 2010–11). The liquidity condition was largely in
deficit mode arising out of: (a) transient factors (such as advance tax collections), (b) frictional factors (large government surplus balances), and
(c) structural factors (i.e., high increase in currency in circulation and
higher credit growth relative to deposit growth). These were managed
through an appropriate mix of SLR, OMO, and LAF. Monetary policy
in 2011–12 changed its primary objective of mitigating inflation pressures during the first half of the financial year to addressing concerns
of a significant slowdown in domestic growth in the second half of the
financial year (RBI, Annual Report, 2011–12). Monetary policy stance
during 2012–13 aimed at calibrated easing in the face of 'a significant
growth slowdown, persistent inflationary pressures and rising macroeconomic and financial vulnerabilities in the economy' (RBI, Annual
Report, 2012–13). During June–August 2013, monetary policy also had
to face the challenge of considerable depreciation in the exchange rate of
the rupee.

Fiscal Consolidation Efforts in India

Fiscal Trends since the 1990s

Fiscal roots of the Indian economic crisis of the early 1990s are well known.[11] Accordingly, the reform measures undertaken since 1991 had a distinct fiscal component. Measures like cessation of automatic monetization of budget deficit and the resultant signing of the agreement between the Government of India and the RBI, a number of measures towards improvement in tax administration and cutting current spending were undertaken. Consequently, the combined fiscal deficit (i.e., both of the central and the state governments) improved to little over 6 per cent by 1996–7. However, these trends were short lived, and by 2001–2 the combined fiscal deficit was about to touch the 10 per cent mark. Consequently, the period 1991–2002 has been seen in terms of 'resurgence of deficits in the 1990s' (Dasgupta and De 2012). Some are of the view that fiscal correction was inadequate to redress the 'profligacy of the 1980s' and that fiscal adjustment underway since 1991 was not able to eliminate the 'spectre of insolvency' (Buiter and Patel 1997).

However, the enactment of the Fiscal Responsibility and Budget Management (FRBM) Act, 2003 and the consequent FRBM rules (which became operational on 5 July 2004) was a major positive step towards fiscal consolidation in India. Under this Act, the central government was mandated to eliminate revenue deficit and to reduce fiscal deficit to 3 per cent of GDP by March 2009. The FRBM Rules 2004 specified, 'reduction of revenue deficit by 0.5 per cent of GDP or more and reduction of gross fiscal deficit by 0.3 per cent or more every year ... progressive reduction of this limit by at least one percentage point of GDP in each subsequent year; and no central government guarantee in excess of 0.5 per cent of GDP in any financial year' (Chidambaram 2012, p. 244).

In some sense, the period 2003 through 2007–8 can be seen as an illustration of 'successful fiscal consolidation' (Dasgupta and De 2012) as can be seen from the following facts. First, during the four-year period covering 2004–5 through 2007–8, the fiscal deficit came down from 4.5

---

[11] For example, it has been observed: 'The major mistake of macroeconomic policy lay in neglecting the danger signs evident in 1985/86 on the fiscal front' (Joshi and Little 1994, p. 190).

per cent in 2003–4 to 2.7 per cent in 2007–8 and the revenue deficit declined from 3.6 per cent to 1.1 per cent. Second, the states' GFD came down to 1.53 per cent of GDP in 2007–8 with a revenue surplus of 0.87 per cent from a fiscal deficit of 4.38 per cent and a revenue deficit of 2.3 per cent of GDP in 2003–4. Third, the combined central and state GFD thus fell to 4.12 per cent with a combined revenue deficit of 0.19 per cent of GDP.

Apart from the enactment of the central FRBM Act in August 2003, there are other dimensions of fiscal reforms in India during this period. First, a system of VAT was adopted by nearly all the states and by the centre by 2004. Second, specific measures towards improvement of tax administration and widening the tax base were initiated. Third, following the agreed FRBM Act, expenditure on subsidies and other current spending was sought to be controlled, not only at the centre, but also at the state level (Dasgupta and De 2012). More importantly, as the Finance Minister pointed out in his interim budget speech of February 2009:

The buoyant growth of Government revenues facilitated fiscal consolidation as mandated in the FRBM Act (Chart 7.2). The tax to GDP ratio increased from 9.2 per cent in 2003–4 to 12.5 per cent in 2007–8

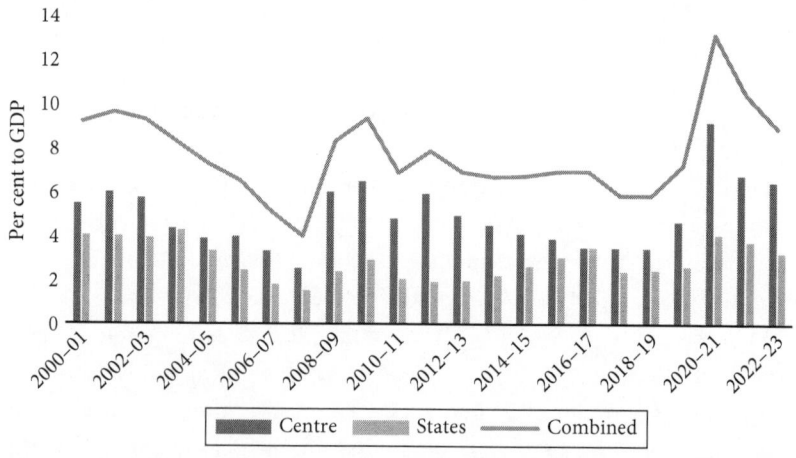

Chart 7.2 GFD of the Centre, of the States, and Combined (Percentage of GDP)

Source: *Handbook of Statistics on the Indian Economy*, RBI, 2022–23.

bringing us within striking distance of the target for fiscal correction. This also enhanced our capacity to raise resources internally to finance our growth at the rate of 9 per cent per annum during the Eleventh Five Year Plan.

Crisis Management and Derailment of Fiscal Consolidation

However, as already noted, efforts towards fiscal consolidation got derailed in tackling the impact of the global financial crisis on the Indian economy. Admittedly, there are divergent views about the appropriateness of the 2008 component of fiscal stimulus. Illustratively, there is a prevalent view: 'luckily for India, its electoral cycle pushed up public expenditure and coincided with the global recession, helping India overcome the negative impact of the crisis' (Kumar and Soumya 2010, p. 20).

There is a contrarian view that there were signs of the Indian economy losing steam long before the outbreak of the global crisis. Rakshit (2009) in fact stated categorically:

India's gross domestic product (GDP) growth . . . had started decelerating in the first quarter of 2007–08 . . . nearly six months before the outbreak of the US financial turbulence and considerably ahead of the surge of recessionary tendencies in all developed countries from August–September 2008. That the beginning of the deceleration of the Indian economy predates the global meltdown is also attested to by the sharply downward trend since March 2007 of the year-on-year (y-o-y) rise in the index of industrial production (IIP), the bellwether of the country's economic performance . . . Indeed, the slowdown in industries during 2007–08 was much more pronounced than that in GDP growth; while the latter registered a 0.5 percentage fall (to 9.2 per cent) from the earlier year, the decline in industrial GDP amounted to as much as 3.1 percentage points. (pp. 94–5)

After the general elections (held during April and May 2009), the second UPA government took office in end-May 2009 and the final budget for 2009–10 was presented on 6 July 2009. Though the Finance Minister in his budget speech of 6 July 2009 explicitly mentioned his desire to return to the FRBM target for fiscal deficit, 'as soon as the negative effect of the global crisis on the Indian economy has been overcome', in broad terms, this budget was a continuation of the fiscally stimulating budget with fiscal deficit as a percentage of GDP projected at 6.8 per cent compared to 6.2 per cent in the provisional accounts of 2008–9. The budget for 2010–11 was presented taking into account the explicit recommendation of the Thirteenth Finance Commission.

Retrospectively, against a fiscal deficit of 7.8 per cent in 2008–9 (inclusive of oil and fertilizer bonds), the comparable fiscal deficit turned out to be 6.9 per cent as per the Revised Estimates for 2009–10. The fiscal deficit for 2010–11 was budgeted at a much lower level of 5.5 per cent of GDP in 2010–11. Actual outturn emerged much better at 4.7 per cent of GDP. Compared with a GFD of 6.4 per cent of GDP in 2009–10, this was indeed a marked improvement. Was it temporary or permanent? It is interesting to turn to the RBI Annual Report for 2011–12, which stated:

> A qualitative assessment of fiscal correction during 2010–11, however, raises concerns. Not only did the correction in revenue account reflect more than anticipated non-tax revenues from spectrum auctions, there has been a spillover of subsidy expenditure from the last quarter of 2010–11 to the current fiscal year . . . Improved fiscal position had a large temporary component arising from a business cycle upswing and one-off revenue gains . . . Not counting for the revenue proceeds of two main one-off items—spectrum auction and the disinvestment—the GFD/GDP ratio works out to be 6.3 per cent of GDP during 2010–11. Also, revenue buoyancy was supported by a cyclical upswing that led to above trend growth. So the one-off gains and higher growth in nominal GDP of 20 per cent against the budgeted 12.5 per cent contributed largely to lower deficits, while the permanent component of fiscal consolidation was rather weak. Clearly, a more enduring fiscal consolidation strategy . . . needs to be put into place without any further delay.

For 2011–12, the fiscal deficit was projected at 4.6 per cent of GDP. The reality turned out to be different and the revised estimates for fiscal deficit for 2011–12 stood at 5.9 per cent of GDP; for 2012–13 the fiscal deficit is budgeted at 5.1 per cent of GDP.[12] Was it an instance of poor fiscal marksmanship or was the situation different? One can turn to the Finance Minister's Budget speech for 2012–13, which stated:

> Our fiscal balance has deteriorated in 2011–12 due to slippage in direct tax revenue and increased subsidies. On both counts our underlying assumptions at the time of Budget presentation last year were belied by subsequent developments. The profit margins came under pressure due to higher interest rates and material costs. This impacted growth in corporate taxes. Further, as against an assumption of US Dollar 90 a barrel, the average price of crude oil in 2011–12 is likely to exceed US Dollar 115. This has necessitated higher outlay on subsidies than projected. The continuing uncertainty in the global environment makes it necessary for us to strike a balance between fiscal consolidation and strengthening macroeconomic fundamentals to create adequate headroom to deal with future shocks. (Para 16)

It needs to be noted that some of the factors mentioned as responsible for fiscal slippage (or delayed exit from the fiscal stimulus) like slippage in direct tax revenue or increased subsidies are essentially home-grown conditions and may have less to do with the global situation of euro area debt crisis.[13]

States' Finances

There has been remarkable improvement in the consolidated fiscal position of the state governments since the mid-2000s. In fact, the period 2004–5 through 2007–8 witnessed almost zero revenue deficits for all the states on a consolidated basis; despite the onslaught of the global financial

---

[12] The total debt stock at the end of 2012–13 is worked out at 45.5 per cent of GDP as compared to the TFC target of 50.5 per cent of GDP.

[13] Having accepted the main recommendations of the Kelkar Report, in the Budget of 2013–14, the Finance Minister had made the following announcements: (a) the fiscal deficit for 2012–13 has been contained at 5.2 per cent; (b) the fiscal deficit for 2013–14 is estimated at 4.8 per cent; (c) the revenue deficit for 2012–13 will be 3.9 per cent; (d) the revenue deficit for the year 2013–14 is estimated at 3.3 per cent; (e) by 2016–17 the fiscal deficit will be brought down to 3 per cent, the revenue deficit to 1.5 per cent, and the effective revenue deficit to 0.

Table 7.4 Key Fiscal Indicators of States

	2004–05	2007–08	2008–09	2012–13	2017–18	2020–21
Revenue Deficit / GDP	1.21	−0.86	−0.23	−0.20	0.11	1.87
Fiscal Deficit / GDP	3.32	1.51	2.39	1.97	2.40	4.06
Primary Deficit / GDP	0.66	−0.49	0.56	0.45	0.69	2.11
Interest Payments / Revenue Receipts	23.77	16.01	14.82	12.02	12.63	14.96
Outstanding Debt / GDP	31.28	26.63	26.11	22.23	25.12	31.04

Source: RBI, State Finances: A Study of Budgets of 2012–13, RBI Bulletin, January 2012.

crisis states have been able to maintain fiscal health (see Table 7.4). In order to combat the unforeseen outbreak of the COVID-19 pandemic, the central government as well as the state governments provided considerable fiscal stimulus as a measure of countercyclical expansionary fiscal policy to boost aggregate demand in the economy, and thereby, the revenue deficit got inflated in recent times.

This may be attributed to initiation of state-level fiscal reforms since the mid-2000s. Introduction of state-level VAT, enactment of state-level FRBM legislations and related incentives provided in the Twelfth Finance Commission were all positive steps in this direction. In fact, by 2005, almost all the states enacted fiscal responsibility legislations and by 2008 almost all of them introduced VAT. Besides, new pension schemes were introduced and ceilings on guarantees were imposed (see Table 7.5). Furthermore, factors such as higher share in central transfers (as a follow-up of the recommendations of the Twelfth Finance Commission), states' own efforts at revenue augmentation, and rationalization of revenue expenditure all added to fiscal health of the states (Gopinath 2009).

An important development in this regard is the market flotation of states' loans. Interestingly, as small savings collections increased sharply during this period and states had to absorb the predominant share of small savings collections earmarked to them, their recourse to market borrowings declined substantially. By 2006–7, the states were allowed to raise market borrowings entirely through the auction route to allow market determination of yields on their loans (RBI 2013).

Table 7.5 Institutional Fiscal Reforms by State Governments in India

State	Value Added Tax (VAT) Implemented	Fiscal Responsibility Legislation (FRL) Enacted#	New Pension Scheme (NPS) Introduced	Ceilings on Guarantee Imposed	Consolidated Sinking Fund (CSF) Set Up*	Guarantee Redemption Fund (GRF) Set Up*
Andhra Pradesh	Apr-05	Jun-05	Sep-04	Yes	Yes	Yes
Arunachal Pradesh	Apr-05	Mar-06	Jan-08	Yes	Yes	No
Assam	May-05	Sep-05	Feb-05	Yes	Yes	No
Bihar	Apr-05	Apr-06	Sep-05	Yes	Yes	No
Chhattisgarh	Apr-06	Sep-05	Nov-04	Yes	Yes	No
Goa	Apr-05	May-06	Aug-05	Yes	Yes	Yes
Gujarat	Apr-06	Mar-05	Apr-05	Yes	Yes	Yes
Haryana	Apr-03	Jul-05	Jan-06	Yes	Yes	Yes
Himachal Pradesh	Apr-05	Apr-05	May-03	Yes	No	No
Jammu & Kashmir	Apr-05	Aug-06	Jan-10	No	No	No
Jharkhand	Apr-06	May-07	Dec-04	No	No	No
Karnataka	Apr-05	Sep-02	Apr-06	Yes	No	No
Kerala	Apr-05	Aug-03	No	Yes	Yes	No
Madhya Pradesh	Apr-06	May-05	Jan-05	Yes	No	Yes
Maharashtra	Apr-05	Apr-05	Nov-05	Yes	Yes	No
Manipur	Jul-05	Aug-05	Jan-05	Yes	Yes	Yes
Meghalaya	Apr-06	Mar-06	Apr-10	Yes	Yes	No

(continued)

Table 7.5 Continued

State	Value Added Tax (VAT) Implemented	Fiscal Responsibility Legislation (FRL) Enacted#	New Pension Scheme (NPS) Introduced	Ceilings on Guarantee Imposed	Consolidated Sinking Fund (CSF) Set Up*	Guarantee Redemption Fund (GRF) Set Up*
Mizoram	Apr-05	Oct-06	Sep-10	Yes	Yes	Yes
Nagaland	Apr-05	Aug-05	Jan-10	Yes	Yes	Yes
Odisha	Apr-05	Jun-05	Jan-05	Yes	Yes	Yes
Punjab	Apr-05	Oct-03	Jan-04	Yes	No	No
Rajasthan	Apr-06	May-05	Jan-04	Yes	No	No
Sikkim	Apr-05	Sep-10	Apr-06	Yes	No	No
Tamil Nadu	Jan-07	May-03	Apr-03	Yes	Yes	No
Tripura	Oct-05	Jun-05	No	Yes	Yes	No
Uttarakhand	Oct-05	Oct-05	Oct-05	Yes	Yes	Yes
Uttar Pradesh	Jan-08	Feb-04	Apr-05	No	No	No
West Bengal	Apr-05	Jul-10	No	Yes	Yes	No

Source: State Finances: A Study of Budgets 2012–13, RBI.

Did the states' fiscal position suffer in the aftermath of the financial crisis? Admittedly, some states initiated fiscal stimulus packages to get the economy going by continuing various developmental and welfare programmes (Government of India, *Economic Survey*, 2008–9) and since 2008–9, there have been some interruptions in progress on fiscal consolidation at the states' level as well. The gross fiscal deficit of all the states increased from 1.5 per cent of the GDP in 2007–8 to 2.4 per cent in 2008–9 and further to 3.2 per cent of the GDP in 2009–10, reflecting inter alia slowdown in growth of revenues and the implementation of the Sixth Central/State Pay Commissions on expenditures.[14] The stimulus packages of the states contained both tax cuts and expenditure augmentation—perhaps with more emphasis on expenditure increases. A brief account of these stimulus measures is in order.

First, as far as tax cuts are concerned, only a few states initiated such measures. Illustratively, the Rajasthan government proposed measures like: (a) exemption from entry tax on inputs for the Micro, Small, and Medium Enterprises (MSMEs); (b) reduction in Central Sales Tax (CST) rate; and (c) exemption of 75 per cent of electricity duty for units located in rural areas. The Karnataka government extended VAT exemption available on food grain items like paddy, rice, wheat, and pulses till 2009–10.

Second, measures for expenditure augmentation were more prevalent at the states' level. While the aggregate capital outlay of the State Governments was budgeted to rise marginally by 1.9 per cent during 2009–10 as compared with 32.3 per cent in 2008–9 (RE [Revised Estimate]), the behaviour varied across states. Although some states like Andhra Pradesh, Rajasthan, Karnataka, and Jammu and Kashmir had not announced dedicated fiscal stimulus packages as countercyclical measures, a significantly higher capital outlay was budgeted in 2009–10 as compared with that in 2008–9. In contrast, a number of states, such as Gujarat, Maharashtra, Punjab, Bihar, Odisha, Assam, West Bengal, Jharkhand, Arunachal Pradesh, Himachal Pradesh, Manipur, Mizoram, and Sikkim budgeted a decline in their capital outlay during 2009–10.

---

[14] As part of the fiscal stimulus, the Central Government enhanced the borrowing limits of the State Governments and relaxed the targets by 100 basis points so that States could raise the GFD limit up to 4 per cent of GSDP during 2009–10 (RBI 2013).

Table 7.6 Major Deficit Indicators of the State Governments (Per cent to GDP)

	2008–10 (Average)	2010–11	2012–13	2017–18	2020–21
Revenue Deficit / GDP	0.1	–0.0	–0.2	0.1	1.9
Fiscal Deficit / GDP	2.7	2.1	2.0	2.4	4.1
Primary Deficit / GDP	0.9	0.5	0.5	0.7	2.1

Source: State Finances: A Study of Budgets, RBI (various years).
Note: Negative (–) sign indicates surplus.

The fiscal consolidation process of the states had resumed in 2010–11 after a setback in 2008–9 and 2009–10; but such a renewed effort was somewhat hampered by a slowdown in economic activities in 2011–12 (see Table 7.6). Consequently, 'the consolidated gross fiscal deficit which had declined significantly in 2010–11, increased marginally in 2017–18. However, most states have shown an increase in their fiscal deficit–GSDP ratio during 2020-21 due to the COVID-19 pandemic'.

Fiscal Situation: An Assessment

A few distinguishing characteristics of Indian fiscal can be noted. First, have the Fiscal Responsibility and Budget Management (FRBM) legislations created fiscal space in India? There are various ways in which the term *fiscal space* is used in the literature. A common understanding is in terms of the presence of a space for 'financing the deficit without either a sharp increase in funding costs or undue crowding out of private investment' (Ostry et al. 2010). With private investment on a downward trend, identification of fiscal space in the Indian context from this standpoint could be problematic. However, following Ostry et al. (2010), if fiscal space is identified as the difference between the current level of public debt and the debt limit implied by the country's historical record of fiscal adjustment, then without any marked increase in the debt profile, there is no denial of the fact that fiscal space was created as a result of effective implementation of the FRBM rules. This came handy in times of crisis and/or recession in India. Counterfactually, had the efforts towards

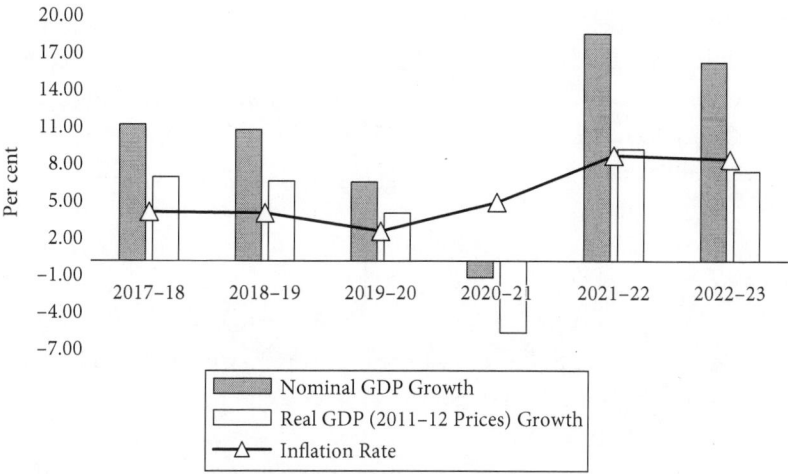

Chart 7.3 Real and Nominal GDP and Inflation Rate (Based on GDP Deflator)

Source: Handbook of Statistics on Indian Economy, 2022–23, RBI.

fiscal consolidation not been initiated, fiscal stimulus could have been macroeconomically costly.

Second, presence of high inflation since 2008–9 produced a bulge in the GDP at current market prices (the denominator in calculating the deficit indicators to GDP ratio) and consequently could have made the GFD–GDP ratio look smaller (relatively speaking). In order to decipher this effect, Chart 7.3 plots rates of nominal income growth (i.e., rate of growth of GDP at current market price) along with rate of growth of real GDP (at 2011–12 prices) and rate of inflation (derived from GDP deflator). The typical trend in recent years has been an increase in the rate of inflation, with or without being accompanied by an increase in real GDP growth. Thus, it seems that the substantial growth of nominal GDP could also be on account of an increase in inflation and part of the respectability of GFD–GDP ratio could be illusory in nature and have stemmed from the inflationary situation prevailing in the economy. In fact, in commenting on the revised lower estimates of fiscal deficit of the Central Government for 2010–11, the RBI Annual Report, 2010–11, ob-served that, 'Centre's lower deficit ratios reflect one-off unanticipated revenue and higher nominal GDP growth'. After all, the receipts from

3G/BWA spectrum auctions turned out to be Rs 1,06,262 crore, which was more than three times the budgeted expectations of Rs 35,000 crore.

Third, there is a view that the inertia in withdrawing stimulus subsequently could have led to a spike in inflation that prompted monetary policy tightening and dampened aggregate demand; gross private investment and private savings could have slowed as a result (Chan 2012). There are, thus, elements of structural weaknesses in the Indian fiscal situation; this could have constrained the fiscal space to a great extent. Where do all these trends lead us to? Was Indian fiscal stimulus too big and too early? Or, even if to begin with it was appropriate, could delay in exit have created complications in macroeconomics management? In order to answer these questions, the next two sections will quickly review major macro developments in two spheres, namely, (a) the financial sector, and (b) the external sector.

Financial Sector Stability

The chapter has already presented an account of the contagion as well as resilience of the Indian financial sector in the period immediately following the crisis, that is, post September 2008. What has been the situation in recent years? Standard financial stability indicators paint a situation of strength.

Aggregate capital-to-risk adjusted assets ratio (CRAR) at around 13 per cent (under Basel I) looks impressive. However, while Indian banks as a group are perceived to be well-capitalized, any bond is only as strong as its weakest link. In this context, sometimes there are apprehensions that while on the average Indian banks may be sound in terms of capital, there could be wide variations among different banks. Such apprehensions are not, however, borne out from the actual data. The distribution of commercial banks in terms of CRAR indicates that in the recent period there is no bank with CRAR less than 9 per cent. Non-performing assets (NPAs), though looking to be manageable, have registered a jump in between.

Besides, asset quality of banks has seen considerable deterioration during the half year ended September 2012 (RBI, Financial Stability Report, 2012). Of course, the stability of NPAs during the crisis was partly as a result of a relaxation of prudential norms whereby banks were allowed to restructure loans in the period October 2008–June 2009 without classifying them as non-performing. Admittedly, there is a natural tendency of NPA to rise after any crisis. In the Indian case, increase in NPAs of banks can be traced to factors such as switchover to system-based identification of NPAs by Public Sector Banks (PSBs), current macroeconomic situation in the country, increased interest rates in the recent past, lower economic growth, and aggressive lending by banks in the past, especially during good times (Government of India, *Economic Survey*, 2012–13). Already some initiatives have been taken by the authorities to handle the problem of NPAs; these include the proposal to increase provision for restructured standard accounts from the existing 2 per cent to 2.75 per cent or close watch on NPAs by picking up early warning signals and ensuring timely corrective steps by banks.

What is the relationship of the fiscal with the financial sector in this connection? The discussion will focus on two specific issues: (a) capital requirements of the Indian banking sector, and (b) presence of implicit sovereign guarantee.

Going forward, Indian banks are in need of capital, at least on account of moving to Basel III. Quick estimates released in the Financial Stability Report of the RBI (December 2012) placed the additional capital requirement of banks on account of Basel III at Rs 5 trillion, of which non-equity capital will be to the order of Rs 3.25 trillion while equity capital will be to the order of Rs 1.75 trillion. These are large numbers. The RBI further noted that, 'Additional challenges could be posed by the recent trends in asset quality of banks, regulatory changes in restructuring guidelines and the proposed implementation of dynamic provisioning norms that may increase the provisioning requirements of the banking sector'. However, while mentioning that 'additional capital requirements of banks' could pose some concerns, the RBI in its *Systemic Risk Survey* of October 2012 classified it as a low-risk event.

A number of concrete steps have been taken in this regard.[15] During 2011–12, Rs 12,000 crore was infused in seven PSBs to enable them to

---

[15] In passing, it may be recalled that as early as in 2009, during the heyday of the financial crisis, the World Bank sanctioned a loan to the Government of India for providing financial support for implementing the economic stimulus program. An important part of the overall stimulus programme is the provision of capital support to public sector banks. India's Banking

maintain a minimum Tier-I CRAR of 8 per cent. In 2012–13 also, the government has infused capital in PSBs to augment their Tier-I capital so that they maintain their Tier-I CRAR at a comfortable level and remain compliant with the stricter capital adequacy norms under BASEL III. For this purpose an amount of Rs 12,517 crore has been allocated in the REs 2012–13 under the Plan. The Budget, 2013–14 proposed to provide a further amount of Rs 14,000 crore for capital infusion in 2013–14.

However, the *Economic Survey, 2012–13* has rightly noted: 'Given the budgetary constraints, it may not be feasible for the government to infuse huge sums into the PSBs.' Hence, a High Level Committee to assess the capitalization of PSBs in the next 10 years (Chair: Finance Secretary) was formed, which has recommended the formation of a non-operating financial holding company under a special act of Parliament with the following key objectives: (a) to act as an investment company for the Government of India, (b) to hold a major portion of the Government of India's holdings in all PSBs, and (c) to raise long-term debt from domestic and international markets to infuse equity into PSBs. Going forward, the implementation of such measures will redefine the nature of relation between the fiscal and the financial sector.

India's predominant public ownership of the banking sector is another feature that can have fiscal implications. What has been the market performance of Indian public sector banks vis-à-vis private sector banks? Viral Acharya reports three important stylized facts in this context (Acharya 2012). First, if one measures the dynamics of the private sector banks vis-à-vis the public sector banks by the stock price differential, then there is evidence of substantial gains by the private banks till about January 2008. All such gains were almost entirely wiped out by the global financial crisis. Second, the difference in market reaction between the public and private sector banks can also be gauged from the widening of

Sector Support Loan was for a quantum of $3 billion programmatic operation with a first phase of $2 billion and was expected to provide budgetary support to the Government of India. (The details of the Banking Sector Support Loan to India are available at http://www.worldbank.org/projects/P116020/banking-sector-support-loan?lang = en.) The loan, requested in December 2008, was approved in September 2009 and was supposed to be disbursed in April 2010 but, 'it was apparently delayed at the request of the government' (Independent Evaluation Office, World Bank, 2012: *The World Bank Group's Response to the Global Economic Crisis*, available at http://ieg.worldbankgroup.org/content/dam/ieg/crisis/crisis2_full_report.pdf).

credit default swap (CDS) spreads for two illustrative firms, namely, State Bank of India (SBI) and ICICI Bank during the crisis of 2008. Third, deposit and credit growth of the private sector and foreign banks suffered vis-à-vis those of the PSBs.

Acharya (2012) sees such a relative underperformance of private sector banks during the crisis in terms of an implicit and explicit sovereign backing of public sector banks. He, thus, concludes, 'At any rate, examining the performance of state-owned banks in a systemic crisis relative to private sector banks, that have access to a weaker set of government guarantees, is not a sound basis of assessing the overall attractiveness of state presence in the financial sector' (p. 223).

Thus, going forward, these two issues may emerge as key to the link between the sovereign and banks. In particular, the creation of a holding company in the banking sector could increase leverage, but in the case of the public sector it may not decrease the overall public sector borrowing requirements. Further, a weak fiscal position with dominant public ownership in financial intermediation may result in intensification of transmission of risks between the two. Further, the implications of public sector banks holding more than half of the stock of government securities impacts the choices available for effective and efficient management of public debt.

External Sector

Finally, what has been the behaviour of the external sector? The indicators show some elements of slippage in external sector 2007 through 2012. The following stylized facts may be noted in particular.

First, there has been a huge increase in trade deficit—from around 4 per cent of GDP during 2000–1 through 2007–8 to little higher than 9 per cent of GDP during 2008–9 through 2011–12.

Second, these have been financed by a modest increase in the capital account. Within the capital account, two major items, namely foreign investment and loans, financed the current account deficit. Interestingly, while on average foreign investment turned out be mildly higher in recent years, there has been some volatility indicating uncertainty in the global markets. Expectedly, foreign portfolio investment has shown much volatility indicating symptoms of *flight to safety/familiarity* during any period of crisis.

Third, as far as external debt indicators are concerned, the proportion of concessional debt has been experiencing a secular decline. Nevertheless, some adverse developments are noticeable in the external debt sphere. Illustratively, short-term debt as percentage of total debt has gone up in the recent period, so has debt–service ratio.

Finally, the exchange rate of the rupee has indicated a two-way movement. This coupled with the prevalence of the current account deficit could be indicative of the fact that India is an atypical South Asian economy which did not contribute to global imbalance and which may not have systemic currency misalignment. Of course, in the recent period, the exchange rate has shown considerable volatility. In particular, following hints of tapering off of quantitative easing by the US Fed triggering substantial outflows on account of foreign institutional investment, the period June–August 2013 witnessed significant depreciation in the exchange rate of the rupee. While the rupee recovered subsequently following a series of measures by the Indian authorities and announcements regarding temporary postponement of tapering off decisions, to the extent the external account represents the fiscal position in an economy, these developments need to be watched carefully.

Fiscal Dominance and Implications for Monetary, Financial, and External Sectors

The issue of fiscal dominance in India is intimately interlinked with monetary and financial sectors (Reddy 2004) through two key channels. First, the continued fiscal dominance could warrant large involuntary financing of credit needs of Government by the RBI. Second, the predominance of publicly owned financial intermediaries and non-financial public enterprises, tends to blur the demarcation between funding of and by Government vis-à-vis the public sector as a whole.

Admittedly, with the cessation of automatic monetization, debarring the RBI in the primary auction of government securities, and enactment of the FRBM Act, the extent of fiscal dominance has come down in India in recent years. But, even without automatic monetization large fiscal deficits could have inflationary consequences. Illustratively, suppressed inflation arising from an administered price regime could remain a significant drag on inflation management. Furthermore, the story told so far tends to indicate return of fiscal dominance in the Indian economy during the post-crisis years. In such a situation, newer challenges have emerged, namely, (a) the inflationary potential of large fiscal deficits, (b) pro-cyclicality of fiscal spending exerting demand management pressures on monetary policy, and (c) debt dynamics causing crowding out of private investment and impacting monetary management (RBI, Report on Currency and Finance, 2013). It is pertinent to turn to what the RBI Governor said in this context:

> Even setting aside crisis related developments, 'fiscal dominance' of monetary policy continues to be a concern. The long-term interest rates are influenced significantly by the yields on government securities and hence on the size of the government borrowing programme, thereby eroding to some extent the efficacy of monetary transmission. The credibility of the Reserve Bank's inflation management, therefore, is critically dependent on the credibility of Government's fiscal consolidation. (Subbarao 2010)

In terms of the implication of fiscal dominance on the financial sector, it may be noted that domestically the debt is held in the commercial banks' portfolio primarily prompted by a rather high (globally speaking) SLR. While this is normally seen as a key element of a financially repressive regime, in the aftermath of the global financial crisis, policy makers across the globe are rediscovering its utility as a means of improving the soundness of banks' balance sheets. It is, however, difficult to decipher how much of the SLR is enhancing banks' solvency and how much of it turns out to be repressive in India. How is the issue of fiscal dominance linked to the external sector?

Interestingly in 2014, with an increasing current account deficit and a fiscal deficit of around 8 per cent, the Indian situation could be compared closely with that of Spain! Nevertheless, despite a rather large debt–deficit configuration India did not face any major economic crisis after 1991. Indian authorities scrupulously avoided the temptation of committing the *original sin* of floating sovereign debt denominated in a foreign currency. Both by design and in hindsight, it seems to have served India well. But then it could well be argued that lack of opening up the capital account did not expose India to market discipline of rating agencies and CDS spreads. In the end, it is a matter of opinion.

To sum up, fiscal dominance has limited the operational autonomy of monetary policy, created issues regarding vulnerabilities of PSBs and financial institutions, and constrained the choice and freedom in managing the capital account.

* * *

Going forward, how do we see the fiscal situation? The outcome would depend on the shape of things to come both domestically and globally.

Globally, Europe and the eurozone accounts for a significant market for India with the EU accounting for nearly one-fifth of Indian exports and nearly 13 per cent of India's imports. Bilateral trade between India and the euro area too has been growing on an average of nearly 10 per cent during 2006–10. Besides, the total FDI from the EU during 2010 amounted to €3 billion (Anand et al. 2012). Thus, any recession in Europe is going to affect Indian export growth (Anand et al. 2012).

Following the enactment of the FRBM legislations, India commenced a strategy of fiscal consolidation quite effectively. Such efforts received a jolt due to the global financial crisis turning into a global recession, which India could not escape being part of the globalized world. Nevertheless, the hard-earned fiscal space provided India the opportunity to undertake fiscal stimulus. At the current juncture when a number of domestic developments did not give the leeway to exit from the fiscal stimulus, it is imperative that the country goes back to a renewed path of fiscal consolidation. Otherwise, without being alarmist, if and when any serious deterioration happens in the global economies, given the ever-increasing trends in India's globalization, India could be exposed to the crisis and contagion. A further deterioration in the euro area (such as a double dip) could be an illustration of such a problem.

To conclude, we can do no better than to quote from a recent article of the former Indian Finance Minister who in emphasizing the imperative and ethos of fiscal consolidation in India said:

The process of fiscal consolidation needs to be sustained over the medium term. The concept of a counter-cyclical policy should be applied both during bad as well as 'good' years. Only this will help in creating the necessary fiscal space for undertaking unconventional measures during crisis periods. Developing economies like India have enormous demands on the expenditure side to fulfil the gap in the provision of physical as well as social infrastructure. However, with scarce and limited resources available with the government, the focus should be on just allocation and closer monitoring of deliverables. Outcomes should get more emphasis than mere outlays and financial expenditures. The concept of the 'government as a whole' needs to permeate the decision making process and the concept of incremental allocation of resources to all the sectors needs to be looked at afresh. (Chidambaram 2012)

8

Public Debt, National Income, and Growth

A Selective Review

The descriptive illustrative analytical account of the book is reflective of the current state of significant uncertainty in three spheres, namely, (a) economic policies, (b) prospects for the global economy, and (c) economic theory. While the present book is primarily concerned with (a) and (b), it may be worthwhile for the sake of completeness to attempt a synoptic account of the economic theories underlying fiscal policy and public debt and its impact on national income and growth. This would help place the cross-country experience (already discussed in Chapters 5, 6, and 7) in perspective and also provide a platform to analyse policy issues in the subsequent chapters. Needless to say, this account is in the nature of a selective survey without any claim to originality or exhaustiveness.[1] Parenthetically, we may, however, note that all the major strands of economic theories failed to either explain or predict the crisis.[2] Even the empirical academic literature is quite divided on the relationship between public debt and growth. Though we may not be able to infer a cohesive set of lessons, a selective review of relevant literature is attempted in view of its contemporary relevance.

---

[1] See for example, Elmendorf and Mankiw (1999), Rakshit (2005), and Panizza and Presbitero (2013) for detailed surveys on mainstream views on public debt and growth.

[2] It may be interesting to note that the Queen of England in her visit to the London School of Economics (LSE) on 5 November 2008 asked the members of academia, 'If these things related to the global financial crisis were so large, how come everyone missed them?' In their response, a group of academicians from the LSE concluded: 'So in summary, Your Majesty, the failure to foresee the timing, extent and severity of the crisis and to head it off, while it had many causes, was principally a failure of the collective imagination of many bright people, both in this country and internationally, to understand the risks to the system as a whole.'

Financial and Fiscal Policies. Second Edition. Y. V. Reddy, Partha Ray, and Pinaki Chakraborty, Oxford University Press.
© Y. V. Reddy, Partha Ray, and Pinaki Chakraborty 2024. DOI: 10.1093/9780198934288.003.0008

The next section begins with a discussion on what may be considered as the mainstream literature that looks at and considers short-run and long-run impact of government deficit and debt on national income and growth. This is followed by an account of the Barro-Ricardo equivalence propositions (whereby the impact of debt-finance and tax-finance are equivalent). This is followed by a discussion of the relevant non-mainstream literature. Empirical literature and related controversies following Reinhart and Rogoff's (2010) contention on the subject is taken up next. The chapter ends with some brief concluding remarks.

Mainstream Views

The issue of public debt has historically evoked extreme reactions. In his bestselling textbook on macroeconomics, Mankiw illustrated this as 'Alexander Hamilton believed that "a national debt, if it is not excessive, will be to us a national blessing", while James Madison argued that "a public debt is a public curse"' (Mankiw 2009, p. 431). What explains such opposite views? Is it economic philosophy of the exponent or the macroeconomic context that determines the view? While a priori it is difficult to answer such a question, in the presence of such multiplicity of views (often contradictory to each other) it may be useful to start with a brief survey of the major strands of the relevant theoretical and empirical literature.[3]

Till the advent of the Keynesian revolution (or the publication of *The General Theory of Employment, Interest and Money* in 1936) stigmas were consistently attached to budget deficit. Among the classicists, Ricardo refers to debt as 'one of the most terrible scourges which was ever invented to afflict a nation' (Sraffa 1951, p. 197). Essentially, 'budget deficits were

---

[3] There is large political economy literature explaining the emergence and bias in favour of debt and deficits in a democracy. Such bias can emanate in various situations, such as, when voters favour public spending but do not understand the government's inter-temporal budget constraint and taking advantage of this, politicians run deficits in order to win elections; when current government may over-issue debt so as to tie the hands of the next government with different preferences for public spending; or when in presence of coalition governments, debt accumulation could be the result of a war of attrition between different parties forming a coalition. This literature is not covered in this chapter. See Persson and Tabellini (2000), and Balassone, Franco, and Zotteri (2004) for a discussion of these models.

considered signs of profligacy, which as in the case of individuals living beyond their means and persistently piling up debt, would eventually lead to bankruptcy of the government or economic chaos like hyperinflation' (Rakshit 2005, pp. 339–40). This philosophy towards debt and deficit changed in the period following the Keynesian revolution and notwithstanding a critique from the monetarist school, an activist role of fiscal policy came to be accepted as standard doctrine (Blinder and Solow 1973).

It appears that the mainstream literature on public debt, national income, and growth currently sprang from two distinct sources: the conventional/extended Keynesian view, and the Barro-Ricardo equivalence hypothesis. In the conventional view it was increasingly believed that while in the short run incurring debt could be beneficial (particularly faced with an adverse demand shock) the long-term effect could be quite different. Such beneficial effects of incurring public debt and the activist role of fiscal policy were questioned by the exponents of rational expectations (i.e., those who believe economic agents do not make systematic errors). It was explained that farsighted individuals who care sufficiently for the welfare of future generations may treat bond financing and tax financing with equal disapproval—such an action would nullify the effects of fiscal policy.

Short-Term versus Long-Term Impact of Public Debt

The conventional view makes a distinction between short-term and long-term effects of public debt (Panizza and Presbitero 2013). In the short run, Keynesian multiplier effect will be operative so that increased government expenditure or tax cuts will lead to increase in aggregate demand that would raise national income. Even if agents are rational and make no systematic errors in perceiving government policy, as long as there are some nominal/real rigidities in the system expansionary fiscal policy tends to be effective; these rigidities may come via the presence of sticky wages, sticky prices, or some temporary misperception (Elmendorf and Mankiw 1999).

Long-term impact of public debt could entirely be different. In order to get the long-term analytics clear, one can refer to the national accounting identity whereby the sum of private saving and public saving (difference between government expenditure and taxes net of subsidy) would be equal to national investment (i.e., sum of domestic investment and net foreign investment). With an increase in budget deficit, both national saving and national investment could go down. Reduced domestic investment will lead to reduced capital stock that would lead to lower productivity, low average real wage, and total labour income. As the sum of current account and capital account is zero (neglecting reserve accumulation/drawdown), decline in net foreign investment, on the other hand, would be matched by decline in net exports with associated effects like appreciation of currency, making domestically produced goods more expensive (Elmendorf and Mankiw 1999). Thus, longer-term effects of continuously increasing public debt could be adverse.

Apart from these short-run and long-run effects of public debt, there could be other effects as well.

First, there could be *deadweight loss* (i.e., a loss of real incomes that comes out of the distortions in economic behaviour due to additional taxation) caused by the higher tax rates, that are necessary to service the debt (Feldstein 2004).[4]

Second, in the presence of huge debt, the government could force the monetary authority to finance the increasing deficit through seigniorage (i.e., difference between the value of money and the cost to produce it), and the resultant inflation could be a fiscal phenomenon (Sargent and Wallace 1981).

Third, foreign-financed government debt could make the country vulnerable to possible crisis of global confidence. This phenomenon, termed as *original sin*, is defined as the inability of a country to borrow abroad in its own currency (Eichengreen et al. 2004).

Fourth, another key issue is sustainability of public debt. Domar (1944) pointed out that fiscal sustainability is assured when the growth rate in nominal GDP is higher than the rate of increase in outstanding

---

[4] Feldstein (2004) noted, 'this deadweight loss is potentially quite substantial. For example, in the United States in the second half of the 1990s, the interest paid on the federal debt averaged 34 percent of total personal income tax revenue. If the debt did not exist, the personal taxes could have been 34 percent lower.'

nominal government bonds; thus, when the GDP growth rate exceeds the interest rate, debt stock will be sustainable.[5]

Barro-Ricardo Equivalence

The other important theoretical strand on public debt is what has come to be known as Barro-Ricardo equivalence.[6] The basic intuition of Barro-Ricardo equivalence is as follows. Let there be a representative individual who has a strong bequest motive so that the utility of the current generation depends upon her own consumption as well as consumption of all the future generations. Thus, the intertemporal utility of the individual becomes dependent on the utility of the whole family—generation after generation. Now, in such a situation, it will not matter for the individual whether government finances happen through debt or taxation. After all, the individual would view debt as equivalent to future taxation on subsequent generations. Given that she has a high altruistic motive, she will not change her current consumption and the entire amount of tax cuts will be saved and passed on to future generations. Hence, public debt will not be able to generate the increased aggregate demand that a Keynesian model would have otherwise predicted.

The Barro-Ricardo equivalence has been criticized from a number of viewpoints. Even within mainstream literature, it has been pointed out that the equivalence of tax financing and debt financing is valid only under very restrictive assumptions. In particular, the following assumptions need to be valid, namely, '(a) successive generations are linked by altruistically motivated transfers; (b) capital markets are either perfect, or fail in specific ways; (c) the postponement of taxes does not redistribute resources within generations; (d) taxes are nondiscretionary; (e) the use of deficits cannot create value (that is, through bubble); (f) consumers are rational and farsighted; and (g) the availability of deficit financing

---

[5] Subsequently, Blanchard et al. (1990) proposed two necessary conditions for sustainability: (a) the ratio of debt to GNP eventually converges back to its initial level; (b) the present discounted value of the ratio of primary deficits to GNP is equal to the negative of the current level of debt to GNP.

[6] Barro (1974) did not make any specific reference to Ricardo but the ideas were contained in David Ricardo's 1817 classic *Principles of Political Economy and Taxation* as well as his 1820 'Essay on the Funding System'.

does not alter the political process' (Bernheim 1987, pp. 264–265). Empirically too, testing Ricardian equivalence yielded quite inconclusive evidence. While debate on Ricardian equivalence has been intense during the 1970s and till end-1980s, since then the debate has reduced in importance (Ricciuti 2003).

Interestingly, in the context of the current global crisis, Ricardian equivalence made a phoenix-like comeback. While articulating the basis of the fiscal stimulus, the then Chief Economist of the World Bank, Justin Lin, went on to say, in a speech on 28 February 2011:

In my view, a global push for investment along the line of Keynesian stimulus is the key for a sustained global recovery; however, the stimulus needs to go beyond the traditional Keynesian investment . . . *how can the Ricardian trap be avoided, i.e. an outcome where the government stimulus fails to boost aggregate demand because economic agents expect future tax increases to pay for larger deficits and thereby increase savings?* (Lin 2011, p. 2; emphasis ours).

Subsequently, Lin's position of raising the possibility of Ricardian equivalence has attracted severe criticism from a number of economists. The prototype position emerged from Krugman (2011), who commented:

Here's what we agree on: if consumers have perfect foresight, live forever, have perfect access to capital markets, etc., then they will take into account the expected future burden of taxes to pay for government spending. If the government introduces a new program that will spend $100 billion a year forever, then taxes must ultimately go up by the present-value equivalent of $100 billion forever. Assume that consumers want to reduce consumption by the same amount every year to offset this tax burden; then consumer spending will fall by $100 billion per year to compensate, wiping out any expansionary effect of the government spending.

But suppose that the increase in government spending is temporary, not permanent—that it will increase spending by $100 billion per year for only 1 or 2 years, not forever. This clearly implies a lower future tax burden than $100 billion a year forever, and therefore implies a fall in consumer spending of less than $100 billion per year. So the spending program *is* expansionary in this case, *even if* you have full Ricardian equivalence. (Krugman 2011; emphasis original)

Thus, the spectra of Ricardian equivalence still haunts the fiscal stimulus package in the current crisis and often a strong case for austerity is made from a misconceived notion of Ricardian equivalence of neutrality between tax financing and debt financing.

How do we see the conventional view of an activist fiscal policy? Looking from the vantage point of the Great Recession, the world seems to have traversed a full circle from the Great Depression period of the 1940s to the inflationary era of the 1970s to the recent era of the Great Moderation. So, the intellectual foundation of fiscal policy is found to be contextual in nature and Krugman seems almost prophetic when he wrote in 2005, after giving due credit to the monetarists, 'Still, the next time there is a slow-down, there will be a pretty strong case for supplementing monetary expansion with discretionary fiscal policy' (Krugman 2005, p. 523).

Non-Mainstream Views

Apart from the mainstream theories, there is a large theoretical literature from non-mainstream schools on the impact of fiscal policy. While the debate between the schools of economic thought becomes, at one level, an abstract discourse of the prior postulates that are adopted, at another they reflect the ideologies of the exponents. To caricature the essential ingredients of difference between the mainstream and non-mainstream views, it may not be an exaggeration to say that the non-mainstream schools, in general, are more favourably disposed towards fiscal activism. Our coverage of the non-mainstream literature is, however, primarily confined to post-Keynesian economics.[7]

---

[7] Post-Keynesians attempt to resurrect Keynesian ideas in the modern context without going through a rational expectationist way of establishing microfoundations of individual behaviour. There is a large literature on fiscal policy from the post-Keynesian viewpoint; see Tcherneva (2008) for a recent survey.

Expectedly, Ricardian equivalence has been criticized from the non-mainstream theoretical paradigms. From a post-Keynesian paradigm, Arestis and Sawyer (2003) pointed out that if the propositions of Ricardian equivalence theorems (RET) are valid, then the size of the budget deficit would not matter for the level of aggregate demand and when there is no paucity of effective demand then fiscal policy would be ineffective. However, 'when fiscal policy is approached in "functional finance" terms, that is, a budget deficit is run by the government because there is a difference between savings and investment at the desired income level, then the RET approach is scarcely relevant' (Arestis and Sawyer 2003, p. 15). The functional finance can also be operative from the standpoint of direct job creation by the government (Tcherneva 2008).

In the context of the current crisis, Arestis and De Antoni (2007) resurrected Hyman Minsky's notion of fiscal policy wherein, 'Government intervention is not only necessary to reach and maintain full employment; it is also indispensable to contain capitalism's instability, avoiding financial crises followed by debt deflations and deep depressions' (Arestis and De Antoni 2007, p. 2). It was pointed out that the Minsykian fiscal policy is even more potent than the Keynesian one.

Against the backdrop of the current crisis in the US and the clamour for reduction of deficit, Baker (2012) re-examined the arguments for and against deficit reduction. While noting the existence of theoretical arguments behind deficit reduction leading to higher investment and higher net exports, he pointed out that such a relationship could be weak. After all, a reduction in deficit could be accompanied by declines in demand.[8] Besides, as the link between interest rate and exchange rate is also weak, net exports may not go up much. In fact, Baker (2012) found that the current attempts towards deficit reduction in the US was completely misguided, as 'they curtail useful public investment at a time when, despite historically low interest rates, private investment is anemic and unemployment is rampant' (p. 262).

To sum up, two comments are in order. First, fiscally the non-mainstream views on fiscal policy and public debt are much more expansionist and hence are often against fiscal austerity. Second, income

---

[8] In fact, Cynamon and Fazzari (2013) termed the period since the mid-1980s in the US as 'consumer age' and the current period in the US as end of 'consumer age'.

distribution often plays a crucial role in these models in determining the final fiscal impact on the economy.[9]

Empirical Evidence

There is large empirical literature, both country-specific as well as at cross-country levels seeking to delve into this issue.[10] For convenience, we start with the recent evidence on this issue that came from Reinhart and Rogoff (2010, 2010a).[11] In particular, Reinhart and Rogoff (R-R) used a new multi-country historical dataset on government debt and examined the experience of 44 countries spanning up to two centuries of data on central government debt, inflation, and growth. They found that across both advanced countries and emerging markets, high debt/GDP levels (90 per cent and above) are associated with notably lower growth outcomes and that much lower levels of external debt/GDP (60 per cent) are associated with adverse outcomes for emerging market growth. More formally, their major results are three. First, median growth rates for countries with public debt over 90 per cent of GDP are roughly 1 per cent lower than otherwise. Second, average (mean) growth rates are several per cent lower. Third, countries with debt-to-GDP ratios above 90 per cent have a slightly negative average growth rate.

The evidence presented in R-R tends to indicate some non-linearity in the relationship between public debt and growth, where after the 90 per cent threshold level of debt, growth becomes negative. This result gave credence to initiation of austerity programmes in a number of countries where the debt-GDP ratio was and exceeded 90 per cent. The increase in debt ratio in 2020–21 again crossed the 90 per cent mark due to the COVID pandemic-related fiscal shock.

---

[9] There is interesting literature relating to income distribution and the present crisis that we did not cover in this chapter; see Rohit (2011, 2012) and Stiglitz (2013).

[10] As Cecchetti et al. (2010) commented sharply, 'Like a cancer victim who cannot wait for scientists to find a cure, policymakers cannot wait for academics to deliver the synthesis that will ultimately come. Instead, authorities must do the best they can with the knowledge they have' (p. 148).

[11] See Balassone, Franco, and Zotteri (2004) for a discussion of the early empirical work on public debt and growth.

In a recent paper, Herndon, Ash, and Pollin (2013) questioned the validity of R-R (2010). In replicating the R-R results from the same data set, they highlighted three issues. First, there seemed to be a spreadsheet error in R-R empirical exercise whereby five countries (Australia, Austria, Belgium, Canada, and Denmark) were excluded completely from the sample; this resulted in significant error of the average real GDP growth and the debt-GDP ratio in a number of categories.

Second, there was selective exclusion of available data in the sense that R-R excluded Australia (1946–50), New Zealand (1946–9), and Canada (1946–50), which led to a significant reduction of the estimated real GDP growth in the countries that exceeded public debt-GDP threshold of 90 per cent.

Third, they questioned the weighting of summary statistics, whereby R-R arbitrarily weighted equally by country rather than by country-year. Thus, Herndon-Ash-Pollin concluded that, 'the average real GDP growth rate for countries carrying a public debt-to-GDP ratio of over 90 per cent is actually 2.2 per cent, not (-)0.1 per cent as Reinhart-Rogoff claim'. Furthermore, probing the data set, they were unable to find a threshold level of debt/GDP ratio after which growth tended to fall.

These studies have used a long-term dataset. But what is the more recent evidence? Using a new dataset on debt levels in 18 OECD countries from 1980 to 2010, Cecchetti, Mohanty, and Zampolli (2010) examined the impact of debt on economic growth after controlling for different sets of variables.[12] Their results indicated that beyond 85 per cent of GDP, government debt turned out to be growth reducing.

While the results turned out to be robust with respect to different sets of control variables, these have been criticized on two grounds: (a) public debt variable turned out to be statistically insignificant in regressions without time or country fixed effects; and (b) their evidence of non-linearity was inconclusive (Panizza and Presbitero 2013).

How can one sum up the recent empirical evidence following R-R? True to the spirit of clashes between the different schools, various views

---

[12] The following countries were included in their sample: Australia, Austria, Belgium, Canada, Denmark, Finland, France, Germany, Greece, Italy, Japan, the Netherlands, Norway, Portugal, Spain, Sweden, the UK, and the US.

have emerged and various economists have taken sides. Three major views are presented below.[13]

First, a somewhat neutral conclusion could be, 'there is no simple relationship between debt and growth . . . there are many factors that matter for a country's growth and debt performance . . . there is no single threshold for debt ratios that can delineate the "bad" from the "good"' (IMF, World Economic Outlook October 2012, p. 109).

Second, Krugman, on the contrary, arrived at a strong conclusion and in his op-ed of 13 April 2013 in the *New York Times* he went on to say:

> What the Reinhart-Rogoff affair shows is the extent to which austerity has been sold on false pretenses. For three years, the turn to austerity has been presented not as a choice but as a necessity. Economic research, austerity advocates insisted, showed that terrible things happen once debt exceeds 90 percent of G.D.P. But 'economic research' showed no such thing; a couple of economists made that assertion, while many others disagreed. Policy makers abandoned the unemployed and turned to austerity because they wanted to, not because they had to.

Third, commenting on this debate, Rajan (2013) lamented the high-profile economic tussles turning to 'ad hominem attacks', and went on to say:

> In fairness, given Krugman's strong and public positions, he has been subject to immense personal criticism by many on the right. Perhaps the paranoid style in public debate, focusing on motives rather than substance, is a useful defensive tactic against rabid critics. Unfortunately, it spills over into countering more reasoned differences of opinion as well. Perhaps respectful debate in economics is possible only in academia. The public discourse is poorer for this.

* * *

At the risk of over-simplification, in conclusion, following broad trends in the literature can be noted.

---

[13] See Black (2013) for a detailed account of the difference of opinion of Stiglitz and Krugman on the one hand and Reinhart and Rogoff on the other hand.

First, in mainstream literature a distinction is often made between the short-term and the medium-term effect of public debt on growth. Existence of short-term favourable effect does not necessarily mean similar longer-term effect. Second, even if evidence is ambiguous in terms of discerning any threshold over which further increase in debt may influence growth adversely, the following determinants are important in determining the debt-GDP relationship, namely, openness of the country, currency composition of public debt, and type of the country (as to whether it has issuing capability of a reserve currency). Third, it is difficult to arrive at a set of linear unconditional conclusions on the empirical relation between public deficit, debt, and growth. Fourth, globalized financial markets complicate an assessment of debt sustainability based entirely on macroeconomic factors of the relevant country in isolation. Against this background of considerable plurality, emerging issues are explored in the succeeding chapters.

9

Crisis and Public Debt Management

It is evident from the narration in previous chapters that in most of the
countries the cumulative impact of monetary and fiscal measures in managing the crisis is reflected in the magnitude of public debt. The stress on
public debt could be the result of financial sector vulnerabilities and fiscal
stimulus or through their mutually reinforcing nature. Global public
debt appears to have increased manifold, mainly on account of fiscal
stimulus in advanced economies. It is undeniable that new dimensions of
public debt in the global economy have emerged from the global financial
crises, which are identified in the first section of the chapter. These have
to be viewed in the context of new thinking on macroeconomic policies
as elaborated in the second section. Further, there are some lessons on
public debt that could be drawn from the unfolding of the global crisis,
which are explored in the third section. The management of public debt
in future should also capture recent developments in global financial
architecture and the outlook for global public debt, which are described
in the succeeding sections. Against this background, the tasks and challenges ahead for management of public debt are listed in the concluding
part of the chapter.

New Dimensions of Public Debt

In the management of the global financial crisis, several new and entirely unexpected dimensions of public debt came to the fore. First, new
sources of sovereign debt crisis emerged, namely, advanced economies.
In recent decades, till the onset of the crisis, sovereign debt crisis was almost wholly confined to developing countries. During the crisis, sovereign debt crisis erupted in countries such as Greece, Portugal, Iceland,
Ireland, Italy, Spain, etc. Second, there are new sets of creditors and

Financial and Fiscal Policies. Second Edition. Y. V. Reddy, Partha Ray, and Pinaki Chakraborty, Oxford University Press.
© Y. V. Reddy, Partha Ray, and Pinaki Chakraborty 2024. DOI: 10.1093/9780198934288.003.0009

debtors in sovereign debt markets. Among the new debtors is an advanced economy, namely, the US; and among the new notable creditors is a developing country, namely, China. Third, there are a few new sources of safe assets, among the non-reserve currencies. Fourth, as mentioned in previous chapters, the growth of public debt has been significantly higher in advanced economies, as opposed to the pre-crisis period (see Table 3.3). Fifth, the aggregate public debt of all the sovereigns in the global economy as a percentage of global GDP has increased manifold. Sixth, there have been changes in the maturity profiles of government securities of both advanced and emerging market economies. In particular, many advanced economies are now issuing government securities with shorter-term maturities. The changes in the maturity profiles, however, have been varying between different countries as the financial crisis unfolded. Finally, the debt of the reserve currency countries in the global economy has increased to disturbing proportions. Indeed, sovereigns within a reserve currency (namely, euro) have also been affected by the sovereign debt crisis.

As a result of the unprecedented challenges faced with regard to management of public debt, mainly in advanced economies, consequent to the global financial crisis, their monetary operations are also significantly affected (see Table 3.4). First, the level of issuance of government bonds has been very high, partly because of increased fiscal deficits and partly because of shorter maturities. Second, fiscal sustainability has become an important consideration in monetary operations in view of the large supply of government securities. Third, and as a consequence of the above, assets on an unprecedented scale, including government securities, have been purchased by central banks. Central bank balance sheets in advanced economies, thus, contain government securities on a larger scale than before. Fourth, the new prudential requirements laid down by financial sector regulators and central banks have resulted in increased demand for government securities, though the increased demand is relatively small, compared to the large supply of government debt. Fifth, the choice of maturity has become critical not only for debt management in view of large issuance and uncertain global financial conditions, but also in view of monetary conditions. Sixth, the currency denomination of issue of sovereign debt seems to be shifting in favour of domestic currencies possibly in recognition that foreign currency denominated sovereign debt has often complicated management of the crisis. Finally, it is inevitable that central banks which had acquired government assets on a large scale during the crisis would be required to sell these assets in the market, thus adding to the supply of government securities in the financial markets in future. The sale of such assets by central banks may be expected when the growth in public debt by the sovereigns is moderated.

New Thinking on Macroeconomic Policies

Public debt management must be viewed in the context of the overall framework that governs macroeconomic policies while being recognized as an important component of these policies. The global financial crisis has sparked a change in thinking about what constitutes the right macroeconomic policies. The major elements of changes in thinking in the context of monetary policy were highlighted by Stanley Fischer (Fischer 2011). But, as indicated by Blommestein and Turner, 'Policy interactions have changed in ways that are difficult to understand. The current delineation of policy mandates may need to be reassessed' (Blommestein and Turner 2012). There are no simple answers to many of the macroeconomic policy issues that have come into focus as a result of the crisis. However, a few generalizations are attempted in subsequent sections to broadly reflect current tentative thinking on relevant policies, despite a lack of consensus.

There is recognition that exclusive focus on price stability, as the single objective of monetary policy, is inappropriate; financial stability is also a key objective of monetary policy. Similarly, monetary policy cannot be indifferent to asset bubbles, and must be formulated taking into account the importance of countercyclicality in public policy. In addition, indicators of macroeconomic conditions cannot be confined to money supply alone but should also incorporate credit conditions. Using interest rate as the single instrument of policy may often prove less than adequate. There is realization that regulation of the financial sector should take into account cyclical conditions and other macro prudential factors. To the extent that it is countercyclical, regulation of the financial sector should be coordinated with monetary policy. It is possible that there are institutions which are too big to fail, and if so, they should be treated differently from others.

In other words, there are limits to setting a level playing field among regulated entities. In addition to interests of depositors and micro-prudential regulations required to conduct their business, liquidity aspects, and risks associated with products available in financial markets should be reviewed on a continuous basis and the regulatory framework should reflect countercyclical policies. Banking services have an important and direct impact on the population at large, and regulating the links between retail banking, including payment system services and non-bank financial services, is critical for effective regulation of the financial sector.

In managing the external sector, it has become clear that persistent large current account imbalances, be they a deficit or a surplus, may not be desirable for the global economy. Large current account deficits in particular may contain risks of instability, though it may not be easy to define the level at which a current account deficit may be regarded as undesirable. Capital flows can be volatile and, in certain circumstances, capital controls may be warranted. In regard to exchange rates, a totally fixed or a totally floating regime is not necessarily the optimal approach and intermediate regimes are acceptable. Foreign exchange reserves provide some cushion for national authorities to manage volatility, particularly in times of stress in global financial markets. Likewise, fiscal policy must not only play a critical role in the overall countercyclical public policy, but also be coordinated with monetary policy, financial sector regulation, and policies relating to an open capital account. It goes without saying that fiscal consolidation in good times provides headroom for stimulating the economy when economic conditions are stressful. Recourse to fiscal consolidation measures may also be warranted at times when capital flows are exceptionally strong.

It is now recognized that there is a need for fundamental review of public policy relating to growth in output, employment, and financial stability. The balance between the role of the state and that of the market is being reassessed in favour of more effective and purposeful regulation of markets. Further, the risks of global finance regulated principally at the national level have been recognized, thus warranting a well-crafted harmonization between global coordination and formulation of countries' own public policy. Moreover, a new balance is sought between growth of the financial sector and growth of the real sector, whereby both excessive financialization and excessive leverage are contained. The severe limitations of the existing global financial architecture in ensuring growth and stability on a sustainable basis have been recognized. The international monetary system is an integral part of global financial architecture and reflects the absence of a level playing field for individual countries in the management of their public debt.

Finally, governance has been found wanting in both public sector and private sector institutions. The rigid compartmentalization of various public sector functions among institutions such as those between monetary authorities, regulators, and fiscal authorities to avoid conflict of interest has, to some extent, led to ineffectiveness of public policy, particularly with regard to coordination in the management of money and finance. Concomitantly, the emergence of large financial conglomerates in the private sector has brought into sharp focus the dangers of conflicts of interest within these institutions, despite assurances that firewalls have been built between different functions and functionaries. As a result, an observable preference is emerging in favour of emphasis on coordination in public policy to ensure effectiveness on one hand, and on institutional mechanisms in the private sector that lower the risk of conflict of interest and minimize incentives for excessive risk taking on the other hand.

Lessons for Public Debt Management from the Global Financial Crisis

By studying the impact of the global financial crisis on different countries, it is possible to make some generalizations which are in the nature of lessons for the management of public debt. The first of these is that the pre-existing level of public debt does not, by itself, have a direct bearing on the impact of the financial crisis. Some countries with large public debt in relation to GDP such as Greece were severely affected while others, for example India and Japan, were not.

Second, in this regard it is necessary to consider the origin and nature of this crisis. While it is true that, in the past, banking crises were not unusual and could impact both developed and advanced economies, it was primarily developing economies that were affected by currency crisis or faced difficulties in discharging sovereign debt obligations. The recent crisis originated in advanced economies and, at the outset, was essentially a banking crisis, but for some countries, particularly in Europe, it evolved into a sovereign debt crisis. As is well known, serious banking crises often lead to sovereign debt crises because the sovereign assumes some of the risks associated with the banking sector, or comes to the rescue of the financial institutions involved. So, whereas previously sustainability of sovereign debt was essentially a challenge for public policy in developing economies, it has now become a challenge for public policy in advanced economies too.

The third lesson relates to financial support in times of crisis. In the past, it was multilateral development institutions that provided support to countries affected by crises in sovereign debt management, with the IMF acting as some sort of lender of last resort. In the current crisis, problems of liquidity were managed initially through coordination between advanced economies, and subsequently some developing countries were also included. Multilateral development institutions also played a pivotal role in providing support to both advanced and developing economies to avoid default on sovereign debt. However, some countries eligible for bilateral swap arrangements under the Chiang Mai Initiative (CMI) preferred to approach the Federal Reserve of New York, on a bilateral basis, for liquidity support. Most of these arrangements took place among central banks, presumably with the implicit approval of their respective governments.

Fourth, it is interesting to note that while the global financial crisis originated in the US and its impact was acute, the Federal Reserve of New York was still in a position to extend liquidity support to some of the countries impacted by the crisis, including Korea and Singapore.

The fifth lesson from the crisis is that where residents held most of the public debt and it was denominated in local currency, a higher level of public debt could be sustained with less disruption in financial markets. Most of the public debt of Japan is denominated in its domestic currency, yen, and public debt in the eurozone countries is primarily denominated in euro. However, whereas Japan's public debt is primarily held by residents, the public debt of countries in Europe most severely affected by the global financial crisis is mainly held by large financial institutions based outside the jurisdiction of the country that issued the debt. Similarly, India has a large public debt-to-GDP ratio and a relatively large fiscal deficit, but public debt is mostly held by residents and denominated in the domestic currency and managed by its central bank. The impact of the financial crisis on management of public debt has been negligible in India, although on account of the crisis the rate of growth of GDP has been constrained and liquidity conditions in financial markets were impacted for a very brief period. Article 293 of the Indian Constitution imposes restrictions on the borrowings by the state governments. Under the Constitution, only central government can borrow externally. Externally aided projects at the state level are back-to-back loans implying central government holds the authority to transfer the external debt to the states with some conditions. Therefore, this leaves limited scope for fiscal profligacy at the state level predominantly because of these borrowing controls that are being exercised by the central government (Gopinath 2009). As a result, there has been no instance of bankruptcy by any state government to date, and further State FRBM Acts impose limits on state borrowing. From these examples, it is evident that debt sustainability depends not only on the broad indicators of debt sustainability, but also on whether (a) residents or non-residents hold the debt; (b) debt is denominated in national currency or an external currency, and on the institutional arrangement for management of public debt.

Sixth, the boundaries of public debt obligations or liabilities assumed significance in the context of the global financial crisis. It has once again highlighted the fact that public debt obligations often extend beyond debt issued by the sovereign. They clearly include the obligations of public or private institutions where formal guarantees of payment have been given by the sovereign. However, they may also extend to letters of comfort that have been issued to public or private enterprises or debt incurred by state-owned enterprises. These obligations often arise as a result of cross-default clauses or, in some cases, reputational risks attached to the sovereign. In addition, the crisis has brought to the fore the potential obligations that may arise on the sovereign from cross-currency exposures of its financial system, in particular, the banking system. Iceland and Ireland are clear examples of countries where large-scale obligations of the banking system have been passed on to the sovereign in one form or another. The essential lesson is that, in the wider context of macroeconomic policy, the debt obligations of government may, at times, extend beyond the debt directly incurred by the government.

The Global Financial Architecture—Recent Developments

Public debt management must also recognize that macroeconomic policies at the national level take account of the global financial architecture and that, consequently, public debt management and global financial architecture are also closely linked. The crisis has exposed the inadequacies of the existing global financial architecture and prompted a comprehensive review based on the insights gained from the financial crisis (Reddy 2011). There has been a debate as to whether new global institutions should be created to address these inadequacies or whether existing multilateral institutions should be revamped. The consensus seems to have evolved in favour of the latter. In the IMF, changes in governance have been initiated and resources available to the IMF have been augmented. The surveillance mechanism has been expanded to include both bilateral and multilateral aspects in a comprehensive manner and its effectiveness and objectivity has been enhanced. These developments provide some comfort to policymakers at the national level, but do not add significantly to the global environment of managing public debt at the national level, especially in large economies. The World Bank has made changes in governance, its resources have been augmented, and a wide-scale review of its thinking on macroeconomic policy is taking place. Several global financial safety nets have been launched both in IMF and in the World Bank, but it is not clear whether they fundamentally alter the lessons from the global financial crisis for management of public debt or not. Above all, it is gratifying that the need for a global perspective with regard to economic thinking and policy is being emphasized and particular attention is being paid to systemically important economies in the world, and to the spillover effects of their national policies on global economic and financial stability.

The G20 was established after the Asian crisis but its mandate and importance have been greatly enhanced in the context of the global financial crisis, particularly with its elevation as a forum for the heads of states since November 2008 (see Table 9.1). It has been recognized as an important pillar in the global financial architecture and at times described as the fourth pillar, alongside the IMF, the World Bank, and the World Trade Organization (WTO). However, it is important to note that the

G20 is a group and not an institution bound by national treaties. The G20 played an impressive role in enhancing cooperation at the global level and coordinating measures of policy-stimulus to avert collapse of financial markets and economic depression. However, coordination of national policies relating to exit from stimulus measures has proved more contentious, due mainly to uneven recovery across nations and sectors. The fact that economic imbalances were an important cause of the crisis has been recognized, but no cognizable agreement has been reached on ways in which these can be unwound or on the role of exchange rate management in this regard. The Financial Stability Board (FSB) is little more than a revised version of the Financial Stability Forum with an enlarged membership and a broader mandate. Its primary task has been to formulate more stringent regulatory standards for financial sectors in the light of experience from the crisis.

The international monetary system has been described as basically a non-system dominated by one currency, the US dollar. The management of the dominant global reserve currency is, in reality, not subject to market discipline or governed by globally binding rules. On the contrary, the legal mandate of the authority issuing the global reserve currency is to serve the interests of its own country, the US. This would be true, to different degrees, of management of any national currency that happens to be a reserve currency for the global economy. The international monetary system is being reviewed but there is as yet no agreement on the way forward. The global financial system continues to be dominated by large powerful conglomerates that move between jurisdictions and are prone to herd behaviour. Similarly, a few ratings agencies, a few business news agencies, and a few auditing giants with ties to each other dominate the financial system. The adjudication of disputes in global finance is concentrated in a limited number of jurisdictions.

In sum, there has not been any significant change in the global financial architecture in so far as it is relevant to public debt management. For example, important recommendations on debt restructuring by the Stiglitz Commission, which calls for an International Debt Restructuring Court and Foreign Debt Management (UN 2009), have not, as yet, received serious consideration. Deficiencies persist with regard to debt reduction mechanisms and measures to address questions of odious debt. It can be argued that, in the absence of orderly debt restructuring, irresponsible

Table 9.1 Evolution of G20 Agenda

Summit	Date	Headline Priorities
Washington	November 2008	• Financial reform
London	April 2009	• Global stimulus • Financial reform • International financial institutions
Pittsburgh	September 2009	• G20 governance • Re-balancing of world economy • Financial reform
Toronto	June 2010	• Re-balancing of world economy • Financial reform
Seoul	November 2010	• Re-balancing of world economy • International financial institutions
Cannes	November 2011	• International monetary system • Commodity prices • Euro crisis
Los Cabos, Mexico	June 2012	• Reaffirmation to increase IMF's resources • Resist and roll back protectionist trade and investment measures to the end of 2014 • Progress on the G20 development agenda, particularly on food security, financial inclusion, sustainable development, and inclusive green growth
Saint Petersburg, Russia	September 2013	• Financing for investment • Fiscal consolidation: Addressing base erosion and profit shifting, tackling tax avoidance, and promoting tax transparency and automatic exchange of information
Brisbane, Australia	2014	• Reforming global financial system • Strengthening tax systems • Creating jobs and empowering development
Antalya, Turkey	2015	• Support the global climate agreement • Migration and refugee movement
Beijing, China	2016	• Favour international trade and investments and opposition to protectionism • Tax evasion reduction • Fiscal stimulus and innovation to boost economic growth
Berlin, Germany	2017	• 'Issues of Global Significance': Migration, digitization, occupation, health, women's economic empowerment and development aid
Mendoza, Argentina	2018	• Infrastructure for development • A sustainable food future

Table 9.1 Continued

Summit	Date	Headline Priorities
Tokyo, Japan	2019	• Eight focussed areas (themes) were 'Global Economy', 'Trade and Investment', 'Innovation', 'Environment and Energy', 'Employment', 'Women's Empowerment', 'Development', and 'Health'
Riyadh, Saudi Arabia	2020	• Empowering people by creating the conditions in which all people can live, work, and thrive
Rome, Italy	2021	• International financial stability • Climate change mitigation and sustainable development
Bali, Indonesia	2022	• Global health architecture • Sustainable energy transition • Digital transformation
New Delhi, India	2023	• Territorial integrity and sovereignty, advocating for peaceful conflict resolution through diplomacy and dialogue

Source: Authors' compilation based on Angeloni and Pisani-Ferry (2012) and various G20 websites.

lending to sovereign and sovereign-backed entities will continue, particularly in view of the dominance of jurisdictions favouring lenders in the resolution of disputes.

The Outlook for Global Public Debt

There are reasons to believe that public debt management in the aftermath of the global financial crisis is likely to be different from what it was before the crisis took place. Restructuring of sovereign debt has already taken place in Greece and such restructuring in some other advanced economies cannot be ruled out. Consequently, the risk premium for government paper in some advanced economies may be higher than before, and the differential between risk premium in advanced economies and developing economies may become narrower. Many advanced economies have incurred significant new public debt to avoid collapse of their financial sectors and to stimulate their economies. As a result, the public debt of advanced economies, as a percentage of their GDP, has

Table 9.2A Select Fiscal Indicators for the G20 Countries: IMF Forecasts

		2014	2015	2016	2017	2018	2019
Overall Balance	G20 Advanced	−4.8	−4.1	−3.6	−3.3	−3.2	−3.2
	G20 Emerging	−2.4	−2.2	−2.0	−2.0	−1.9	−1.9
Primary Balance	G20 Advanced	−2.6	−1.8	−1.2	−0.7	−0.4	−0.3
	G20 Emerging	−0.6	−0.4	−0.3	−0.2	−0.2	−0.1
Cyclically Adjusted Balance	G20 Advanced	−3.80	−3.4	−3.2	−3.1	−3.1	−3.2
	G20 Emerging	−2.3	−2.0	−2.0	−1.9	−1.9	−1.9
Gross Debt	G20 Advanced	113.8	113.4	112.6	111.5	110.3	109.3
	G20 Emerging	31.8	31.0	30.2	29.5	28.7	28.2

far surpassed that of developing economies as a group, and is expected to continue to do so for several years (see Table 9.2). Global public debt, as a percentage of global GDP, is likely to be very high for the foreseeable future since the combined GDP of advanced economies in relation to global GDP is high, and public debt in advanced economies has escalated rapidly.

The global allocation of capital will have to contend with the new dynamics of high public debt requirements in advanced economies and the increasing demand for capital by private sectors in developing countries which are poised to grow rapidly in the coming years. It is conceivable that the trade-off between yield and quality of the public debt of advanced economies, relative to developing economies, will assume greater complexities. Advanced economies also have to cope with servicing large public debt burdens while, in parallel, meeting the costs of maintaining ageing populations and, in many instances, the need to adjust wage levels in the face of growing competition from developing economies.

Experience has clearly demonstrated that, from the macroeconomic viewpoint, large public debt burdens need to be managed through a combination of policy responses. These include: (a) higher taxes and austerity, (b) financing through inflation, and (c) financial repression. To quote two eminent economists:

> It is conjectured here that the pressing needs of governments to reduce debt rollover risk and curb rising interest expenditure in light of the

Table 9.2B Select Fiscal Indicators for the G20 Countries: IMF Forecasts

		2023	2024	2025	2026	2027	2028
Overall Balance	G20 Advanced	−5.16	−4.39	−4.20	−3.95	−3.81	−3.95
	G20 Emerging	−5.65	−5.51	−5.28	−5.24	−5.22	−5.28
Primary Balance	G20 Advanced	−3.50	−2.57	−2.24	−1.84	−1.61	−1.63
	G20 Emerging	−3.43	−3.12	−2.82	−2.72	−2.65	−2.67
Cyclically Adjusted Balance	G20 Advanced	−5.58	−4.64	−4.43	−4.22	−4.12	−4.28
	G20 Emerging	−5.95	−5.82	−5.67	−5.72	−5.71	−5.72
Gross Debt	G20 Advanced	112.07	112.75	113.79	114.60	115.27	116.29
	G20 Emerging	68.33	70.09	72.29	74.26	76.18	78.06

Source: Compiled from IMF Fiscal Monitor, 2023.

substantial debt overhang (combined with the widespread 'official aversion' to explicit restructuring) are leading to a revival of financial repression —including more directed lending to government by captive domestic audiences (such as pension funds), explicit or implicit caps on interest rates, and tighter regulation on cross-border capital movements. (Reinhart and Rogoff 2011a)

It is quite possible that social and political circumstances, particularly in advanced economies, will dictate changes in public policy when selecting the combination of instruments to manage the burdens of public debt. In turn, such measures may introduce added uncertainties to the challenges of public debt management in both advanced and developing economies.

Tasks and Challenges Ahead

Public debt management has to be considered in the context of the new thinking that is evolving with regard to macroeconomic policies, and in particular, fiscal policy. The links between fiscal management and the financial sector have become very intertwined in the context of crisis management and are likely to remain so for several years to come. These include bailout expenses, quasi-fiscal operations of central banks, taxation of the financial sector and, above all, debt management. Debt sustainability has to be considered more broadly, taking into account the fiscal risks associated with contingent liabilities. There is realization that sovereign debt obligations are not confined just to debt incurred by the sovereign. They also encompass a variety of contingent liabilities, including guarantees, letters of comfort, liabilities of state-owned enterprises, as well as implicit contingent liabilities arising from weaknesses in the banking system.

Public debt management will have to cope with deficiencies in the global financial architecture, the international monetary system, and the global financial system. These are likely to be corrected gradually and only somewhat marginally. Debt managers will also have to contend with a shift in the dynamics of global public debt with the advanced economies accounting for a large share of global public debt. This has serious implications in terms of the possible crowding-out effect on public debt in developing economies or resources available for the private sector globally.

The linkages between management of public debt and financial stability are better appreciated now than ever before. Considering the importance of the linkages to stability, the Committee on the Global Financial System commissioned a study group to report on Interactions of Sovereign Debt Management (SDM) with Monetary Conditions and Financial stability. It commented:

> The Study Group has found little evidence that existing arrangements for operational independence of SDM and monetary policy functions have created material problems. Modifying these arrangements would be risky. But in the current circumstances, or where financial systems are still developing, there is benefit in debt managers taking a broad view of cost and risk. Central banks can likewise benefit from keeping abreast of SDM activities. Recent experience confirms that medium-term strategic outcomes for the maturity structure and risk characteristics of outstanding debt do matter for financial stability in particular. This underscores the importance of close communication among the relevant agencies, yet with each agency maintaining independence and accountability for its respective role. (BIS 2011, p. 1)

The institutional arrangements for debt management appropriate to the new realities may need to be addressed. There is a growing recognition of the core role for central banks in the management of public debt, in view of the consequences of the global financial crisis and its management in advanced economies. As Professor Goodhart has underscored:

Debt management has again become a critical element in the conduct of overall macro-economic policy, as evidenced by events in Greece. It can no longer be viewed as a routine function to be delegated to a separate, independent body. On the contrary, debt management lies at the crossroads between monetary policies (both inflation targets and systemic stability) and fiscal policy. When markets get difficult—and government bond markets are likely to do so—the need is to combine an overall fiscal strategy with high caliber market tactics. The latter is what central banks must have as their métier. During the coming epoch of central banking they should be encouraged to revert to their role of managing the national debt. (Goodhart 2010)

Goodhart believes there is also considerable merit in developing economies adopting existing models that combine monetary authority, financial sector regulation, and public debt in the central bank. He noted that such arrangements in developing countries where they exist have demonstrated that they can operate effectively. This would help policy coordination in the light of large uncertainties in the future, and would make best use of the limited availability of skills, and the prestige associated with central banks.

The IMF and World Bank had issued guidelines for public debt management in 2003 (IMF/World Bank 2003). Developments since the eruption of the crisis have been, to some extent, captured by the Stockholm Principles for managing sovereign risk and high levels of public debt, which were promulgated by debt managers and central bankers from 33 countries drawn from both advanced and emerging market economies (IMF 2013). This points towards a review in the thinking on the ideal organizational structure for public debt management, and best practices for public debt management in the light of the experience of the global financial crisis.

Finally, the challenges of managing large public debt may compel examination of several policies with fiscal implications, such as retirement age. A study on the future of public debt draws some important conclusions (Cecchetti et al. 2010). The first conclusion is that fiscal problems confronting industrial economies may be bigger than suggested by official debt figures. These may be, for instance, on account of ageing populations and unfunded liabilities. The second conclusion is that such large public debts have significant financial as well as real consequences. The third conclusion is the risk that persistently high levels of public debt will drive down long-term potential growth through its adverse impact on capital accumulation and productivity growth. The fourth conclusion is that long-term fiscal imbalances pose significant risk to the prospects for future monetary stability. Finally, it is suggested that any fiscal consolidation plan should include credible measures to reduce future unfunded liabilities.

Challenges of management of large public debt have close linkages with not merely financial sector and monetary stability but also the real sector. Although, such linkages do not diminish, but perhaps enhance the importance of paying attention to the efficient management of public debt within fiscal policy, and indeed within overall macroeconomic management.

* * *

The global financial crisis has brought about a dramatic change in the magnitudes of public debt, sources of debt-crisis, profiles of creditors and debtors, and maturity structures. The management of fiscal policy and large public debt in the advanced economies in the context of the crisis has influenced monetary management in several ways. Some of the lessons to be drawn from the impact of the crisis include the critical role of financial sector in public debt, the changing role of multilateral institutions, the criticality of residence of holders of debt securities as well as currency of denomination, and the somewhat porous boundary of fiscal obligations. The recent improvements in global financial architecture do not significantly improve the global environment for management of public debt. The outlook for global public debt is different from the past, requiring close coordination between fiscal and monetary policies as well as regulation of the financial sector. The tasks and challenges warrant a review of the organizational structures and best practices for management of public debt. Such a review should be one component of a more integrated view of macro-policies that recognizes the implications of large public debt and other liabilities for growth, stability, and equity.

10

Fiscal Implications and Central Banking

The global financial crisis compelled not only significant coordination between central banks, particularly of advanced economies, but also necessitated close collaboration between monetary and fiscal authorities, as explained in detail in previous chapters. The fiscal implications of operations of central banks, however legally independent, cannot be ignored in assessing macroeconomic conditions. More important, the globally coordinated stimulus has the potential to build fiscal liabilities that could result in fiscal dominance over monetary policy, while theory and practice of central banking is also likely to change on account of the experience of the global crisis. This continued during the active pursuit of monetary and fiscal stimulus during the pandemic.

The introductory part of the chapter gives an overview of the well-recognized links between central banking and fiscal environment. This is followed by an account of the role of central banks, with particular reference to fiscal aspects, in causing the crisis, in managing the crisis, and in the conduct of exit policies. The succeeding part is devoted to a brief assessment of fiscal implications and to the elements of a new framework of central banking consequent upon the global crisis. The concluding part focuses on the issues that need to be considered in view of the new fiscal dominance of central banking in future, in the context of such a new framework.

Links between Central Banking and the Fisc

Most of the operations of central banks have fiscal implications. First, profits of the central bank are generally, sooner or later, transferred to the government. Hence, in a way all the financial actions of central banks have in the final analysis fiscal implications. Second, most of the open

Financial and Fiscal Policies. Second Edition. Y. V. Reddy, Partha Ray, and Pinaki Chakraborty, Oxford University Press.
© Y. V. Reddy, Partha Ray, and Pinaki Chakraborty 2024. DOI: 10.1093/9780198934288.003.0010

market operations of central banks deal with government securities and, hence, impact supply of and demand for government securities in the market, with potential fiscal consequences. Third, setting policy interest rates is a monetary function, but it impacts the cost of debt and hence it has implications for debt burden of the government. Fourth, where management of public debt becomes a critical element of conduct of macro policies, as it often does when levels of public debt are high, the inflation target cannot be divorced from the management of public debt. Often, when government bond markets dominate the system or they become volatile or highly uncertain, fiscal strategies are coordinated with market tactics of central banks, in the interests of stability. Fifth, as a lender of last resort, central banks do provide liquidity but it is well recognized that in reality the boundaries between liquidity and solvency become difficult to identify at the time decisions are taken. Hence, there is a potential burden on taxpayers if the central bank provides liquidity assuming a lack of liquidity, but in reality, the problem turns out to be a case of insolvency. Sixth, intervention in foreign exchange markets, and capital account management have quasi-fiscal costs through their impact on profits of the central bank while their positive impact on fiscal position by avoiding excess volatility cannot be quantified. Finally, in view of all these considerations, the boundaries between monetary and fiscal measures often overlap, but they do so significantly during periods of crisis.

Role of Central Banks in Causing the Crisis

Central banks have been held responsible for causing the crisis on several accounts and the arguments may be summarized as follows. Monetary authorities, particularly in advanced economies, permitted excess liquidity by adopting relatively loose monetary policy since they focused excessively on inflation or price stability. Thus, they neglected credit booms and asset bubbles. They did not assume responsibility for financial stability on the ground that financial stability was not part of their mandate, and that they had responsibility mainly for price stability and, to some extent, for employment or output objectives. They left it to the corrective mechanisms of the market to address any risks building up in the financial system. In their view, they had no way of determining whether the markets had under-priced risks and, in any case, they believed that they could not justify possessing better perception of risks than the market mechanisms. They were generally convinced that they did not have necessary policy tools and instruments to take effective actions to correct asset bubbles. In their view, rather than trying to restrain the possible build-up of such bubbles, it is desirable to take appropriate actions after the bubbles, if any, burst. Those who were uncomfortable with the build-up of excessive risks often took the view that because of financial innovations, the risks were highly dispersed, and hence, there was no serious threat to the stability of the financial system.

Some central bankers expressed concern at the excessive build-up of risks because investors were searching for yield in an era of ample liquidity, but they were confident that banks were very well regulated by the regulators, and hence the banking system was safe. The non-banks, particularly non-deposit taking institutions were, in their judgement, expected to assume the risks if they were to materialize, and they were considered capable of assuming such risks. In any case, they were expected to have viable resolution mechanisms in case of distress. Large financial institutions were generally assumed to have sophisticated risk assessment models, and many central banks and concerned regulators assumed that self-regulation by such individual institutions was adequate to ensure the stability of the system. More generally, central banks had neglected issues like sudden drying up of liquidity in the system and prolonged procyclical biases in the functioning of markets. Above all, they assumed that if individual institutions in general were solvent, the system as a whole would be risk-free.

Generalizations about responsibility of all the central banks or central banks only in a global financial crisis could be misleading. First, the crisis in the financial sector did not occur in all the countries. Most of the developing economies were spared the severity of the financial crisis, while the financial sectors of many advanced economies such as Canada were, by and large, resilient. Second, the failures in the financial sector were all pervasive, and were not confined to central banks or regulators. The regulated institutions had several prescribed layers of governance, such as Board of Directors, Audit Committees, Risk Management Units, etc., and all these seem to have failed. Similarly, accounting and auditing bodies, credit rating agencies, and self-regulatory organizations have all contributed to the enormous leverage and risk taking. Third, among those countries which were seriously affected, the monetary and regulatory structures were varied. In other words, there was no particular regulatory structure or governance arrangement involving central banks that could be identified as common to all the countries where the financial crisis occurred. The crisis occurred in a country like the US with multiple regulators and the UK with a single regulator. Anecdotal evidence of those countries that were not affected by the serious financial crisis also shows diversity in regulatory structures and consequential governance arrangements. Fourth, the most affected countries are, however, found to be those where the growth of the financial sector was significantly ahead of the growth of the *real* sector.

Fifth, countries where retail banking dominated the financial sector and where less sophisticated financial instruments were used were less affected compared to those economies in which large-scale financial innovations dominated. Sixth, in many developing economies, the financial crisis did not occur domestically, but severe problems arose as a result of the contagion from the advanced economies. The extent to which the financial sector of developing economies was affected depended on the extent of integration of their financial markets with markets of advanced economies. Further, those countries with heavy dependence on commodity exports were also affected through the secondary impact of the financial crisis on real economic activity in the advanced economies, resulting in recession or fear of recession. Seventh, those developing economies which had maintained significant forex reserves, and those which did not have high current account deficits, were less affected by the contagion from advanced economies to their financial markets and financial institutions. Finally, some argue that there is no evidence that fiscal dominance played a role in advanced economies adopting the accommodative monetary policies that they did. However, some analysts argue that the easy monetary policy was, in some cases, meant to accommodate the large fiscal deficits or help governments manage public debt. It is also held that the US was in a privileged position to adopt such a policy in view of its exorbitant privilege as the dominant reserve currency.

There is, however, general consensus on the failure of most central banks in anticipating the crisis and exploring suitable measures. The reasons for this failure include a belief in ideology of unfettered markets, dependence on unrealistic models, capture of monetary authorities and regulators by political economy considerations and regulatory institutions, a failure of governance in central banks and possibly in several institutions, and finally a combination of these. Further, the structures relating to monetary and regulatory authorities seem to have played a lesser role than the policies adopted, especially those which related to growth and regulation of the financial sector, and, to some extent, monetary policies. The policies adopted could be explained in terms of either ideological commitments or political economy considerations, both at national and global level.

There is considerable agreement that regulatory systems and market failures in the financial sector were the main causes of the global crisis, while the enabling role of monetary policies cannot be denied. However, the role of fiscal policy in causing the crisis is less clear. There are cases where problems arising out of the crisis in the financial sector triggered issues of fiscal sustainability, warranting coordination with monetary policies. There is little or no evidence to show that fiscal mismanagement, by itself, contributed to the onset of the crisis. Some of the actions taken by central banks to manage the crisis have fiscal impact. In addition, fiscal stimulus may also add to the fiscal burden. As exit from stimulus is managed, monetary authorities have to reckon with fiscal dominance in the conduct of their policy.

There are some indications that in the US, considerations of political economy, including fiscal profligacy, could have prompted easy monetary policy and indeed excess leverage, particularly among households. It has been argued that despite impressive growth in national output, the per capita real income for a major part of the population remained constant in the US. However, growth in per capita consumption of these sections was in excess of growth in income. Political economy considerations, it is argued, prompted such a policy and that the central bank was a willing party to accommodate a combination of high growth, high asset prices, growing inequality, and large fiscal deficits to avoid social tensions. It is less clear whether similar explanations of fiscal mismanagement, being the main reason for the crisis, will hold with regard to other economies deeply affected by the crisis. The close links between monetary, regulatory, and fiscal policies became evident while managing the crisis, in which operations of central banks provided the first line of defence.

Role of Central Banks in Managing the Crisis

There is a general consensus that in times of financial crisis, central banks are at the forefront in managing the crisis and are often described as the first line of defence. In a narrow sense, they are lenders of the last resort to vulnerable institutions, and in a broader sense, they are finally responsible for stability of the financial system as a whole, which the public expects. In brief, to the extent central banks are critical to the smooth functioning of the system, they would have to be the first line of defence in times of stress in the system. As soon as the crisis erupted, coordinated monetary actions were taken by systemically important countries. However, in view of the nature, spread, and intensity of the financial crisis, the lines between solvency and liquidity of individual institutions became blurred and uncertain. Further, central banks had to purchase financial instruments of uncertain value. Any resultant losses would have quasi-fiscal implications. Normal functioning of markets virtually collapsed in the sense that there were no transactions to guide either the market or the authorities on the right price (since the process of price discovery collapsed in the light of absence of normal market transactions), and this occurred almost across the board in many systemically important financial markets.

Central banks, which were in the forefront of managing the crisis, had to take a call in determining whether they were taking serious risks by supporting insolvent institutions or market instruments, with uncertain value as collaterals. The large-scale operations involving provision of liquidity to markets and institutions required significant assumption of risky assets on the balance sheets of central banks with attendant quasi-fiscal implications. Central banks were the first line of defence as soon as it became clear that it was a large-scale financial crisis requiring massive liquidity injections through open market operations, with significant uncertainty about solvency of the institutions concerned. They had little choice except to obtain assurances of firm support from fiscal authorities about their operations, in view of their huge latent quasi-fiscal implications because of large-scale collaterals of uncertain value.

There were many systemically important financial institutions whose solvency was seriously questioned by the financial markets themselves. Since financial markets were on the verge of collapsing, many of the affected institutions were not in a position to raise capital. Hence, it was not possible to ensure their normal functioning without prompt injection of capital. It was, therefore, necessary to undertake nationalization as in the UK and bailout operations as in the US, and both of these operations possibly proposed by the central banks required firm fiscal actions or full fiscal endorsement. In brief, in managing the crisis, there were significant overlaps between illiquidity and insolvency warranting fiscal and monetary actions that often ignored the distinction between monetary and fiscal implications.

The moment the magnitude of the crisis was recognized as large, close involvement of fiscal authorities particularly in regard to judgement on the range and magnitudes of actions mentioned above became inevitable. More generally, the intensity and magnitude of the financial crisis were such that it quickly transformed into an economic crisis. Fiscal stimulus thus became inevitable, and hence, very close coordination between fiscal and monetary authorities was compelling. The extent and nature of coordination between central banks and governments in countries depended on the requirements of liquidity, threat of solvency in the financial sector, and potential dampening of economic activity.

Soon after the onset of the financial crisis, it was realized that coordination between systemically important countries comprising both advanced and developing economies was essential. It was also realized that the crisis required action not only on the part of finance ministers and governors of central banks, but also on a broader scale. Hence, the heads of states had to take the initiative for international coordination through the convening of meeting of heads of governments of G20 countries. In such arrangements, it becomes necessary for central banks to reconcile national interests with global obligations. It is not necessary that national and global compulsions for action always converge, though at the time of crisis management, there was considerable convergence in terms of direction. The compulsions of coordination at global level on broader economic issues necessarily involve initiatives at the level of governments. These considerations that combine coordination of policies at national level at the level of governments and coordination between national authorities at global level, further reinforce the need for central banks to actively align their policies with those of governments in general, and fiscal policies in particular.

Governance arrangements in most central banks are predicated on the assumption of operational autonomy to the central banks for discharge of their functions with insistence on transparency and accountability. These governance arrangements are meant for normal circumstances and designed essentially to respond to domestic issues. It is quite possible that extraordinary measures required to meet a crisis would normally call for unconventional accountability procedures. The balance sheet of a central bank in dealing with the crisis generally expands significantly, and given the nature of problems during crisis management, several decisions taken will be inherently less transparent at the time they are taken. Further, it is virtually impossible to assess the value of assets and liabilities on a mark-to-market basis when markets have collapsed. At best, there can be only what may be termed as retrospective transparency and expected accountability. At the same time, there are serious reputational risks for central banks in regard to these operations. These risks may unfold as time passes and not necessarily when the crisis is at its worst.

It is necessary to note that most of the processes and the issues described are essentially applicable to select advanced economies which were most affected. In most others, including developing economies, there have been pressures on the financial markets, and in response, some unconventional measures were undertaken, but these related essentially to liquidity with insignificant implications for solvency. In the few cases where financial markets were affected and the external sector was under serious pressure with consequent serious impact on the real economy, the actions by central banks were considerably influenced by the programmes, if any, under IMF and assistance from the World Bank. Hence, for most developing economies, the governance arrangements in central banks may not be a noticeable issue in the context of managing the crisis.

The case of the eurozone is unique in the sense that the ECB had to undertake monetary actions whose fiscal impacts were a combination of national-level obligations and those of member states of the eurozone jointly. This, indeed, is a special case warranting separate treatment; but the fundamental overlaps between fiscal and monetary policies remain, though the distribution of fiscal burden between member countries may be somewhat unclear.

There is general consensus that in managing the crisis all central banks succeeded in avoiding collapse of financial markets. However, in doing so, central banks in systemically important advanced economies undertook extraordinary monetary measures involving significant fiscal costs.

Role of Central Banks in Exit Policies

Central banks acted in response to the crisis on an emergency basis, addressing both liquidity and solvency issues. In terms of general direction, the crisis was common to all economies and, hence, both central banks and fiscal authorities in all the countries moved in the same direction. The measures were unconventional in many cases. They were coordinated because the crisis happened about the same time on a global scale. While financial markets resumed functioning globally in a fairly smooth manner, the immediate impact of the crisis and the stimulus on individual national economies was uneven across countries in terms of initial slowing down of growth and subsequent recovery. Hence, the compulsions to exit and the manner of exit from unconventional monetary measures involving fiscal consequences and fiscal stimulus are also uneven among the countries. Despite differences in timing and sequence, many common issues are being addressed by all central banks.

First, exit policies are coordinated and sequenced between central banks and fiscal authorities. While central banks consider medium- to long-term horizons, fiscal authorities, and possibly financial markets, lay greater emphasis on avoiding shorter-term risks. Second, coordination is required between central banks of different countries with regard to exit also, which is extremely complex when the response of economies to stimulus varies significantly among countries. The policies towards stimulus and the response of financial markets and economies are necessarily different. The inherent preference of fiscal authorities to delay initiation of exit or prolong its process (due to political compulsions) may be common between advanced economies and developing economies. But the objective conditions warranting priority in many advanced economies are to avoid deflation or double-dip depression, while for many developing economies management of volatile inflation assumes priority.

In view of divergence in economic cycles among countries, divergence in policies—particularly monetary policies—becomes inevitable. The challenge facing monetary authorities, particularly of systemically important countries (issuing reserve currencies) is to take risks that appear reasonable for stimulating their domestic economies; at the same time, they cannot ignore the risks that may arise to the rest of the global economy due to their actions. An interesting issue in this context is whether the spillover effects of fiscal stimulus in advanced economies are benign to global economy relative to monetary stimulus in their economies, at a time when there is divergence in economic cycles between countries.

In view of the inherent tendency of fiscal management to be subjected to political compulsions, monetary authorities have to fine-tune their operations relating to exit policies whenever coordination is critical. In brief, fiscal dominance in determining monetary actions at the time of exit is not uncommon, and is not inconsistent with the basic objectives of monetary policies.

Policymakers, particularly in advanced economies, face acute dilemmas in considering exit policies. The fiscal position is stretched, warranting assurance of fiscal consolidation. Hence, some policymakers took recourse to fiscal austerity while continuing with monetary stimulus. Some others, who did not launch austerity in the short run, provided assurance of consolidation for the longer term while continuing with monetary stimulus. More recently, there is a perception that monetary stimulus is not having the desired effect on output and employment since it is operating through the financial sector which is yet to overcome several infirmities. Hence, some of them seek monetization of government debt, in a way, bypassing financial markets till conditions stabilize. There is noticeable attention to the recently increasing amounts of government securities in the balance sheets of central banks. In any case, there is growing realization that fiscal and monetary policies, at the time of crisis and exit, have a supplementary role and may also be substitutes.

An Assessment of Fiscal Implications

Management of crisis and exit from stimulus have both monetary and fiscal dimensions, with considerable overlap between the two. There are difficulties in quantifying the fiscal implications of monetary actions, even in the limited context of balance sheets of central banks. For instance, stimulus often involves fiscal concessions to financial entities and instruments, which could have a positive impact on the value of assets in the books of central banks.

A pragmatic approach would be to identify the broad magnitudes of both fiscal and monetary actions and assess their consequences for fiscal conditions. In the current global environment, there are countries where exit from both fiscal and monetary stimulus has commenced, especially among emerging market economies. There are countries where the exit from fiscal stimulus is evident but monetary stimulus may persist, such as the UK or countries in the euro area. There are others like the US where both fiscal and monetary stimulus persist, but with a stated commitment to exit from fiscal stimulus (see Chapter 5). But monetary policy in general and in a number of cases unconventional monetary policy (in the face of near zero interest rate) attempted to stimulate the economy. Several measures were adopted (see Table 10.1).

As a result of such unconventional policies, balance sheets of all the leading central banks have experienced huge expansion during the period of global financial crisis. This continued during the pandemic as well.

Ideally, the combined impact of both fiscal and monetary measures needs to be captured through some sort of consolidated balance sheet of the sovereign that includes the balance sheets of both the government as well as the central bank. However, absence of data of such a consolidated balance sheet makes this task difficult empirically (Stone et al. 2011).

Much of such expansion in central banks' balance sheets continued during the pandemic. Illustratively, the size of the US Fed balance sheet increased from US$922 billion on 2 January 2008 to around US$3.9 trillion on 4 December 2013 and further to around US$8.9 trillion on 14 May 2022. Similar expansions took place in the case of other advanced

Table 10.1 Examples of Central Bank Unconventional Balance Sheet
Policies during the Global Financial Crisis

	Purpose	Central Bank	Measure
Measures for financial stability	Liquidity provision to funding and credit markets	US Fed	Active use of repo operations, TAF, TSLF, CPFF, AMLF, and TALF
		ECB	Fixed-rate full allotment refinancing operations, covered bonds purchases and Security Market Program
		Bank of England	Active use of LTRO, purchase of corporate bonds and CPs by Asset Purchase Facility
		Bank of Japan	Active use of term operations, Special Funds—supplying operations to facilitate corporate financing, outright purchase of corporate bonds and CPs
		Bank of Canada	Term PRA, Term PRA for Private Sector Instruments
		Reserve Bank of Australia	Active use of term operations, active use of repo operations against private debts
	Foreign exchange liquidity provision to local markets	Many central banks	USD operations
		Sweden, Denmark, Poland and Hungary	Euro operations
		ECB, Poland and Hungary	Swiss franc operations
Measures for macroeconomic stability	Purchase of long-term public securities	US Fed	Large-scale purchase of agency MBS, agency debt and US Treasury
		Bank of England	Gilt purchase by Asset Purchase Facility

Table 10.1 Continued

Purpose	Central Bank	Measure
	Bank of Japan	Purchase of JGB under Asset Purchase Program
Large-scale	Bank of Israel	FX purchases
Foreign exchange intervention	Swiss National Bank	FX purchases
Central bank involvement in credit provision	Bank of Japan	Purchase of commercial paper, corporate bonds, ETF and REIT under Asset Purchase Programme, fund-provisioning measure to support strengthening the foundations for economic growth

Source: Constructed by authors based on Stone et al. (2011).

economies' central banks as well. In fact, some commentators have ascribed the exuberance in the global equity markets to such massive monetary stimuli and the expansions in central banks' balance sheets.[1]

In fact, post pandemic, the return of inflation in the advanced countries invited comments such as the following:

Central bankers of industrialized countries have fallen tremendously in the public's estimation. Not long ago they were heroes, supporting feeble growth with unconventional monetary policies, promoting the hiring of minorities by allowing the labor market to run a little hot, and even trying to hold back climate change, all the while berating paralyzed legislatures for not doing more. Now they stand accused

---

[1] Illustratively, Ray and Pal (2022) noted a total disconnect between the movements of indicators in the Main Street and in the Wall Street in the US, whereby the number of deaths in the United States went up consistently and the GDP growth nosedived to negative territory, stock indices like the Dow-Jones industrial average (DJIA) index or the Nasdaq composite index moved up during the pandemic. They argued that the clue to understanding this phenomenon lies in the active pursuit of quantitative easing and other aggregative monetary and fiscal stimulus measures by the authorities of the developed countries.

of botching their most basic task, keeping inflation low and stable. Politicians, sniffing blood and mistrustful of unelected power, want to reexamine central bank mandates. (Rajan 2023)

New Framework for Central Banking

Will there be, as a consequence of the global crisis, a new framework of economic policies within which central banks have to function? The structural changes brought about through legislative actions in the US and the UK do seem to be indicative of a paradigm shift in central banking. The changes under contemplation in the eurozone are also indicative of fundamental changes in central banking. There are changes in structural aspects relating to money, banking, and finance in systemically important countries, and hence, these changes are significant for thinking on macroeconomic policies in general. However, it is noteworthy that there have been no legislative changes in central banking in most other countries. Similarly, significant unconventional measures were adopted by the central banks in the US, the UK, and the eurozone, and far less so, by others. Yet, there is a profound change in the thinking that governs the future of central banking. Goodhart certainly seems to think so and went on to say:

> The first (Victorian) and third (1980–2007) epochs of central banking were characterized by highly successful monetary regimes (the gold standard and inflation targeting), reliance on market mechanisms and independent central banks. After an interregnum post-World War I, the first epoch came to a crashing halt in the 1929–33 Depression, and deflation then led to a period of government domination, direct controls and subservient central banks. Now there is a good chance—but not a certainty—that we are entering a fourth epoch, in the aftermath of the financial crisis of 2007–10. (Goodhart 2010, p. 15)

Similar sentiments have been expressed by some others. 'Central banking will never be quite the same again after the global financial crisis. The crisis will no doubt prove to be one of those rare defining moments in the history of this institution—an institution that, from its faltering first steps in the 17th century, has grown to become widely regarded as indispensable' (Borio 2011, p. 13).

Having recognized that the future of central banking will be very different from the past, there is less clarity about what the future would be like. There is a view that it will be a period of experimentation and that central banks 'face a three-fold challenge: economic, intellectual, and institutional' (Borio 2011, p. 14).

There are several reasons for expecting a paradigm shift in the framework within which central banks operate. First, the mandate of central banks is being widened formally, to include financial stability. In some ways, this widening could include growth and employment objectives. Second, there is greater emphasis on coordination with other regulators in the financial sector which has the potential to undermine their sense of independence though operational autonomy may be maintained. Third, there is a greater emphasis on accountability than before, especially to elected representatives, in view of the social costs incurred on account of the crisis and the enhanced role of central banks in the crisis. Fourth, there is preference for explicit recognition of the costs of preventing a crisis and the costs of managing it. Thus, the costs and benefits of preventive and curative aspects may have to be continuously kept in view. Fifth, the wider mandate may warrant several judgements and trade-offs, requiring a greater role for discretion in monetary policy. Sixth, with regard to banking, there is an implicit recognition of the special nature of banks in view of the criticality for smooth functioning of financial markets. Consequently, central banks have to be closely involved in regulation of banking, where banking regulation is not with them. In the UK, the Bank of England has regained overall responsibility for supervision of banks while the ECB is acquiring it through proposed banking union. Seventh, the management of large public debt in systemically important countries, especially those that are issuers of reserve currency, may require closer coordination between management of public debt and monetary policy. The preference for an independent public debt office may be moderated in view of the compulsion of coordinated actions between monetary and fiscal authorities. Eighth, the aftermath of balance sheet expansion of central banks may warrant government support in terms of capital infusion or loss absorption. This may imply some sort of dependency in the relationship between central banks and fiscal authorities. More generally, central banks have monopoly over interest rate policy, but not over balance sheet policy. The balance sheets of central government and central banks are part of the larger public sector balance sheet.

As pointed out by Borio, central banks' purchases of long-term government bonds can be frustrated if government debt managers lengthen maturity to lock in unusually low yields. 'In this context, the very meaning of operational independence becomes somewhat unclear' (Borio 2011, p. 20).

Ninth, the management of capital flows by central banks involving forex market intervention and reserves management, especially in the context of excess volatility in global flows, has significant fiscal implications. The emerging concerns relating to macroeconomic imbalances in terms of persistent large current account deficits or surpluses would warrant policy actions on several fronts, with central banks playing a critical role always being conscious of the fiscal implications.

Tenth, the recent proposals for taxation of the financial sector will necessarily have implications for it. Taxing the financial sector has gained significance in the context of the crisis, for several reasons. For example, taxation of the financial sector is proposed to moderate speculative elements or reduce excess volatility in financial markets, especially currency markets. However, there could be overlap between taxes on the financial sector and effectiveness of transmission of monetary policy. There was, indeed, a controversy in India on the subject, which eventually led to the exit of the Governor of Reserve Bank of India (RBI). The Finance Minister had, at one stage, contemplated interest tax in 1965, but was dissuaded by the Governor of RBI. However, on an earlier occasion, in November 1956, an increase in stamp duty was effected and the RBI took the stand that the steep increase in stamp duty had implications for the viability of the Reserve Bank's bill market scheme. The Governor, Rama Rau, in a memorandum submitted to the Central Board of the Bank in December 1956 pointed out that the Finance Minister's move meant that there would be 'two authorities who would operate the Bank rate—The Reserve Bank in the usual manner under Section 49 of the Act, and the Government by variation of the stamp duty by executive order of the Finance Ministry' (Balachandran 1998, p. 718). The 'consequences of this dual control of the Bank rate', Rama Rau added, 'need hardly be emphasized'. The Board's response to the subject is also significant. 'Thereupon the Central Board resolved that while the stamp duty might be regarded as a "fiscal matter" its steep increase had, by the Finance Minister's own admission, "monetary implications" which could not be "ignored". The stamp duty "added substantially to the Bank Rate" which was the "statutory responsibility of the Reserve Bank to fix every week"' (Balachandran 1998, p. 718). It seems clear that the complexity and the growing recognition of the links between central banking and the fiscal position lead to a redefinition of the relationship between central banking and government.

Finally, complexity appears to have been injected into central banking after the disastrous experience with the global crisis based on a simplistic approach to objectives and operational independence. A paper by Turner calls into question a number of widely held assumptions about monetary policy, in particular about the linkages between monetary policy, debt management policy, and financial stability policy when expectations of future real and nominal interest rates are not well anchored by strong fiscal positions and credible policy frameworks (Turner 2010).

New Fiscal Dominance

There is reasonable consensus that central banking, in particular in advanced economies, will be different in future. Its balance sheets may warrant fiscal support. Management of sovereign debt and its impact on interest rates may impinge on operations of central banks. There may be considerable overlap between financial sector policies, especially those relating to the banking sector, and monetary policies. As Blommestein and Turner put it eloquently, 'Worries about both "fiscal dominance" and "financial repression" have certainly gained ground. Whatever view is taken of this, the boundary between monetary policy and government debt management has become increasingly blurred. Policy interactions have changed in ways that are difficult to understand. The current delineation of policy mandates may need to be reassessed' (Blommestein and Turner 2012, p. iii).

More recently, the February 2023 *Financial Report of the United States Government* had indicated, 'Under current policy and based on this report's assumptions, [government debt relative to GDP] is projected to reach 566 percent by 2097. The projected continuous rise of the debt-to-GDP ratio indicates that current policy is unsustainable.' This had led some economists to point out that fiscal dominance is a serious possibility for the United States in the near future, and in that case various policies related to the banking system could change; e.g., interest on reserves would likely be eliminated (Calomiris 2023).

The nature and magnitude of new fiscal dominance will, no doubt, depend on several factors and may vary significantly between countries. First, as part of orthodoxy during great moderation, many advanced economies considered sovereign debt management to have no relationship with monetary policy. In some developing countries, this has not happened. Hence, the movement towards what may be described as new fiscal dominance will be noticeable in advanced economies. Second, the inherited size and structure of public debt would be relevant for the intensity of fiscal dominance. For example, a large share of short-term debt may imply significant risks of refinancing. Similarly, the home bias of holders of sovereign debt will impact the scope for fiscal dominance. Third, persistence of sporadic troubled conditions in financial markets may warrant direct monetization of sovereign debt through a process of participation of central banks in primary markets. Fourth, the levels and leverages of household savings, corporate savings, and of the financial sector would also influence the nature of fiscal dominance. Demography and inherited contingent fiscal liabilities will also be relevant.

Finally, openness of the economy determines the scope for and limits to fiscal dominance over money and finance. For example, increasing globalization of trade, labour, and capital limit the capacities of fiscal authorities with regard to both fiscal management and monetary management. A recent IMF study has shown that, in meeting the challenges of surges of capital inflows, even advanced economies may find the recourse to fiscal policies by themselves inadequate, and may need to consider other policies also (Atoyan et al. 2012). Obviously, the other policy tools refer to monetary and regulatory policies also. In brief, the new fiscal dominance may, no doubt, be warranted by high public debt but the policies of central banks may be compelled to meet threats to financial stability from other sources. Developing economies will naturally be affected by such developments in central banking and fiscal management.

* * *

The global financial crisis has drawn attention to the significant links be-tween central banking and fiscal management. The role of central banks in causing the crisis is a matter of considerable interest. However, central banks had to play a critical role in managing the crisis, and in the process, they had to operate in close coordination with fiscal authorities due to fiscal implications, particularly in advanced economies which were most affected. Monetary and fiscal policies may supplement, and may often substitute for each other in managing stimulus of the economy. Such tradition continued during the pandemic as well. An assessment of large fiscal implications in systemically important economies indicates poten-tial for a new framework for central banking whose contours continue to be unclear. A paradigm shift in the framework for central banking was expected. Correspondingly, new fiscal dominance may emerge which re-quires central banks to incorporate it along with other sources of threat to financial instability and inflation.

11
Sovereign Debt Restructuring

A significant fallout of the global financial crisis is the expansion of liquidity facilities for economies in distress, through bilateral currency swaps, multilateral arrangements between central banks, and through the IMF. A recent report of the World Bank (2022) noted that '(I)n the pandemic-induced global recession of 2020, global debt levels surged. The rise in debt has led to several countries initiating debt restructurings, while many others are in or at high risk of debt distress and may also eventually need debt relief.'

This report further noted that 'Historically, several umbrella frameworks coordinated debt relief to multiple debtor countries from multiple creditors on common principles. They offered substantial—but protracted—debt stock reductions that were typically preceded by a series of less ambitious debt relief efforts. The G20 Common Framework provides a structure to initiate debt restructuring for low-income IDA eligible countries, but largely avoids the issue of outright debt reductions. Future umbrella frameworks for debt restructuring will face greater challenges than those in the past due to a more fragmented creditor base.'

Inevitably, these pose issues of fiscal solvency or sovereign debt sustainability and sovereign debt restructuring, all of which have features very distinct from individuals and corporate entities. These are not entirely new issues, but they have acquired new significance after the global crisis, for several reasons (Sturzenegger and Zettelmever 2006). In particular, de facto debt restructuring of an advanced economy, Greece, in the eurozone has led to renewed interest in the history and policy of debt restructuring. Several fresh proposals for orderly sovereign debt resolution mechanisms have been mooted. The April 2012 communiqué of the G24 stated that 'the Euro area crisis has also highlighted the need for

Financial and Fiscal Policies. Second Edition. Y. V. Reddy, Partha Ray, and Pinaki Chakraborty, Oxford University Press.
© Y. V. Reddy, Partha Ray, and Pinaki Chakraborty 2024. DOI: 10.1093/9780198934288.003.0011

further study of sovereign debt restructuring mechanisms'.[1] The conduct of fiscal policy and its constituent part, management of public debt by national authorities in the future, is likely to be influenced by developments with regards to liquidity facilities available and mechanisms for debt restructuring. Such developments have acquired relevance for the first time since 1950, to advanced economies as much as to developing countries.

This chapter is devoted to exploration of emerging new realities of liquidity facilities for the sovereigns and sovereign debt restructuring in the global economy. The first section provides a backdrop of conceptual clarity on liquidity, solvency, and debt restructuring with regards to a sovereign. The second section reviews in detail the experiences with regards to liquidity support facilities. The third section provides some clarity on debt restructuring and related concepts, followed by a brief history of debt-restructuring mechanisms, and sums up the features of sovereign debt restructuring so far. The fourth section focuses on the proposals for improvements in mechanisms for debt restructuring consequent upon the global financial crisis. The fifth section discusses Chinese debt and the global financial system. The concluding part is devoted to an exploration of the emerging issues with regards to both liquidity and debt restructuring, which are interrelated.

Background

In discussing sovereign debt restructuring, it may be useful to start with some conceptual issues with an analogy of a firm. In the case of a firm, the terms *liquidity* and *solvency* are used to describe its ability to pay off its debts. The extent of debt can easily be determined from a firm's balance sheet identity. If a firm is illiquid it would mean that the firm does not have enough cash to pay off the debts readily when they are required to. If, however, the value of its asset is not sufficient to pay off its debt, it is a situation of *insolvency*. Essentially, *illiquidity* is a temporary situation of shortage of cash or other liquid assets, while *insolvency* is a situation where

---

[1] 'Intergovernmental Group of Twenty-Four on International Monetary Affairs and Development Communiqué' (19 April 2012), available at http:// www.imf.org/external/np/cm/ 2012/041912.htm.

the firm is bankrupt and has to face the prospect of closure in a market economy. When a sovereign is not in a position to discharge its cash obligations, it faces problems of liquidity; but there are complexities in assessing solvency because the government's access to assets and resources depends on its willingness and ability to mobilize resources from a variety of sources, including powers to legislate and tax. The limits to availability of liquidity and the scope for debt restructuring for the sovereign are, thus, mostly with regard to discharge of external obligations usually in foreign currency and occasionally to restructuring of debt owed to residents.

A related issue is the applicability of the concept of bankruptcy to sovereign. In the case of the US, for example, there are two relevant chapters of the Bankruptcy Codes, namely Chapter 7 (relating to 'straight bankruptcy liquidation', mostly for individuals) and Chapter 11 (primarily applicable to commercial enterprises that want to continue business operations while repaying creditors through a court-approved reorganization plan) that deserve special attention. A bankrupt firm uses Chapter 11 of the Bankruptcy Code to reorganize its business and try to become profitable again. In this case, management continues to run the day-to-day business operations but all significant business decisions must be approved by a bankruptcy court. This procedure represents some sort of holding operation for orderly restructuring of business and debt. On the contrary, under Chapter 7, the company stops all operations and goes completely out of business. A trustee is appointed to liquidate (sell) the company's assets and the money is used to pay off the debt, which may include debts to creditors and investors. Obviously, a sovereign cannot go out of business, and hence Chapter 7 is inapplicable. This conceptual uniqueness of sovereign debt needs to be appreciated in the context of sovereign debt restructuring. In any case, mechanisms for obtaining liquidity in the case of fiscal stress often, though not invariably, precede restructuring of sovereign debt. Hence, it is necessary to appreciate the liquidity support facilities available to a sovereign as a prerequisite to understanding the restructuring of sovereign debt.

Liquidity Support Facilities

In order to meet the liquidity demands under stressful conditions, a central bank or government has to depend on some sort of external liquidity support. The major forms of such liquidity support can occur either through central bank swap lines or from multilateral institutions like the IMF.

Swap Lines among Central Banks

A swap line is an arrangement whereby each of two central banks deposits an equivalent amount of its currency in the other central bank, usable by the respective central banks. Illustratively, a swap line between the US Fed and the Bank of England would involve two transactions. To begin with, when the Bank of England draws on its swap line, it sells a specified quantity of pound sterling to the US Fed in exchange for dollars at the prevailing market exchange rate. At the same time, the US Fed and the Bank of England enter into an agreement for which the Bank of England is obligated to buy back pound sterling at a future date at the same exchange rate. Because the exchange rate for the second transaction was set at the time of the first, there is no exchange rate risk associated with the swaps (Fleming and Klagge 2010). The Bank of England then may lend the dollars it obtained via the swap line to the UK institutions; the US Fed is, however, not a counterparty to any loan extended by the Bank of England to depository institutions. Thus, the Bank of England would bear the credit risk associated with such loans that it makes to the UK institutions.

The idea of swap when needed is not new, but in recent times, the idea of a swap line was first suggested by the Bank of France in the early 1960s. The first swap of $50 million was opened by the central bank of the US and France in March 1962. Swap arrangements totalling $2 billion were established between the Federal Reserve and eight other central banks by the end of 1962. The swaps were activated and used by Canada in 1962 and by Italy in 1963–4 (when the Bank of England and the German Bundesbank also provided credits), as well as by the US in the 1960s. Most of the activated swaps were quickly repaid. By 1975, the total had grown to $20 billion with 14 central banks and the Bank for International Settlement. Most of these older swap lines were phased out by mutual agreement in 1998, although Canada and Mexico retained swap lines of a small magnitude under the auspices of the North American Free Trade Agreement.

The 1997–8 East Asian crisis led to an initiative for creating a financing facility through which economies in the region can prevent or respond effectively to currency crises. ASEAN+3 leaders noted that there is a need for 'enhancing self-help and support mechanisms in East Asia through the ASEAN+3 Framework'.[2] The finance ministers of ASEAN+3 agreed in Chiang Mai in May 2000 to establish a regional network of swap arrangements for its members, thus launching the Chiang Mai Initiative (CMI). The CMI consists of two elements: (a) expansion of the existing ASEAN Swap Arrangement (ASA), and (b) creation of a new network of bilateral swap arrangements (BSAs) among APT members. By July 2007, 16 BSAs had been concluded, amounting to a total of $83 billion (Kawai and Houser 2007).

Subsequently, in February 2008, the fund was expanded to $120 billion. It is useful to note that most of the amount of swap can be drawn only if an IMF programme is put in place within a specified time. In a way, these liquidity support facilities are mostly in the nature of bridge loans in anticipation of an IMF programme.

The CMI, a multilateralized currency swap arrangement among the 10 members of the Association of Southeast Asian Nations (ASEAN), the People's Republic of China (including Hong Kong), Japan, and South Korea, draws from a foreign exchange reserves pool worth $120 billion and was launched on 24 March 2010. The APT also agreed to adopt the Chiang Mai Initiative Multilateralization Precautionary Line (CMIM-PL), which is designed on the model of Precautionary and Liquidity Line (PLL) programme within the IMF in order to prevent financial crisis.

Following the terrorist attacks of 11 September 2001, the US Fed had instituted a system of swap lines to ensure the continued smooth functioning of global financial markets. In the wake of the global financial crisis, the US Fed entered into temporary dollar liquidity swap arrangements with 14 foreign central banks between 12 December 2007 and 29 October 2008. In its press release, the Fed indicated that the swap lines,

[2] Members of ASEAN are: Brunei Darussalam, Cambodia, Indonesia, Lao PDR, Malaysia, Myanmar, Philippines, Singapore, Thailand, and Vietnam. The *plus three* countries are China, Japan, and South Korea. ASEAN plus three (APT) being a forum that functions as a coordinator of cooperation between the ASEAN and the *plus three* East Asian nations, under the aegis of APT framework, government leaders, ministers, and senior officials from these 10 member states, have consultations on an increasing range of issues.

like the Term Auction Facility created at the same time, were intended 'to address elevated pressures in short-term funding markets'. The arrangements expired on 1 February 2010. Subsequently, in May 2010, in response to the reemergence of strains in short-term dollar funding markets abroad, the dollar liquidity swap lines were initiated by the US Fed with five foreign central banks through January 2011. On 21 December 2010, these lines were extended further till 1 August 2011.

Faced with the euro area debt crisis, on 15 September 2011, the ECB announced additional US dollar liquidity-providing operations over year end and decided that in coordination with the US Fed, the Bank of England, the Bank of Japan, and the Swiss National Bank, to conduct three US dollar liquidity-providing operations with a maturity of approximately three months covering the end of the year. These operations were in addition to the ongoing weekly seven-day operations announced on 10 May 2010.

In June 2008, a BSA between Japan and India was signed. The BSA enabled both countries to swap their local currencies (i.e., either Japanese yen or Indian rupee) against the US dollar for an amount up to $3 billion. The arrangement aimed at addressing short-term liquidity difficulties and supplementing the existing international financial arrangements, as one of the efforts in strengthening mutual cooperation between Japan and India. The BSA gets activated when an IMF support programme already exists or is expected to be established in the near future. Nevertheless, up to 20 per cent of the maximum amount of drawing could be disbursed without an IMF support program. Both the countries are to have biannual consultations on economic and financial conditions of each country (RBI 2008). The BSA, which was originally operational for three years, has been renewed in December 2012 and the swap amount enhanced up to $15 billion and valid for three years (RBI 2012a).

It needs to be recognized from its history that most swap lines are typically available to select advanced country central banks. Admittedly, the CMIs gave birth to some sort of reserve pooling mechanism, but the mechanism is linked to a time-bound IMF programme. As of now, when faced with a sovereign debt crisis, most countries continue to approach the IMF for some support in terms of liquidity under several programmes.

IMF Liquidity Support

This section gives a very brief account of the broad contours of liquidity support from the IMF.[3] If a member country of the IMF faces a potential or actual balance of payments problem, it can approach the IMF for financial assistance or liquidity support. Any crisis period typically witnesses large increases in IMF liquidity support. Illustratively, during the debt crisis of the 1980s, there were sharp increases in IMF lending. More recently, in the wake of the global financial crisis, IMF lending started rising since late 2008.

Generically, IMF loans can be subdivided into two broad groups, concessional and non-concessional. Low-income countries may borrow on concessional terms through various types of IMF facilities, such as the Extended Credit Facility (ECF), the Standby Credit Facility (SCF), and the Rapid Credit Facility (RCF). Non-concessional loans are provided mainly through Stand-By Arrangements (SBA), the Flexible Credit Line (FCL), the Precautionary Credit Line (PCL), and the Extended Fund Facility (which is useful primarily for longer-term needs). Of these, SBA and FCL deserve special mention. The bulk of non-concessional fund assistance is provided through SBAs, the length of which is typically 12–24 months, and repayment is due within 3¼–5 years of disbursement. In the wake of the financial crisis, the IMF has introduced another new facility, namely, FCL. The FCL is for countries with very strong fundamentals, policies, and track records of policy implementation. These are particularly useful for crisis prevention purposes. Another version of FCL, namely PCL, has recently been introduced by the IMF. The PCL is similar to FCLs with one exception. Countries qualified under PCL may face moderate vulnerabilities and they may not qualify for FCL but at the same time they will not require the same large-scale policy adjustments normally associated with traditional SBAs.

It should be noted that both the central bank swap lines and IMF loans are intended to be liquidity support for a country for a limited period. Their effectiveness will be limited when a country faces an acute debt

---

[3] This section draws on the Factsheet on 'IMF Lending', available at http://www.imf.org/exter nal/np/exr/facts/howlend.htm (accessed in September 2024).

crisis that cannot be resolved by temporary liquidity support without un-acceptable disruptions to public policy. In such cases, sovereign debt re-structuring becomes relevant, in which the IMF may also play a role.

Concepts and Features of Debt Restructuring

Debt restructuring may involve debt rescheduling with or without a re-duction in the face (nominal value) of the old instruments. When there is a restructuring involving reduction in the value of outstanding debt obligations, it is treated as debt relief. Debt buybacks, with or without dis-count, may also be considered as debt restructuring, but they have been rare in the recent past.

The concept of credit event has become relevant now since it is used in the context of CDS, which have grown exponentially in the recent past. A credit event in the context of CDS contracts occurs when there is a de-fault or restructuring or repudiation. Thus, a credit event could be on the account of failure to pay a coupon or principal on a bond or loan. It could also be due to distressed debt restructuring that changes the terms of a debt obligation to the disadvantage of investors. This may happen through an extension of maturities, cutting the debt's face value or interest rate, or a change in the payment ranking or currency of the outstanding debt obligations. Finally, the event may occur when the announcement is made by an authorized official of the intention to suspend payments due to debtors. Sovereign debt restructuring, which till recently was essen-tially between governments and banks, and more recently the dispersed bondholders, has now become complex with ripple effects on financial markets through extensive prevalence of CDS.

Debt incurred by a sovereign merely to strengthen itself in the context of a popular movement without any regard to the needs or interests of the state is described as *odious*. Such debts are treated as those incurred by the regime and not the state. There are only a very few instances in his-tory when governments succeeded in refusing to honour the debt obliga-tions on this account. A recent instance is that of Ecuador in 2008, when President Rafael Correa declared Ecuador sovereign debt as illegitimate odious debt. He held that such debts were incurred by corrupt and des-potic regimes of the past. Ecuador had some success in reducing the debt obligations before paying the debt. There are proposals to declare ex ante that borrowings by a particular regime are odious in order to dissuade lenders in advance, but this is found to be infeasible.

A review of the characteristics of debt restructuring since the 1950s by a recent IMF paper provides some interesting features which are worthy of recall here (Das et al. 2012). There has been no distressed sovereign debt restructuring in an advanced economy since 1950. All restructurings occurred in developing or emerging market economies. Sovereign debt restructurings have taken place both with private creditors (foreign banks and bondholders) and restructured bilateral debt with the Paris Club. Most restructurings were with bank loans, and some were sovereign bond restructurings. Some involved a cut in face value (debt reduction), while most implied only a lengthening of maturities (debt rescheduling). Both operations can involve a *haircut*, that is, a loss in the present value of creditor claims. A majority of cases of restructuring occurred post-default though others took recourse to restructuring, to pre-empt default. An overwhelming majority of restructuring implied the exchange of old into new debt instruments.

Some of the developing countries have utilized the mechanism of the Paris Club to restructure external bilateral sovereign debt, mainly official debt. The Paris Club is an informal group of creditors and is an ad hoc negotiation forum. The London Club restructuring refers to negotiations between governments and commercial banks that have lent to governments. This is also ad hoc and, in fact, was taken recourse to only on a case-by-case basis for restructuring of debt owed by sovereign entities of developing countries to the banks.

In 1982, when Mexico suspended current payments to its creditors, the sovereign debt situation assumed crisis proportions. Consequently, there was reluctance on the part of the private lenders to provide new loans, while slow growth, inflation, and capital flight affected some developing countries. In this context, the US Secretary of the Treasury, James Baker, made a proposal in 1985, which has been described as the Baker Plan. He proposed a *programme for sustained growth* to deal with the debt problem. The programme had three major elements. The principal debtor countries would adopt comprehensive macroeconomic and structural policies, supported by the international financial institutions. A continued central role for the IMF, in conjunction with increased and more effective structural adjustment lending by the multilateral development banks had to be ensured. Increased lending by the private banks in support of comprehensive economic adjustment programmes was to follow.

In 1989, the US Treasury under then Treasury Secretary Nicholas F. Brady formulated a new strategy for dealing with developing country debt. The strategy, known as the Brady Plan, recognized that reversing the capital flight from debtor nations was critical to the strategy. The main focus of the Brady Plan was on debt and debt service reduction by commercial bank creditors for those debtors who agreed to implement substantial economic reform programmes.[4] The Plan offered banks credit enhancements in exchange for their agreement to reduce claims. These credit enhancements were created by two stages: (a) first converting commercial bank loans into bonds, and (b) then collateralizing principal and rolling interest payments on those bonds with US Treasury zeroes purchased with the proceeds of IMF and World Bank loans. Brady restructurings have been implemented in approximately 16 countries, resulting in a $150 billion-plus market in Brady bonds, which are fundamentally US dollar-denominated bonds issued by an emerging market and collateralized by US Treasury zero coupons having 10- to 30-year maturity.[5]

The sovereign debt was dominated by bank financing till the 1990s. However, in the 1990s, sovereign debt was increasingly held by a large number of bondholders, and hence restructuring through informal negotiations became operationally very difficult. There have been many proposals for debt-restructuring mechanisms, but there are really only three basic approaches (Dodd 2002). First, a proposal from the IMF called for the creation of an institution to act as an arbiter along the lines of an international bankruptcy court. Known as the Sovereign Debt Restructuring Mechanism (SDRM), it was inspired by the US corporate bankruptcy reorganization law under Chapter 11 of the 1978 Bankruptcy Act (Krueger

---

[4] It is interesting to note that Mr Brady said in an interview to *Time Magazine*, 'Our objective is to rekindle the hope of the people and leaders of debtor nations that their sacrifices will lead to greater prosperity in the present and the prospect of a future unclouded by the burden of debt' ('Enter The Brady Plan', *Time*, 20 March 1989).

[5] The ghosts of the Brady Plan haunts us even at the present time, as in the context of the recent Greek debt crisis, a headline in the *Financial Times* mentions: 'The monetary union now needs an ambitious and comprehensive solution: it should commit to a Brady plan for Europe' (*Financial Times* 2011).

2002). Second, another proposal from the US Treasury advocated the involvement of a majority of creditors to set the terms of restructuring. A related proposal was in line with an adaptation of US sovereign bankruptcy laws, known as Chapter 9, to the needs of developing countries. Third, there was a model code of conduct for the borrower countries.

The SDRM proposals faced strong opposition.[6] Apart from the investor community, the middle-income countries were against it. This has led commentators to label it as 'The SDRM project nobody liked' (Simpson 2006). The private sector, the Wall Street-based investment banks were against it as the SDRM, in some sense, transgressed the market mechanism. Two proposals emerged as strong alternatives: (a) the US Treasury proposal and (b) the model code of conduct for the borrowers of the Institute of International Finance.

In April 2002, the US Treasury proposed a reform strategy that expanded upon traditional collective action clauses. John B. Talyor, the then Undersecretary of the US Treasury, proposed a variant of the SDRM. This approach with its *contractual* emphasis wanted to retain the market-oriented approach towards restructuring while utilizing some additional tools. The approach called for sovereign borrowers and creditors to insert a package of new *contingency clauses* into future bond contracts, which would describe the process that would be followed if a restructuring proved necessary (Taylor 2002).

The call for a code of conduct originally came from the then Governor of the Banque de France, Jean-Claude Trichet. Subsequently, in November 2004, major sovereign issuers of international bonds and global leaders of private finance announced agreement on a set of 'Principles for Stable Capital Flows and Fair Debt Restructuring in Emerging Markets' under the aegis of the Institute of International Finance (IIF). The Principles focused on four areas, namely, transparency and timely flow of information, close debtor–creditor dialogue and cooperation to avoid restructuring, good faith actions, and fair treatment.

---

[6] The main response to SDRM has been a sharp revival of interest in contractual restructuring procedures based on collective-action clauses. These clauses, which facilitate debt workouts by providing for majority decision making by bondholders, have traditionally been included in bonds issued under British law. By custom, they are generally not included in bonds issued under New York law; see Group of Thirty (2002) for details.

The SDRM proposal failed to take off. At its spring 2003 meeting, the IMFconcluded that it was not feasible to establish the SDRM. It did, though, agree that work should continue on the issues raised in discussion of the SDRM that relate more generally to the orderly resolution of financial crises, including aggregation. While there are technical reasons behind its failure to take off, there are political economy-related angularities, which have been summed up cogently as:

> *Different constituencies with a stake in the sovereign bankruptcy process had very different conceptions of what a sovereign bankruptcy regime should do. Groups who agreed on the need for an international bankruptcy regime in theory often had radically different visions of what sovereign bankruptcy should look like . . .* The debate in the IMF executive board left many constituencies with a stake in emerging market debt, and thus in an international sovereign bankruptcy regime, with a sense that their concerns were represented only indirectly. These difficulties . . . were not the product of outdated voting weights that leave Europe over-represented and Asia under-represented on the IMF board. Rather, they stemmed from the conflicting interests of many of the IMF's leading countries. The countries of the Group of 7 (G7) had to choose between representing the interest of the private financial institutions inside their countries and their interest in limiting the need to commit public resources provided by the G7's taxpayers to rescue troubled emerging economies. The major emerging economy borrowers were even more torn. They had to choose between defending their interest as borrowers seeking access to private capital in the markets, their interest in preserving their ability to borrow large sums from the IMF, and their interest in a better restructuring process. (Setser 2008, pp. 2–3; emphasis ours)

Proposals for Improvement

The global financial crisis has triggered interest in sovereign debt restructuring globally. The first comprehensive proposal after the global crisis came from the Stiglitz Report in 2010. It proposed the creation of an

'International Debt Restructuring Court' similar to national bankruptcy courts. The Report suggests that, as an interim step to the establishment of such a court, an International Mediation Service be created. This is meant to be a kind of *soft law* to facilitate the creation of norms for sovereign debt restructurings. The Report adds that even after the creation of the court, there is a presumption that judicial proceedings would be preceded by mediation.

A five-point agenda for global arrangements for resolving sovereign debt crisis has been proposed by the Centre for International Governance Innovation (CIGI) under the aegis of the Institute for New Economic Thinking (INET) in August 2012 (Schadler 2012).

In October 2012 a special event took place at UN headquarters. The event considered the proposals made by UNCTAD. The participants noted that earlier work on the creation of a sovereign debt-restructuring mechanism focused on credit coordination which is a problem that can be partly solved with the introduction of collective action clauses. The participants recognized that problems of fairness, seniority, interim financing, and delayed restructuring are more important than creditor coordination. A report on this event is very comprehensive and worthy of note:

> The first problem is that of lengthy debt negotiations which, in some cases, do not restore debt sustainability . . . The second problem is the need to coordinate the interest of dispersed creditors, and to deal with bondholders, who have an incentive to hold out from debt restructuring deals . . . The third is lack of access to private interim financing during the restructuring process. In the corporate world, interim financing is guaranteed by the presence of debt-in-possession financing provisions, but sovereign debt lacks a mechanism able to enforce seniority. Lack of access to private interim financing may amplify the crisis and further reduce the ability to pay . . . And the final area of priority is delayed debt defaults. While most economic models of sovereign debt assume that countries have an incentive to default too much or too early, there is evidence that countries often try to postpone the moment of reckoning and may sub-optimally delay the beginning of the debt restructuring process. (Muchhala 2013)

The special event was followed by a technical stakeholders' meeting during which experts discussed the pros and cons of different institutional set-ups of a possible debt-restructuring mechanism. The UNCTAD Expert Group on Responsible Sovereign Lending and Borrowing also held a meeting to discuss the guidelines on implementation of the principles.

At the event, a paper authored by the Chief Economist of South Centre was presented, giving justification and mechanisms for statutory debt workout (Akyuz 2013). There were extensive references to the fact that the restructuring of some Greek debt that was owed to private creditors shows that private debtors could be persuaded to share the burdens of resolving sovereign debt crises. Of particular interest to developing countries are the comments attributed by South Bulletin to Professor Kenneth Rogoff in the event.

Rogoff stressed that a deeper question remains of why such a large percentage of international capital flows get channelled through debt, and whether it can be shaped in the future in a more balanced way. Equity and direct foreign investment are arguably somewhat more robust than debt. Thus, an international bankruptcy regime that weakens creditors' rights is not necessarily inefficient. Perhaps an ideal regime is one with strong creditor rights but with extensive indexation of debt to GDP, commodity price, etc., depending on country circumstances.

The bulletin further reports:

A big challenge in re-doing the international financial architecture, Rogoff argued, is to try to redirect some of the financial flows that currently go through loans (about 75 per cent of the international tradable market supply is funnelled via debt), and instead channel it through other instruments such as indexation, commodity prices and so on. (Muchhala 2013)

Two important implications of the noteworthy observations of Professor Rogoff are: that the discussion on international architecture should encompass the composition of capital flows, and that sovereign debt instruments are in dire need of innovations.

Chinese Debt and the Global Financial System

Global debt servicing costs are increasing rapidly while annual refinancing needs have tripled to about $60 billion (Allison and Pazarbasioglu 2024). This is 'about three times the average in the decade through 2020. But with many competing demands for financing, including from advanced and emerging market economies that are also trying to adapt to climate change, there's a significant risk of a liquidity crunch—failure to raise sufficient financing at an affordable cost. That could in turn lead to a destabilizing debt crisis' (Allison and Pazarbasioglu 2024). In the face of rising debt servicing cost, complexity of debt management has only compounded due to the rising Chinese investment and lending to the low-income developing countries. In this section, we briefly discuss the rising Chinese lending and its implications for global debt management. While China's dominant footprint in world trade and global output is well known, its expanding role in international finance is poorly understood (Horn et al. 2019). As observed by Horn et al., when it comes to Chinese lending, the data is scarce and the process of lending is not transparent and there is little research available on the subject. In this section, we have collected some information on Chinese lending from the International Debt Statistics 2022, published by the World Bank, to understand the magnitude of the lending and investment operation by China.

China has become the largest borrower and lender among low- and middle-income countries. As evident from the International Debt Statistics (2022):

(O)ver the past decade almost 60 percent of net aggregate financial flows to low- and middle-income countries from external creditors and investors went to China. Over this period China received inflows close to $4 trillion, of which 40 percent were debt-creating flows and 60 percent were foreign direct investment and portfolio equity flows. In 2020, aggregate financial flows to China rose 32 percent to $466 billion, driven by a 62 percent increase in net debt inflows to $233 billion and a 12 percent rise in net equity inflows also to $233 billion.

At the same time China has emerged as one of the major lenders to low-income developing economies.

Low- and middle-income countries' combined debt to China was $170 billion at end-2020, more than three times the comparable level in 2011. To put this figure in context, low- and middle-income countries' combined obligations to the International Bank for Reconstruction and Development were $204 billion at end-2020 and to the International Development Association $177 billion. Most of the debt owed to China relates to large infrastructure projects and operations in the extractive industries. Countries in Sub-Saharan Africa, led by Angola, have seen one of the sharpest rises in Chinese debt although the pace of accumulation has slowed since 2018. The region accounted for 45 per cent of end-2020 obligations to China. In South Asia, debt to China has risen from $4.7 billion in 2011 to $36.3 billion in 2020, and China is now the largest bilateral creditor to the Maldives, Pakistan, and Sri Lanka (International Debt Statistics 2022).

The nature of Chinese loans to various countries is given in Box 11.1. How important is Chinese debt? Horn, Reinhart, and Trebesch (2021) point out:

As of 2017, China surpassed the outstanding claims of the World Bank, IMF, or all 22 Paris Club governments combined. Unlike other major economies, much of China's external lending is official, meaning that it is undertaken by China's government, state-owned policy banks, or other state-owned entities. The lending terms of China's official overseas loans, however, resemble commercial lending transactions in that most loans have short maturities and relatively high interest rates.

Rising Chinese debt poses several challenges to the global financial system. First, the 'hidden debts' owed to China are consequential for debt sustainability in recipient countries and pose serious challenges for macroeconomic surveillance work and the market pricing of sovereign risk (Horn et al. 2019). Second, available literature shows that around 50 per cent of Chinese lending is collateralized (Horn et al. 2019). This poses a major risk for debt restructuring and has the potential to reduce public revenues of the debtor countries. Third, since one of the key drivers of

---

Box 11.1   The Nature of Chinese Loans to Low- and Middle-Income Countries

China extends loans to low- and middle-income countries on concessional and non-concessional terms. There are four main types of loans. The first type is concessional loans extended by the government of China at very low interest rates or interest-free, funded from tax revenues. These loans are denominated in renminbi and managed by the China International Development Cooperation Agency. The second type is concessional loans from the Export–Import Bank of China (Chexim) managed by the Preferential Loans Department. There are two types of loans: (1) concessional loans denominated in renminbi funded by the government and (2) US-dollar-denominated 'preferential buyers' credits financed from Chexim's own resources. The third, and largest type, is non-concessional loans extended by policy banks, Chexim, the China Development Bank, and the Agricultural Development Bank of China. Policy banks fund their operations through bond issuance in the domestic (CIBM) and international capital markets. Loans from policy banks are denominated in US dollars and have market interest rates and medium-term maturities. The fourth type is loans from Chinese commercial banks and suppliers insured by China's official export credit agency, SINOSURE.

Source: Box O.1, World Bank 2022, pp. 8–9. International Debt Statistics 2022. Washington, DC: World Bank. doi:10.1596/978-1-4648-1800-4. License: Creative Commons Attribution CC BY 3.0 IGO.

---

low-income developing countries' debt is due to the Chinese lending at higher than other alternative sources of borrowing, this has implications for development spending and fiscal space. Going forward Chinese debt is going to be of significant importance to the global economy.

Emerging Issues

A by-product of the global financial crisis was the large public debt of advanced economies relative to their GDP. The pandemic has resulted in significant increase in debt in both advanced and emerging market economies. As mentioned in the World Bank (2022) report: 'In 2020 total global debt reached 263 percent of GDP, its highest level in half a century. The buildup has been broad based, with rapid growth in both government and private debt; advanced-economy and emerging market and developing economies (EMDEs) debt; and external and domestic debt (Kose, Nagle et al. 2021).' As debt vulnerabilities have increased, some countries have already defaulted on their debt, some have been restructured, and some are in the process of debt restructuring (World Bank 2022).

During the pandemic, the World Bank Group President David Malpass and IMF Managing Director Kristalina Georgieva made a proposal

for a debt moratorium to help countries cope with the COVID-19 pandemic, [and] the G20 announced the Debt Service Suspension Initiative (DSSI). The DSSI offered debt payment suspension on official sector debts for the poorest countries to create fiscal space to increase social, health or economic spending in response to the crisis but did not reduce debt stocks or require private sector participation. In November 2020, the G20 announced the 'Common Framework' which would provide a forum for DSSI-eligible countries to seek debt relief if their debt is considered unsustainable by the IMF and the World Bank (G20 2020).

Going forward, fiscal stress may be experienced by the advanced economies as well as the developing countries. For the advanced economies when the demographic profile reduces the share of working age population and increases the share of those that need social welfare benefits, the fiscal stress will arise to meet these obligations. In view of the size of their economies and their systemic importance, the impact of fiscal stress of advanced economies on the global economy is likely to be significant. For the developing and emerging economies, the issues are primarily related to creating fiscal space for development and growth recovery on a sustainable basis.

The fiscal stress often brings about issues of liquidity facilities and debt sustainability, including the scope and limit for debt restructuring. Further, unlike in the past when developing countries faced sovereign debt crisis, the share of debt in the capital flows in the global economy has increased substantially. The public debt is held by widely dispersed bond holders. Further, the proportion of public debt being held by non-residents of a country is considerably larger than ever before. The global crisis has also brought into focus the close links between the financial sector and fiscal management. In brief, the environment for liquidity facilities and sovereign debt restructuring in future may be complex and history may be less helpful in facing the policy challenges of the future in this regard.

A recent study by Saakai Ando et al. (2023) observed that 'debt restructuring has a significant and long-lasting impact on the debt-to-GDP ratio. The impact is even larger when combined with fiscal consolidation. In the short run, restructurings with face value reduction and higher creditor coordination tend to be more effective, compared to the average. In the long run, however, the depth of treatment is important, irrespective of how restructuring is executed.'

It is clear from the narration in the chapter that liquidity support facilities for countries are conceivable from several sources, namely, bilateral sources which are mostly ad hoc, and IMF. It has also been noticed that the reserve currency country has a critical role to play. In fact, at the time of the global crisis for which the epicentre was the US and with which the US Fed was grappling, the necessary liquidity had to be provided to other central banks by the US Fed. In brief, therefore, it is necessary to appreciate the role of reserve currencies and the IMF, in addition to the bilateral swaps in the availability of liquidity support facilities. Currently, the global monetary system is characterized by what has been described as a non-system with the dominance of the US dollar as the reserve currency. It is also recognized that this non-system may be undergoing change in future, in view of the experience with the global financial crisis and other developments in the global economy. The issue then would be the implications for liquidity support facilities of changes in the current non-system dominated by the US dollar. In brief, the evolution of the international and monetary financial system will have an important bearing on the future of liquidity facilities.

It is clear that in the past the IMF had a critical role to play in the provision of liquidity to most developing economies, and more recently to countries within the reserve currency area, namely, the eurozone. However, it must be recognized that there are limitations for the IMF on its own and in its discretion to expand global liquidity and withdraw such liquidity as appropriate, and in a prompt manner. Further, its capacity to distinguish between liquidity and solvency of a country, particularly of an advanced economy, has still not been tested. In any case, the IMF may not be in a position to assume the risk of solvency if its assessment of a country's economic stress as one of liquidity rather than solvency turns out to be wrong. There is recognition that the IMF is already stressed in terms of resources and greater demand on its resources may not be unexpected if the global uncertainty continued. In addition, there is a growing feeling that the conditionality that has been suggested to an advanced economy like Greece is significantly diluted relative to developing economies. Whether approaching the IMF entails reputational risk is still a moot point. Above all, any liquidity from the IMF has a senior creditor status and, therefore, comfort of other creditors with the IMF programme may not be entirely unmixed. In brief, the limits to the IMF's ability to provide liquidity support in future should be continuously assessed.

There has been some evidence of regional mechanisms in the nature of self-insurance, of which CMI is the most striking. CMI is meant to be a mechanism of *regional insurance* in the sense that it assures liquidity facilities within a group of countries in the region. The mechanism, as already described, is meant to assure the financial markets also of the availability of liquidity when needed. At the same time, there is peer pressure through regional surveillance to incentivize policies that are conducive to the success of the arrangement. It has enormous significance for boosting confidence of the national authorities in their macroeconomic management and promoting harmonization of their macro policies. The mechanism of multilateral surveillance incorporated into the arrangement enables such harmonization and thus may also help insulate the participants' economies of the region from individual national policies that may endanger regional economy. The size of the fund has been increased recently with a credible promise of making available resources when called upon.

The CMI, in terms of bilateral swaps, did not stand the test of time in 2008. The affected countries approached mainly the US Federal Reserve for bilateral swaps, partly due to the size of requirements and partly to win the confidence of financial markets, in addition to the need for rapid response. The multi-lateralization of the fund made attempts in

2010 to correct some of the infirmities, but the need to approach IMF with its accompanying stigma, perhaps, continues to operate for CMI also. Improvements suggested for enhanced effectiveness of the CMIM (Chiang Mai Initiative Multilateralization) include increasing the size of its lendable resources, broadening its membership to include India, improved surveillance among member states, and introducing a Regional Monetary Unit within the member states (Hill and Menon 2012).

As a consequence of the success of trade integration in East Asia, there was considerable enthusiasm for a common currency. The Asian Development Bank had pursued some research work on the subject. However, the global financial crisis has moderated the enthusiasm for further financial integration within the region and has also put on hold serious consideration of currency union. Experience with the EU demonstrates the importance of political convergence as either a precondition or a goal for such a union. It is difficult to hold that such preconditions exist in East Asia.[7]

While there has been a call for establishing a sovereign debt-resolution mechanism, there have been three main objections to formalization of such mechanisms. First, it is argued that such mechanisms will have an element of moral hazard, resulting in higher borrowing cost for the borrowing countries. However, there is no empirical evidence to establish this. Second, it has been argued that market-based arrangements, including collective action clauses, have been useful and, therefore, they need to be extended. However, experience in this regard has been limited, and prima facie, the coordination issues may persist. Third, it is argued that it is extremely difficult for having a formal official mechanism that would carry out the task of differentiating between the capacity to take and willingness to pay the debts by a sovereign. This argument is not without basis.

The distinction between illiquidity and insolvency is particularly complex in respect of the sovereign which has no scope for *exit* and is thus

---

[7] A related development is the proposed launching of a BRICS Development Bank (BRICS Bank). However, as decided earlier, the BRICS Bank was not launched at the 2013 BRICS Summit in Durban, South Africa. While the 2013 Summit agreed to establish the BRICS Contingent Reserve Arrangement (a stabilization fund of $100 billion in reserves) and a BRICS Business Council to stimulate trade and investment, the actual launch of the BRICS Bank itself was postponed until the next summit in Brazil in 2014; see Institute of Development Studies (2013) for details.

not amenable to being subject to a *bankruptcy* code. Consequently it becomes very difficult to judge whether a sovereign is unwilling to pay or unable to pay, since ability to pay depends on economic consequence on the economy of discharging all obligations of sovereign debt. Further, at times of economic shock, the distinction between willingness and ability is blurred, impacting the process of debt restructuring.

Interestingly, there is a view that delays in debt-restructuring negotiations due to non-existence of formal mechanisms may be mutually beneficial for the defaulting country and the debt holder. The argument is based on some important features of the real world whereby *waiting for a larger cake* would be helpful for all concerned (Ran Bi 2008). The study, however, is based on the cases of sovereign debt restructurings mostly during 1982–94. All the countries covered were developing countries. These cases related to a pre-crisis situation. There seems to be considerable global interest in formal mechanisms for sovereign debt restructuring after the crisis, than before, when the study was undertaken.

It is useful to explore the constraints on and the prospects for establishing debt-restructuring mechanisms. An important consideration in the prospects for debt restructuring relates to the laws governing the issue of bonds. In regard to almost all the bonds issued by the emerging economies, the laws and the jurisdictions for enforcement and adjudication governing them are mostly in the US, followed by the UK, Germany, and Japan. On the other hand, bonds issued by Greece were governed by its own laws, which seem to have made it easier to *persuade* bond holders to accept voluntary cuts, thus avoiding the trigger for a credit default event for purposes of CDS transactions. It is not only Argentina which has been subjected to litigation relating to debt default but also poorer countries including those that are beneficiaries of special dispensation by multilateral institutions like the IMF and World Bank. Thus, the governing laws of most bonds issued by sovereigns are loaded heavily against emerging economies.

On a different plane, there have been instances of restructuring of domestic sovereign debt also. Where it happened, the adjudication was domestic and barring a few exceptions such as Russia, the debt was mostly held by residents. No doubt, complications due to exchange rate risks will not devolve on the sovereign when domestic sovereign debt is denominated in domestic currency. It needs to be recognized that even in cases where sovereign bonds are issued in domestic currency by emerging economies, non-resident bond holders will necessarily be comfortable with jurisdiction of the emerging economy for enforcement and arbitration.

It must be noted that similar considerations will apply in regard to *quasi-sovereign debt* that is debt issued by public enterprises or guaranteed by the sovereign. While restructuring of their default does not constitute a sovereign debt restructuring, it has serious reputational risk for the sovereign and often impacts the sovereign credit rating by rating agencies. In particular, developing countries are vulnerable to such risks in view of the significant use of public enterprises and guarantees as instruments of public policy.

More recently, CDS are being issued and traded extensively. These have grown exponentially. CDS is a derivative contract similar to an insurance policy on a bond, namely, that the debt will be serviced. Those sovereign debt restructurings which are legally considered *voluntary* between the sovereigns and bond holder are not treated as a triggering *credit event*. Barring one stray case of Ecuador, there is no experience with regard to a trigger event. An issue for developing countries is the implications of CDS on the debt markets as a whole, and the possible impact on the scope for debt restructuring, if the need were to arise.

It is evident that the prospects for establishing orderly sovereign debt-restructuring mechanisms are very limited. The disorderly case-by-case debt restructuring appears to favour the financial markets relative to sovereigns. The financial market, and arguably the financial system as a whole, has considerable advantages in ensuring that there exist credit risk-free financial instruments to operate as benchmarks to assess and price other risks. Efforts at enforcing good creditor conduct and good debtor conduct for debt restructuring are bound to fail as long as creditors and debtors are located in different jurisdictions and the governing law of dominant international financial centres favours creditors.

To sum up, there are considerable uncertainties with regard to the liquidity support facilities available in future in the global economy, particularly for meeting the needs of developing economies. The prospects for formal debt-restructuring mechanisms that would give comfort to sovereigns at the time of fiscal stress do not appear to be very bright. In such a situation, the assessment of debt sustainability by policymakers will have to take account of the perception of financial markets, the prospects for liquidity, and in the extreme case, the scope for relatively smooth debt restructuring. Second, the links between the nature and composition of global capital flows and the scope for crisis as well as debt restructuring need to be visited in the light of the comments made by Professor Rogoff. Finally, fiscal management and the closely related subject of regulation of financial markets in each country, particularly in developing economies, will have to take note of the developments in the international financial architecture as well.

Some Evidence of New Approaches in Policy

There is some evidence of consideration of new approaches among policy circles to taxation of the financial sector. First, the European Commission supported the establishment of ex-ante resolution funds based on the *polluter pays* principle, outside the financial stability framework. An EU approach was sought for financing the fund through contributions based on the relevant institution's assets, liabilities, or its profits. The Commission had planned to adopt legislative proposals to this end in early 2011 (European Commission [EC] 2011). Second, there was a proposal for levy of a financial transactions tax at 0.1 per cent on trading of stocks and bonds, and 0.01 per cent for derivatives contracts. The tax was to be applied throughout the euro area. The proposal originally envisaged implementation from January 2014 but was deferred considerably in view of notable opposition to this proposal, especially from the UK. While the details of the proposal are yet to be finalized, in April 2014, the EU's Court of Justice rejected the UK's challenge to the introduction of a financial transactions tax.

Third, the US proposed a Financial Crisis Responsibility fee to recover intervention costs. The proposal originally envisaged an annual levy of 0.15 per cent on total liabilities (Claessens et al. 2010). Fourth, the UK and France have introduced temporary bonus taxes. The Bank Pay Roll Tax, taxing all bonus payments at 50 per cent, expired in 2010, while in France a similar tax was levied for the accounting year 2009 (IMF 2011). Fifth, four alternative forms of taxation have been developed, which include tax on bonuses, and tax on financial transactions that have been described. In addition, the IMF considered a Financial Securities Contribution linked to a resolution mechanism and Financial Activities Tax (EEAG 2011).

Shared Objectives

The objectives and focus of regulation of the financial sector have been refined in the light of the experience with the global crisis. These include a review of adequacy of level of risk capital and definition of the required capital ratio. It also includes putting in place mechanisms that will dissuade excessive risk taking by financial intermediaries. Regulations seek to reduce the likelihood of failure of individual institutions, particularly banks, and they also seek to put in place mechanisms for orderly resolution of stresses in individual institutions, if they arise.

The objectives of taxation of the financial sector are also being reviewed in the light of the experience with the crisis. First, taxes on financial intermediaries have been proposed in order to defray the expenses incurred by governments in bailout operations. The objective is clearly to make the financial sector pay for externalizing its costs. No doubt, several issues arise with regard to computing the fiscal cost of bailout and unfairness in imposing burden of past deeds on current or future operations of economic agents. Second, taxes are proposed for creating a fund to facilitate support to the financial sector in the case of distress in future. This is essentially in the nature of insurance for the future. The design of the tax is critical, since there are possibilities of moral hazard in instituting such funding sources. However, the purpose of the tax is forward looking and is aimed at supplementing the regulatory objective of putting in place orderly resolution mechanisms in cases of distress. Third, there is interest in taking recourse to taxes on financial transactions, which in any case do exist in many countries in several forms, with a specific regulatory objective of moderating excess volatility in financial markets. There is considerable experience with regard to such taxes in several jurisdictions but the objective of such taxes on financial transactions is revenue to exchequers, and not related to regulation of the financial sector. In some cases, such a tax was leviable by sub-national governments. In the context of the crisis, there has been considerable discussion on the desirability of such taxes to moderate risks. However, their effects on volatility, liquidity, and price discovery are debatable. Their feasibility, in the absence of global coordination, is also questionable. In this context, there has been revival of interest in taxes on foreign exchange transactions, namely, the Tobin Tax.

It is necessary to recognize that the report of the IMF to the G20 on the subject of taxation of the financial sector was restricted in its scope of mandate, namely, the consideration of fair and substantial contribution towards paying for any burden associated with government interventions in the banking system. In doing so, it is clear that the IMF was primarily concerned with what it considered as excess burden on the financial sector. The Report of the OECD Secretary General to the G20 in February 2023 highlighted the progress made in the implementation of a global minimum tax on corporates but was silent on the taxation of the financial sector (OECD 2023).

Regulation and Taxation

The major tool of regulation to mitigate the effects of excess leverage is prescription of desired capital or leverage ratio. It is possible to argue that the same objective can be met by taxing leverage. Similarly, the buffers against instability that are sought to be built within each financial intermediary through regulation seek to internalize the issue of externalities but taxes can provide mechanisms for encouraging building of such buffers.

The Report of the IMF to the G20 noted the prevailing practices in relation to taxes on financial transactions, but were not favoured primarily on the ground that they are not focused on core sources of financial instability and not related to financing of resolution mechanisms. It was also observed that the real burden of financial transactions tax may fall largely on final consumers rather than on earnings of the financial sector.

It is also clear that the proposals for taxation in the context of the crisis were motivated by the public outcry on bailout of the financial sector at the expense of taxpayers. The proposals were aimed at collecting revenues to meet pre-specified expenditures. The proposal of the EC was also in a similar context. However, at an analytical level, the inter-reactions between taxation and regulation have attracted serious attention.

It is possible to levy taxes in a way that they favour appropriate equity relative to debt. With regard to liquidity management too, taxes can be designed to provide incentives that favour longer-term instruments over shorter-term ones. Yet, regulation reforms have been preferred to taxation to address the issues of externalities in the financial sector.

There are several reasons for greater reliance on regulation of the financial sector than taxation. First, there is a long history of regulation, and both experience and institutional arrangements make it attractive to build on them. Second, there are severe problems of designing a tax regime that meets the objectives. The route of regulation provides greater scope for discretion and flexibility in application to evolving circumstances relative to taxation. Third, it is operationally smoother to ensure coordination at a global level among regulators than through fiscal authorities involving legislative sanctions.

There is, however, a broader issue, namely, whether the tax system has elements that undermine regulatory intent. The exemption from VAT and more favourable tax treatment of debt relative to equity are cited as examples of such tax distortions.

Tax Distortions in the Financial Sector

Tax regimes in most countries provide incentives for leverage since payment of interest is treated as business expense while payment of dividend is taxed. In addition, the limited liability of corporates provides a safety net to equity holders to take excessive risks. In particular, banks are believed to be justifiably bailed-out in many cases, which adds to the behaviour of excessive risk taking. Further, banks, as lenders, have considerable access to information on their borrowers, in addition to expertise in assessing risks of their borrowers. On the other hand, creditors to banks have relatively less access to information on the operations of banks. The bonus systems prevalent in banks provide incentives to management also to take excessive risks, protected as they are at the higher likelihood of bailout than of other industries. There is also evidence of aggressive tax planning by the financial sector, which is yet to be firmly dealt with by fiscal authorities, particularly with regard to its cross-border activities. Excessive financialization is thus attributed not only to soft regulation reflected in inadequate capital and leverage ratios, but also due to prevalent tax regimes. In any case, an integrated view of regulation and taxation of the financial sector, despite its complexities, would be of value for public policy.

At an operational level, taxation of the financial sector, in particular financial transactions, may enhance regulatory effectiveness. Information generated for the purposes of taxation is likely to be of significance for monitoring the activities of the financial sector. Cross-border activities

can also be brought under regulatory ambit by tax authorities adopting *issuance principle* and *residence principle* (Reddy 2012).

Tobin Tax

A tax on financial transactions in foreign currency markets was advocated by Professor James Tobin in the 1970s. He made the suggestion with two objectives, namely, to make exchange rates reflect, to a larger degree, the long-run fundamentals relative to short-term expectations and risks, and to preserve the autonomy of national macroeconomic and monetary policies. The levy of the tax has been subject to policy debates since it was mooted. Excessive financialization was noticeable in the rising volume of forex transactions relative to trade in goods and services, but the Tobin Tax attracted significant attention only with the onset of the global crisis, for several reasons. However, monetary measures, such as imposition of reserve requirements without remuneration was resorted to in Chile for some time, which had an effect similar to Tobin Tax. Such a tax was also advocated in order to finance what have been described as global public goods.

The levy of the Tobin Tax is debated on grounds of desirability and feasibility (Reddy 2011). The desirability of the tax has been questioned on the grounds that it is difficult to differentiate between real variable and speculative elements that drive markets; the tax distorts market mechanisms, it increases transaction costs, and the revenue yield from it is highly uncertain. However, the arguments against such a levy are based on the assumption that financial markets always play an optimal role in reflecting the fundamentals, without fully recognizing that incentive systems, herd mentality, etc., could distort markets to discharge their role with minimum friction.

The arguments relating to feasibility focus on lack of international consensus and difficulties in enforcement. It is true that it has not been possible to obtain international consensus. However, enforcement may not be an insurmountable difficulty since settlement in currency markets is centralized or centrally overseen. Further, information technology infrastructure enables effective monitoring.

Several countries have taken recourse to measures that have effects similar to the Tobin Tax and they were essentially elements of their overall policy of management of capital account. There is renewed interest in the usefulness of capital account management in the light of experience with the crisis.

Developing Country Perspectives

The policy debate on taxing of the financial sector appears to have arisen in response to popular backlash against incurring of fiscal costs to bail out the financial sector and excessive remuneration of senior management. Further, interest in the links between taxes and regulation of the financial sector was evinced in the context of their relevance to financial stability. Developing countries have a special interest in currency markets due to their vulnerability to currency crisis. Further, developing countries confront challenges of accelerated economic growth which cannot be divorced from considerations of stability of the financial sector. An integrated approach to regulation of the financial sector and fiscal management, including taxation, may have special relevance to developing economies in achieving their goals of inclusive development while minimizing potential for instability.

* * *

There are many ways in which fiscal management, including taxation and regulation of the financial sector have links. The crisis resulted in renewed interest in taxation of the financial sector. But the main focus of such interest was to tax the financial sector to defray the fiscal costs of bailout of the finance sector in the past or costs likely to be incurred in future. This interest was, perhaps, in the context of public outcry in advanced economies. To achieve regulatory objectives, it is possible to envisage taxes that dissuade excessive leverage, but several practical considerations stand in the way of their adoption. However, there are elements of the current tax system which may contribute to excessive financialization, including volatility in financial markets. There is, therefore, the need to consider regulation and taxation in an integrated manner for policy purposes.

13

Sub-national Finance and Crisis

This chapter notes the growing importance of sub-national finance and identifies the recent trends. This is followed by exploration of the effects of the global financial crisis and pandemic on sub-national finance. The policy responses to the impact of the crisis on sub-national finances are mentioned in the penultimate part. The emerging issues in this regard, along with a reference to recent experience, are identified in the concluding part.

The global crisis and the pandemic have impacted fiscal management and an important component of government finances is sub-national finance (also described as sub-central government finances), in addition to states or provinces in respect of federations. The sub-national tiers of government refer to local governments such as metropolitan or city governments, counties, and rural decentralized governments. Sub-national tiers of government may not have systemic importance in general, but many of the functions discharged by them, such as water supply, sanitation, roads, etc., have special relevance to the day-to-day life of large segments of the population. Hence, the impact of the crisis on sub-national finance is obviously varied, but some generalizations are possible. In fact, there are several emerging issues with regard to fiscal arrangements as a consequence of the experience with the crisis, which cannot be ignored by any study of fiscal impact of the crisis.

In the context of the pandemic a recent OECD report observed that

Subnational governments (SNGs) were at the forefront of the 2008–09 financial crisis, since they were severely hit by it as well as important actors in overcoming it. Today, SNGs are again at the forefront, as they are important actors in the implementation of the public health measures to prevent the spread of the virus (through screening, population monitoring, crisis communications, coordinated care for vulnerable

Financial and Fiscal Policies. Second Edition. Y. V. Reddy, Partha Ray, and Pinaki Chakraborty, Oxford University Press.
© Y. V. Reddy, Partha Ray, and Pinaki Chakraborty 2024. DOI: 10.1093/9780198934288.003.0013

populations, enforcing confinement policies, ensuring public order, among others), and in some countries, in providing the health treatment and services to those infected. Moreover, in many countries, SNGs are also a key player in social protection, providing financial support to citizens who cannot work, and on business support.[1]

A study of sub-national finance is made difficult by the fact that data is limited, and often either incomplete or outdated. Comparisons are also difficult due to the nature of data. However, some generalizations are possible in the light of existing literature, based significantly on qualitative observations and anecdotal evidence to supplement the limited available data (Canuto and Liu 2010a; IMF 2012a; OECD 2010; United Cities and Local Governments [UCLG] 2009). It is essential to note that the institutional arrangements that govern sub-national finances in countries vary significantly. In addition, the impact of the crisis and the nature of crisis are also varied among countries. Despite several common features of macroeconomic environment within a country, the impact of the crisis varies among its regions.

Importance of Sub-national Finance

Finances of sub-national governments are a significant part of general government finances in many countries. For example, in OECD countries, sub-national governments account for 31 per cent of total government spending, 22 per cent of tax reserve, and 66 per cent of public investment (OECD 2010, p. 5). The available evidence seems to indicate that the importance of sub-national entities may be of similar magnitudes in the developing world also, in particular in larger countries such as India, Brazil, Turkey, Indonesia, China, and Russia. For example, the debt of Indian states is about 27 per cent of GDP and the number would be higher if debt on the balance sheets of companies at state level such as power and water, which are wholly or largely owned by the states, are included (Canuto and Liu 2010b).

---

[1] See 'COVID-19 and fiscal relations across levels of government' (oecd.org) (accessed 2 December 2023).

(d) restructuring debt owed by sub-national governments to central government, and (e) facilitating flow of other resources such as those from the World Bank. A significant contribution from national governments was apparently with a view to align the activities of sub-national governments with national policy initiatives to manage the crisis.

Emerging Issues

The available evidence does not indicate that finances of sub-national governments were threatened by a collapse; but they do point to a reasonably rapid restoration to what may be described as a steady state. These generalizations may conceal many nuances. Further, these generalizations may not capture the possible deterioration in the quality of services on the account of the stress on sub-national finances. Further, mounting unfunded liabilities may escape attention and slip through the available data. Hence, further work in these areas would be necessary.

An interesting issue is whether the observed pre-crisis favourable trends of the increasing role of sub-national governments will continue in future, in view of the likely continued fiscal stress of national governments. Also, it remains to be seen whether their enthusiasm for reliance on financial markets may be moderated in view of their bitter experience of dealing with financial markets during the global financial crisis. Some advanced economies are likely to face acute fiscal stress due to mounting public debt and ageing populations. The central governments in advanced economies may find constraints on supporting sub-national governments through fiscal transfers. Some sub-national governments may face problems inherited from the crisis, such as raising additional debt in financial markets, as they may have to reckon with central governments under fiscal stress.

Trends favourable to sub-national governments during the pre-crisis period are likely to continue insofar as developing countries are concerned. The national governments of these economies are less fiscally stressed. They were not subject to the turbulence of financial markets; moreover, their sub-national governments had relatively low exposure to debt markets. The growing urbanization in developing countries may strengthen forces favourable to the increasing role of sub-national governments.

There could be a debate on the need to review the structures of fiscal relations between central and sub-national governments in the light of experience from the crisis. The evidence so far does not indicate high volatility or severe pro-cyclicality in the finances of sub-national governments. At the same time, they do not have the manoeuvrability to adopt countercyclical fiscal policies. The issue is whether such a flexible regime will be consistent with prevailing fiscal rules that need to balance several considerations. A related issue is the lack of adequate buffers in many sub-national governments against *shocks*. There are costs and benefits of pooled buffers at the central government level which need to be assessed in the context of the circumstances of each country.

In Spain, as a result of the bursting of the property bubble, the impact of the financial and debt crisis varied across its regions. Thus, some regions were affected more than others. Illustratively, the north-eastern region of Catalonia (with Barcelona as its capital) faced a plunge in home sales by more than 40 per cent in 2011. Accordingly, sub-national finance faced a hard time. By end-August 2012, Catalonia sought aid from the Spanish central government to prevent defaulting on its debt. Catalonia, whose debt is more than €42 billion, became the third region after Valencia and Murcia to officially solicit aid from the Spanish central government. Given that politically there is clamour for Catalonia to secede from Spain the situation is fraught with complications. With fiscal stress getting accentuated, these separatist demands have been increasing in the recent period. This is a classic case where an economic crisis with sub-national fiscal dimensions fuels separatist forces within a state.

In the US too, sub-national finance took a hit. The American Recovery and Reinvestment Act of 2009 provided nearly $135 billion in emergency funding; it helped states avoid draconian cuts in services (Canuto and Liu 2010b).[2] The situation in states like California is alarming—so much so that in describing the state of sub-national finance, Michael Lewis has coined the term 'too fat to fly' and went on to say, 'The relationship

---

[2] For example, with $87 billion in additional Medicaid funding via increased federal medical assistance percentage rates and $48 billion as part of the State Fiscal Stabilization Fund, states were able to maintain critical funding for social services.

between the people and their money in California is such that you can pluck almost any city at random and enter a crisis' (Lewis 2011, p. 193).

To sum up, the increasing importance of sub-national governments in the provision of public services, in public investment, and in fiscal operations has to be recognized despite data limitations, in the context of the global crisis and the pandemic. Their finances have been adversely affected by the global financial crisis, though in varying ways in different countries. As a consequence, the possible deterioration in the quality of public services due to the crisis may be going unnoticed. Most of the policy responses to the crisis have been from the central governments in several forms. Transfers to sub-national governments have been biased in favour of earmarked transfers to subserve national goals, having regard to absorptive capacity. Drawing from the experience of sub-national finance, in the context of the global crisis and the pandemic, it is possible to identify some emerging issues: Will the crisis be positive or negative for further decentralization in governments? Will the space for fiscal management in sub-national levels increase? Could their policies be countercyclical? Should the buffers against shocks be built at sub-national levels also? Should there be debate on the review of structures of fiscal relations between central and sub-national governments on the basis of experience with the global financial crisis and the COVID-19 pandemic?

14

Emerging Challenges

The underlying narrative of the book is the ineluctable interrelationship between the fisc, finance, and monetary policy. Against the backdrop of the global financial crisis since 2007, the sovereign debt crises during the first half of 2020, the COVID-19 pandemic, and the Russia-Ukraine war, it focuses on this broad theme. As noted in the introductory chapter, the book attempts to capture some aspects of the rapidly unfolding events, endeavouring, however, not to miss the wood for the trees. The concluding chapter presents, as a supplement to the analyses and policy issues narrated earlier in the book, a brief overview of some emerging challenges to fiscal and financial sector policies.

The links between fiscal management, financial regulation, and conduct of monetary policy are closer than were perceived by policy circles before the global financial crisis and the pandemic. There are efforts to put in place appropriate institutional arrangements at the national level to ensure coordination between such policies, keeping in view the objective of financial stability. Since growth and financial stability are closely linked, in particular in the case of developing economies, the institutional arrangements may have to consider the related issues of employment and output. However, in designing such arrangements for coordination, there is a danger that the focus of institutions such as the central bank and financial regulators will get diluted. It is also possible that accountability will be difficult to enforce in the absence of well-defined objectives and operational freedom to each of the institutions to pursue such objectives. This is a complex reality that has to be faced by each country in devising both institutional arrangements and policy parameters for such coordination.

It is also necessary to examine how institutional arrangements at a global level would affect coordination arrangements at the national level. Such global arrangements for coordination should have adequate

Financial and Fiscal Policies. Second Edition. Y. V. Reddy, Partha Ray, and Pinaki Chakraborty, Oxford University Press. © Y. V. Reddy, Partha Ray, and Pinaki Chakraborty 2024. DOI: 10.1093/9780198934288.003.0014

legitimacy. More important, elements of enforceability of such arrangements would also be relevant. Further, such global arrangements for coordination may have to recognize that institutional arrangements at the national level may be diverse, while governments, mainly fiscal authorities, would be the preferred channel for representing the interests of the sovereign in the global forum. The current focus is appropriately on crisis management, but institutional and structural issues at the global level are yet to be addressed. No doubt, there are a series of arrangements, other than treaty-based or legally binding ones, such as the G20, to enhance coordination of such policies among larger economies, but these remain somewhat ad hoc. Though the G20 forum has become an important forum for exchange of ideas and played a key role in sensitizing global leaders on key social and economic challenges, as an institution, it is yet to become an operational arm of global governance to implement policies. Translating G20 intent into policy action needs to overcome this challenge.

There is increasing awareness of the capacity of the financial sector, especially of large conglomerates, to undermine effectiveness of policies relating to both taxation and regulation at the national level. In some ways, taxation and regulation can complement each other at the national level, and they have combined impact on the financial sector. The fiscal issues relating to exchange of information on taxation and the cross-border tax avoidance mechanisms discussed in the G20 will also influence the future of global finance, while simultaneously impacting the fiscal measures; in particular, the provisions relating to tax avoidance may come under review.

Cross-border capital flows have shown significant gyrations in the twenty-first century so far. There is a continuous debate about capital account management and use of capital controls. At the same time, it is recognized that some of the bilateral treaties restrict the freedom of countries to manage their capital account. The future of global finance would be influenced by the manner in which policies relating to capital flow evolve, considering that capital account can be managed through a combination of fiscal measures, regulatory prescriptions, and administrative measures. At the same time, the benign role of global finance in current account transactions, especially trade in goods and services, is bound to continue.

In the global financial markets, the low interest rate regime seems to be over. Higher inflation in the post-COVID period, all over the world, had prompted the authorities to increase interest rates, leading to some financial instability in the US (e.g., fall of the Silicon Valley Bank). With higher inflation, markets in some cases behaved abnormally, making conduct of fiscal policy more complex. In any event, with a large public debt in advanced economies, the conflicts between conduct of fiscal policies and monetary policies could accentuate in the days to come.

The search for safe assets appears to have resulted in a rush towards gold. This tendency appears to be widely prevalent after the crisis. It is interesting that central banks have also exhibited preference for holding their reserves in the form of gold since the onset of the global financial crisis. This is a reversal of the trend of selling of gold by central banks of advanced economies earlier, when some advanced economies coordinated their significant operations to off-load gold, but such sales have now stopped. Further, some developing countries, including India, seemed to have enhanced the gold component of their foreign exchange reserves since the crisis. This could be symptomatic of the challenges being faced in the reserve currency system (non-system) with very feeble signs of an acceptable substitute to the US dollar. In brief, there is little or no evidence of improvements in the international monetary system and international financial architecture that would reassure developing countries to desist from policies of self-insurance. The costs, especially fiscal costs, of such self-insurance, would, therefore, continue to be relevant vis-à-vis benefits of such self-insurance in an increasingly uncertain global economic environment. The impact of inevitable but far from clear structural changes in the economies of the US, China, and the euro area add considerable uncertainties to the policy challenges for many national authorities.

Where does our quest for safe assets lead us to? In view of the fluidity of the concept of safe assets and its practical usage, instead of any definitive conclusions, some conjectures are presented below. First, the euro imitative was essentially an attempt to question the hegemony of the US dollar. However, the lack of a unified fiscal policy, different inflationary thresholds, and differences in social and political norms—have all led to its partial failure. Effectively, the euro initiative has failed to some extent in the absence of a global institutional monetary institution, and the IMF could not deliver those functions in the absence of global safe assets. Second, insofar as non-dollar trade is concerned, the recent Indian experience is worth considering. In recent times there has been a number of bilateral ties between India and a number of other countries. In the recent past, the RBI has allowed banks from 18 countries to open Vostro accounts for trade in rupee: Botswana, Fiji, Germany, Guyana, Israel, Kenya, Malaysia, Mauritius, Myanmar, New Zealand, Oman, Russia, Seychelles, Singapore, Sri Lanka, Tanzania, Uganda, and the UK.[1] While these are encouraging developments and could pave the way for making the rupee an international currency, two words of caution may be noted: (a) what would be the usage of the rupee in the hands of our trading partners?; and (b) to that extent, what is the cost of having such bilateral arrangements of rupee trade?

While clarity is yet to emerge for answers to this question, it is pertinent to note the following:

> Currently, the Indian rupee is not freely convertible and cannot be bought or sold in global markets freely. Speculative buying or selling of the rupee without a corresponding underlying trade in goods or services is not permissible as per Indian law. Buying and selling the underlying asset denominated in rupees depends on the prevailing policy regarding acquisition of Indian rupee assets by non-residents. However, trade in rupee-denominated assets outside the country cannot be controlled by the Indian government. Capital account convertibility and the progress towards full capital account convertibility has remained slow for India. While foreign investment flows, especially direct investment, are encouraged, debt flows in the form of external commercial borrowings are generally subject to ceilings and with some end use restrictions. (Reddy 2023)

The experience with regard to the euro area provides critical lessons on the links between political union, fiscal management, and banking union in the context of a monetary union. The lessons with regard to linkages can be distilled from the diverse experiences of the countries within the

---

[1] Vostro is a Latin word that means 'your', therefore, a vostro account literally means that it is 'your account'. An example of such an account would be HSBC vostro account held by SBI in India.

euro area and outside the euro area in Europe. At a broader level, the interlocking of banking crisis, growth crisis, and sovereign debt crisis may provide significant lessons for issues relating to coordination at supra-national level in future. There is a perception that the political and bureaucratic elites may be driving the integration in the euro area, but popular resistance is palpable. It is not clear how these will pan out in future. The COVID-19 pandemic has forced the European Union to reimagine its fiscal rules and bring flexibility to the fiscal operation.

This change in fiscal rules with country-specific flexibility also shows that currency union has several advantages but, in no way, can it substitute the benefits of a fiscal/political union. In fact, mere presence of a currency union without strict adherence to a tight set of rules (e.g., various convergence criteria) creates a number of complications, both for the constituent economies as well as market participants. Going forward, while one would expect firming up of the various criteria for joining a currency union, market participants are also expected to be more careful in distinguishing between various constituent countries within a currency union, depending upon their fundamentals. These lessons may not be lost in the design of future regional arrangements, such as CMI in Asia.

The cross-country experience shows that the global financial crisis and the COVID-19 pandemic were not simply events from the perspective of macroeconomic management, though manifested initially in that fashion. Like in the case of the global financial crisis, after the COVID-19 pandemic also, the crisis in the financial sector has been evolving and unfolding into sovereign debt crises in some countries, great recession in some, and slowdown in most countries, and near collapse of some of the small-income developing economies. The macro impact on countries has also been diverse. It is still not clear whether the global economy is in the middle of a crisis or it is towards the end of the crisis. It is interesting to note that the forecasts of the IMF with regard to the growth prospects of the global economy have been more often revised downwards than upwards since the onset of the crisis. There is evidence that new risks to the global economy are emanating.

The emerging market economies, as a group, were affected during the global financial crisis. However, they appeared less vulnerable than the advanced economies then. The post-COVID challenges are of a different nature and its impact has been asymmetric across countries. However, continuing risks and uncertainties in the advanced economies, which still account for a large output and dynamism, would be interacting with the brighter prospects for emerging market economies. While there could be a rebalancing in the global economy, the path for such rebalancing may have to reckon with interactions between international financial architecture and fiscal stresses at the national level.

There appears to be a dichotomy between the growth performance and growth prospects of advanced economies and developing economies. The growth, fiscal deficit, and inflation dynamics appear to be divergent among them with consequential difficulties for global coordination of national policies. The disconnect between macroeconomic indicators such as growth and inflation, and the real economy reflected in human suffering due to unemployment, and livelihood crises after the pandemic is evident in most economies. Similarly, the divergence between the indicators of macro economy as well as employment, and the impressive performance of financial markets, especially equity markets, is noticeable. The interesting issue is whether in the near term the growth impulses of developing economies would make up for the loss in growth momentum of advanced economies, in a possible new twist to coupling. While the global economy has been witnessing a series of crises with observable inter-linkages between the economies of the countries, one factor that is common for most, though not all, countries is the increasing challenge of fiscal management.

There are three important areas where the trade-off for macroeconomic management is distinctly different for advanced economies relative to emerging market economies. The *first* relates to the growth versus austerity debates, the *second* to monetary versus fiscal policy stimulus, and the *third* to the tensions between the short term and medium term. In all these areas, the country-wise differences in policy challenges seem to be significantly more acute at the current stage relative to the trade-offs prior to the crisis and during the period of management of the crisis.

Among the emerging market economies, India seems to be faced with daunting challenges in view of its relatively higher dependence on external flows and the structural deterioration in its fiscal situation subsequent to the onset of the crisis. Financial stability does not seem to be under threat, though the financial sector is under stress. Debt sustainability in terms of the normal indicators is not as severe as the magnitudes may indicate, but the fact that the banking system holds a major part of the tradable government securities indicates potential complexities. However, India has strong fundamentals, including, in particular, demographic dividend and a strong entrepreneurial base. India's post-pandemic growth recovery is stable and is expected to continue supported by increase in private sector investment.

It is possible to hold that the financial sector has globalized ahead of some sort of globalization of regulation of the financial sector. The Basel standards are indicative of efforts to globalize regulation of the financial sector, in some form or other. However, the close linkages between the financial sector and fiscal management that have been enunciated in the book indicate that globalization of regulation by itself may not assure growth with stability—stability to include price stability, financial stability, and acceptable levels of employment and output for ensuring social stability. Some elements of globalization of fiscal management that could match globalization of finance and its regulation may be essential to maximize benefits from and minimize risks of such globalization. Hence, a benign globalization of the economies warrants synchronization between the extent of globalization of finance and fisc. Indeed, the limits to globalization of finance may be set by the limits to globalization of fisc, the latter being an intensely political process within the confines of nation states. Moreover, owing to a number of events like the US-China trade war, crumbling of the global supply chain during the pandemic, Brexit, or the Russia-Ukraine War, the forces of de-globalization got a fillip.

However, there so many limitations of the current global monetary system primarily emanating out of the close link between Wall Street, the US Treasury, and the Bretton Woods Institutions,[2] that it may not be an exaggeration to term it as a 'global monetary non-system'. Notwithstanding the limitation of the global monetary non-system, monetary policies of different nations are getting increasingly interlinked due

[2] See Yaga Venugopal Reddy, Wall Street Debate, available at https://www.youtube.com/watch?v=x32ZtglrRDw(accessed on 10 August 2024).

to the interlinked nature of financial systems, where Wall Street has huge influence on the financial markets worldwide. All these have significant implications, of differing degrees, for the financial and fiscal policies, directly or indirectly. The future at this juncture looks much cloudier than how it would have appeared at the end of the last millennium.

References

(Note: All URLs have been accessed during January 2013–April 2014)

Abidin, Mahani Zainal. 2010. 'Fiscal Policy Coordination in Asia.' ADBI Working Paper: 232.

Acharya, Shankar. 2012. *India after the Global Crisis*. New Delhi: Orient Blackswan.

Acharya, Viral. 2012. 'What Saved the Indian Banking System: State Ownership or State Guarantees?' *World Economy*, 5(1): 19–31.

Akyuz, Yilmaz. 2013. 'Statutory Sovereign Debt Mechanism: Why and How?' *South Bulletin*, 70, article 21, January. https://www.southcentre.int/wp-content/uplo ads/2022/03/SV53-130206.pdf

Allison, H., and C. Pazarbasioglu. 2024. 'How to Ease Rising External Debt-Service Pressures in Low-Income Countries.' Available at https://www.imf.org/en/Blogs/ Articles/2024/01/24/how-to-ease-rising-external-debt-service-pressures-in-low-income-countries?utm_medium = email&utm_source = govdelivery (accessed in October 2024).

Anand, M.R., G.L. Gupta, and Ranjan Dash. 2012. 'The Euro Zone Crisis: Its Dimensions and Implications.' Working Paper, Ministry of Finance, Government of India.

Angeloni, Ignazio, and Jean Pisani-Ferry. 2012. 'The G20: Characters in Search of an Author.' Bruegel Working Paper.

Arestis, Philip, and Elisabetta De Antoni. 2007. 'Rediscovering Fiscal Policy through Minskyan Eyes.' Working Paper No. 01/2007, Department of Economics, University of Trento.

Arestis, Philip, and Malcolm Sawyer. 2003. 'Reinventing Fiscal Policy.' *Journal of Post Keynesian Economics*, 26(1): 3–25.

Atoyan, Ruben, Albert Jaegar, and Dustin Smith. 2012. 'The Pre-crisis Capital Flow Surge to Emerging Europe: Did Countercyclical Fiscal Policy Make a Difference?' IMF Working Paper No.12/222, 1 September 2012.

Aziz, Jahangir, Ila Patnaik, and Ajay Shah. 2008. 'The Current Liquidity Crunch in India: Diagnosis and Policy Response.' NIPFP Working Paper.

Bajpai, Nirupam. 2011. 'Global Financial Crisis, its Impact on India and the Policy Response.' Working Paper No. 5, Columbia Global Centres.

Baker, Dean. 2012. 'Fiscal Policy: The Recent Record and Lessons for the Future.' In *After the Great Recession: The Struggle for Economic Recovery and Growth*, edited by Barry Z. Cynamon, Steven M.Fazzari, and Mark Setterfild, pp. 244–263. Cambridge: Cambridge University Press.

Balachandran, G. 1998. *The Reserve Bank of India 1951–1967*. Delhi: Oxford University Press.

Balassone, Fabrizio, Daniele Franco, and Stefania Zotteri. 2004. 'Public Debt: A Survey of Policy Issues.' Proceedings of the Banca d'Italia Workshop held in

Perugia, 1–3 April 2004. Available online at http://www.bancaditalia.it/studiricer che/convegni/atti/publ_debt.

Barro, R.J. 1974. 'Are Government Bonds Net Wealth?' *Journal of Political Economy*, 82(6): 1095–1117.

Benediktsdóttir, Sigriður, Gauti B. Eggertsson, Eggert Þórarinsson. 2017. 'The Rise, the Fall, and the Resurrection of Iceland', Brooking Papers on Economic Activity.

Berger, Helge, Giovanni Dell'Ariccia, and Maurice Obstfeld. 2018. 'The Euro Area Needs a Fiscal Union', IMF Research Department Policy Paper, available at http://www.imf.org/en/Publications/Departmental-Papers-Policy-Papers/Issues/2018/02/20/Revisiting-the-Economic-Case-for-Fiscal-Union-in-the-Euro-Area-45611

Bernheim, Douglas B. 1987. 'Ricardian Equivalence: An Evaluation of Theory and Evidence', in *Macroeconomics Annual 1987, Volume 2*, edited by Stanley Fischer, pp. 263–316. Cambridge, MA: MIT Press.

Bi, Ran, 2008. ' "Beneficial" Delays in Debt Restructuring Negotiations', IMF Working Paper No. 38.

BIS. 2011. 'CGFS Paper No. 42: Interactions of Sovereign Debt Management with Monetary Conditions and Financial Stability', BIS May 2011.

Black, Bill. 2013. 'Rajan Calls Krugman "Paranoid" for Criticizing Reinhart's and Rogoff 's Research', 14 August 2013. Available online at http://www.nakedcapital ism.com/2013/08.

Blanchard, O., J.C. Chouraqui, R.P. Hagemann, and N. Sartor. 1990. 'The Sustainability of Fiscal Policy: New Answers to Old Questions', OECD, *Economic Studies*, 15. https://www.researchgate.net/publication/5183200_The_Sustainability_of_Fiscal_Policy_New_Answers_to_An_Old_Question

Blanchard, Olivier. 2006. 'Adjustment within the Euro: The Difficult Case of Portugal'. Available online at http://economics.mit.edu/files/740.

Blinder, Alan. 1982. 'Issues in the Coordination of Monetary and Fiscal Policy', Fed Kansas City Conference Proceedings. Available online at http://www.kansascity fed.org/publicat/sympos/1982.

Blinder, Alan, and Robert M. Solow. 1973. 'Does Fiscal Policy Matter?' *Journal of Public Economics*, 2: 319–337.

Begg, Iain, and Fabian Mushövel. 2019. 'The Economic Impact of Brexit: Jobs, Growth and the Public Finances', LSE Research Online, available at https://epri nts.lse.ac.uk/67008

Blommestein, Hans J., and Philip Turner. 2012. 'Preface', in *Threat of Fiscal Dominance?* BIS Papers No. 65, Proceedings of a BIS/OECD Workshop on 'Policy Interactions between Fiscal Policy, Monetary Policy and Government Debt Management after the Financial Crisis', Basel.

Bordo, Michael D., Agnieszka Markiewicz, and Lars Jonung. 2011. 'A Fiscal Union for the Euro: Some Lessons from History', NBER Working Paper No. 17380.

Borio, C. 2011. 'Central Banking Post-crisis: What Compass for Uncharted Waters?' BIS Working Papers No 353, https://www.bis.org/publ/work353.pdf.

Brigitte, Young, and Willi Semmler. 2011. 'The European Sovereign Debt Crisis: Is Germany to Blame?' *German Politics and Society*, 29(1). https://www.researchg ate.net/publication/233647034_The_European_Sovereign_Debt_Crisis_Is_G ermany_to_Blame

Brittan, Samuel. 2012. 'Come on Bernanke, Fire up the Helicopter Engines.' *Financial Times*, 30 August 2012.

Broyer, Claudia, Ann-Katrin Petersen, and Rolf Schneider. 2012. 'Impact of the Euro Crisis on the German Economy', Working Paper, *Allianz*, 154. Available online at https://www.allianz.com/media/economic...papers/.../euroimpact.pdf.

Buiter, Willem H. 2012. 'Testimony of Williem Buiter to UK House of Lords, quoted in "The Euro Area Crisis"', House of Lords, European Union Committee 25th Report of Session 2010–2012. Available online at http://www.publications.parliam ent.uk/pa/ld201012/ldselect/ideucom/260/260.pdf (accessed in October 2012).

Buiter, Willem H., and Urjit R. Patel. 1997. 'Solvency and Fiscal Correction in India: An Analytical Discussion.' In *Public Finance: Policy Issues for India*, edited by Sudipto Mundle, pp. 30–75. Delhi: Oxford University Press.

Bulmera, Simon, and Lucia Quaglia. 2018. 'The Politics and Economics of Brexit', *Journal of European Public Policy 2018*, 25(8): 1089–1098.

Calomiris, Charles W. 2023. 'Fiscal Dominance and the Return of Zero-Interest Bank Reserve Requirements', *Fed St Louis Economic Research, Fourth Quarter*, 105(4), 1–11. https://www.stlouisfed.org/-/media/project/frbstl/stlouisfed/publications/ review/pdfs/2023/10/02/fiscal-dominance-and-the-return-of-zero-interest-bank-reserve-requirements.pdf?sc_lang=en&hash=34322211A452FEFFDC3BF8179 111FDBE

Canuto, Otariano, and Lili Liu. 2010. 'Sub-national Debt Finance and the Global Financial Crisis', *Economic Premise*, The World Bank, number 13, May.

Canuto, Otariano, and Lili Liu. 2010a. 'Sub-national Debt Finance: Make it Sustainable.' In *The Day after Tomorrow—A Handbook on the Future of Economic Policy in Developing World*, edited by Canuto Ottarianol and Marcelo Gingale, pp. 219–37. The World Bank, Washington DC.

Carballo-Cruz, Francisco. 2011. 'Causes and Consequences of the Spanish Economic Crisis: Why the Recovery is Taken so Long?' *Panoeconomicus*, 3: 309–28. Available online at: http://www.doiserbia. nb.rs/img/doi/1452-595X/2011/1452-595X1103309C.pdf

Cecchetti, Stephen G., M.S. Mohanty, and Fabrizio Zampolli. 2010. 'The Future of Public Debt: Prospects and Implications', BIS Working Paper No. 300, March.

Chakraborty, Pinaki. 2007. 'Implementation of the National Rural Employment Guarantee Act in India: Spatial Dimensions and Fiscal Implications.' *Levy Institute Working Paper No. 505*.

Chan, Sarah. 2012. 'Is India's Current Economic Slowdown Due to Cyclical or Structural Factors?' Available online on the VOX website: http://www.voxeu.org/ article/india-s-economic-slowdown-andwhat-should-be-done-about-it.

Chidambaram, P. 2012. 'Fiscal Policy Reforms since 1991.' In *The Oxford Companion to Economics in India, Vol. 1*, edited by Kaushik Basu and Annemie Maertens, pp. 242–46. Delhi: Oxford University Press.

Claessens, Stijn, Keen Michael, and Ceyla Pazarbaslogu (Eds). 2010. 'Financial Sector Taxation: The IMF's Report to the G20 and Background Material', IMF, September.

Claessens, Stijn, Giovanni Dell'Ariccia, Deniz Igan, and Luc Laeven. 2010. 'Lessons and Policy Implications from the Global Financial Crisis', IMF Working Paper WP/10/44, February.

Clinton, Bill. 2011. *Back to Work: Why We Need Smart Government for a Strong Economy*. New York: Random House.

Cœuré, Benoît. 2012. Speech at the Conference 'Bank funding—Markets, Instruments and Implications for Corporate Lending and the Real Economy', Frankfurt, 8 October 2012. Available online at http:// www.ecb.int/press/key/date/2012/html/sp121008_1.en.html.

Constâncio, Vítor. 2012. 'Contagion and the European Debt Crisis', *Banque de France Financial Stability Review*, 16, April.

CRS (Congressional Research Service). 2023. 'Section 301 of the Trade Act of 1974', available at https://crsreports.congress.gov (accessed on 3 October 2023).

Cynamon, Barry Z., and Steven M. Fazzari. 2013. 'The End of the Consumer Age.' In *After the Great Recession: The Struggle for Economic Recovery and Growth*, edited by Barry Z. Cynamon, Steven M. Fazzari, and Mark Setterfield, pp. 129–157. Cambridge: Cambridge University Press.

Darvas, Zsolt. 2012. 'The Euro Crisis: Ten Roots, But Fewer Solutions', *Bruegel Policy Contribution*, no. 2012/17, October 2012. Available online at http://www.bruegel.org/publications/publication-detail/ publication/755-the-euro-crisis-ten-roots-but-fewer-solutions/.

Das, Udaibir S., Michael G. Papaioannou, and Christoph Trebesch. 2012. 'Sovereign Debt Restructuring 1950–2010.' IMF Working Papers, WP/12/203, August.

Dasgupta, Deepak, and Supriyo De. 2012. 'Fiscal Deficit', in *The Oxford Companion to Economics in India, volume 1*, edited by Kaushik Basu and Annemie Maertens, pp. 233–8. Delhi: Oxford University Press.

De, Supriyo. 2012. 'Fiscal Policy in India: Trends and Trajectory', Government of India. Ministry of Finance Working Paper.

Demetriades, Panicos. 2012. 'Cyprus Financial Crisis: The Framework for an Economic Recovery within the Eurozone.' Speech of Governor of the Central Bank of Cyprus, at a discussion organized by the Hellenic American Bankers Association and the Cyprus-US Chamber of Commerce, New York on 11 December 2012. Available online at http://www.centralbank.gov.cy/nqcontent.cfm?a_id = 12472.

Deng, Yongheng, Randall Morck, Jing Wu, and Bernard Yeung. 2011. 'Monetary and Fiscal Stimuli, Ownership Structure, and China's Housing Market.' NBER Working Paper No. 16871.

Desai, Padma. 2011. *From Financial Crisis to Global Recovery*. New York: Columbia University Press.

Deutsche Bundesbank. 2010. 'Financing and Representation in the International Monetary Fund', *Monthly Bulletin*, March.

De Grauwe, Paul. 2022. 'Towards a New Euro Crisis?', *Intereconomics*, 57(5): 273–277, available at https://www.intereconomics.eu/contents/year/2022/number/5/article/towards-a-new-euro-crisis.html

Di Quirico, Roberto. 2010. 'Italy and the Global Economic Crisis', *Bulletin of Italian Politics* 2(2): 3–19.

Dixit, Avinash, and Lambertini Luisa. 2001. 'Monetary-Fiscal Policy Interactions and Commitment versus Discretion in a Monetary Union', *European Economic Review*, 45: 977–87.

Dodd, Randall. 2002. 'Sovereign Debt Restructuring', *Financier* 9: 1–4.

Domar, E.D. 1944. 'The "Burden of the Debt" and the National Income', *American Economic Review*, 34(4): 798–827.

EC. 2012. *Banking Union: Commission Proposals for a Single Supervisory Mechanism*. Available online at http://ec.europa.eu/internal_market/ finances/

The Economist. 2012. 'Stimulus: The Same Old Debate', *The Economist*, 7 June.

Edwards, Sebastian. 2000. 'Interest Rates, Contagion and Capital Controls.' NBER Working Paper No. 7801, National Bureau of Economic Research.

EEAG. 2011. 'The EEAG Report on the European Economy', Taxation and Regulation of the Financial Sector, CESIFO, Munich, 2011.

Eichengreen, Barry, Ricardo Hausmann, and Ugo Panizza. 2004. 'Currency Mismatches, Debt Intolerance, and Original Sin.' https://www.nber.org/system/ files/chapters/c0150/c0150.pdf

Eijffinger, Sylvester C.W., and Rob Nijskens. 2012. 'Banking Union and a Single Banking Supervisory Mechanism.' Note prepared for the European Parliament. Available online at www.europarl.europa.eu/.

Elmendorf, D.W., and G.N. Mankiw. 1999. 'Government Debt.' In *Handbook of Macroeconomics, vol. 1*, edited by J.B. Taylor and M. Woodford, chapter 25, pp. 1615–1669. Amsterdam: Elsevier.

European Central Bank. 2011. *The International Role of the Euro*, July 2011. Available online at http://www.ecb.int/pub/pdf/other/eurointernational-role201107en.pdf.

European Central Bank. 2013. 'Intra-euro Area Trade Linkages and External Adjustment', *ECB Monthly Bulletin*, January: 59–74.

European Commission. 2010. 'Bank Resolution Funds', Communication from the Commission to The European Parliament, The Council, the European Economic and Social Committee, and the European Central Banks, Brussels, 26 May 2010.

European Commission. 2011. 'The Economic Adjustment Programme for Portugal', European Economy Occasional Papers 79, Directorate-General for Economic and Financial Affairs.

European Economic Advisory Group (EEAG). 2011. EEAG Report on the European Economy 2011, Munich: CESifo Group (on behalf of Ludwig-Maximilians University's Center for Economic Studies and the Ifo Institute for Economic Research). Available online at http://www.kof.ethz.ch/static_media/fi ler_public/ 2012/09/16/none_1402.

Fajgelbaum, Pablo, Pinelopi K. Goldberg, Patrick J. Kennedy, Amit Khandelwal, and Daria Taglioni. 2021. 'The US-China Trade War and Global Reallocations', NBER Working Paper 29562.

Feldstein, Martin S. 2004. 'Budget Deficits and National Debt', text of the L.K. Jha Memorial Lecture at the Reserve Bank of India in Mumbai, delivered on 12 January 2004. Available online at http://rbidocs.rbi. org.in/rdocs/Publications/PDFs/50483.pdf.

Feldstein, Martin S. 2011. 'The Euro and European Economic Conditions', NBER Working Paper No. 17617.

Financial Times. 2010. 'Time to End the Denial over Mortgage Debt', *Financial Times*, 4 November.

Financial Times. 2011. 'A Brady Plan to End Europe's Crisis', 3 July 2011.

Fischer, Stanley. 2011. *Central Bank Lessons from the Global Crisis*, Third Brahmananda Memorial Lecture, Reserve Bank of India, Mumbai.

Fleming, Michael J., and Nicholas J. Klagge. 2010. 'The Federal Reserve's Foreign Exchange Swap Lines', *Current Issues in Economics and Finance*, 16(4): 1–7.

Francesca Caselli, Vitor Gaspar, Gee Hee Hong, and Paulo Medas. 2023. *Fiscal Policy Can Promote Economic Stability and Address Risks to Public Finances*, https://www.imf.org/en/Blogs/Articles/2023/04/12/fiscal-policy-can-promote-econo mic-stability-and-address-risks-to-public-finances

Freedman, Charles, Michael Kumhof, Douglas Laxton, Dirk Muir, and Susanna Mursula. 2011. 'Global Effects of Fiscal Stimulus During the Crisis', Stanford University Working Paper. Available at http:// www.stanford.edu/~johntayl/car negie1march.pdf

Gelpern, Anna. 2009. 'Financial Crisis Containment', *Conneticut Law Review*, 41(4) (May): 493–549.

Gerstman, B.B. 1998. *Epidemiology: An Introduction to Classic and Modern Epidemiology*. New York: John Wiley.

Gibson, Heather D., Stephen G. Hall, and George S. Tavlas. 2012. 'The Greek Financial Crisis: Growing Imbalances and Sovereign Spreads', *Journal of International Money and Finance*, 31: 498–516.

Global Economic and Financial Crisis: Essays from Economic and Political Weekly. 2009. New Delhi: Orient Blackswan.

Goodhart, C.A.E. 2010. *The Changing Role of Central Banks*, BIS Working Paper No. 326.

Gopinath, Shyamala. 2009. 'Sub-national Fiscal Reforms and Debt Management— The Indian Experience', *RBI Bulletin*, August.

Gorton, Gary. 2010. *Slapped by the Invisible Hand: The Panic of 2007*. Oxford: Oxford University Press.

Gourinchas, Pierre-Olivier, Thomas Philippon, and Dimitri Vayanos. 2017. 'The Analytics of the Greek Crisis'. *NBER Macroeconomics Annual*, 31(1): 1–81.

Government of India. 2009. *Economic Survey, 2008–09*. New Delhi: Government of India.

Government of India. 2010. *Economic Survey, 2009–10*. New Delhi: Government of India.

Government of India. 2013. *Economic Survey, 2012–13*. New Delhi: Government of India.

Grauwe, Paul De. 2009. 'The Politics of the Maastricht Convergence Criteria', 15 April 2009. Available online at http://www.voxeu.org/ index.php?q = node/3454.

Group of Thirty. 2002. 'Key Issues in Sovereign Debt Restructuring', Working Paper, Washington DC.

Gulati, Mituand, and Lee C. Buchheit. 2010. 'Responsible Sovereign Lending and Borrowing', UNCTAD Discussion Paper No. 198, 4 January. Available online at http://scholarship.law.duke.edu/faculty_scholarship/2318.

Hannoun, H. 2009. 'Long Term Sustainability versus Short Term Stimulus: Is There a Trade-off?' Paper Presented at the 44th SEACEN Governors Conference on Preserving Monetary and Financial Stability in the New Global Financial Environment, Kuala Lumpur, 7 February.

Harrington, Carrie. 2011. 'The Spanish Financial Crisis'. Available online at http://blogs. law.uiowa.edu/ebook/sites/default/files/BP. Spanish % 20Financial % 20Crisis.pdf.

Herndon, Thomas, Michael Ash, and Robert Pollin. 2013. 'Does High Public Debt Consistently Stifle Economic Growth? A Critique of Reinhart and Rogoff ', Working Paper, Political Economy Research Institute, University of Massachusetts, Amherst.

Hill, Hal, and Jayant Menon. 2012. 'Chiang Mai Initiative Designed not to be Used?' 25 July. Available online at http://www.voxeu.org/article/chiang-mai-initiative-designed-not-be-used.

Hoffmann, Daniel. 2011. 'The Impact of the Financial Crisis in Brazil and Germany: A Comparative Analysis of Distinct Developments', mimeo. Available online at http://www.ie.ufrj.br/fgr/arquivos/Finan cial % 20Crisis % 20in % 20Brazil % 20and % 20Germany.pdf.

Horn, S, C.M. Reinhart, and C. Trebesch. 2019. 'China's Overseas Lending', Working Paper 26050, http://www.nber.org/papers/w26050, National Bureau of Economic Research, Cambridge, MA.

Horvath, Julius. 2003. 'Optimum Currency Area Theory: A Selective Review', Bank of Finland Discussion Paper No. 15/2003.

IFO Institute. 2012. 'Germany's and France's Potential Losses if Greece Declares Insolvency'. Available online at www.cesifo-group.de/. . . PDFs/Potential_Germa n_and_French_Losses.

IMF. 2004. *The IMF and Argentina, 1991–2001*. Washington DC: IMF Independent Evaluation Office.

IMF. 2008. *Iceland: 2008 Article IV Consultation—Staff Report*. Available online at http://www.imf.org/external/pubs/ft /scr/2008/cr08367.pdf

IMF. 2009. 'Fiscal Implications of the Global Economic and Financial Crisis', IMF Staff Position Note SPN/09/13.

IMF. 2009a. 'India: 2008 Article IV Consultation— Staff Report; Staff Statement; Public Information Notice on the Executive Board Discussion; and Statement by the Executive Director for India.' Available online at http://www.imf.org/external/pubs/ft /scr/2009/cr09187.pdf.

IMF. 2011. 'Euro Area Policies: Spillover Report for the 2011 Article IV Consultation and Selected Issues'. Available online at www.imf. org/external/pubs/ft /scr/2011/cr11185.pdf.

IMF. 2012. 'Euro Area Policies, 2012 Article IV Consultation', IMF Country Report No.12/181. Available online at http://www.imf.org/ external/pubs/ft /scr/2012/cr12181.pdf.

IMF. 2012. *Euro Area Policies: 2012 Article IV Consultation—Selected Issues Paper*, July 2012.

IMF. 2012a. 'Fiscal Monitor; Balancing Fiscal Policy Risks' [Appendix 3. The Impact of the Financial Crisis on Sub-national Government Finances], IMF April 2012, Washington DC, USA.

IMF. 2012b. 'IMF Country Report No. 12/190: United Kingdom, 2012 Article IV Consultation'. Available online at www.imf.org/external/ pubs/ft /scr/2012/cr12190.pdf

IMF. 2012c. 'Portugal: Third Review under the Extended Arrangement and Request for Waiver of Applicability of End-March Performance Criteria'. Available online at http://www.imf.org/external/.

IMF. 2013. 'Stockholm Principles'. Available online at http://www.imf.org/external/np/mcm/stockholm/principles.htm.

IMF Fiscal Monitor. 2021. 'Strengthening the Credibility of Public Finances'. Available online at https://www.elibrary.imf.org/display/book/9781513584140/9781513584140.xml

IMF. 2022. 'Global Financial Stability Report'. Available online at https://www.imf.org/en/Publications/GFSR/Issues/2022/10/11/global-financial-stability-report-october-2022

IMF/World Bank. 2003. 'Guideline for Public Debt Management', IMF/ World Bank, Washington DC.

Institute of Development Studies. 2013. 'What Next For The BRICS Bank?' *Policy Briefing*, 3, May. Available online at http://www. ids.ac.uk/fi les/dmfi le/Rapid3.pdf.

Issing, Otmar. 2008. *The Birth of the Euro*. Cambridge: Cambridge University Press.

Jones, Claire. 2012. 'Lagarde Calls for Caution on Austerity', *Financial Times*, 11 October.

Joshi, Vijay, and I.M.D. Little. 1994. *India: Macroeconomics and Political Economy, 1963–1991*. Delhi: Oxford University Press.

Jost, Thomas, and Franz Seitz. 2012. 'The Role of the IMF in the European Debt Crisis'. Discussion Paper No. 32, http://www.haw-aw.de/fileadmin/user_upload/Aktuelles/Veroeffentlichungen/WENDiskussionspapier/wen_diskussionspapier32.pdf.

Joyce, Michael. 2012. 'Quantitative Easing and Other Unconventional Monetary Policies: Bank of England Conference Summary', *Bank of England Quarterly Bulletin*, 2012 1st Quarter, 52(1): 48–56.

Kawai, Masahiro, and Cindy Houser. 2007. 'Evolving ASEAN + 3 ERPD: Towards Peer Reviews or Due Diligence?' ADB Institute Discussion Paper No. 79.

Kenen, Peter B. 1990. 'Organizing Debt Relief: The Need for a New Institution'. *Journal of Economic Perspectives*, 4(1): 7–18.

Khatiwada, Sameer. 2009. 'Stimulus Packages to Counter Global Economic Crisis: A Review'. Discussion Paper, International Institute for Labour Studies.

Khor, Martin. 'Resolving Debt Crises: How a Debt Resolution Mechanism Would Work', *South Bulletin*, 70, 21 January.

Kishore, Adarsh, Michael D. Patra, and Partha Ray. 2011. *The Global Economic Crisis through an Indian Looking Glass*. New Delhi: Sage.

Krueger, Anne. 2002. *A New Approach to Sovereign Debt Restructuring*. Washington DC: International Monetary Fund.

Krugman, Paul. 2005. 'Is Fiscal Policy Poised for a Comeback?' *Oxford Review of Economic Policy*, 21(4): 515–523.

Krugman, Paul. 2011. 'Ricardian Confusions (Wonkish)', *New York Times*, 10 March 2011. Available online at http://krugman.blogs.nytimes. com/2011/03/10/ricardian-confusions-wonkish/.

Krugman, Paul. 2012. 'Revenge of the Optimum Currency Area', *New York Times*, 24 June 2012. Available online at http://krugman.blogs.nytimes.com/2012/06/24/revenge-of-the-optimum-currency-area/.

Krugman, Paul. 2013. 'I nequality and Recovery', *New York Times*, 20 January. Available online at http://krugman.blogs.nytimes.com/2013.

Krugman, Paul. 2020. 'The Case for a Permanent Stimulus.' In *Mitigating the COVID Economic Crisis: Act Fast and Do Whatever it takes*, edited by Richard Baldwin and Beatrice Weder di Mauro, VoxEU.

Kumar, Rajiv and Alamuru Soumya. 2010. 'Fiscal Policy Issues for India aft er the Global Financial Crisis (2008–2010)', ADBI Working Paper Series No. 249.

Lafrance, Robert and Pierre St-Amant. 1999. 'Optimal Currency Areas: A Review of the Recent Literature', Bank of Canada Working Paper No. 99-16.

Lane, Philip R. 2012. 'Th e European Sovereign Debt Crisis', *Journal of Economic Perspectives*, 26(3): 49–68.

Lewis, Michael. 2011. *Boomerang*. London: Allen Lane.

Lin, Justin Yifu. 2011. 'Beyond Keynesianism and the New "New Normal"', speech delivered at the Council on Foreign Relations, New York on 28 February 2011. Available online at http://siteresources. worldbank.org/DEC/Resources.

Liu, Henry C.K. 2008. 'Too Big to Fail versus Moral Hazard', *Asia Times*, 23 September 2008. Available online at http://www.atimes.com/ atimes/Global_Economy/ JI23Dj12.html.

Lybeck, Johan A. 2011. *A Global History of the Financial Crash of 200710*. Cambridge: Cambridge University Press.

Mankiw, N. Gregory. 2009. *Macroeconomics*. New York: Worth Publishers.

Mishkin, Frederic S. 2009. 'Is Monetary Policy Effective During Financial Crises?' NBER Working Paper No. 14678.

Ministry of External Affairs, Government of India. 2023. 'G20 New Delhi Leaders' Declaration.' Available at https://www.mea.gov.in/Images/CPV/G20-New-Delhi-Leaders-Declaration.pdf (accessed 1 October 2024).

Mohan, Rakesh. 2011. *Growth with Financial Stability: Central Banking in an Emerging Market*. Delhi: Oxford University Press.

Mohanty, Deepak. 2011. 'Lessons for Monetary Policy from the Global Financial Crisis: An Emerging Market Perspective', paper presented in the Central Banks Conference of the Bank of Israel, Jerusalem, 1 April 2011.

Morsy, Hanan, and Silvia Sgherri. 2010. 'After the Crisis: Assessing the Damage in Italy', IMF Working Paper No. WP/10/244.

Moss, David. 2002. *Government as the Ultimate Risk Manager*. Cambridge, MA: Harvard University Press.

Muchhala, Bhumika. 2013. 'UN General Assembly Special Event on Sovereign Debt and Debt Resolution Mechanisms', *South Bulletin*, 70, January.

Mundell, Robert A. 1961. 'A Theory of Optimum Currency Areas', *American Economic Review*, 51(4): 657–665.

Mundle, Sudipto, M. Govinda Rao, and N.R. Bhanumurthy. 2011. 'Stimulus, Recovery and Exit Policy: G20 Experience and Indian Strategy', Working Paper No. 2011–85, National Institute of Public Finance and Policy, New Delhi.

Notre Europe. 2012. 'Completing the Euro: A Road Map Towards Fiscal Union in Europe, Report of the "Tommaso Padoa-Schioppa Group".' Available online at http://www.eng.notre-europe.eu/ media/CompletingTheEuro_ReportPadoa-SchioppaGroup_NE_ June2012_01.pdf.

OECD. 2010. 'Sub-national Governments and the Economic Crisis: Impact and Policy Responses', OECD Economics Department Working Paper No. 752.

OECD. 2012. *OECD Economic Surveys: Euro Area*. Paris: OECD.

OECD. 2016. 'The Economic Consequences of Brexit: A Taxing Decision', OECD Economic Policy Paper No. 16, Paris: OECD, available at https://www.oecd.org/economy/The-Economic-consequences-of-Brexit-27-april-2016.pdf (accessed on October 1, 2023).

OECD. 2023. 'OECD Secretary-General Tax Report to G20 Finance Ministers and Central Bank Governors', https://www.oecd.org/tax/oecd-secretary-general-tax-report-g20-finance-ministers-india-february-2023.pdf

Ostry, Jonathan D., Atish R. Ghosh, Jun I. Kim, and Mahvash S. Qureshi. 2010. 'Fiscal Space, Staff Position Note, No. SPN/10/11', Washington DCL International Monetary Fund. Available online at http://www. imf.org/external/pubs/ft /spn/ 2010/spn1011.pdf.

Panizza, Ugo, and Andrea F. Presbitero. 2013. 'Public Debt and Economic Growth in Advanced Economies: A Survey', Money and Finance 78.Research group (MoFiR) Working Paper No. Available online at http://ideas.repec.org/e/ppr57.html.

Patra, Michael Debabrata, and Indranil Bhattacharyya. 2022. 'Priming Monetary Policy for the Pandemic', *Economic and Political Weekly*, 57(20): 41–48.

Persson, T., and G. Tabellini. 2000. *Political Economics: Explaining Economic Policies.* Cambridge, MA: MIT Press.

Pisani-Ferry, Jean, André Sapir, and Guntram Wolff. 2013. 'EU-IMF Assistance to Euro-Area Countries: An Early Assessment, Bruegel Blueprint Series'.

Prasad, Eshwar, and Isaac Sorkin. 2009. 'Assessing the G-20 Stimulus Plans: A Deeper Look', Brookings Working Paper. Available online at http://www.brookings.edu/research/articles/2009/03/g20-stimulus-prasad.

Rabinovitch, Simon. 2012. 'China Tells Banks to Roll Over Loans', *Financial Times*, 12 February.

Rajan, Raghuram. 2010. *Fault Lines*. Princeton, NJ: Princeton University Press.

Rajan, Raghuram. 2013. 'The Paranoid Style in Economics', Project Syndicate, 8 August. Available online at http://www.project-syndicate.org/ commentary.

Rajan, Raghuram. 2023. 'Less is More', *Finance and Development*, IMF, March 2023, available at https://www.imf.org/-/media/Files/Publications/Fandd/Article/2023/March/RAJAN-Central-banks-less-More.ashx

Rakshit, Mihir. 2005. 'Budget Deficit: Sustainability, Solvency and Optimality.' In *Readings in Public Finance*, edited by Amaresh Bagchi, chapter 19. Delhi: Oxford University Press.

Rakshit, Mihir. 2009. 'India amidst the Global Crisis', *Economic and Political Weekly*, 64(13), 28 March: 94–106.

Ran Bi. 2008. '"Beneficial" Delays in Debt Restructuring Negotiations', IMF Working Paper No. 38.

Rangarajan, C., and Abha Prasad. 2012. 'Managing State Debt and Ensuring Solvency: The Indian Experience', World Bank Policy Research Working Paper 6039, April 2012.

Ravallion, M., and S. Chen. 2009. 'The Impact of the Global Financial Crisis on the World's Poorest.' Available online at the VOXEU website: http://www.voxeu.org/article/impact-global-financial-crisisworld-s-poorest.

Ray, Partha, and Parthapratim Pal. 2022. 'Festival of Death: Global Stock Markets During the Pandemic.' In *The Impact of COVID-19 on India and the Global Order*, edited by M. Dutta, pp. 189–210. Delhi: Springer.

Reddy, Y.V. 2004. 'Monetary and Financial Sector Reforms in India: A Practitioner's Perspective.' In *India's Emerging Economy*, edited by Kaushik Basu. Cambridge, MA: MIT Press.

Reddy, Y.V. 2009. *India and the Global Financial Crisis*. New Delhi: Orient Blackswan.

Reddy, Y.V. 2011. *Crisis, Recession and Uneven Recovery*. New Delhi: Orient Blackswan.

Reddy, Y.V. 2012. 'Society, Economic Policies and Financial Sector', Per Jacobsson Lecture 2012, Bank for International Settlements, June.

Reddy, Y.V. 2012a. 'Sub-national Finance: Indian Experience', address delivered at the Sub-Sovereign Finance Forum 'Debt, Insolvency and Market: Lessons Learned from Emerging Issues', The World Bank, Washington DC, 20 June.

Reddy, Y.V. 2023. 'The Rupee as an International Currency', The India Forum, 21 June, available at https://www.theindiaforum.in/rupee-international-currency (accessed in December 2023).

Reinhart, Carmen M. 2010. 'Time to End the Denial over Mortgage Debt' (with Vincent R. Reinhart), *Financial Times*, 'Opinion', 4 November.

Reinhart, C.M., and K.S. Rogoff. 2010a. 'Growth in a Time of Debt', *American Economic Review*, 100(2): 573–578.

Reinhart, C.M., and K.S. Rogoff. 2011a. 'From Financial Crash to Debt Crisis', *American Economic Review*, 101(5): 1676–1706.

Reinhart, C.M., and K.S. Rogoff. 2011b. 'A Decade of Debt', NBER Working Paper No. 16827.

Reserve Bank of India. 2008. 'Signing of the Bilateral Swap Arrangements between Japan and India', Press Release dated 30 June 2008.

Reserve Bank of India. 2010. *Report on Currency and Finance, 2008–09*. Mumbai: Reserve Bank of India.

Reserve Bank of India. 2012. 'Report on State Finances: 2010–2011', Supplement to *RBI Bulletin*, March 2012.

Reserve Bank of India. 2012. 'Signing of the Bilateral Swap Arrangement between Japan and India', Press Release dated 4 December 2012.

Reserve Bank of India. 2013. *State Finances: A Study of Budgets of 2012–13*.

Reserve Bank of India. 2014. 'State Finances: A Study of Budgets of 2013–14', Supplement to the *RBI Bulletin*, February

Reserve Bank of India. 2023. *State Finances: A Study of Budgets of 2022–23*, December 2023

Ricciuti, Roberto. 2003. 'Assessing Ricardian Equivalence', *Journal of Economic Surveys*, 17(1): 55–78.

Rohit. 2011. 'Income Distribution, Irrational Exuberance, and Growth: A Theoretical Model of the U.S. Economy', *Review of Radical Political Economics*, 43(4): 449–466.

Rohit. 2012. *It's not Over: Structural Drivers of the Global Economic Crisis*. Delhi: Oxford University Press.

Sakai Ando, T. Asonuma, P. Mishra, and Alexandre Sollaci. 2023. 'Sovereign Debt Restructuring and Reduction in Debt-to-GDP Ratio', https://papers.ssrn.com/sol3/papers.cfm?abstract_id = 4605287

Sargent, Thomas J., and Neil Wallace. 1981. 'Some Unpleasant Monetarist Arithmetic.' *Federal Reserve Bank of Minneapolis Quarterly Review*, 5(3): 1–17.

Schadler, Susan. 2012. 'Sovereign Debtors in Distress: Are our Institutions up to the Challenge', CIGI Papers, No. 6, August.

Schuman, Michael. 2012. 'Why China Will Have an Economic Crisis', *Time*, 27 February.

Setser, Brad. 2008. 'The Political Economy of the SDRM.' Background Paper for the IPD Task Force on Sovereign Debt. Available online at www.cfr.org/content/publi cations.

Shambaugh, Jay C. 2012. 'The Euro's Three Crises.' *Brookings Papers on Economic Activity*, Spring 2012.

Sheel, Alok. 2012. 'IMF and the Eurozone—A Developing Country Perspective', *Economic and Political Weekly*, 29 December 2012.

Simpson, Lucio. 2006. 'The Role of the IMF in Debt Restructurings: Lending into Arrears, Moral Hazard and Sustainability Concerns.' G24 Discussion Paper.

Sraffa, P. (Ed.). 1951. *David Ricardo: Works and Correspondence*. Cambridge: Cambridge University Press.

Stephanou, Constantinos. 2011. 'The Banking System in Cyprus: Time to Rethink the Business Model?' *Cyprus Economic Policy Review*, 5(2): 123–130. Available on-line at http://www.ucy.ac.cy/data/ecorece/ STEPHANOU_123-130.pdf.

Stiglitz, Joseph. 2013. 'Inequality Is Holding Back the Recovery', *New York Times*, 19 January. Available online at http://opinionator.blogs.nytimes.com/2013/01/19/ inequality-is-holding-back-the-recovery/.

Stone, Mark, Kenji Fujita, and Kotaro Ishi. 2011. 'Should Unconventional Balance Sheet Policies be Added to the Central Bank Toolkit? A Review of the Experience So Far', IMF Working Paper No. WP/11/145.

Sturzenegger, Federico, and Jeromin Zettelmever. 2006. *Debt Defaults and Lessons from a Decade of Crises*. Cambridge, MA: MIT Press.

Subbarao, D. 2008. 'The Global Financial Turmoil and Challenges for the Indian Economy', speech by Governor, Reserve Bank of India at the Bankers' Club, Kolkata on 10 December 2008. Available online at www.rbi.org.in.

Subbarao, D. 2009. 'Impact of the Global Financial Crisis on India Collateral Damage and Response', speech delivered at the Symposium on 'The Global Economic Crisis and Challenges for the Asian Economy in a Changing World', organized by the Institute for International Monetary Affairs, Tokyo on 18 February 2009 by Governor, RBI. Available online at www.rbi.org.in.

Subbarao, D. 2010. 'India and the Global Financial Crisis: Transcending from Recovery to Growth', comments at the Peterson Institute for International Economics, Washington DC, 26 April 2010.

Subbarao, D. 2013a. 'India's Macroeconomic Challenges Some Reserve Bank Perspectives', Fifth I.G. Patel Memorial Lecture delivered by Governor, RBI at the London School of Economics on 13 March 2013.

Subbarao, D. 2013b. 'Is There a New Normal for Inflation?' Speech delivered by Governor, RBI at the Bankers' Club, New Delhi on 8 March 2013. Available online at http://rbidocs.rbi.org.in/rdocs/Speeches/PDFs/ GSP080313FLS.pdf.

Subbarao, D. 2013c. 'The Global Financial Crisis and the Indian Financial Sector— What Have We Learnt and How Have We Responded?' Address by Governor of the Reserve Bank of India at the 7th International Banking and Finance Conference

2013, organized by the Indian Merchants' Chamber, Mumbai, 5 June 2013. Available online at rbi.org.in.

Taylor, John B. 2002. 'Sovereign Debt Restructuring: A U.S. Perspective,' remarks at the Institute for International Economics Conference on 'Sovereign Debt Workouts: Hopes and Hazards', Washington, 2 April 2002.

Tcherneva, Pavlina R. 2008. 'The Return of Fiscal Policy: Can the New Developments in the New Economic Consensus be Reconciled with the Post-Keynesian View?' Levy Economics Institute Working Paper No. 539.

Ter-Minassian and Fedelino Annalisa. 2011. 'Impact of the Global Crisis on Subnational Government Finances', Bank of Italy Working Paper.

Trichet, Jean-Claude. 2012. 'Reflections on Unconventional Monetary Policy Measures and on European Economic Governance: Towards an Economic and Fiscal Federation by Exception', Mandeville Lecture 2012 delivered at Erasmus University, Rotterdam on 6 June 2012. Available online at http://www.eur.nl/fileadmin/ASSETS/press/2012/Juni/speech_Jean-Claude_Trichet_Mandeville_Lezing_2012.pdf.

Turner, Philip. 2010. 'Fiscal Dominance and the Long-Term Interest Rate.' Special Paper 199, Financial Markets Group Special Paper Series, London School of Economics, May 2011, 47.

UCLG, United Cities and Local Governments. 2009. 'The Impact of the Global Crisis on Local Governments', October.

United Nations. 2009. 'Report of the Commission of Experts of the President of the United Nations General Assembly on Reforms of the International Monetary and Financial System' (Chair: Joseph Stiglitz), 21 September 2009. Available online at http://www.un.org/ga/econcrisissummit/docs/FinalReport_CoE.pdf.

United Nations. 2012. 'World Economic Situation and Prospects 2012'. Available online at www.un.org/en/development/desa/.../2012wespupdate_pr_en.pdf.

United Nations. 2013. World Economic Situation and Prospects 2013, 17 January 2013. Available online at http://www.un.org/en/development/desa/policy/wesp/wesp_current/2013wesp_pr_europe_en.pdf.

Watson, O.J., G. Barnsley, J. Toor, A.B. Hogan, P. Winskill, and A.C. Ghani. 2022. 'Global Impact of the First Year of COVID-19 Vaccination: A Mathematical Modelling Study.' The Lancet Infectious Diseases, 22(9): 1293–1302.

Webb, Stephen B. 2004. 'Fiscal Responsibility Laws for Subnational Discipline: The Latin American Experiences', Policy Research Working Paper 3309, The World Bank, Washington, DC.

Wolf, Martin. 2011. 'Ireland Needs Help with its Debt', Financial Times, 23 February.

World Bank. 2022. 'Resolving High Debt After The Pandemic: Lessons from Past Episodes of Debt Relief', https://thedocs.worldbank.org/en/doc/cb15f6d7442ea dedf75bb95c4fdec1b3-0350012022/related/Global-Economic-Prospects-January-2022-Topical-Issue-1.pdf

Young, Brigitte, and Willi Semmler. 2011. 'The European Sovereign Debt Crisis: Is Germany to Blame? German Politics & Society, 29(1): 1–24.

Young, H. 1998. This Blessed Plot: Britain and Europe from Churchill to Blair. London: Macmillan.

Zhang, Zhiwei, and Wenlang Zhang. 2009. 'The Road to Recovery: Fiscal Stimulus, Financial Sector Rehabilitation, and Potential Risks Ahead', BIS Working Paper 18/

2009. Available online at http://www.bis.org/repoffi cepubl/arpresearch201003.14. pdf.

World Bank, 2022. International Debt Statistics 2022, Washington DC: World Bank, available at https://documents.worldbank.org/en/publication/documents-repo rts/documentdetail/552361634028314881/international-debt-statistics-2022 (accessed in October 2024)

G-20. 2020. Leaders' Declaration, Riyadh Summit, November 21, 2020, available at https://g20.utoronto.ca/2020/2020-g20-leaders-declaration-1121.html (accessed in October 2024)

Index

For the benefit of digital users, indexed terms that span two pages (e.g., 52–53) may, on occasion, appear on only one of those pages.

Tables, figures, and boxes are indicated by an italic *t*, *f*, and *b* following the page number.

Acharya, Viral 222–23
ad hominem attacks 239
advanced economies 53, 84, 87, 88
    current account deficit of 103
    deterioration in fiscal balances during crisis 49*t*
    fiscal balances 51
    fiscal deficits 99
    fiscal stimulus during COVID-19, 70*t*
    GDP growth during global financial crisis 101
    growth of non-European 108, 116*t*
    growth performance and growth prospects of 326
    inflation 97*f*, 97–98, 102
    monetary policy responses and implications 64
    net borrowing of general governments of 99
    primary fiscal balances 51, 52*t*
    productivity growth and aging demographics in 90–91
    real GDP growth and share in global GDP 85*f*
    re-capitalization of banks 64–65
ageing populations, on financial crisis 27
Arestis, Philip 236
ASEAN Swap Arrangement (ASA) 281
Asian Development Bank 297
asset-backed securities purchase programme (ABSPP) 168–69

Association of Southeast Asian Nations (ASEAN) 281
austerity measures, dangers of 32
    corporate profitability, falling 32
    curtailment of public spending 32, 33
    emergence of primary deficit, revenue deficit, and fiscal deficit 32–33
    government deficits 34
    high unemployment levels and falling incomes 33
    incomes of developing countries 32
    increase in interest rates 32–33
    increasing debt to GDP ratios 32
Australian economy 103, 109
    Australian dollar, collapse of 109
    unemployment 109
Austrian economy
    current account surplus 120–22
automatic stabilizers 45–46, 70–72, 74

Baker, Dean 236
Banking Union 171
Bank of International Settlement (BIS) 154
bankruptcy 279
Bankruptcy Act, 1978, 286–87
Bankruptcy Code 279
Barro–Ricardo equivalence 14–15, 231, 233
    assumptions 233–34
    criticism 233–34
    Lin's position 234
Basel Committee 302–3

BBVA 146–47
Berlusconi, Silvio 142–43
Bernanke, Ben 66
Biden, Joe 3–4
bilateral swap arrangements
  (BSAs) 281, 282
  between Japan and India 282
Blanchard, Olivier 139–40
Blommestein, Hans J. 243
book money 119
borrowings by government 46
Brady, Nicholas F. 286
Brady Plan 286
Bretton Woods Institutions 327–28
Brexit 1, 3, 11–12, 89–90, 104, 107
  impact on UK economy 108t
  implications for UK 3
budget deficits 130, 163, 209, 230–32, 236

cajas de ahorros 11–12
Cameron, David 3
Canadian economy, impact of global
  financial crisis 109
capacity of financial sector 31, 72–73,
  315–16, 322
central bank debt 57–59t, 59
central banking and fiscal environment
  build-up of risks 259
  controversy in India 272–73
  creating crisis, role in 258
  exit policies 265, 267
  fiscal implications of monetary
    actions 257, 267, 268t
  fundamental changes in 270
  governance arrangements 259–60, 264
  management of capital flows 272
  management of large public
    debt 271–72
  managing crisis, role in 262
  nature and magnitude of new fiscal
    dominance 273
  political economy considerations 261
  purchases of long-term government
    bonds 272
  regulatory systems and market
    failures 261
  taxation of financial sector 272–73

central banks 17
  asset purchase programmes 5
Centre euro area economy 125 see also
  euro area economies
  energy prices 129
  impact of pandemic on 129
  select indicators 126t
Centre for International Governance
  Innovation (CIGI) 289
Chiang Mai Initiative (CMI) 281, 296–
  97, 325
Chiang Mai Initiative
  Multilateralization Precautionary
  Line (CMIMPL) 281, 296–97
China 84, 188
  as a cheap channel of outsourcing 96
  Chinese currency appreciation 105
  contribution to Australia's
    resilience 109
  current account surplus 105
  current account surpluses of 103
  fiscal stimulus measures, effectiveness
    of 75–76
  growth in economy 105
  restrictive trade practices 90
  share in global GDP 103, 104f
China's bilateral lending 18–19
Chinese debt 18–19, 241–42, 291
Chinese loans
  to low-income developing
    economies 292
  nature of 292, 293b
Chinese trade policy 3–4
Clinton, Bill 67–68
Coeure, Benoit 172
commodities markets, impact of
  economic recession 44–45
corporate sector purchase programme
  (CSPP) 168–69
Correa, Rafael 284–85
counter-cyclical fiscal policies 47
covered bond purchase program
  (CBPP) 168–69
COVID-19 pandemic 48, 62, 83, 187,
  301, 325
  demand shock and supply
    shock 91–92

economic impact of 91
fiscal stimulus measures
during 70–72*t*
Indian economy during 190
most-affected countries 92*t*
post-COVID fiscal consolidation 82
Covid-19 pandemic 1–2
economic implications of 4–5
macroeconomic vulnerability
post 13
credit event 284, 299
crisis containment 61
crisis- ridden GIIPS countries 11–12
cross-border capital flows 322
cross-border spillover effects 31, 76,
78–79
crowding out effect 51
current account surpluses 24
cutbacks in expenditure 46

dangers of financial crisis 32 *see also*
austerity measures, dangers of
curtailment of public spending 32, 33
high unemployment levels and falling
incomes 33
reduced consumption 40–41
severity and global spread of 41
deadweight loss 232
De Antoni, Elisabetta 236
debt buybacks 284
debt configuration 11–12
debt default 39
debt sustainability 15, 18–19, 77, 79–80,
178*t*, 240, 246–47, 253–54, 277–78,
289, 292–93, 294–95, 299–300,
326–27
debt-to-GDP ratio 14, 32, 33, 37–38
deficit- financed public investment
program 15
de Larosiere Group 172–73
devaluation of currency 88
developed and developing economies,
growth of 2, 84
discretionary fiscal measures 63–64,
70–72
discretionary spending 45–46
Domar, E.D. 232–33

dot-com bubble in 2001, 84
Draghi, Mario 177–78, 180

East Asian crisis, 1997–1998, 281
economic area of a nation 170
economic imbalances 248–49
economic recession, impact of
in China 44
earnings of migrant workers 45
on export-dependent economies 44
in fiscal balances 47
flow of grants 44
movements in commodity prices 44–45
negative consequences on non- tax
revenues 43–44
in public debt 51
reduction in public revenues 43–44
economic recovery 62, 78–79, 87
2014–2019, 89
economies and emerging and
developing economies
(EMDEs) 10
Ecuador sovereign debt 284–85
emerging market and developing
economies (EMDEs) 84, 87, 88,
97, 293–94, 325–27
capital inflow 98
debt- GDP ratios 99
fiscal deficits 99
inflation 97*f*, 97–98
real GDP growth and share in global
GDP 85*f*
emerging markets 84
euro area crisis of 2011–13, 1, 7–8, 25–26,
33, 83, 87–88, 181
channels of contagion of 152
characteristics of crisis countries 156,
157*f*
common features 161
European response 164
financial rescue package 164
financial spillovers 153
fiscal irresponsibility and 181
general patterns 12–13
IMF rescue actions 165
indebtedness and leverage in select
economies 162*t*

euro area crisis of 2011–13 (*cont.*)
mechanisms of economic
shocks 152–53
optimum currency area (OCA) 157
patterns and solution packages
of 155
policy initiatives for 12–13
euro area crisis of 2012–2015, 180–81
euro area economies 184
bailouts 120–22
centre (or core) 122, 125
crisis in 119–20
economic weight in global GDP 120,
121*t*
genesis and transmission of 122–23,
123*t*
groups 122
intra–euro zone fiscal and financial
linkages 119–20
macroeconomic fundamentals 120–
22, 123*t*
smaller economies 122
Europe
fiscal deficit in 105–6
share in global GDP 103, 104*f*
European Banking Authority
(EBA) 171–72
European Central Bank (ECB) 167,
168, 177–78
asset purchase programme
(APP) 168–69
monetary policy rates 169*f*
net asset purchases by programme
under APP 171*f*
Pandemic Emergency Purchase
Programme (PEPP) 170
powers for banking supervision 172
Single Supervisory Mechanism
(SSM) 172
US dollar liquidity- providing
operations 282
European Financial Stability Facility
(EFSF) 12–13, 131, 164
European Free Trade Association
(FETA) 151–52
European Monetary Union
(EMU) 128, 174–75, 177

European Stability Mechanism 12–13
European Stability Mechanism
(ESM) 165, 167
European Systemic Risk Board
(ESRB) 172–73
European System of Financial
Supervision (ESFS) 172–73
European Union 89–90, 184
economic and monetary union 173
fiscal governance 178
new fiscal rules 178*t*
exit policies 187, 207, 257, 265–66
exit strategy 79
exorbitant privilege 105–6
expenditure implications of financial
crisis 45
automatic stabilizers 45–46
borrowings by government 46
cutbacks in expenditure 46
discretionary spending 45–46
non-discretionary
expenditures 45–46
expenditure management 60
Extended Credit Facility (ECF) 283
Extended Fund Facility 283

Fannie Mae 86–87
Feldstein, Martin 160
financial crisis, phases of 61
Financial Crisis Responsibility fee 305
financial stability 17–18, 19–20, 72–73,
78–79, 87–88, 141, 164–65, 177,
221, 243, 326–27
Indian context 187, 193–94, 203, 220
Financial Stability Board 302–3
Financial Stability Report of the
RBI 221
Fini, Gianfranco 143
fiscal balances, impact of economic
recession 47
in advanced economies 51
among euro area countries 48
in Canada 48
in China 48, 53
decline in global public debt 48
deterioration in onset of financial
crisis 49*t*

in emerging economies 48
in G20 emerging market
    countries 51, 52t
in India 51, 53
in Middle East and North Africa 51
in US 48
fiscal deficits 60
in advanced economies 99
in euro area economies 99
level of public debt 51
in Middle East and North African
    (MENA) economies 99
fiscal management and regulation 6–8,
    19–20, 25–26, 60, 321
debt reduction following financial
    crisis 38–39
exit strategies 61
reduced consumption 40–41
restructuring of debts 40
revaluation and readjustment of
    exchange rates 40
fiscal policies 33, 51–53, 60, 61,
    80–81, 82, 102–3, 141, 153,
    170, 174, 175, 176, 177, 189,
    207, 208, 229, 231, 235, 236, 244,
    253–54, 256, 261, 274, 277–78,
    318, 323
Fiscal Responsibility and Budget
    Management (FRBM) Act,
    2003, 209, 210–11, 226
fiscal space in India 218–19
fiscal stimulus measures 64, 67, 69–72t,
    73–74, 99
case of China 75–76
cross-border spillover effects 31, 76,
    78–79
from domestic funding
    resources 72–73
effectiveness of 75–76, 80–81
employment measures 68
fiscal consequences 81
global stimulus spending 68
long-term 79
lowering of interest rates 64–65,
    73, 81
packages 95
during pandemic 70–72t

role of credit rating agencies 80
short-term 77–78, 79
social transfers 68
stabilization measures 67–68
stimulation measures 67–68
tax cuts 68
three 'T's', 67
fiscal sustainability 15–16, 51, 64, 73–
    74, 77–78, 80, 81, 95, 178, 232–33,
    242–43, 261
fiscal union 174
Fischer, Stanley 243
fixed rate full allotment (FRFA) 168
Flexible Credit Line (FCL) 283
flight to familiarity syndrome 196–97,
    223–24
foreign exchange reserves 194,
    244, 281
in form of gold 323
foreign financed government
    debt 232
Freddie Mac 86–87
French economy
    energy prices in 128–29
    during euro area crisis 128–29
    global GDP share 120
    inflationary risks 128–29
    macroeconomic
        fundamentals 120–22
    sovereign CDS spread 128–29
Friedman, Milton 66

Gaza war, 2023, 1–2, 14
G20 countries 248–49
    agenda 250t
    current account balance position
        of 103, 115t
    discretionary fiscal stimulus during
        crisis 69t
    fiscal balances of 27, 51, 52t, 102,
        114t
    GDP growth 101, 112t
    inflation 102, 113t
    primary fiscal balances 52t
    select fiscal indicators 252–53t
Gelpern, Anna 61
Georgieva, Kristalina 294

German economy
  banking sector in 125–28
  current account surplus 120–22
  during euro area crisis 125–28
  German exports to euro area 128
  global GDP share 120
  impact of global financial crisis 125
  macroeconomic
    fundamentals 120–22
  OECD Economic Survey for,
    2011, 125–28
GIIPS (Greece, Ireland, Italy, Portugal,
    and Spain) 120, 122, 128–29 see
    individual countries
global debt servicing costs 291
global economic developments during
    2001–2022, 83
  during 2001–6, 84
  factors responsible for
    slowdown 90–91
  period of marked volatility and
    uncertainty (2000–2022) 93
  real GDP growth and share in global
    GDP 85f
global financial crisis of 2008–2009, 1,
    2–3, 5–6, 7–8, 16–17, 23, 83, 85
  ageing populations, impact of 27
  asset values, effect on 26–27, 36
  causes 24
  cost of raising debt 27–28
  debt incurred by government
    69–70
  financial market volatility 87–88
  fiscal stimulus measures to 26–28
  genesis of 86–87
  levels of debt 53
  link between fiscal health of countries
    and 26
  macroeconomic factors 24–25
  public debt, issue of 34
  severity and global spread 41
  in US 47–48
  World Bank estimate of impact 46
global imbalances
  as contributory cause of financial
    crisis 40, 98–99, 100f
  role of flows of budget balances 99

  in terms of current account
    balance 99
globalization of finance 327
G20 New Delhi declaration 15–16
Goldilocks scenario of pre-crisis
    years 101, 110–11
Goodhart 2010, 255
Great Depression of 1930s 83
Great Moderation 2
Greece 129, 162, 241–42, 277–78
  Association Agreement with
    European Economic Community
    (EEC) 129–30
  association with euro area 129–30
  budget deficit, 2009, 130
  debts 130
  economic adjustment
    programme 131
  economic recovery 134
  fiscal calamity 134
  formation of optimum currency area
    (OCA) 133–34
  Greek borrowing costs 130–31
  Greek CDS spread 133
  Greek government bonds 131–33
  impact of global financial crisis 133
  macroeconomic indicators 132t
  Standard & Poor's (S&P)
    rating 134
Greek crisis 6–7, 11–12, 33
Greek law bonds (GGBs) 131–32

Halifax Bank of Scotland
    bankruptcy 107
helicopter money 66
Herndon, Ash, and Pollin (2013) 238
Hole, Jackson 66

Iceland 149, 241–42
  anti-terrorism legislation
    against 151–52
  basic problems of 149
  diplomatic disputes, 2008, 151–52
  GDP growth 149
  gross external indebtedness 149
  Icelandic banking system 149–50
  Icesave dispute 151–52

IMF's Financial System Stability
Assessment Update 149–50
impact of financial crisis, 2008, 150–51, 152
króna depreciation 149, 151
liquidity problems 151–52
macroeconomic imbalances 149
select macroeconomic
indicators 150*t*
Icelandic Bank collapse 63
Icesave 151–52
illiquidity 278–79
IMF 130, 248–49
Article IV Report for the euro
area 160
Article IV report of UK 106
Article IV Report on Euro Area
Policies 172
bilateral swap arrangements
(BSAs) 282
country groupings 182
Financial Sector Assessment Program
(FSAP) Report of EU 155
on fiscal austerity 78
fiscal packages for GIIPS 138, 140–41, 145–46
Global Financial Stability Report 20
liquidity support 283
rescue actions for euro area crisis 165
sovereign debt restructuring 18–19
World Economic Outlook (WEO)
report 85–86, 87, 88, 89, 90–91,
93*t*, 96
incipient stage of financial crisis 61
India Infrastructure Finance Company
Limited (IIFCL) 205
Indian economy and crisis
accounting practices 193–94
banking sector 220–23
capital-to-risk adjusted assets ratio
(CRAR) 220
cash reserve ratio (CRR) 201–2
corporate performance 199
crisis management 211
dealing with liquidity pressures 195
debt-deficit configuration 225–26
economic growth, 2000–2008, 188

exchange rate of rupee 224
exports and imports 194, 226
extent of globalization 194–95
external commercial
borrowings 197–98, 202–3
external funding 201
external sector, behaviour of 196, 223
financial markets 195
financial sector stability 220
fiscal and monetary policies 189
fiscal consolidation efforts 209–11,
218, 226–27
fiscal deficit 51, 102–3, 209, 211–13
fiscal stimulus 204
foreign direct investments 196–97
FRBM legislations 209, 210–11, 226
GDP growth 198, 209–10, 211
industrial and services sectors 198
inflation 189, 190–93, 219–20
institutional fiscal reforms 215*t*
investment portfolios of Indian
commercial banks 193–94
issue of fiscal dominance 224
liquidity adjustment facility
(LAF) 195–96, 202
liquidity injection/availability 200*t*,
201–2
macroeconomy, 2000–2022, 187, 213
Market Stabilisation Scheme
(MSS) 201–2
measures for expenditure
augmentation 217
measures to augment forex
liquidity 202–3
monetary measures 199
monetary policy preceding the
crisis 194
monetary stimulus packages 203
money market 195–96, 197*f*
openness indicators 194
during pandemic 190, 203, 204*t*
policy repo rate 201
pro-cyclical provisioning norms 203
recovery and exit policies 207
reform measures 209
regulatory practices 193–94
resilience of financial sector 220

Indian economy and crisis (*cont.*)
  resilience post global financial
    crisis 193
  revenue measures 205
  select macro indicators 191*t*
  Sixth Pay Commission
    recommendations 205–7
  stability of NPAs 220–21
  states' finances 213, 214*t*, 218*t*
  states' GFD 209–10, 210*f*
  statutory liquidity ratios 201–2, 207,
    208, 225, 301–2
  tax cuts 217
  trade credit 197–98
  unconventional measures 205
Indian rupee, as international
    currency 323–24
inequality 25
inflation 96, 97*f*
  in advanced economies and
    EMDEs 97–98
  aftermath of global financial crisis 98
  control of 96
  in recessionary period 97
inflationary trends 10–11
insolvency 278–79
Institute for New Economic Thinking
    (INET) 289
International Centre for Settlement of
    Investment Disputes (ICSID) 18
International Monetary Fund
    (IMF) 7–8
international monetary system 249
intra-euro area trade 154
Ireland crisis 135, 162, 241–42
  budget surplus problem 35–36
  Credit Institutions Eligible Liabilities
    Guarantee Scheme (ELG
    Scheme) 136–37
  Credit Institutions Financial Support
    Scheme (CIFS) 136–37
  credit rating during 136–37
  debt-GDP ratio 135
  foreign currency denominated
    financial assets 135–36
  growth rate post 138
  IMF's Article IV report on 135

IMF's loan (the Extended
    Arrangement program) 138
  real estate prices and mortgage
    lending 135
  role of financial integration 137
  select macroeconomic
    indicators 136*t*
  transferring private and bank debt to
    government 36–37
Irish banks, risk management practices
    of 11–12
Issing, Otmar 159
Italy 141, 162, 241–42
  average maturity of Italian debt 141
  credit rating 143
  debt-GDP ratio 144–45
  foreign asset position 144–45
  GDP contraction during crisis 141–42
  household balance sheets 144–45
  IMF report on 141–42
  pension system and labour
    market 144
  political uncertainties 143
  public debt situation 141, 142–44
  select macroeconomic
    indicators 142*t*
  stimulus package during
    crisis 142–43
  total factor productivity (TFP)
    contributions 144
  World Bank's Doing Business
    indicators 144

Japanese economy
  ageing Population, effect of 109
  fiscal balance 102–3
  impact of global financial crisis 109
  recovery from Great East Japan
    earthquake, 2011, 109

Keynes, Lord 21
Khatiwada, Sameer 68
Krugman, Paul 15, 25, 145, 234, 235, 239

Lagarde, Christine 78
Lehman Brothers collapse 23, 62, 63,
    85–87, 107, 195–96, 205–6

Lewis, Michael 34
Lin, Justin 234
liquidity 278–79
London Club restructuring 285
long-term refinancing operations
(LTROs) 168

Maastricht Treaty 12–13, 160, 161
Maastricht treaty 131–32
macroeconomic policies 243
macroeconomic uncertainties, adverse
effects of 43, 63–64
expenditure implications 45
revenue implications 43
Madison, James 230
Malpass, David 294
management phase of financial
crisis 61
May, Theresa 3
Middle East and North African
(MENA) economies
fiscal deficits 99
Minsky, Hyman 37, 236
monetary policy responses and
implications 64 see also fiscal
stimulus measures
Monti, Mario 143, 144
moral hazard in financial system 29
Mundell, Robert 157–58

nationalization of banking sector 6–7
National Rural Employment Guarantee
Act (NREGA) 205–6
net government debt 53–56
of Australia 56–59
of Canada 56–59
of France 56–59
general 56–59
of Germany 56–59
of Italy 56–59
of Japan 56–59
of New Zealand 56–59
of Spain 56–59
of US 56–59
Netherlands economy
current account surplus 120–22
global GDP share 120

NextGeneration EU (NGEU) plan of
2020 170
non-European advanced economies
growth in 108, 116t
inflation 117t
normalcy 41
North American Free Trade
Agreement 280

odious 284–85
optimum currency area (OCA) 133–
34, 157, 170
advantages of 157–58, 161
criteria for 159, 161
formation 159
Mundell's analysis 157–58

Padoa-Schioppa, Tommaso 142–43
Paris Club restructuring 285, 292
policy responses and their effectiveness
case of China 75–76
cross-border spillover effects 31, 76
easing credit crunch 73
of fiscal stimulus 73–74
job creation 74
liquidity management 73
of monetary policy 74
multiplier effects of stimulus
programmes 74–75, 78–79, 95
restoration of confidence 73–74
political union 179
Portugal 11–12, 162, 241–42
anaemic productivity growth 139–40
austerity measures 140
average annual real GDP growth 138
competitiveness gap 139–40
current account deficit 139–40
economic growth 138, 141
fiscal deficit 140
IMF's Economic Adjustment
Programme 140–41
impact of global financial crisis 140
Moody's rating 154
select macroeconomic
indicators 139t
Standard & Poor's (S&P) rating 140
unemployment 139–40

Prasad, Eshwar 63–64
Precautionary and Liquidity Line (PLL)
    programme 281
Precautionary Credit Line (PCL) 283
private debt 35–37
    link between banking crises
        and 36–37
protectionist measures 40
public debt 51, 53, 54t, 60, 99, 230, 241
    adverse consequences of high 35, 37
    beneficial effects 231
    burdens 16–17, 34
    in China 53
    consolidated central government and
        central bank debt 57–59t
    conventional views 230
    as cumulative effect of fiscal
        deficits 36
    empirical literature 229, 237
    financial crisis and 36
    of G7 countries 36
    growth of 241–42
    in India 53
    Italy 141, 142–44
    in Japan 56
    Keynesian multiplier effect on 231
    link between fiscal deficits and 51
    management 15–16
    new dimensions of 241
    non-mainstream views 235
    during peace time and post- Second
        World War 53
    as a percentage of global
        GDP 241–42
    relationship between growth and 237
    R–R empirical exercise 237–38, 239
    short-term vs long-term impact
        of 231, 240
    sustainability of 232–33
    in UK 56
    in US 56
public debt management
    boundaries of public debt obligations
        or liabilities 247
    capital flows 244
    challenges 242–43, 253, 255–56
    combination of policy responses 252
    debt restructuring 249–51
    of dominant global reserve
        currency 249
    of external sector 244
    financial stability 254
    financial support 246
    global allocation of capital 252
    global financial architecture 248
    during global financial crisis 245
    governance 245
    identifying origin of crisis 245–46
    IMF and World Bank guidelines 255
    institutional arrangements
        for 254–55
    liquidity support 246
    outlook for 251
    prudential requirements 242–43
    public debt-to-GDP ratio 246–47
    surveillance mechanism 248
public money for rescuing the financial
        sector 303, 303t
public policy 47
public sector purchase programme
        (PSPP) 168–69

quantitative easing 65–66, 95–96, 98
quantitative easing measures 5, 15–16

Rajan (2013) 239
Rapid Credit Facility (RCF) 283
Rau, Rama 272–73
regulation of financial sector 301–2,
        327
    globalization of 327
    new approaches 305
    objectives and focus of 305–6
    polluter ays principle 305
Reinhart, C.M. 14–15, 237
reputation risk 38–39
responses to crisis 62
    ad hoc measures safeguarding
        national interests 63
    discretionary measures 63–64, 70–72
    effectiveness of policy responses 73
    expansionary measures 66–67

increase in liquidity 63
issue of exit policy 79
monetary policy responses and
    implications 64
policy issues and lessons 77
quantitative easing 65–66
quasi-fiscal effects 70–72
re-capitalization of banks 64–65
stimulus measures 64
tax cuts 64
timing and pace of retreat of
    emergency measures 67
revenue balance
    current receipts vs current
        expenditures 47
    golden rule 47
    total receipts (tax and non-
        tax) of government vs total
        expenditures 47–48
revenue deficit 47
revenue implications of financial
    crisis 43
Ricardian equivalence theorems
    (RET) 236
Rogoff, Kenneth 14–15, 237, 290
Rompuy, Herman Van 177
Russia 102–3, 298–99
Russia–Ukraine war 2, 10–11, 14, 62,
    91–92, 123–24, 129, 147–48, 177–
    78, 181

Santander 146–47
Saudi Arabia 101, 102–3
Schuman, Michael 75
securities market programme
    (SMP) 168
'Severe acute respiratory syndrome
    coronavirus 2' (SARS-CoV-2) 91
short-term stimulus measures 77–78,
    79
Single Resolution Mechanism
    (SRM) 167, 173–74
Single Supervisory Mechanism
    (SSM) 167, 173–74
solvency 278–79
solvency of financial institutions 62

Sorkin, Isaac 63–64
sovereign debt crises 2–3
sovereign debt of emerging
    markets 85–86
sovereign debt restructuring 5, 18–19,
    277–78
    applicability of concept of
        bankruptcy 279
    Brady Plan 286
    case of quasi-sovereign debt 299
    CDS transactions 299
    characteristics of 285
    Chinese lending and its
        implications 291
    code of conduct 287
    concepts and features 284
    consideration of currency union 297
    constraints on formalization of 297,
        298
    debt reduction and debt
        rescheduling 285
    in developing or emerging market
        economies 285
    distinction between willingness and
        ability 297–98
    good creditor conduct and good
        debtor conduct 299
    IMF liquidity support 283, 295–96
    liquidity support facilities 278, 279,
        294–95, 299–300
    mechanism of regional
        insurance 296
    in Mexico 285
    with private creditors 285
    program for sustained growth 285
    proposals for improvement 288
    prospects for establishing
        orderly 299
    subject to bankruptcy code 279,
        297–98
    swap line arrangement 280, 296–97
    UNCTAD's role 18
    US Treasury proposals 286–87
Sovereign Debt Restructuring
    Mechanism (SDRM) 286–87, 288
    criticism 287

sovereign default 38–39
Spanish banking system 11–12, 146–47
Spanish crisis 11–12
Spanish economy 145, 241–42
   cajas de ahorros 146–47
   creation of Financial Assets
      Acquisition Fund (FAAF) 147
   debt-GDP ratio 120–22
   financial support during crisis 147
   financial support from state-owned
      recapitalization vehicle (FROB) 147
   GDP growth 145–46, 147–48
   global GDP share 120
   growth cycle 145
   housing boom 145–46
   IMF's Financial Sector Assessment
      Programme (FSAP) 145–46
   interrelated shocks 145
   loan loss provisioning requirements
      for credit institutions 147
   select macroeconomic
      indicators 148*t*
Stand-By Arrangements (SBA) 283
Standby Credit Facility (SCF) 283
statutory liquidity ratios 301–2
Stiglitz, Joseph 25
Subbarao, D. 190
sub-national finance 5, 20–21
   effects of global crisis and pandemic
      on 313
   emerging issues 317
   importance of 311, 312
   policy responses of 316
subnational governments
   (SNGs) 311–12
sub-prime crisis in US 10, 24, 62, 84–87,
   188
sustainability of debt 38
swap arrangements 280

taxation of financial sector 19–20
tax system 301
   backward looking 304
   on bonuses 304
   bonus systems 308
   as complementary 304

   developing country perspectives 310
   on financial transactions 306
   forward looking 304
   IMF report 306–7
   issuance principle 308–9
   objectives 306
   at operational level 308–9
   regulation and 307
   residence principle 308–9
   taxation on banks 304
   tax distortions 308
terrorist attacks of 11 September
   2001, 281–82
third covered bond purchase
   programme (CBPP3) 168–69
Thomsen, Paoul 155
Tobin Tax 301, 304, 309
Tobin tax 19–20
Tommaso Padoa-Schioppa
   Group 174
trade-off for macroeconomic
   management 326
Troubled Asset Relief Program
   (TARP) 8–9
Truman, Edwin M. 61
Trump, Donald 83, 90, 104–5
Turner, Philip 243

UK economy
   fiscal balance 102–3
   impact of global financial crisis 106
UK–EU relationship 107–8
UNCTAD Expert Group on
   Responsible Sovereign Lending
   and Borrowing 290
under-taxation of financial sector 301
United States Trade Representative
   (USTR) 90
US 84, 236, 260, 261
   balance sheet expansion 95–96
   banking sector 87
   fiscal balance 102–3
   growth in economy 104–5
   income and wealth inequalities 25
   reduced consumption in 40–41
   share in global GDP 103, 104*f*

temporary dollar liquidity swap
 arrangements 281–82
US debt to GDP ratio 95
US Dollars to Euro spot exchange
 rate 124*f*
US–China trade war 1, 3–4, 10, 83, 99,
 110–11, 327
 in terms of tariffs 3–4, 90
US Trade Act of 1974, 90

Vostro accounts for trade
 323–24

World Bank 248–49, 293–94
World Inequality Report 20
World Trade Organization
 (WTO) 248–49

Y2K-related problems 1